D1159888

Novozhilov, Valentin Valentinovich, 1910–
    Problems of cost-benefit analysis in optimal planning
[by] V. V. Novozhilov. [Translator: Henry McQuiston].
White Plains, N. Y., International Arts and Sciences Press
[c1970]

    viii, 362 p. 24 cm.

    Translation of Проблемы измерения затрат и результатов при
оптимальном планировании (romanized: Problemy izmereniia zatrat
i rezul'tatov pri optimal'nom planirovanii)
    Includes bibliographical references.

    1. Industrial management. 2. Cost effectiveness. I. Title.

    HD36.N6913   658.1'55   69–10004
                                                          MARC

    Library of Congress   [2]

PROBLEMS OF COST-BENEFIT
ANALYSIS IN OPTIMAL PLANNING

PROBLEMS OF COST-BENEFIT
ANALYSIS IN OPTIMAL PLANNING

V. V. Novozhilov

 INTERNATIONAL ARTS AND SCIENCES PRESS, INC.
White Plains, New York

Originally published as
*Problemy izmereniia zatrat i rezul'tatov
pri optimal'nom planirovanii,*
by "Ekonomika" Publishing House,
Moscow, 1967

Translator: Henry McQuiston

Library of Congress Card Catalog
Number: 69–10004

Translation © 1970 by International
Arts and Sciences Press, Inc., 901 North
Broadway, White Plains, New York 10603

Printed in the United States of America

CONTENTS

CHAPTER 1

FORMULATION OF THE PROBLEM

Cost-benefit analysis is the key problem in economic science and practice. Problems of planning, economic calculation, distribution according to labor, and organizing management of the national economy are all interconnected in this key problem. The use of incorrect methods of cost-benefit analysis orients economic activity toward excessive expenditures and the pursuit of imaginary results, gives rise to contradictions between economic accountability and the plan, and between the interests of the enterprise and those of the national economy, hinders distribution according to labor, and obstructs democratization of management of the national economy and development of the creative initiative on the part of the working masses.

The significance of cost-benefit methods is explained by the fact that the solution of any economic question — both general ones concerning the national economy as a whole and particular ones affecting only a small section of socialist economics — is linked with cost-benefit analysis. Consequently, the correct solution to all questions of socialist economics depends on the correctness of cost-benefit methods.

Naturally, considerable attention has been paid to the principles and methods of these calculations. Many books and articles have been written on questions of calculating production costs, price formation, measuring labor productivity, determining the effectiveness of capital investments, etc. Many scientific conferences and meetings have dealt with these questions.

However, all this enormous amount of work still has not led to

1

a solution of the problem. Cost-benefit methodology comprises one of the most controversial problems of economic science. In practice the cost-benefit criteria that were applied long ago diverged from the conclusions of our economic science. In some cases this divergence occurred because practice outstripped the development of theory. In other cases practice lagged behind the level attained by science.

1. Divergence Between Theory and Practice in Measuring Costs

According to theory national economic expenditures consist of labor and labor alone. In practice, however, the use of certain limited resources such as capital investments, fixed and circulating capital, and natural resources are taken into account in the composition of expenditures. This is understandable. Every practical person knows that both costs and benefits depend on the effective use of these resources. It is important that limited resources be used most effectively. Consequently, norms are necessary for effective utilization. These norms require that, for it to be used, one or another limited resource should attain a result no lower than a specific level. Such norms were first applied by Soviet planners to provide the economic basis for projects. They consisted of normative periods of recoupment on capital investments and of normative coefficients of effectiveness for the utilization of scarce materials (for example, nonferrous metals). In 1958 the principle of applying norms of effectiveness of capital investments in project calculations was recognized at the All-Union Scientific and Technical Conference on Problems of Determining the Economic Effectiveness of Capital Investments and New Technology in the National Economy of the USSR.

"The Standard Procedure for Determining the Economic Effectiveness of Capital Investments and New Technology in the National Economy of the USSR" (Gosplanizdat, 1960), developed on the basis of this conference's resolutions, recommends, together with the formula for a recoupment period, two formulas for overall expenditures:

$$K + T_0 C, \qquad (1.1)$$

$$C + E_0 K, \qquad (1.2)$$

where K is the capital investment for each variant;

C is the annual production cost for each variant;

T_0 is the branch normative recoupment period on capital investments;

E_0 is the branch normative coefficient of effectiveness of capital investments.

The standard procedure does not clarify the economic meaning of these formulas. It designates them as "overall expenditures," not explaining just which labor outlays are expressed in the products

$T_0 C$ and $E_0 K$.

The application of norms of effectiveness in project calculations paved the way for their introduction into the operations of existing enterprises. It could not be otherwise. It is inconsistent to introduce a normative payment for capital investments $(E_0 K)$ into the operating costs of projected enterprises and not to include it in existing enterprises. Payments for capital were established by the 1965 reform. Still earlier the use in project calculations of coefficients of the scarcity of certain materials gave way to calculation of scarcity in the increased prices of these materials. Thus considerations of scarcity (via prices of materials) were extended to existing enterprises.

However, the "legalization" of scarcity of resources as an element of costs made the question of the basis of this calculation still more critical. One of two things is true; either certain outlays of labor are the basis for increases in the prices of scarce goods or these increases distort the measurement of labor outlays. Either the normative effect of capital investments reflects labor outlays or it is not possible to add this quantity to production costs.

Solution of these questions is necessary for practical calculations: for computing norms of effectiveness of capital investment, capital payments, and payments for use of natural resources. Although in practice there are no doubts about the necessity for taking account of scarcity, in theory for a long time there was no doubt about the reverse. Although there are no doubts in practice as to the necessity of calculating capital investments as a special form of expenditures together with production costs, this seemed to many theoreticians to be double counting.

It is true that production costs incompletely reflect outlays of social labor. That part of expenditures of live labor that creates a product for society is not taken into account in production costs. Hence it might seem that we need to supplement production costs

3

with a monetary expression of labor for society, distributing the surplus labor proportionally to wages. Such proposals have been presented in our literature by Academician S. G. Strumilin and others. However, the contrary is done in practice. Production costs are supplemented not by what has not been taken into account in them, but by those expenditures that are already completely reflected in them — investments in fixed and circulating capital. By adding to production costs the normative effect of capital investments according to formula (1.2), in actual practice we derive not value but a modified form of it similar to the price of production.

The question arises: what conditions of socialist economics lie at the basis of this modification of value?

Marx's theory of value examined only one modification of value, the price of production. Its formation was explained by specific conditions of capitalism — by competition among capitalists. Its formula reflects only the process of redistribution of surplus value via the interbranch equalization of rates of profit. It is not possible to explain the formation of the socialist modification of value in the same way. The socialist economy needs prices first of all for measuring the outlays of social labor. Consequently, it is not possible to explain the calculation of outlays according to the formula (1.2) for the formation of a general rate of profit, because at once the question arises, why is a general rate of profit necessary? What labor costs does it reflect? In exactly the same way it is not possible to explain the introduction of payments for capital only by the desire to stimulate its better utilization. On the contrary, if these payments do not reflect any real labor expenditures, they will stimulate the ineffective use of productive capital.

The question of the introduction of payments for the use of natural resources arises in connection with the 1965 economic reform. The inclusion of a differential rent in calculations of production costs confronts economic theory with a question: On what basis must "false social value" be included in the costs of socialist enterprises? If the normative effect of capital investments, computed according to the formula $E_0 K$, can be interpreted as expenditures of surplus labor for expanding the production of a given product at rate of growth E_0, then in regard to differential rent this semblance of an explanation disappears. What labor expenditures reflect this element of costs of production of socialist enterprises?

4

2. Modification of Value as the Consequence of Modification of Labor Costs

It is customary to think that outlays of social labor for each product can be reduced to the labor expended in producing the given and *only* the given product. Of course, this does not signify general agreement concerning just what costs consist of. Marxist-Leninist theory teaches that costs consist only of labor expenditures. Bourgeois economists adhere to other views. However, in questions of computing the labor costs of a product, even some supporters of Marxist political economy presume that there is only one expression for labor costs, namely, the labor used in producing the given product.

The conviction that this expression of labor costs is the only possible one and therefore the unchangeable one is the main obstacle to further development of the theory of value and to progress in the systematic use of the law of value. Such a concept, which is neither historically nor dialectically correct, creates a convenient position for a superficial criticism of the labor theory of value. [1] This concept does not follow from the foundations of Marxist-Leninist theory, however; moreover, it is incompatible with them. It arose only because the development of the practice of cost measurement was insufficiently studied. The experience of socialist construction was not generalized.

Above all, the concept of the independence of labor cost expressions from the level of development of the social economy does not correspond to dialectical materialism.

It must not be forgotten that the measurement of social costs is a social process. It presumes the formation of a multitude of social norms, such as prices, various charges, and norms for labor inputs. In an unplanned economy, value norms are determined by the market. In a planned economy, they are planned. Yet always, under any historical conditions, norms for calculation of costs depend on the condition of the social economy — on its production relationships and, especially, on the social division of labor. With the development of the social division of labor, the interrelationships between the expenditures of different links of social production become complicated. This complication influences social norms of expenditures. They change not only quantitatively but also qualitatively, according to the composition of the outlays taken into account and according to the method by which they are calculated.

The historical example of such a change is the transition from price formation according to value to price formation according to price of production. The expression of labor costs in value was changed into their expression as a converted form of value.

Nevertheless, to those who are convinced of the invariability of forms of expression of labor costs, the converted forms of value inevitably appear as a distorted expression of labor costs. In consequence of this, the entire process of development of social norms of expenditures appears as some sort of exception to the laws of dialectical materialism. According to these laws the process of development consists of a gradual, progressive movement from a lower to a higher level. There are no grounds for thinking that the development of social norms of expenditures is not subordinate to this law. Yet if we consider that labor costs of a product are expressed only by the labor involved in the production of the given product, then the entire historical course of development of cost norms proves to be not a progressive but a reverse movement, from a higher to a lower level.

Indeed, the prices of goods tend toward value only in the age of simple commodity production. With the appearance of capitalism prices begin to deviate systematically from values. In this process, with the development of capitalist production these deviations increase by virtue of inequality in the growth of the organic composition of capital in different branches of production.

It is even more significant that in socialist practice also, outlays on a product are calculated not according to its value, but according to a scheme that embodies systematic deviations from this value. It appears that under socialism, when economy of labor becomes more important than at some previous time, labor costs are measured less exactly than even under feudalism. A strange "principle" emerges, namely, the more fully the law of economy of labor functions, the less satisfactory is the measurement of outlays. [2] Thus, if the labor involved in producing a product (accordingly, its value) is considered as the sole expression of the labor cost of the product, then the development of social norms of costs seems incompatible with one of the most general laws of materialist dialectics. The choice is either that the development from a lower to a higher level is not a universal law or that the labor involved in producing an individual product is not the sole expression of labor costs.

How do we resolve this dilemma? Obviously we must give preference to the more general law — the law of dialectics. Further on we will become convinced that only by applying dialectics to the measurement of costs is it possible to overcome difficulties both in the explanation of history and in our practice of measuring costs.

The concept of the invariability of forms of measuring costs does not even correspond to Marx's theory of value. According to this theory the methods of measuring social costs do not remain unchanged in practice. The exchange of goods according to value gave way to exchange according to prices of production. Although under the conditions of simple commodity production only the labor involved in the production[3] of a given commodity was taken into account in measuring costs, under capitalism the costs of production and the price of any commodity became a function not only of the labor involved in its production but also of the labor associated with the production of all other commodities.[4] Measurement of costs according to prices of production is more appropriate to a higher degree of development than calculating costs according to values.[5]

Let us note, however, that the price of production is formed in the process of competition among capitalists, in the process of equalizing rates of profit. On this basis the opinion was formed that under socialism a return to the calculation of costs through values is unavoidable. Yet this conclusion rests on the supposition that the price of production does not have any other basis than competition among capitalists. But this supposition does not at all follow from Marx's theory. On the contrary, Marx asserted something else: that the price of production has a material basis, namely, a growth in the relative importance of one-time expenditures for the creation of means of production, especially implements of labor.[6] This basis is obviously more permanent than capitalism itself. It remains in the socialist economy and will remain even under communism. Furthermore, under the conditions of socialism and communism it becomes more developed than under capitalism. Experience in socialist construction confirms this conclusion.

In determining the effectiveness of capital outlays, of new technology, and of the work of enterprises, precisely those material factors are taken into account that are considered by capitalist competition and that cause deviations of prices of production from value, namely, investment in fixed and circulating capital, the utilization of productive capital, expenditures of scarce means of production, construction time, etc. The introduction of payments for capital extends the calculation of costs according to the formula for modified value to the sphere of price formation and economic calculation. The result

7

is that the absence of prices of production makes necessary other, indirect procedures for calculating those labor costs that are not taken account of in value but are taken account of in the price of production.

Yet if this is so, is not the price of production a specifically capitalist (and incomplete) form of that expression of labor costs which is necessary in every highly developed economy, an incomplete form of that expression of costs which is more important the higher the level of development and which can only be fully realized under communism?

This hypothesis is prompted by the logic of Marx's theory of value. In contrast to other theories of value, Marx's theory explains systematic deviations of prices from values with the same law of value. Even Ricardo, the most consistent of those who preceded the Marxist theory of value, believed that the relative value of goods depends not only on the labor expended but also on the time required for the circulation of capital (on the different longevities of elements of capital and on the different periods of turnover of capital). Marx demonstrated why and how under the conditions of capitalism a different center of gravity of prices, the price of production, is regularly formed. Interbranch competition leads to this. If the theory is correct, then the price of production must be formed not only in the distribution process but also in the production process. This means that under the conditions of capitalism production must take into account not only those labor costs that are reflected in value but, in addition, certain other labor costs, i.e., the price of production must have its own labor substance. Finally, the same logic leads to the supposition that the formula for labor costs forming the substance of the price of production, the formula for the optimal price, and also the formula for value have something in common. This general formula for price formation must obviously reflect the law of value as a law of prices in any commodity economy. These are the hypotheses prompted by the logic of the theory of value and whose analysis is dictated by the requirements of our economic practice.

3. Divergence Between the Theory and Practice of Measurement of the Results of Labor

The problem of measuring the results of labor is more complex than the problem of measuring the expenditures of this labor. We saw that in methods of measuring expenditures our practice (above all, planning and project practice) proceeded ahead of theory, clearing the way for optimal planning. In the sphere of measuring results practice lagged behind the level attained by science.

It is well known that according to the labor theory of value results must be expressed in socially necessary labor. Then comparison of socially necessary costs for the production of given output with actual costs will reveal the degree of effectiveness of the actual costs. For example, if actual costs are half the socially necessary ones, this means that labor in the given production yields a result twice as large as is assumed according to social norms.

Nevertheless, until the 1965 reform the planning of prices was the major bottleneck in organizing a socialist economy. Methods of optimal planning were partially used in planning production and in calculating expenditures, but were not applied to price formation. Consequently, the system of prices diverged considerably from the law of value, since the most exact use of this law finds its expression precisely in optimal prices. According to the law of value only those labor expenditures form value whose product is socially necessary. If the product does not correspond in quality or quantity to demand, part of the expenditures made do not form value. In practice prices frequently did not satisfy this requirement. They were oriented mainly toward costs, as if every expenditure of labor created value. Naturally such prices contributed to the production of low quality products and goods which did not meet demand. Therefore the noncorrespondence of prices with socially necessary outlays hindered measuring the results of expenditures of social labor. In addition, the task of bringing prices close to labor costs, which is socially necessary in optimal planning, was complicated by the fact that socially necessary expenditures as they are usually understood form the substance of value, whereas prices in optimal planning correspond to a modified form of value. Consequently, bringing prices close to socially necessary labor costs as they are usually understood is equivalent, as a rule, to making them diverge from optimal prices. Here, naturally, one may surmise that socially necessary labor costs have a dual expression. One lies at the basis of value and the other at the basis of its modification in optimal planning.

Although in measuring the results of *overall* expenditures of labor (living and past) a divergence occurs between theory and practice, this divergence emerges still more strikingly in measuring the results of *living* labor.

It is difficult to imagine a cruder error in economic calculations than confusing income with expense, benefits with costs. Moreover, elements of this error are contained in the most prevalent methods of measuring the results of living labor, namely, by gross output on a factory basis and by the quantity of produced output.

In fact, an enterprise's gross output reflects the results of the work not only of the given enterprise but also of a number of other enterprises, which have delivered means of production used for producing the first enterprise's output. Accordingly, the enterprise's gross output can increase as a result of increased consumption of means of production obtained "on the side." (Gross output can be viewed as the sum of an enterprise's net output and of its material expenditures.) This confusion of income with expense contained in the plan indicator frequently led to the enterprise's increasing material costs to the detriment of the net product. Costs are easier to increase than benefits. This error was manifested in extreme form in measuring fulfillment of the production plan as a sum of actually consumed inputs (this occurred, for example, in geological prospecting).

Measuring the results of an enterprise's work according to the weight of its output suffers from a similar defect. It is well known that the weight of output depends not only on the volume of the net product of the enterprise's personnel but also on the consumption of materials purchased.

Finally, the indicators used to measure the results of an enterprise's work suffer from the important defect that economies of past labor are not taken into account in them. But the consumption of past labor depends on living labor. Consequently, economies (or overexpenditures) of past labor are a component part of the results of living labor. Moreover, they are an extremely important factor. The consumption of past labor forms, on the average, four-fifths of the production costs of industrial output.

It is true that the consumption of past labor is taken into account in calculating the enterprise's profit. Until the 1965 economic reform, however, the role of this indicator was unclear and limited. On the one hand, this was the most general indicator of an enterprise's work. On the other hand, the assignment to increase profits often contradicted other important plan assignments (for example, the assortment plan). Defects in price formation showed up here. In addition, profit did not properly reflect such elements of the results of living labor as the use of fixed and circulating capital. The use of this capital influenced profit only to the extent that it was reflected in production costs. Moreover, the connection between the use of capital and production costs is not an obvious one. An improvement in the use of capital is accompanied in some cases by a reduction and in others by a rise in production costs.[7] This is precisely why it was necessary to supplement the indicator of production costs with special indicators of the utilization of productive capital.

Finally, using the relationship of profits to production costs as a profitability norm was incompatible with logic. With a rise in production costs, profits, as a rule, should decrease, not increase.

Thus, until the 1965 reform, profit and profitability indicators suffered from substantial defects.

Since a genuine overall indicator of the results of living labor was not available, the practice was to use several indicators for evaluating the success of an individual production link's work. The multiplicity of indicators hindered forming a general conclusion as to the degree of success in the production link's work and thereby hindered payment according to the results of labor. In particular, because of the absence of general rules for weighing individual indicators against other ones, qualitative indicators were underestimated in comparison with quantitative ones, and among the qualitative indicators those that concerned the use of fixed and circulating capital were usually underestimated.

The economic reform is introducing fundamental changes into the system and methods of calculating indicators of benefits. These new methods are more profound than those for the cost indicators, since the principles of optimal planning began to penetrate into the sphere of computation of costs even before the reform, which cannot be said concerning the computation of indicators of benefits. The 1965 reform is eliminating the evaluation of an enterprise's work according to gross output by introducing for this purpose profitability calculated on the basis of productive capital. The confusion of benefits with costs is thereby being eliminated and the information capacity of the profitability indicator is increasing. [8] In addition, the system of price formation is being reorganized with the objective of bringing prices closer to the socially necessary labor costs, i.e., for the purpose of enhancing prices as carriers of economic information.

Permeated with the principles of optimal planning, the 1965 economic reform should ultimately bring practice and theory together in that sphere in which the gap between them was especially great — in the sphere of measuring benefits. Success in this matter depends largely on the achievements of economic science, since the problem of measuring the benefits of social labor is more complex and less developed than the problem of measuring costs.

4. Significance of the Problem of Measuring Costs and Benefits

Because of the complexity of economic interrelationships, losses caused by shortcomings in calculations of costs and benefits affect a multitude of links. Therefore, it is not easy to notice and define them. If a worker spoils an article, the loss is obvious and easy to calculate. It is much more difficult to take account of losses from poor organization of a shop's or plant's production, although these losses can be much greater than those from rejected material. Yet the estimation of losses resulting from the application of incorrect methods of calculating costs and benefits is almost an impracticable task. We do not have in mind random errors in calculations of costs and benefits (these are not dangerous since, according to the law of large numbers, they will cancel each other out in the mass of calculations), but rather systematic errors engendered by incorrect methods of calculating. Errors in the principles of calculating costs or benefits are factors that operate on a massive scale. An error introduced into a plan indicator takes on the force of law for all executors of the plan and acts upon millions of persons, inducing them to consider an expenditure as a revenue and a reduction in the quality of output as a desirable result.

We will present an example illustrating the nature of losses to the economy arising from the lack of a common norm of effectiveness of investments. Let us assume that in some branches the design of projects presupposes a normative recoupment period of two years, while in others this norm is twenty years.

Let there be two design projects A and B, relating to different kinds of production and with the following expenditures associated with variants of these projects (Table 1).

Table 1

Variants	Project A Capital investment, in millions of rubles	Project A Production costs of annual output, in millions of rubles	Project A Recoupment period, in years	Variants	Project B Capital investment, in millions of rubles	Project B Production costs of annual output, in millions of rubles	Project B Recoupment period, in years
I_A	50	75	2	I_B	50	50	20
II_A	100	50	2	II_B	100	47.5	20
				III_B	550	25	20

Let us assume that for each project all variants fulfill identical tasks (yield identical output) and are identical in terms of the qualitative elements of their effect (labor conditions, etc.). Each of the combinations of variants of projects A and B will then also fulfill identical tasks. Furthermore, let us also agree that additional investments in both kinds of production are not associated with additional outlays of scarce types of means of production.[9]

Let us examine the costs required by combinations of variants of A and B given the different normative recoupment periods: For $A \leqslant 2$ years, for $B \geqslant 20$ years (Table 2).

Table 2

Composition of the combination	Investment, in millions of rubles	Production costs of annual output, in millions of rubles
$I_A + II_B$	150	122.5
$I_A + III_B$	600	100

The first combination is formed if current outlays of investment in producing B are relatively constrained, and the second is formed given less binding constraints on present outlays of investment.

We will now examine the combination of variants of A and B that is formed given a general normative recoupment period that lies within the range of two to twenty years (Table 3).

13

Table 3

Composition of the combination	Investment, in millions of rubles	Production costs of annual output, in millions of rubles
$II_A + I_B$	<u>150</u>	<u>100</u>

Let us compare this combination with the two preceding ones. Both preceding combinations are associated with large losses. The first combination $(I_A + II_B)$ involves additional production costs of 22.5 % for the same overall investment (compare the numbers underlined once in Tables 2 and 3). The second combination $(I_A + III_B$ in Table 2) requires an investment four times as large as the combination formed with a common recoupment period and does not yield any economies in production costs (compare the numbers underlined twice in Tables 2 and 3).

We recall that the combinations compared yield identical output. This means that those combinations that are formed with unjustified differences in recoupment periods can cause net losses. Moreover, these losses can become enormous on a national scale.

These losses are greatest when we are guided by minimum production costs (or individual value) of output, because when capital expenditures are limited, the principle of minimum production costs is associated with the greatest differences between recoupment periods for investment. Actual practice is guided by branch norms for the recoupment period. Differences between these periods are less than in the example presented. Relative overexpenditures on production costs and investment (caused by incorrect determination of norms of investment effectiveness) is accordingly less than in our example. Nevertheless, absolute overexpenditures probably amount to billions of rubles yearly.

Let us consider our example further.

If we examine separately the variants presented in Table 1 we notice that not one of them can be regarded as ineffective in itself. This means that if a given variant is "worse" than another in production costs, then it is "better" in terms of investment, and vice versa. There is no variant in the example that is worse than others without some compensation. Yet it turns out that ineffective combinations of variants can arise from individually

14

effective variants. Accordingly, planners, each working in his own sphere, are not in a position to notice or to prevent economically ineffective combinations of variants in the national economy unless they are guided by a proper normative recoupment period.

We have examined only one of the forms of losses resulting from the incorrect measurement of costs. But costs are calculated not just for determining the effectiveness of capital investment: the correct use of existing means of production, both reproducible and nonreproducible, also depends on cost calculations.

Let us assume that the headings in our example have been changed. Instead of the heading "Capital investment, in millions of rubles" we put "Annual consumption of scarce raw materials, in thousands of tons," and instead of the heading "Recoupment period" we put "Consumption of scarce raw materials, in kilograms per ruble of savings in production costs." It then turns out that if the prices of the scarce raw material do not properly govern its use, combinations of variants arise that may require either four times greater expenditures of a scarce raw material (for the same production costs) or greater production costs with the same total expenditure of a scarce raw material.

Similar examples could be presented for any means of production. Almost every means of production (a piece of land, a deposit of ore, a building, a lathe, etc.) can be used differently and with varying effectiveness. In this process (just as with capital investment) ineffective combinations of variants can arise from individually effective variants of the use of each relatively better means of production.

It is difficult to determine the scale of losses from insufficiently effective use of productive capital and natural resources. They probably significantly exceed losses from errors in calculating the effectiveness of investment, because annual investment constitutes only a small part of all productive capital. Our example illustrates those losses that arise in the course of preparing the plan, but defects in measuring costs and benefits also affect the fulfillment of the plan. Losses in this area stem mainly from discrepancies between economic accounting and the plan.

It is well known that until recently plan assignments were by no means always reinforced by financial stimuli for their fulfillment. There are profitable and unprofitable plan assignments. These discrepancies between the plan and financial considerations relate both to the question of *what* to produce (the assortment of output) and to the question of *how* to produce (with what means). In this way the managerial apparatus of the economy

15

worked under an unnecessary burden in overcoming this self-imposed obstacle.

There was a time when the discrepancy between economic accounting and the plan exemplified by the unprofitable operation of a number of production units which were advantageous from a national standpoint was treated by certain economists as one of the advantages of socialism over capitalism. This was true in the first stages of the socialist transformation of the national economy. This is true even now in certain cases (which will be discussed below). Nonetheless, the conformity of economic accounting with the plan is such an important aspect of organizing the management of the economy that the degree of this conformity can be considered as the criterion of completeness of organization of this management. Realization of the most important advantages of the socialist system depends on the extent of this conformity.

Proportionality in developing the national economy can be complete only when that composition of output and those means of producing it that correspond to the national economic plan are also most advantageous according to local (economic accounting) indicators. In the opposite case it becomes necessary to have centralized determination of every enterprise's entire production program as well as of all technical methods of producing all goods, a situation that is not feasible.

The growth of productivity of social labor can be greatest when local (economic accounting) advantage coincides with overall advantage, and local (economic accounting) increases in benefits coincide with the growth of the national income. For, under the conditions of democratic centralism, the principle of maximum benefits with minimum costs is fulfilled only to the extent that partial mimimum costs are compatible with the overall mimimum costs, and partial maximum benefits are compatible with the overall maximum benefits.

Distribution according to labor will be most complete when local indicators of the results of labor exactly reflect what each individual gives to society.

Finally, what is most important: only under conditions in which there is a conformity between individual (partial) indicators and the overall ones can the creative activity of the broad masses have the greatest scope and the most correct direction. The Program of the CPSU has set the task of the greatest possible development of democratic foundations of management together with the strengthening and improvement of centralized state

16

leadership of the national economy. But the expansion of economic independence (of state enterprises, collective farms, and districts) is appropriate only for that group of operations for which local indicators of costs and benefits are coordinated with the overall indicators. In the opposite case the expansion of operational independence of enterprises, collective farms, and districts expands the possibility of utilizing local advantage even when this advantage does not coincide with that of the national economy. Such consequences are probable even if there is a conscious desire to subordinate local interests to the general interest. In order to actually subordinate local interests to the general interest we first need local indicators of the general interest.

This means that the most complete combination of democratization of management with centralization is attained only when minimum costs from the standpoint of enterprises' economic accounting are compatible with overall minimum costs and maximum local benefits are compatible with overall maximum benefits.

Thus, the degree of conformity of local (individual) indicators to the overall indicators actually can serve as the criterion of optimality of organization of management of the economy. The conformity of local indicators to the overall indicators provides the greatest opportunities for developing the working people's creative initiative in an optimal direction for all of society, i.e., with adherence to optimal national economic proportions, with maximum growth of productivity of social labor, and with the best material and moral incentives for the working people. The problem of best using the creative energy of the millions of working people is, figuratively speaking, the problem of using the enormous internal energy of the "atoms of society." The importance of this problem can perhaps be compared to the importance of the problem of using atomic energy. Of course, there are substantial differences between these two problems. In particular, the reserves of internal energy of the "atoms of society" are not available to every social system. They are completely available to the socialist system, and, accordingly, the methods of using these reserves deserve the special attention of our science.

How should we set prices and economic accounting indicators so that economic calculation will serve as a reliable implement of the plan?

17

Notes

1. We have in mind what is called the "contradiction" between Volumes I and III of *Das Kapital.*

2. It is interesting that this strange principle was not observed in the development of simple commodity production. According to Engels, "the more completely simple commodity production develops, the more average prices for prolonged periods not interrupted by external forcible disturbances coincide with values with an accuracy corresponding to a quantity that can be disregarded" (K. Marx and F. Engels, *Soch.*, 2nd Edition, Vol. 25, Part II, p. 474).

3. The reader should bear in mind that for brevity Professor Novozhilov expresses the concepts of "labor necessary for producing a product" and "costs connected with producing a product" with the words "labor involved in producing a product" and "costs of producing a product." These abbreviated designations of the concepts named have been used in all of Professor Novozhilov's previous works, and accordingly the Editorial Board considered it possible to retain them in this book [Editorial Board].

4. The price of production "is determined not only by the value of the given commodity but also by the gross value of all commodities" (K. Marx and F. Engels, *Soch.*, 2nd Edition, Vol. 25, Part I, p. 225).

5. "The exchange of goods according to their values or approximately according to their values requires . . . a much lower stage than exchange according to prices of production, for which a rather high stage of capitalist development is necessary" (K. Marx and F. Engels, *ibid.*, p. 193).

6. For more detail on this, see Chapters 5 and 9.

7. For example, a decrease in the size of a batch of articles in serial machine-building accelerates the turnover of circulating capital but raises production costs.

8. However, another plan indicator, realized output, includes not only the result of an enterprise's work but also material expenditures. Accordingly it is not yet possible to consider the problem of measuring benefits as solved.

9. This condition is necessary since in the opposite case savings of production costs would be the result not only of additional investment but also of additional expenditures of scarce materials, etc.

CHAPTER 2

OPTIMAL PLANNING AND ITS CONTROLLING NORMS

The principle of an optimum arises from the economic laws of socialism. It is manifested above all in the fundamental economic law of socialism. No matter how the formulations of this law encountered in our literature may differ, in one way or another they are concerned with the maximum welfare of the working people and with the highest rates of its growth. This in turn presumes the minimization of labor costs, maximum effectiveness in the use of all material resources, optimal relationships between necessary and surplus labor, an optimal distribution of surplus labor among different uses, an optimal organization of management of the economy, etc. In this respect the laws of economics are somewhat similar to the laws of nature. Many of them represent movements or activities in accordance with extremal principles. An example is the propagation of light. Of course, an optimum in the economy differs substantially from the kind of optimum with which physics is concerned. Economic laws are historical in nature. Accordingly, the tendency toward an optimum is manifested differently under different economic conditions of place and time.

The law of labor economy dominates all human history, yet every economic structure has rates of growth in the productivity of labor that are specific to it alone. Socialism's rates are inaccessible to capitalism, and capitalism's rates are inaccessible to feudalism. In the economy the principle of the optimum governs not only quantitative relationships within the limits of a given structure but also qualitative changes – changes in production

19

relations. In Marx's theory of economic development, all of economic history is regarded as a steady advance toward the optimal social structure — communism. Marx determined both the law conditioning this movement (the law of correspondence of production relations to productive forces) and the factors constraining the action of the principle of the optimum. The law of labor economy lies at the basis of the development of productive forces, and the law of correspondence of production relations to productive forces lies at the basis of development of production relations. The reestablishment of a disturbed correspondence of production relations to the state of productive forces is dictated by the law of labor economy. In this lies the profound meaning of V. I. Lenin's well-known thesis that "in the final analysis it is labor productivity that is the most significant, most important element in the victory of the new social structure."

When the social structure begins to restrain the further growth of labor productivity (possible with a given level of productive forces), it is inevitably replaced by another economic structure, one that corresponds to the more developed productive forces and therefore ensures higher rates of growth of labor productivity. Hence it follows that the progressive development of production relations is as normal as is the tendency to an increase in labor productivity. Sooner or later this tendency breaks down those forms of social relationship that obstruct it and finds new forms that makes its realization possible. While the development of production relations proceeded spontaneously and by uncontrolled routes, in presocialist structures under socialism there arose not only the possibility but also the economic necessity of controlling the development of production relations. In accordance with this, planning the Soviet economy was permeated from the very beginning with the principle of the optimum. Naturally, however, at various stages of development of the socialist economy this principle was realized in a nonuniform way in various spheres, in different degrees, and by different methods.

1. The Pioneering Role of Soviet Science in Creating the Theory of Optimal Planning

In the first years after the October Revolution, the operation of the principle of the optimum in the economy was expressed mainly by the qualitative transformation of production relations.

A rise in the relative importance of the socialist sector in the national economy formed the basis for achieving high rates of labor productivity in the future. Even at the beginning of socialist reconstruction of the national economy there arose quantitative problems involving the principle of an optimum, such as problems of a long-run maximum rate of development, an optimal relationship between consumption and accumulation, and the most effective distribution of capital investments among construction projects. The decisions of the Fifteenth Congress of the All-Union Communist Party (Bolsheviks) contain not only the formulation of these problems but also instructions on the means of solving them.

New problems posed by the socialist transformation of the economy gave a powerful impetus to the development of economic science. Consequently, Soviet economic science systematically outstripped bourgeois science in formulating and solving new economic problems. Thus, even in the first half of the 1920s, our economic science posed and solved those specific problems of planned reconstruction of an underdeveloped economy that began to be discussed in bourgeois science a good quarter of a century later. In solving these problems bourgeois science very often "discovered" truths that had been discovered long before by Soviet economists.[1]

In the 1920s the first chessboard-type balance of interbranch connections for 1923-1924 was prepared by workers of the Central Statistical Administration, anticipating the input-output analysis developed by W. Leontief in the USA.

In practice, we realized, at the end of the 1920s and the beginning of the 1930s, the necessity of taking into account various constraints involved in microeconomic problems by use of the principle of the optimum, such as capital investment constraints, the limited availability of the best natural resources, and the scarcity of a number of materials. In scientific discussions concerning these problems a basically correct solution in the form of the application of coefficients expressing the normative effectiveness of utilization of scarce resources had already been projected. The need for these norms was confirmed later by the theory of optimal planning.

Finally, it was in our country that the basis was laid for mathematical methods of optimal planning. L. V. Kantorovich's works preceded the development of linear programming abroad (in the USA) by almost ten years.

Thus the principles and methods of optimal planning were first

21

developed in the first country with a planned economy. This was entirely to be expected.

In the 1930s the system of management of our national economy was reconstructed. Centralized direction was strengthened. Centralization was then objectively necessary for rapid industrialization under conditions of limited resources (the more limited are resources in comparison with the demand for them, the more important is centralization of their distribution).[2] But, as usually happens, the centralization entailed excessive "costs." In planning practice these "costs" were expressed in the form of insufficient recognition of the laws of economics (i.e., by voluntarism in planning). In the sphere of economic science the costs of centralization were reflected in the development of dogmatism and in the tendency to limit the functions of economic science to tasks of explaining and propagating existing practice. Of course, during this period our science also continued to develop. It is sufficient to recall that in 1939 L. V. Kantorovich's first work on linear programming was published. At the same time the development of problems of planning capital investments and their most effective distribution among various uses also continued.

Nevertheless, the new ideas were assimilated slowly by our science and were also put into practice slowly. In particular, mathematical methods of optimal planning were scarcely applied for twenty years in economic research or in planning, and therefore were weakly developed. A discussion on whether norms of investment effectiveness were needed was drawn out for three decades. As early as the end of the 1920s and in the 1930s some Soviet economists and engineers proposed the idea that the planning of capital investments should be directed toward achieving the maximum overall effect of all capital investments in the national economy. For this purpose it was proposed to include in production costs a payment for capital corresponding to its minimally acceptable effectiveness. In the 1940s this payment was substantiated by the mathematical theory of optimal planning. However, a norm of effectiveness of capital investments was not recognized by us for project calculations until 1958. Payments for capital are being introduced into economic calculations only now, in the course of implementing the 1965 economic reform.

As we see, the introduction into the economy of the achievements of Soviet economic science and of Soviet mathematics has extended over at least two unnecessary decades. At present twenty years mean much in science. Two-thirds of all scientific knowledge accumulated by mankind is the result of the last two decades.[3] Of course, this is a rough estimate. Yet there is no doubt that the rate of development of economic science until the 1960s lagged behind the progress of mathematics, natural science, and technology. In connection with this, the organization of the socialist economy was not adapted in time to the new conditions of development of productive forces. The lag in economic science was also expressed in the rates of utilization of the results of other sciences in raising our economy and culture. As is well known, the achievements of science and technology are still being slowly introduced into our national economy. The slow introduction of the results of scientific research in turn hinders the further development of science.

A turning point in the development of economic science has already occurred. It began eight or nine years ago. At that time there arose and rapidly developed a movement for the application of new mathematical methods and cybernetics in planning and economic research. In recent years increasing attention has been paid to the question of involving other sciences (sociology, psychology) in working out economic problems. To make up for lost time is difficult but, having the advantages of accumulated experience in planning the national economy and favorable objective conditions for development, Soviet economic science can become in the near future one of our most important productive forces.

At the present time, outlays on the development of economic science are probably more effective than outlays on any branch of natural science, for we must add to the direct benefits from the introduction of the achievements of economic science indirect benefits from the best introduction into production of the achievements of other sciences.

The direct benefits of economic science are most often measured by cost savings achieved by improved methods of planning or organizing production. As experience in the application of methods of optimal planning for the solution of plant and branch problems demonstrates, these benefits exceed by many times the costs involved in the formulation and solution of these problems. Economic science can yield still greater benefits by developing a system of management under which all enterprises would be interested in preparing and fulfilling optimal plans and in applying new technology and the best methods of economic work. It is no accident that we began the creation of mathematical methods of optimal planning in connection with the theoretical elaboration of those auxiliary norms of effectiveness of scarce

23

resources — norms of investment effectiveness, L. V. Kantorovich's resolving multipliers — that are necessary for coordinating economic calculation with the plan, and for coordinating individual interests with social ones and special optima with the overall optimum.

2. Democratic Centralism in Management of the National Economy and the General Principle of Its Development

At first glance the system of management of a socialist economy can be represented as the product of the voluntary creativity of legislators and administrators. Consequently, the replacement of one arrangement of economic management by another often seems like the correction of previously tolerated errors or insufficiently successful decisions. However, this is only the external aspect of the matter. In essence the organization of economic management is subordinate to the objective economic laws of socialism. Any nonconformity between the system of economic management and these laws causes consequences that sooner or later compel us to change this system in order to attain its greater conformity with objective economic laws.

The development of a system of economic management, including methods of measuring costs and benefits, is a law-governed process.

In the first stages of socialist construction, forms of management of the economy were selected purely empirically, by means of repeated corrections of new discrepancies arising in practice between the organization of management of the economy and economic laws. From this came the frequency of rearrangements of forms of organization of planning and management. ". . . Not one reasonable socialist who has written about future prospects ever had in mind that we could immediately put together and assemble, in a single stroke and according to previously given orders, forms of organization for the new society,"[4] wrote V. I. Lenin in 1918. Consequently, "repeated alterations and trials in practice of different systems of management and of different norms for the imposition of discipline are unavoidable . . . ."[5]

Only in proportion to the accumulation of experience does the possibility arise of studying the principles of development of a system for managing a socialist economy. Knowledge of these principles opens the way to the planned improvement of the system of management. Tasks formulated in this sphere by the Program of the CPSU are an organic part of the plan for creating the material and technical basis of communism. Their content reflects the most important principle of development of the system of economic management — the two-sided development of democratic centralism. "Communist construction presumes the greatest possible development of democratic foundations of management together with the strengthening and improvement of centralized state direction of the national economy."

The principle of democratic centralism, formulated by V. I. Lenin as early as 1918, has been applied in one or another form at all stages of socialist construction. Even in the years of intervention and civil war, when specific circumstances required strict centralization in the distribution of scanty resources, local bodies had certain rights in the sphere of managing local industry and of control over large, centrally subordinated enterprises. It is remarkable that the functions and powers of local Councils of the National Economy were expanded even at a time, 1920,[6] when the problem of liquidating the monetary system was formulated. These facts show that democratic centralism is the only possible principle of management of a socialist and, probably, a communist economy.

This proposition is confirmed and explained by cybernetics. A national economy is a very complex stochastic system that is not subject to description in all its details. "In order to obtain the possibility of managing such systems we must provide a controlling mechanism capable of fulfilling functions that are not clear to us although we are building this mechanism ourselves. A regulator with feedback can fulfill precisely these functions. . . . A regulator with feedback guarantees compensation of disturbances not only of a specific kind but also of any possible disturbances."[7] This kind of regulator must keep track of the values of certain variables (for example, the amounts of production of each product, the profitability of production) and act upon the system in such a way as to prevent significant deviations of these variables from their prescribed (normative) values.

The laws of commodity-monetary relationships, characteristic of socialism, perform the role of regulators in a socialist economy. Commodity production is capable of sustaining a certain proportionality among its elements only on the basis of a feedback. Under capitalism the conformity of production to demand is expressed in the equality of the market price and the price of production. A surplus (or shortage) of production in

25

comparison with demand causes deviations of market prices from prices of production that stimulate industrialists to reduce correspondingly to expand) production. The general rate of profit is the regulating variable. The feedback mechanism is directed toward sustaining profits at a certain level. Nevertheless, as is well known, this regulator (the law of value) works very slowly in the most important economic processes, and consequently allows deep disproportions extending all the way to cyclical crises. Frequently a lengthy interval of time ensues between the decision of a particular businessman and the market reaction to this decision (the feedback). During this interval similar decisions may be taken by other businessmen. This interval of time is especially long when production is being expanded through capital investment, that is, by constructing new enterprises or reequipping existing ones. The later the market consequences of businessmen's decisions are discovered, the greater is the probability of the appearance of disproportions. Therefore, periods of upward movement of capitalist industry which are linked with the introduction of new technological means of production terminate in crises of general overproduction.

The great length of time required for feedback to operate is a substantial defect in a system of commodity production. Consequently, the organization of the management of a socialist economy in the form of commodity production by autonomous and self-managing enterprises is clearly inappropriate. In such a case the possibilities of centralized planning and regulation would be completely unused. And yet these possibilities are considerable. No matter how complex a socialist economy is, it lends itself to study of its essential elements and their interrelationships. Their stochastic character can also be taken into account by using statistical methods. A knowledge of the essential elements of the economy and of the interrelationships among them opens the way for constructing a concrete quantitative model of its optimal development, i.e., for constructing a national economic plan. In this model one must necessarily determine those elements and interrelations in which feedback in the form of commodity-monetary relationships operates most slowly. These include plans for technological development, capital investments, and the development of heavy industry. Commodity-monetary relationships can then be used for elaborating and adjusting the plan (with due regard for unforseen changes in the situation).

Thus, democratic centralism presupposes a planned utilization of the law of value as an automatic regulator, i. e., as a regulator with feedback. Such a system of management was basically created at the very beginning of NEP, consisting of the plan and of economic calculation. Joining the two regulators into one system is a bold idea. It seemed to many economists (both here and abroad) that a plan and economic calculation were as incompatible as a plan and spontaneous processes. History, however, has shown the vitality of this system. It has withstood tests under the most difficult conditions. At the same time the possibility and necessity of more strictly coordinating economic calculation and the plan gradually emerged. An economy cannot be managed by two uncoordinated regulators. If the economic decisions of individual production units are based only on economic calculation, the plan loses its directive character to some extent. If, on the other hand, economic decisions are based only on plan directives, economic calculation loses its force.

Thus, with insufficient coordination of economic calculation and the plan, either the plan or economic calculation assumes a formal character.

These two types of interrelations between the plan and economic calculation are not just theoretical possibilities. Depending on historical conditions they can become separate phases in the development of a system of management.

We can perhaps consider the NEP period as the first phase. The system of planning the national economy was then only being formulated. Its methods were still incomplete. The constant and careful calculation of market relations, the mastering of these relations, and the corresponding construction of an economic apparatus then represented the most important problems of economic policy.

The second phase begins when the scientific level of the planning system is sufficiently high for administrative methods of management to be used, but insufficient for the extensive use of economic methods.

Such a situation arose in the period of socialist reconstruction of the Soviet economy and was retained with some changes down to the reform in progress now. The tasks of reconstructing and building up the power of the Soviet economy were so vast and urgent that they could be solved only by the planned concentration of forces and resources. Therefore, when there was a conflict between economic calculation and the plan, the former had to yield.

Coordinating economic calculation with the plan and joining them into a single regulator of production is a most difficult problem. This is the central problem of organizing the management of a socialist economy on the road to communism. It is so complex that its solution can only be gradual and approximate. It is so important that the extent to which it is solved must be considered as the criterion of perfection of the system of managing the economy. Under an optimal system of management the operation of economic laws (including the law of value) is directed toward fulfilling tasks established in the plan. Knowing the quantitative dependency of prices on those conditions that lend themselves to plan direction, it is possible to change these conditions so that the law of value assists rather than counteracts the realization of plan proportions. In such a situation the case proportions dictated by the law of value coincide with the planned ones.

It would be incorrect to consider that in this case production is regulated by the law of value. The law of value operates in a planned economy as an independent regulator only when it counteracts planning.

If planned prices are set contrary to the law of value, this law will give rise to disproportions and to expenditures of effort by economic management to overcome the resulting disproportions. When the law of value assists planning, it plays the role of a subordinate, auxiliary regulator. The plan, as the form in which the requirements of the system of economic laws is realized, serves as the basic regulator of proportions in production. Hence it follows that the basic task in improving economic management consists of coordinating the regulating functions of commodity-monetary relationships with the planned regulation of a socialist economy.

The possibility of coordinating economic calculation with the plan, and local with general advantage, has been demonstrated by the theory of optimal planning.[8] Optimal prices coordinate economic calculation with the plan, and profitability with national economic effectiveness. On this basis it is comparatively easy to construct a system of incentives in which the interests of each enterprise and each worker would coincide with the interests of society. The first and most complex condition for strengthening material and moral interests in the results of production is the coordination of profitability with the plan, the individual unit's economic advantage with that of the national economy. It is appropriate to stimulate material incentives only by the use of those indicators in which local advantage also reflects the general advantage. In the opposite case strengthening the material incentives of executors of the plan can lead to attempts to use local advantage to the detriment of the general advantage. Moral incentives to achieve high indicators are also beneficial only under the condition that these indicators reflect the national economic effectiveness of an enterprise's work.

Coordinating economic calculation with the plan gives the plan a new quality and new force. The plan-directive becomes an economic imperative for all its executors. Only on this basis can the broadest democratization of economic management be carried out in the future, consisting of the ultimate transformation of the planning and accounting agencies into organs of social self-government.

The basic line of subsequent development of the system of direction of the economy is from the plan-directive to the plan-economic imperative.

3. Management of the Soviet National Economy Before the 1965 Reform

An optimal system of management can be realized only with a sufficiently high level of development of productive forces, as well as of computer technology, mathematics, and economic science. The system of economic management before the 1965 reform was far from an optimal one. As we saw, the methods of calculating certain summary indicators were erroneous. Nonetheless, great historic tasks were solved with this system of management. Consequently there can hardly be any doubt that in its time this system of management basically corresponded to the state of productive forces and political circumstances. This system emerged in the period of socialist reconstruction of the national economy. Despite frequent reorganizations, its basic features were retained until recently.

In the period of socialist reconstruction of the national economy the tasks of economic management were much simpler than they are now. The structure of the national economy (the number of different branches and enterprises) was less complex. There were great possibilities for the extensive growth of production. The transition from hand labor to advanced technology ensured a considerable growth in labor productivity even with planning decisions that were not optimal. Finally, the living standards of the people were still low, and the composition of their consumption fund was comparatively simple.

In a sense all these conditions facilitated the centralized

management of the economy. In addition, centralization was historically necessary. Only it could ensure the highest possible rates of socialist reconstruction, which were obligatory in the circumstances of capitalist encirclement and threatening war. Centralized management of the economy made it possible to concentrate our strength and resources on decisive tasks, such as the creation of heavy industry and of cadres capable of mastering new technology, etc.

In the postwar period the conditions for development of the productive forces changed substantially. The structure of the national economy became more complex. The number of branches, enterprises, and construction projects increased. The variety of goods manufactured increased. The sources of extensive growth of production diminished. The significance of intensification of production grew, i. e., the significance of raising the efficiency of utilization of all resources, such as labor, materials, productive capital, capital investments, and natural resources. The rates of technological progress increased and the tasks of choosing the economically best variants became more complicated. With the growth in the workers' well-being their needs became more varied, more changeable, and more demanding. The tasks of economic management became extraordinarily complicated and transcended the possibilities of the former centralized system of management. It became necessary, on the one hand, to broadly democratize economic management, to involve the mass of workers in the search for new reserves of growth of productivity in solving tasks of technological and economic development, and, on the other hand, to reorganize the centralized direction of the national economy on the basis of new mathematical techniques and computer technology.

However, the attempts undertaken before 1965 to carry out the further democratization of economic management did not yield substantial results. The reorganization of management of industry and construction carried out in 1957 was confined to territorial decentralization. The extent of the enterprises' operative and economic independence did not undergo substantial changes despite the fact that expansion of this independence was urgently required in practice. Tasks that had been projected in the course of organizing the Councils of the National Economy were likewise not accomplished, such as strengthening economic calculation, raising the role of profits, and increasing the material interest of enterprises in the results of their production. The accomplishment of these tasks was hindered by the system of measuring costs and benefits that had emerged under conditions of strict centralization of management of the national economy.

The task of coordinating profitability with the plan and of the individual unit's economic advantage with national economic effectiveness was not posed. Prices were mainly oriented toward the costs of producing goods and contained neither normative profits relative to productive capital nor differential rent. The quality of output and the demand for it was insufficiently taken into account in these prices. Such a system of prices and other norms for calculating costs and benefits contains much less economic information than is assumed in the theory of optimal planning, and — we anticipate here a subsequent discussion — in the theory of value. Such prices do not inform the enterprises about what is to be produced (since with these prices the production of equally necessary goods is of varying profitability), nor about the necessary quality of this output (prices do not properly reflect the quality of goods), nor about the socially necessary limits on costs of production. With no charge for capital investments, with the absence of payments for the use of productive assets and natural resources, the system of social norms for calculating costs and benefits also does not contain information about how material resources are to be used and what the minimal level of effectiveness of their utilization should be.

Thus, before the 1965 reform, the law of value was used in our planned economy more in appearance than in essence, and more in form than in content. Naturally, under such conditions economic accounting at enterprises was in many respects a formality. Administrative methods of management prevailed over economic ones, the work of enterprises was regulated by a large number of plan indicators, and the independence and initiative of enterprise collectives were limited.

It could not be otherwise. When prices and norms of effectiveness of resources do not yield the information necessary for economic decisions the missing information must be given in the form of an administrative order. Since the information embodied in prices often diverged from the plan-directive, this directive had to be reinforced by sufficiently vigorous sanctions. But as the economic experience of many centuries demonstrates, administrative sanctions are a less effective stimulus to production than economic or moral incentives. Moreover, the advantages of relying on individual interests are greater the more the results of labor depend on the creative initiative of the worker. Consequently, with the increasing role of science and technological progress the inadequacy of purely administrative methods of managing the economy became increasingly apparent.

However, in the complex system of the modern economy it is not easy to achieve an exact linking of each worker's individual interest in the results of his work with the interests of the entire society. The interrelationships between the costs and benefits of different production units are now so complex that measuring the results of the labor not only of each worker but even of an enterprise as a whole has become a most difficult task. This task is much more difficult than the one that arose forty-five years ago during the transition to NEP, when V. I. Lenin wrote that "it is necessary to base every large branch of the national economy on individual interest." The new 1965 economic reform is a large step forward on the road to communism. It corresponds to the basic principle of development of the system of managing a socialist economy, namely, the two-sided development of democratic centralism.

There are now opportunities for improving the organization of our economy that were not even dreamed of during the NEP period. New mathematical methods of optimal planning have been elaborated. Foundations have been laid for the theory of managing complex systems (cybernetics). High-speed electronic computer technology has been invented and has attained a high level. These new scientific and technological resources permit us to achieve success in coordinating economic calculation with the plan and the interests of the enterprise with those of the national economy. Therefore, the economic reform now in progress can become an important stage on the road to the gradual transformation of the plan-directive into the plan-economic imperative, i. e., into that directive the best fulfillment of which coincides with the individual interests of all executors.

4. The Optimum in Economic Management — the Greatest Democratization with the Greatest Development According to the National Economic Plan

It is easy to expand the rights of enterprises. It is much more difficult to coordinate the interests of enterprises with those of the national economy. A complex system of measures is required for this. Democratization of a planned economy presumes optimizing the planning of production, optimizing price formation, and optimizing economic calculation and distribution according to labor. All these tendencies are interconnected. Obstructing any of these obstructs the coordination of individual interests with general interests. The optimization of planning is the main principle in this matter. This follows from the theory of the duality of mathematical programming. Optimal prices can be found after finding the optimal variant of the production plan, and simultaneously with finding this variant; but it is impossible to find them independently of the optimization of production, for the optimality of prices consists precisely in their conformity to optimal production. Prices must stimulate the realization of optimal production proportions and the minimization of costs in the economically oriented organization of plan fulfillment. Consequently the planning of prices must be closely connected with the planning of production at all levels.

At the level of national economic planning optimal prices will naturally pertain to highly consolidated groups of goods and resources. One of the most general norms used for calculating outlays and establishing prices — the norm of effectiveness of capital investment — is determined at this level of planning. The transition from consolidated prices (the sum of prices for a group of goods or price indices) to optimal price lists and norms of profitability of specific kinds of resources is still an unsolved problem.

The planning of prices would be most closely connected with the planning of production if the detailing of planned prices was done together with the detailing of production plans, i. e., if the consolidated prices and norms of effectiveness of resources in the national economic plan were divided up into smaller groups of goods in the course of branch planning, and, finally, if this was done for the prices of individual goods (price lists) in the course of planning associations' and enterprises' production.

Optimal prices are the basis for optimizing economic calculation. Norms of profitability of fixed productive capital must be determined by proceeding from these prices. For circulating capital this norm must be close to the norm of effectiveness of capital investment. Norms of effectiveness of fixed capital must differ both by enterprises and (with subsequent detailing) by the kinds of fixed capital. The normative profitability of different kinds of fixed capital must lie at the basis

33

of their future revaluation. Differences in the valuation of identical implements of labor in different branches and enterprises will indicate the means of raising the effectiveness of their utilization stemming from their redistribution among branches and enterprises.

In order to achieve the most effective utilization of implements of labor the unification of these valuations according to a certain principle is advisable. This principle is: the same valuation of an implement of a given kind and quality at a given time and given place.

Differential rent must be standardized together with the profitability of productive capital. The rates of differential rent must reflect not the actual effectiveness of utilization of natural resources, but their normative effectiveness in the optimal plan. Then the collection of differential rent and normative profit (in the form of payments for the use of productive capital) will impart to the optimal production plan the force of economic law, the violation of which is unprofitable and the observation of which is profitable for all executors of the plan.

Payments for the use of material resources coordinate the interests of cost accounting organizations with the general interest. On this basis the number of planned effectiveness indicators of the work of individual production units can be reduced to a minimum. The multiplicity of indicators of their work in the absence of objective rules for the common measurement of these indicators excludes the possibility of accurately calculating the effectiveness of economic decisions and the effectiveness of operations. Under such conditions the evaluation of effectiveness unavoidably depends on the subjective judgment of the evaluating authorities.

An optimal system of economic calculation is the basis for optimizing distribution according to labor. The formula for such distribution is: "Each individual producer obtains back from society, after all deductions, exactly as much as he gives to it." [9] The real measure of the results of living labor is net output. But net output depends on the conditions of application of labor, such as the nature of its technological equipment, the quality of natural resources used, location, and other factors. These conditions of application of labor are usually not identical for different enterprises producing the same kind of output. Therefore, the payment of labor according to net output would violate the principle of distribution according to quantity and quality of labor. Workers in the best equipped enterprises, those that have the best resources, would receive for the same work higher wages than workers of enterprises situated in less favorable conditions. This means that distribution according to labor presupposes the conversion of each producer's net output to identical conditions of application of labor, i. e., a conversion such that labor identical in quality and quantity under any necessary conditions of production (within the limits of the optimal plan) would yield an identical corrected net output. Only then will it be possible to calculate correctly how much each producer gives to society, so that distribution according to labor would correspond to Marx's formula indicated above.

The conversion of net output to equal conditions of application of labor presupposes the standardization of profitability in accordance with the effectiveness of the utilized means of production. By deducting from net output the normative profit associated with comparatively better conditions of application of labor, we obtain an indicator depending only on the quality and quantity of individual labor. Thus, an optimal system of prices and economic calculation creates the basis for optimizing distribution according to labor.

Of course, a full accounting of corrected net output is economically sound only for sufficiently large collectives of workers, in which many elements of material expenditures depend on the workers. The results of the labor of small collectives (sections, brigades) and of individual workers must encompass only those elements of corrected net output that depend on the given workers.

Optimizing distribution according to labor presupposes not only refining the measurement of its national economic results, converted to equal economic conditions, but also finding the best relationships between the corrected result and payments for labor. This relationship must be most conducive to obtaining improved results. In other words, it is necessary to determine principles of differentiating the share of deductions for society. This share naturally must be larger in the case of payment for the results of collective labor than of individual labor, and above all it must be larger in the case of payment for scientific and technological achievements (universal labor), for the role of previous labor is great here (and is increasing all the time). Correspondingly, the shares of participation in negative results (losses) must also be differentiated.

The more highly perfected is distribution according to labor, the more exactly it is realized in accordance with Marx's formula presented above, the broader the democratization of economic management can and must be. Thus, the democratization of management of the economy is the final link in the chain of trends of development of organization of a socialist economy under consideration here. The democratization of management is necessary not only because the national economy is too complex a system, whose management cannot be completely centralized, but it is also necessary for developing the creative activity of the masses. The broader the creative participation of the masses in the development of the economy and culture, the more rapid are the rates of growth of production. This is one of the most important historic laws. The most recent confirmation of this law is the acceleration of rates of economic and cultural development of countries following the socialist revolution. The socialist revolution liberated the creative energy of the masses. Although the thousand-year oppression and poverty of the working masses did not pass without traces — they are reflected in their moral and cultural level — this energy has nonetheless already greatly accelerated the rates of economic and cultural development.

Economic progress depends not only on the activity of the masses but also on the organization of the economy. The role of this factor is greater the higher the level attained by the social economy. Therefore, with the growth of large-scale production and the increasing complexity of economic connections (interbranch, interdistrict, etc.), the role of centralized direction is increased. The improvement of centralized direction of the economy is an economic necessity arising from the most important principles of development of the socialist economy. The more correct the proportions between branches of production, the more accurate the calculation of economic interrelationships, the more fruitful is the activity of the masses, and accordingly the higher are the rates of growth of production.

Thus, the two-sided development of democratic centralism fully corresponds to the law of labor economy, both with respect to democratization and to the centralization of management of the economy. The optimal organization of the social economy is attainable given the fullest possible development of both of these principles.

The combination of these two principles proceeds by means of expanding the scope of those economic problems that are solved jointly by the center and the localities. The greater the extent to which economic problems are solved by joint efforts of the center and localities, the more precisely both general state and local interests are reflected in the plans, the higher is the level of

36

planning leadership and the more effective is local initiative. Therefore, we can conceive of the optimum in the organization of the economy as a state of affairs in which all economic questions, down to the smallest ones, are decided by cooperation of the center and the localities. This is possible on the basis of combining two forms of centralization, direct and indirect. Direct centralization consists of the specific solution, in the planning center, of a particular class of questions. Indirect centralization in the solution of a particular class of economic questions consists of establishing norms for calculating costs and benefits by means of which the localities, guided by the principle of "maximum benefits and minimum costs" may themselves find the variants that correspond most to the national economic plan. These norms can be expressed both in monetary and in labor units.

Indirect centralization is necessary both in a socialist and in a communist economy. It has the remarkable property of subjecting all possible local decisions to the plan, including decisions concerning the smallest questions, since all economic questions are decided on the basis of comparing costs and benefits. In particular, in this arrangement the violation of plan directives expressed in value categories is equivalent to the direct infringement of both the collective and individual interests of executors of the plan. It is linked with a reduction in the profitability of an enterprise, with losses, and with the reduction of earnings (bonuses, etc.). The better the use that is made of the law of value in planning, the broader can be the democratization of management of the economy, and the higher can be the general level of centralization, both direct and indirect.

Hence it is apparent that the most rigorous degree of planning the development of the national economy is attained, given the fullest combination of direct and indirect centralization. In this situation the plan regulates all economic decisions. The most important decisions are regulated in a twofold manner, directly and indirectly, and all the remaining ones are regulated only indirectly, through planned norms for calculating costs and benefits.

At the present time the system of indirect centralization corresponds to economic laws (and to the principles of optimal planning) less than the methods of direct centralization. In this connection indirect centralization has become a bottleneck in the system of managing the socialist economy. For example, the prices set before the 1965 reform differed from optimal plan prices in the very principles of their formation – in their very structure.

This cannot be said about the planning of production. The methods of optimal planning, although in an incomplete form, are nonetheless applied to the planning of production. But in price formation and in calculating costs and benefits the methods of optimal planning have not yet received general recognition. Therefore, for optimizing the planning of production it is important, above all, to remove the bottleneck involving the noncorrespondence of prices to the law of value (and this means to the principles of optimal planning). The development of methods of calculating costs and benefits is dictated not just by the special features of the current state of the socialist economy. Prices and norms of effectiveness of the optimal plan are not only an implement for fulfilling the plan on the basis of economic calculation but also are an implement for preparing the plans. Optimal prices cannot be worked out after the preparation of an optimal plan. Such a procedure is possible only for solving small tasks of optimal planning, such as for a shop or a small enterprise. In these cases an optimal plan can be prepared first by using "external" prices, and then internal prices and effectiveness norms can be established for internal economic accounting. In national economic planning the optimal plan and optimal prices can only be determined jointly. Democratic centralism is necessary not only in plan fulfillment but also in its preparation. "In planning, an increasing role must be played by plans and proposals coming from below, beginning from the enterprises."[10]

The task of planning the national economy can be solved by means of dividing this task into a multitude of sub-tasks of varying degrees of consolidation and magnitude. In so doing each sub-task is solved separately, i.e., optimal plans, prices, and norms of effectiveness of resources are found for each part of the national economy. Discrepancies between local prices and effectiveness norms indicate the directions in which it is necessary to change the distribution of resources among the various parts of the national economy. Resources must be redistributed in the direction of those parts of the economy in which the normative effectiveness of resources is higher, and away from those parts in which the effectiveness of utilization of resources is lower. The same must be said concerning goods. In the process of successively recalculating the plans, goods must be shifted from where their prices are lower to where their prices are higher. When equalization of prices and norms of effectiveness of resources in the plans of different economic units is attained in this iterative process, the production plans of all economic units attain a general national economic optimum.

Naturally, such a procedure for bringing plans to the optimum depends on the methods of recalculation (algorithms). In order that the attained optimum be sufficiently stable and not depend on small changes in the situation, it is necessary that prices and effectiveness norms do not reflect an accidental and temporary situation but rather a comparatively stable one. Determining prices on the basis of socially necessary outlays of labor meets this requirement. The law of value regulates the composition of production by means of equating prices that represent the equilibrium of supply and demand with the monetary expression of socially necessary outlays of labor. Correspondingly, in optimal planning models, prices are equal to costs of production, including payments for capital. Hence it follows that optimal prices can be determined not only as a whole but also by parts, by means of summation of elements of expenditures calculated according to socially necessary norms. The value principle of price formation reflecting the law of value consists precisely of this. The optimization of prices and effectiveness norms of resources is an active and independent factor in optimizing production plans precisely on the strength of this principle. Consequently, the gradual approximation of prices to socially necessary outlays of labor is one of the aspects of the gradual optimization of planning.

We will gradually approach the problem of socially necessary outlays of labor, examining its different aspects in turn.

First we will investigate methods of measuring outlays in problems of their minimization in the course of achieving a result prescribed by the plan. Then we will examine methods of measuring results in problems of their maximization with given resources. Lastly, by generalizing models of minimization of costs and maximization of benefits we will construct a model of the formation of socially necessary labor in the process of optimal planning of the national economy. A retrospective view from this model of the essential history of the operation of the law of value will allow us to establish a general formula for price formation.

Notes

1. Collette convincingly demonstrated that the ideas presented by Soviet economists in the middle of the 1920s and at the beginning of the 1930s anticipated by 20 years the ideas presented after the Second World War by Kahn, Lewis, Rosenstein-Rodan, and the authors of the first Indian plan, and that the works of Strumilin, Shaposhnikov, and others on the problems of the First Five-Year Plan anticipated similar works by

Leibenstein, Myrdal, and others by 25-30 years (cf. Collette, *Politique des investissements et calcul economique. L'experience Sovietique,* Paris, 1965).

2. See Oskar Lange, *Niektore zagadnenia centralizacji i decentralizacji w zarzadzaniu,* Warsaw, 1962.

3. See M. Lavrent'ev, "Science and the Rates of the Century," *Izvestiia,* January 17, 1966.

4. Lenin, *Poln. sobr. soch.,* Vol. 36, p. 379.

5. *Ibid.*

6. See A. V. Venediktov, *Organizatsiia gosudarstvennoi promyshlennosti v SSSR,* Leningrad University Publishing House, 1957, pp. 576-577, 590-591.

7. S. Beer, *Kibernetika i upravlenie proizvodstvom* (translated from English), Moscow, Fizmatgiz, 1963, p. 49.

8. For more detail on this, see Chapters 5 and 9.

9. K. Marx and F. Engels, *Soch.,* 2nd Edition, Vol. 19, p. 18.

10. *Programma Kommunisticheskoi partii Sovetskogo Soiuza,* Gospolitizdat, 1961, p. 87.

CHAPTER 3

MEASUREMENT OF RELATIVE EFFECTIVENESS OF OUTLAYS OF LABOR WITHOUT MEASURING THEIR NATIONAL ECONOMIC EFFECT

We will begin with methods of measuring costs in problems concerned with their minimization. In problems of this kind the result is assumed to be prescribed in accordance with social requirements. Such a limitation of the problem is not just procedure facilitating investigation, but can correspond to reality. When prices do not sufficiently take account of conditions of demand and the quality of goods, measuring the results of production in such prices will be incorrect. How do we determine the effectiveness of outlays under such conditions if the value expression of their results is insufficiently reliable? Only one possibility remains — to compare with each other those plan and project variants that yield identical output. Having calculated outlays on each of these variants, we can then choose from them as many variants with relatively lower outlays as are necessary for covering requirements. This is what was done in our economic practice. The magnitude of requirements was calculated by the planning bodies.

Consequently, the effectiveness of plan variants was determined without measuring their national economic effect and only on the basis of comparing outlays. The appropriateness of such a method was rooted not only in the particular features of price formation, but also in the fact that in the period of socialist reconstruction, of fundamental changes in the branch structure of the national economy and in the territorial location of productive forces, the national economic effect of construction was not confined to output. Other results of construction that frequently did not lend themselves to monetary evaluation had substantial significance, together with material wealth. Comparing the effectiveness of plan and project variants without measuring their national economic effect was a justified method of planning work under conditions of reorganization of the economy and given the one-sided use of the law of value, i.e., its use chiefly to measure costs rather than benefit.

With the approximation of prices to socially necessary labor costs and with the development of methods of optimal planning, the effectiveness of plan and project variants will increasingly be measured by their profitability. Yet methods of measuring effectiveness of variants on the basis of measurements of costs without measurements of benefits will undoubtedly also be applied in the future. They will be applied in developing those plan projections that are geared to long-run considerations and that introduce profound changes in the structure of the national economy. Of course, socially necessary labor costs also change in such cases. This means that until completion of the new plan they remain unknown.

1. The Effectiveness of Social Labor

The measurement of costs and benefits helps to solve the most important question of economic practice, that of determining the effectiveness of social labor. The effectiveness of social labor is one of the broadest concepts of economics. This is precisely why it is not easy to define.

First of all we must establish the meaning of effectiveness in general. The general concept of effectiveness is extremely broad and is used in the most varied spheres. Effectiveness usually is the ratio of useful effect (benefit) to the costs of obtaining it. By comparing individual types of costs with the elements of useful effect connected with them we obtain a multitude of effectiveness indicators, namely, labor productivity, the capacity coefficient, the coefficient of utilization of equipment, etc. Effectiveness indicators are often expressed in reciprocal form, i.e., as the relationship of costs to benefits, such as production costs per unit of output, the consumption of fuel per unit of output, etc.

However, all the effectiveness indicators in use are incomplete. Either costs or benefits or (most frequently) both are insufficiently taken into account. Moreover, for economic decisions and for the choice between alternative plans (or projects)

42

it is necessary to know the relationship between the overall national economic effect and all costs in the economy for each of the alternatives compared. It is necessary to know the overall national economic effectiveness of the compared alternatives.

Since in reality all costs consist only of labor costs, the national economic effectiveness of alternatives is nothing but the effectiveness of social labor.

The effectiveness of labor is usually identified with its productivity. However, the product of labor and the effect of labor are not one and the same. The national economic effect of labor is not always confined to output. The construction and operation of new enterprises results not only in deriving output but also in accomplishing other tasks for the national economy. Thus, construction of a plant in a region with a population that is relatively backward culturally assists in raising its cultural level. A variant of an industrial process that facilitates adapting a given kind of production unit to defense needs strengthens the country's defense capacity. Similar types of benefits usually cannot be measured. Nevertheless, they must be taken into consideration in solving the problem of the correspondence of costs to benefits received.

However, the difference between labor productivity and labor effectiveness consists not just of the fact that labor effectiveness depends on certain unmeasurable elements. Even if the national economic effect of labor did not include these factors labor effectiveness still would not coincide with its productivity. Indeed, the productivity of labor is the ratio of the quantity of output to the labor expended on it. The useful effect of output is not measured by its quantity. A product can be useful or useless, necessary or unnecessary. An increase in the production of unnecessary output can raise labor productivity but reduce its effectiveness.

The essence of determining labor effectiveness is expressed in the following comment by Engels on planning under communism. "This plan will be determined in the final analysis by weighing and comparing the useful effects of different objects of consumption with each other and with the amount of labor necessary for producing them."[1] According to Engels, in preparing a plan it is necessary to compare not the amount of products but their useful effects. In this way the relative significance of different lines of production will become apparent. In addition, the useful effects of objects of consumption should be compared with the labor costs required to produce them. In this way both the amount of each product and the total volume of material production will be established.

There is no doubt that in the assertion cited Engels had in mind a communist society operating in historical conditions other than those of the USSR. In particular he assumed that the law of value had already lost its force. Nevertheless, the idea that the plan must be prepared on the basis of comparing not the quantity of products but their "useful effects" retains its full significance even under our conditions. Without comparing qualitatively different use values it is impossible to determine whether a particular kind of output "justifies" the costs required for producing it. If we took into account only the quantity of output and did not pay attention to the correspondence of these quantities to needs, we could not determine in what proportions to produce goods, for quantities of heterogeneous products are incommensurable with each other, and therefore their ratios do not provide any basis for determining the proportions required.

It follows that the effectiveness of social labor is a broader concept than its productivity. The former encompasses not only the quantity of output but also its correspondence to needs, and likewise those elements of the national economic effect of labor that do not lend themselves to measurement.

2. The Basic Rule for Comparing the Effectiveness of Outlays of Labor

Measuring labor effectiveness with due regard for the unmeasurable elements of the overall effect is not possible. But this does not prevent us from measuring the relative effectiveness of labor. Although the effectiveness of social labor may not be capable of expression by a number, the ratio of the effectiveness of outlays on two alternative plans (projects) can be expressed by a number under one condition. This condition is that the national economic effect of the compared alternatives is identical.

We cannot measure the national economic effect, but we can establish whether identical purposes are attained by the variants being compared. This possibility (of determining the identity or difference of national economic effect) is the basis for measuring the national economic effectiveness of alternative plans (projects). Given the identity of the national economic effect of the compared alternatives, the ratio of their national economic effectiveness is inversely proportional to the ratio of the costs required for implementing each alternative. Thus, given an

44

identical effect for all variants being compared, costs become the basis for comparison. The costs of the various alternatives are commensurable.

From this follows the first rule for comparing the national economic effectiveness of alternative projects. It can be called "the rule of identity of effect." It rests on the proposition that the alternative projects being compared must fulfill identical national economic tasks, i.e., must satisy needs that are identical in volume, composition, place, and time and serve goals of economic policy that are identical in nature, volume, place, and time.

Let us examine the various aspects of this rule.

(a) At first glance it seems that differences in the extent to which needs are met do not prevent us from comparing the national economic effectiveness of alternative projects. But this is incorrect. The point is that differences in the amount of production of a planned project exert an influence on the effectiveness of the remaining output of the same product.

In fact, by choosing a variant that meets a certain share of requirements, we thereby determine the amount of output of other new enterprises producing the same product. From the national economic standpoint, indicators of effectiveness that apply to all requirements rather than to a portion of them are of decisive significance. Therefore, we cannot reach firm conclusions by comparing indicators of effectiveness of alternatives that meet different portions of total requirements. If, for example, one alternative meets 100% and the other 50% of national economic requirements for a product, we cannot establish which of them ensures the satisfaction of total requirements at minimum cost by comparing costs. The first alternative meets total requirement whereas the second meets only half of them. Therefore, in the first case all costs are known to us, but in the second case only part of them are. It is quite possible that the costs of production required to satisfy the second half of requirements when the second alternative is used will be much higher than the costs of output in the first alternative. As a result, the costs of total output in the second case will be higher, even if the second alternative (meeting 50% of requirements) yields output that is cheaper per unit than the first alternative.

Hence it follows that comparison of indicators of effectiveness is possible only when the same share of total requirements is being met, i.e., the same volume of production. Only in this case does the effectiveness of producing the remaining part of output not depend on the choice of the particular project.

(*b*) It is hardly necessary to prove that the production costs of one kilowatt-hour of electric power are incommensurable with the production costs of one ton of cast iron. Capital investment per unit of finished output of different kinds is also incommensurable. But this is a minor matter. Differences in the qualitative composition of the effect prevent a comparison of the national economic effectiveness of alternative projects not only where different elements of effect are present in the alternatives being compared but also where the effects of the compared alternatives consist of the same elements but are combined in different proportions.

(*c*) Differences in the location of projected enterprises by themselves do not prevent us from comparing outlays on these enterprises, provided the alternatives compared are intended to meet the same requirements (with respect to place and other characteristics). For the comparison of costs of different projects, not identity of the place of construction but identity of region being supplied is necessary. Outlays on alternative projects of a machine-building plant intended for supplying the entire Soviet Union can be fully commensurable even if the alternative locations are separated by thousands of kilometers.

(*d*) Two variants of outlays for producing output similar in composition, quantity, and place of consumption will not be commensurable if they do not yield output at the same time. Thus, if for one reason or another one plant begins to provide output three years later than a second plant the outlays associated with these variants will be incommensurable, for during the three years the effects of outlays on the construction of these plants will be very different.

(*e*) The complete identity of physical or chemical properties of output is not a necessary conditions for the comparison of the effectiveness of alternatives. If two products that differ in certain physical or chemical properties meet the same requirements we can compare outlays on the production of these products. For example, we can compare the national economic effectiveness of different variants of supplying fuel for power purposes although the chemical composition and physical properties of peat, coal, oil shale, and other types of fuel differ.

(*f*) Differences in "unmeasurable elements of national economic effect," i.e., differences in the content or the extent of realization of alternative projects of such tasks of economic policy as the economic development of backward regions, strengthening of defense capacity, etc., naturally complicate the comparison of national economic effectiveness of these alternatives. Thus, if the alternatives compared yield identical output but one of them promotes the economic and cultural development of a backward region more than another the ratio of the effects of these alternatives will not be inversely proportional to the cost ratios of these alternatives.

3. The Conversion of Alternative Projects to a Common Effect

The rule of identity of effect presents such strict requirements for the procedure of comparing effectiveness that this comparison might appear to be practically unrealizable. Indeed, alternative projects that would yield an identical effect in all respects are rarely encountered in practice.

Nevertheless, alternative projects that differ greatly in their effect can be compared in effectiveness provided they are adjusted in a manner that might be called conversion to a common effect.

The essence of this conversion is extremely simple. We will assume that it is necessary to compare the national economic effectiveness of two alternatives, one of which yields an effect $(a + b)$ and the other an effect $(a + c)$, with the same costs for both.

It would be incorrect in this case to determine the comparative effectiveness of both projects by comparing differences in the indicators of effectiveness with differences in the degree of national economic usefulness of the outputs $(a + b)$ and $(a + c)$. Such a comparison of costs and degrees of usefulness would be required only if the choice of one of the alternatives, say the first instead of the second, excluded the possibility of producing c in the national economy, and the choice of the second alternative instead of the first excluded the possibility of producing b. Then it would be necessary to take into account the values for the national economy of c and b, to compare them with costs, and to decide which one is preferable.

In reality, such a necessity usually does not arise in the comparison of plan (project) alternatives that differ in the composition of their effects. As a rule the choice of one of the alternatives instead of all the others does not at all exclude the possibility of producing those products or of obtaining those effects that exist in the rejected alternatives but that are not obtained in the accepted alternative. The effects absent in the accepted alternative can be obtained by means other than those that were rejected in the given case. This is the situation in our example. If we accept the alternative yielding output $(a + b)$ and

47

reject the alternative yielding $(a + c)$ this does not mean, as a rule, that the national economy will do without c or reduce its consumption of it. This signifies only that c must be produced by other methods that are not included in the alternatives under consideration.

The availability of other methods of producing c makes it possible to convert the alternatives being compared to a common (identical) effect and consequently makes it possible to compare the effectiveness of these alternatives.

If we accept the alternative yielding $(a + b)$ instead of the one yielding $(a + c)$ then we must ascertain by which method and at what cost the requirements for c will be met. On the other hand, if we accept the alternative yielding $(a + c)$ instead of the one yielding $(a + b)$ then we must ascertain by which method and at what cost the requirements for b will be met. In other words, in both cases we must examine what are the costs of producing $(a + b + c)$ by various methods, with $(a + b)$ being produced jointly and c separately in the first alternative, and $(a + c)$ being produced jointly and b separately in the second.

If we allocate to each of the alternatives the production of that output (or of those effects) that are obtained in the other alternative projects but that are absent in the given alternative, we convert the various alternatives to an identical effect. In addition, we must increase outlays on each alternative by the sum of costs necessary for producing the effects allocated to the given alternative. After this the effect associated with all the transformed alternatives will be the same, and consequently the outlays on each will be commensurable.

Thus, conversion to a common effect means finding those combinations of alternative projects that must include the compared alternatives of the particular project and yield an identical national economic effect. It is clear that such combinations can be derived from a different number of alternatives.

However, there is no need for such an expansion in the number of alternatives being compared. We can limit ourselves to the number of alternatives necessary and sufficient to attain identity. For this purpose it is necessary to add to each of the alternatives being compared the production of goods available in other alternatives but absent (or produced in lesser amounts) in the given alternative. In so doing, the goods absent in the given alternative (or available in lesser amounts) must be assumed to be produced in the same amount as in that alternative in which they are obtained in the greatest amounts.

A scheme for adjusting alternative projects to a common effect can have the following form, for example. Suppose that four alternatives that are characterized by the data in Table 4 are being compared.

Table 4

Alternatives	Annual output	Operating costs, in rubles per year	Capital investment, in rubles
I	$100a + 100b$	1000	2000
II	$100a + 50c$	1100	2300
III	$100a + 50c + 50d$	1300	2250
IV	$100a + 150e$	900	200

In such a form the alternatives are incommensurable. Suppose further that products b, c, d, and e can be produced separately, with their separate production being sufficiently effective in comparison with all other methods of their production. Then the common effect for alternatives I — IV is:

$$100a + 100b + 50c + 50d + 150e.$$

We will assume that the individual production of b, c, d, and e will involve the following costs (Table 5).

Table 5

Output	Operating costs, in rubles per year	Capital investment, in rubles
$100b$	200	50
$50c$	200	300
$50d$	100	200
$150e$	50	50

It is now possible to adjust all existing alternatives to a common effect. We do this by adding to each of the alternatives the costs

49

required for producing output equal to the common effect. As a result we obtain the following sums of costs for the adjusted alternatives (Table 6).

Table 6

Alternatives	Output before adjustment	Output added for adustment to the common effect	Operating costs added, in rubles per year	Capital investment added, in rubles	Costs of adjusted alternatives	
					Operating costs, in rubles per year	Capital investment, in rubles
I	$100a + 100b$	$50c + 50d + 150e$	350	550	1.350	2.550
II	$100a + 50c$	$100b + 50d + 150e$	350	300	1.450	2.600
III	$100a + 50c + 50d$	$100b + 150e$	250	100	1.550	2.350
IV	$100a + 150e$	$100b + 50c + 50d$	500	550	1.400	2.550

Since the adjusted alternatives have identical output, their costs are commensurable. It is not difficult to see that of the four alternatives the first is the most effective. It is true that capital investment in this alternative is higher than in alternative III, but the additional amounts for one-time expenditures are covered by savings in operating costs during one year. Accordingly, the question of the choice of alternatives in the given case leaves no doubts.

4. Examples of Adjusting Project Alternatives to a Common Effect

Let us illustrate what has been said with more obvious examples of adjustment to a least common effect.

(a) Adjustment to the same volume of output.

Conditions of the problem. The reconstruction of a condensation plant with the following characteristics is planned:

Generation of electric power

Before reconstruction . . . . . 125 million kilowatt-hours per year
After reconstruction . . . . . . 250 million kilowatt-hours per year

50

Investment for carrying out reconstruction   17.5 million rubles

Production costs of electric power

> Before reconstruction . . . . 10 kopecks per kilowatt-hour
> After reconstruction . . . . 8 kopecks per kilowatt-hour

The question is whether reconstruction is effective.

We will first try to solve this problem without adjustment to a common effect. Reconstruction yields savings in production costs of two kopecks per kilowatt-hour. Consequently, investment in reconstruction will be recouped by savings in production costs. However, the attempt to determine the amounts of annual savings in production costs encounters difficulties. By what volume of annual output should we multiply the savings in production costs per unit of output — the volume prevailing before reconstruction (125 million kilowatt-hours per year) or the output after reconstruction? If the first decision is taken, the result apparently would not reflect those cost savings that will stem from the growth in output. If the savings in production costs are multiplied by output after reconstruction, the savings in this case would obviously be extended to that part of output that did not exist before reconstruction. Consequently, the calculation will include a fictitious saving.

Suppose that we cautiously take the first decision (in order not to exaggerate the effectiveness of reconstruction). It then turns out that the investment in reconstruction is recouped by savings in production costs over seven years $\left(\dfrac{17,500,000}{0.02 \times 125,000,000} \right)$. We can conclude from this that, even with the most cautious calculations, the cost of reconstruction is recouped in a comparatively short period and consequently is effective.

However, this conclusion is based on an incorrect comparison of alternatives differing in volume of output, and therefore it may be correct only by chance. Indeed, even if the reconstruction of our plant is rejected, the need for additional production of 125 million kilowatt-hours must still be met. We will assume that this can be attained by constructing a new installation, investment in which is 20 million rubles, due to a more favorable location with respect to fuel resources, and the average production cost of one kilowatt-hour (for consumers) will be five kopecks.

Having ascertained other possibilities for meeting the need for power we thereby obtain data for adjusting both alternatives to a common effect (Table 7).

Table 7

Alternatives	Output in millions of kilowatt-hours per year	Investment in millions of rubles	Production costs of annual output in rubles per year
I (without reconstruction)	125 (old plant) + 125 (new installation) = 250	20	0.1·125,000,000 + 0.05 X 125,000,000 = 18,750,000
II (reconstruction)	250 (reconstructed plant)	17.5	0.08 X 25,000,000 = 20,000,000

Hence it is apparent that our previous conclusion about the effectiveness of reconstruction is erroneous. When we determined the effectiveness of reconstruction without adjustment to a common effect it seemed that reconstruction yielded savings in production costs and would recoup the capital investment required for it in seven years. After adjustment of the alternatives to a common effect it turned out that reconstruction requires additional production costs of 1,250,000 rubles annually. It is true that it yields savings in capital investment. However, the excess cost of the new plant in comparison with the cost of reconstruction is recouped by savings in production costs in two years: $\left(\dfrac{20,000,000 - 17,500,000}{20,000,000 - 18,750,000} \right)$.

Now it is easy for us to find the source of those difficulties in determining the total savings in production costs from reconstruction that occurred in calculating without adjustment to a common effect. The fact is that this calculation was based on an erroneous comparison of alternatives that were unequal in volume of output. By virtue of this both of the two possible methods of determining total savings was incorrect. In multiplying savings obtained from the reduction in production costs of a unit of output by the volume of production before reconstruction, we did not take into account savings (negative in this case)[2] from the growth of production connected with reconstruction. In multiplying savings obtained from the reduction in production costs of a unit of output by the volume of production after reconstruction, we thereby unjustifiably presumed that in the case

52

of rejection of reconstruction, meeting the need for an additional 125 million kilowatt-hours per year was possible only with the high operating costs of the given old installation.

(b) Adjustment to a common composition and volume of output.

Suppose the problem concerns the construction of a hydrostation producing 200 million kilowatt-hours per year and the accompanying development of navigation that will reduce the transportation costs of two million ton-kilometers of freight yearly between points $a, b, c, \ldots, k$ along river A. If construction of this plant is rejected, the need for electric power and transportation remains. Consequently, it must be met by other means, either by constructing another hydrostation, by constructing a condensation plant and a rail line, or by constructing a condensation plant and carrying out dredging work, all of which are the possible different alternatives. Yet for all their diversity they must have the same purpose, that of meeting the same requirements for which the hydrostation is intended. If the projected hydroelectric power plant is to provide excess power for long-distance transmission, then if construction is rejected it is necessary to show not only how the local shortage of power but also the shortage of those distant points where excess power from the hydrostation was to be transmitted will be met.

Let us assume that another alternative of a hydrostation project in the same region but on another river competes with the project for this hydrostation. The other alternative provides 100 million kilowatt-hours of electric power per year and improves river transportation to the extent of three million ton-kilometers of shipments between points $a_1, b_1, c_1, \ldots, k_1$ along river B. In this form the effectiveness of the second alternative is incommensurable with that of the first. We will adjust both of these alternatives to a common effect. We determine the total effect for both alternatives after deducting the quantities that are repeated:

(1)   200 million kilowatt-hours of electric power;
(2)   the transportation of freight between points $a, b, c, \ldots, k$;
(3)   the transportation of freight between points $a_1, b_1, c_1, \ldots, k_1$.

It is easy to see that we have obtained the sum of the maxima of each kind of output for the alternatives being compared. This sum represents the minimum volume of those sectors of the national economy that, in the first place, have the same output

53

and, in the second place, include one of the alternative stations being compared.

Let us try to describe each of these alternatives more specifically.

Variant 1 (adjusted to a common effect).

Hydrostation on river A

(1) Production of electric power of 200 million kilowatt-hours per year.

(2) Two million ton-kilometers of transportation per year along river A.

(3) Three million ton-kilometers of transportation per year along river B in small craft at comparatively high cost.

Variant 2 (after adjustment to a common effect).

Hydrostation on river B

(1) Production of electric power of 100 million kilowatt-hours per year. Thermal (condensation) plant producing 100 million kilowatt-hours per year.

(2) 1.5 million ton-kilometers of shipments per year by railroad. The same shipments are transported that would be transported along river A in the first alternative (the railroad transports the same amount of freight but requires fewer trips).

(3) Three million ton-kilometers of shipments per year along river B in large craft at low costs.

Both of these alternatives have the same effects. Consequently, to compare their effectiveness it is necessary only to compare annual operating costs and capital outlays on each.[3]

(c) Adjustment to a common region of consumption of output.

We will assume that we are comparing alternative locations of an enterprise such that the regions of consumption of its output do not completely coincide. In this case it is necessary to make clear, in the course of examining each alternative, from which sources and with what outlays requirements will be met for that part of the region that is not covered by the given alternative but is covered by other alternatives.

For example, suppose the first location alternative of the projected enterprise has a consumption region consisting of zones A and B, and a second location alternative has a consumption region consisting of zones B and C. Then, in examining the first alternative it is necessary to make clear how the requirements of zone C will be met, and in examining the second alternative how the requirements of zone A will be met. Having established the outlays required for realizing the alternatives adjusted in this manner, we can determine the alternative for which the requirements of all three zones, *A, B,* and *C,* will be met with minimum outlays.

(*d*) Adjustment to a common consumption time.

Adjustment to a common consumption time is one of the most complicated cases of adjustment to a common effect.

In comparing alternatives we must take into account nonsynchronization (differences in time) of two sorts:

(1) the nonsynchronization of outlays and effects caused by the time of production and circulation;

(2) the times when effects occur, which are different for different alternatives.

The consumption of a product is always asynchronous with the labor producing it. The point is not only, and not so much, that labor in production requires time as it is that the time for production and circulation is longer than working time. The use of implements of labor on the one hand, and the necessity for reserves of objects of labor and finished products on the other hand, lengthen the time between the outlays of labor and the consumption of its product. This gap in time between labor and the consumption of its product is measured by the turnover time of fixed and circulating capital. As we know, the average turnover time of fixed capital is measured in years, reaching several decades. Since people cannot cease to consume, outlays of labor in the national economy are always synchronized with consumption: the products of past labor are consumed. The synchronization of outlays and effects is supported by a specific structure of productive and circulating capital. In this way the possibility arises of adjusting nonsynchronized outlays and effects for each plan (project) alternative to the same time period. For this it is necessary to determine how the given project alternative acts on the relationship between outlays and their synchronized consumption.

Obviously, this is a complex problem. We will approach its solution beginning with an examination of certain individual aspects.

Adjusting outlays made at different times and the effect to the same time for each alternative does not eliminate the possibility of discrepancies between the time of the appearance of output (effect) in the different alternatives.

If one project alternative yields output three years later than another with the same costs of production, it is then necessary to make clear how and with what synchronously adjusted outlays requirements will be met for the product during that interval of time when the second alternative will already be yielding an output while the first will only require outlays but will not yield a product.

This gap in consumption time sometimes can be made up by means of imports or by removing bottlenecks in existing enterprises. But such opportunities are often absent or clearly ineffective. Then there remains the course of weighing the useful effects of products available at different times.

(e) Adjustment to identical goals of economic policy.

The requirements of the example are to compare two variants of producing the same quantity of product A.

Alternative I_A — in a backward region.

Alternative II_A — in a developed region.

Outlays on these variants are presented in Table 8.

Table 8

Alternatives	Capital investment	Annual operating costs
I_A	110	95
II_A	100	90

The question is, which alternative is more effective?

At first glance, to solve this question it is necessary to compare the additional outlays required by alternative I_A with its additional effect in comparison with alternative II_A, i.e., to compare the development of the backward region promised by alternative I_A with the supplementary ten million rubles of capital expenditures and the five million rubles of annual operating costs that it requires in comparison with alternative II_A.

However, such a comparison would be correct only if there were one variant for the economic development of the backward region. In reality it rarely happens that the possibilities of developing a region are limited to only one variant. Accordingly, the question arises whether it is possible to develop the given region economically to the same extent as is accomplished by alternative I_A but with smaller additional outlays.

Suppose that the production of B and C can be undertaken with the following outlays in the given backward region (Table 9).

Table 9

Alternatives	Capital investment	Annual operating costs
I_B	80	60
I_C	60	70
Total	140	130

Suppose the organization of both of these kinds of production units generally will yield the same degree of economic and cultural development of the backward region as alternative I_A. We determine the outlays necessary for producing the same quantity of products B and C in developed regions (Table 10).

Table 10

Alternatives	Capital investment	Annual operating costs
II_B	75	60
II_C	61	67
Total	136	127

We adjust alternatives I_A and II_A to a common national economic effect, taking into account the indicated alternatives for producing B and C (Table 11).

57

Table 11

Combination of alternatives	Adjusted alternatives (combinations of alternatives of producing A, B, and C)	Capital investment	Annual operating costs
I	$I_A + II_B + II_C$	246	222
II	$II_A + I_B + I_C$	240	220

Each of the two combinations of alternatives (I and II) yields the same effect, namely, the same quantity of products A, B, and C, and an identical degree of development of the given backward region. Accordingly, we can judge the comparative effectiveness of these two combinations of alternatives from their outlays. In the given example it is obvious that combination II is more effective than combination I.

The most difficult feature in this case of adjustment to a common national economic effect is determining the identical goals of economic policy being implemented by the compared alternatives. Indeed, by which attributes can we judge the degree of economic and cultural development of the region attainable by implementation of one or another construction alternative? This is a question that has not been worked out. Obviously, its solution depends on the specific tasks that are posed by economic policy in the sphere of developing a particular region. For example, in some cases the fundamental task of development might be raising the material well-being of the local population, which is engaged in backward forms of production. In other cases the main goal might be the utilization of vast natural resources by means of settling an uninhabited region.

In the first case, one of the main indicators of the extent of economic and cultural development will be the number of workers drawn from the local population into industrial, highly productive labor. In the second case, the main indicator will be the effectiveness of utilization of local resources.

Thus, in adjusting the compared alternatives to common goals of economic policy it is necessary above all to determine as specifically as possible precisely which goals of economic policy are accomplished by each alternative. We should not confine ourselves, as was often done by planning organizations, to general considerations concerning how construction will raise a backward outlying district, will promote its industrialization, etc. It is necessary to give a detailed qualitative and quantitative characterization of the tasks of economic policy in the given region. Only under such conditions can we validly judge to what degree the alternatives being compared promote the accomplishment of these goals.

5. Difficulties in Adjusting Project
Alternatives to a Common Effect

Adjusting plan (project) alternatives to a common effect is often associated with complications difficult for planning organizations to overcome. The problem is that those elements that in the alternatives under consideration are obtained jointly with the basic effect cannot always be created separately from other elements of effect. For example, often a product that is a by-product of a certain sector is generally not produced independently and can only be a by-product of other sectors.

Expressing this by means of the general example presented on page 49, we can say that products b, c, d, and e can be produced not only jointly with product a but also jointly with products f, g, and h, i.e., in combination with elements of effect that are not contained in any of the four project alternatives being compared. As a result, the overall common effect of the compared alternatives is extended still further, and complete adjustment of project alternatives to a common effect can become practically impossible for planning institutions. It becomes impossible because planning institutions have a branch character whereas the common effect in the indicated cases transcends the limits of the branch.

In such cases adjustment to a common effect must become the function of the planning bodies. By concentrating in their hands the basic data for each project alternative the planning bodies could derive complex combinations of alternatives with an identical effect.

We will note that sometimes it is possible to determine the comparative effectiveness of alternatives even with an incomplete adjustment to a common effect. This happens in cases in which a partially adjusted alternative yields an obviously greater effect but requires equal or smaller outlays than an alternative with an obviously smaller common effect.

59

Let us examine the difficulties of adjusting to a common effect that arise in designing hydroelectric power plants in undeveloped regions. The simplified example given above of adjusting two alternatives of hydroelectric power plants to a common effect applied to a *developed* region. The hydroelectric power plant was intended to meet requirements that arose independently of its existence. Accordingly, the output of the compared sectors of the national economy was equal to the sum of the maximum values of the separate elements of the direct effect of different alternatives of hydraulic-engineering construction.

In planning hydroelectric power plants in *undeveloped* regions it is necessary first of all to determine the composition of power consumers, since the activity of the hydrostation in this case is completely linked with the needs of consumers who do not yet exist. Consequently, the problem is not only whether to construct or not to construct an electric power plant but also whether or not to create an entire complex of consumers of power from this plant.

Of course, in such a case it is not so much the effectiveness of creating individual consumers that must be considered, but rather the effectiveness of the entire complex of consumers, in other words, the effectiveness of the given alternative of development of the region.

6. Adjustment to a Common Effect
as a Method of Justifying
Projects of Socialist Enterprises

Adjustment to a common effect has the function of specifying by which means and at what cost, in implementing one of the project alternatives, we can meet those needs that are met by other alternatives being compared but not by the given alternative. Hence it follows that this method makes sense only in a society whose purpose is to satisfy the needs of this society. In a capitalist economy it is not possible to use this method to choose between project alternatives with varying composition of output, since it does not answer the question which project alternative yields a higher rate of profit. By comparing the rate of profit of the alternative yielding output $(a + b)$ with the rate of profit of the alternative yielding output $(a + c)$, the capitalist obtains an answer, adequate for him, to the question which alternative should be preferred.

But a socialist economy has as its objective the greatest possible

60

satisfaction of social needs. Therefore, in solving the question of implementing a particular alternative in a socialist society, we must make clear how requirements will be met for those products, or how those tasks will be fulfilled, which are not reflected in the given alternative but are accomplished in other alternatives.

The project alternatives adjusted to a common effect can represent alternatives not of enterprises but of small sectors of the national economy designed to fulfill the same complex of tasks. These sectors of the national economy can consist of spatially separate parts of different enterprises that are not directly linked. Thus, an alternative involving the reconstruction of a number of shops of several existing machine-building plants can compete with an alternative involving the construction of new plants of this type.

Adjustment of alternatives to a common effect does not free the planning bodies from the necessity of comparing nonmeasurable elements of the effect with outlays, and somehow "weighing" and comparing one against the other.

The method of adjusting alternatives to a common effect presupposes that the requirements for the products of the alternatives under consideration have already been determined and that not one of these alternatives exceeds requirement. But this means that the role of individual types of output in the national economy and quantities of production by branches have already been established.

Such a determination of needs and prospects for developing production presumes, of course, precisely that comparison of nonmeasurable elements of effect and outlays, a comparison we are trying to avoid by adjusting alternatives to a common effect. However — and this is the decisive feature — the significance of the method of adjusting alternatives to a common effect does not consist in removing the responsibility from the planning organizations for establishing conformity between goals and outlays on production, the responsibility for comparing and weighing nonmeasurable elements of effect (it is impossible to remove this responsibility, and to strive to do so is harmful). The significance of this method consists in the fact that this "weighing" need not be done in each separate case of comparison of two or three project alternatives, but only in solving basic questions of the structure of the national economy. The main advantage of the method of adjusting alternatives to a common effect is that it makes it possible to find alternatives requiring minimum outlays for fulfilling a particular complex of tasks.

7. Implicit Forms of Adjustment to a Common Effect That Are Applied in Practice

Comparing the effectiveness of project alternatives by adjusting to a common effect is often done in implicit form.

Let us take the simplest case of comparing the effectiveness of alternatives differing in the composition of their effects, that of alternative ways of producing metal articles with the lowest and the highest percentage of by-products. There is considerable disagreement on the methods of valuation. At first glance it may appear that by-products as such are worthless and that the valuation should include only the cost of transporting, storing, and preparing them, and similar operations. However, it is sufficient to consider carefully the example presented below in order to understand how incorrect such a solution of the question would be.

Suppose that two alternative methods of producing metal articles that are similar in quality require identical capital investment and operating costs, but yield different amounts of scrap. Will we obtain a correct answer to the question of the effectiveness of these alternatives if we assume the value of scrap to be zero? Obviously not. Scrap can replace cast iron as a raw material for open-hearth furnaces and thereby can economize on labor outlays in producing a certain amount of cast iron. For this reason the practice in project calculations has been to value scrap according to the producing cost of cast iron.

In the same way, in planning chemical plants by-products are usually valued according to the production costs of analogous products or of substitutes, if they are produced by other means than the projected one.

The practice of valuing by-products according to the production costs of their substitutes is nothing but a concealed form of adjusting the compared alternatives to a common effect.

In fact, suppose that it is necessary to compare the operating costs of the two project alternatives presented in Table 12.

Table 12

Alternatives	Output	Operating costs
I	$100a + 100b$	E_1
II	$100a + 50c$	E_2

Since the outputs associated with these alternatives are dissimilar we must first make appropriate adjustments. This can be done by two methods:

(1) by adjustment to the least common effect;

(2) by valuing by-products b and c according to the production costs of making them by other methods and subtracting this value of by-products from the sum of operating costs.

Both methods require data on the operating costs necessary to produce b and c under alternative conditions.

Suppose that these data are as follows:

Outlays for producing $100b = S_b$,
Outlays for producing $50c = S_c$.

Then, to adjust both alternatives to the least common effect it is necessary to add:

to alternative I — $50c$ of output and S_c of outlays,
to alternative II — $100b$ of output and S_b of outlays.

To determine production costs by subtracting the valuation of by-products it is necessary to deduct:

from alternative I — $100b$ of output and S_b of outlays,
from alternative II — $50c$ of output and S_c of outlays.

In other words, the comparison of alternatives by adjusting to a common effect represents the following inequality:

$$E_1 + S_c \gtreqless E_2 + S_b. \tag{3.1}$$

The comparison of operating costs for the same alternatives after subtracting production costs of by-products obtained from different sources gives the following inequality:

$$E_1 - S_b \gtreqless E_2 - S_c. \tag{3.2}$$

if several products are produced in one technological process we can determine only the general production cost of the entire complex. The production costs of the separate products of the complex are approximate magnitudes.

The approximate nature of the production cost of basic output is especially clearly revealed in those cases in which this production cost emerges as a negative quantity in the calculations. Such cases are possible when other alternative methods of obtaining secondary output require large operating costs.

4. Valuing secondary output according to the production cost when it is produced by other methods permits the comparison of the national economic effectiveness of alternatives with a differing composition of output for only one of the basic indicators of effectiveness — that of operating costs. To compare the effectiveness of such alternatives according to capital investment it is necessary to determine investment in basic output by a method analogous to determining the production cost of basic output, i.e., according to the amount of investment in producing the given secondary output by other methods.

Evaluating by-products and secondary products according to production costs is not the only example of how adjustment of alternatives to a common effect is applied in our project practice. Many similar examples could be presented. In essence, the adjustment of alternatives to a common effect already occurs when the planner, comparing alternatives with a differing composition of effect, poses the question of how, in implementing a given alternative, those requirements will be satisfied and those tasks fulfilled that are not met by the given alternative. This question arises, for example, if one of the alternatives yields output later than another one. In this case the question is how and with what outlays the deficit can be met during the period when the given alternative is not yielding an output but another alternative could yield it. Finding these possibilities is nothing other than the beginning of adjusting alternatives to a common effect with respect to its time of realization.

Thus, project practice makes use of various implicit forms of adjusting compared alternatives to a common effect. But the concealed forms obscure the meaning of the operation carried out and do not make it possible to evaluate the degree of accuracy of the results obtained. Moreover, implicit forms of calculation usually require not less but more labor to attain the same results.

It is obvious that the second inequality is a transformation of the first.

This means that comparing the operating costs of alternatives with dissimilar output by subtracting the production cost of by-products obtained from other sources is equivalent to comparing the operating costs of the same alternatives by adjustment to a common effect.

If properly used, the concealed forms of adjusting project alternatives to a common effect yield the same result as the explicit form of this method. But it should be clear that the proper use of the concealed method of adjustment is considerably more difficult. Furthermore, implicit methods lead to certain errors. In particular, the method of valuing by-products according to the production costs of making them by other means is characterized by the following deficiencies:

1. It replaces adjustment to a common national economic effect by adjustment to a common output. Valuing secondary products and by-products relates all outlays only to output. Thus, the difficulty of comparing the effectiveness of alternatives that meet differing goals of economic policy remains unresolved in this case.

2. It relates the entire difference between operating costs of different alternatives of producing the entire complex of output to only one product taken as the basic one. Thus, the difference between the production cost of $100a$ according to alternatives I and II is $(E_1 - S_b) - (E_2 - S_c)$, which obviously is equal to $(E_1 + S_c) - (E_2 + S_b)$. As a result, the relative significance of this difference is exaggerated. Thus, if $E_1 = 100$, $E_2 = 120$, $S_c = 85$, and $S_b = 70$, the difference between the production costs of the basic product in the two alternatives of our example is 16.7% of the production cost of the basic product of alternative I $[(5:30) \times 100]$. But this difference in relation to the general sum of operating costs in adjusted alternative I is only 2.7% $\{[(120 + 70) - (100 + 85)] \times 100: (100 + 85)\}$. The first ratio (16.7%) is sufficiently large so that, under otherwise identical conditions, the advantage would be with the first alternative. The second ratio (2.7%) is not of decisive significance even assuming otherwise identical conditions, since the difference falls within the limits of probable errors of calculation, at least in the stage of project-making.

3. The implicit form of adjusting to a common effect creates the false impression that we can determine the real production cost of basic output by valuing secondary output according to its production cost if it is produced by other methods. Furthermore,

Accordingly, it is advisable to replace implicit forms of adjusting project alternatives to a common effect with the explicit form of this operation explained above.

It should be noted that the implicit form of adjusting to a common national economic effect is not the most serious fault of project and planning practice at the present time. Much worse methods of comparing the effectiveness of project alternatives are encountered. Various procedures for valuing secondary output and distributing capital investment among individual "components of a complex" that differ from the methods presented above are used in current practice. There is nothing absolutely fixed in these procedures. All the procedures are conditional – or perhaps it is more accurate to say that they are not substantiated. Serious errors are therefore possible.

Cases of extremely large discrepancies in the results of different calculations of indicators of effectiveness of the same project occur in planning practice, discrepancies that arise from differences in valuation of secondary output or by-products. Such a situation is intolerable. Project calculations must not depend upon the subjective judgments of planners. The method of adjusting to a common national economic effect provides an objective basis for comparing the effectiveness of alternatives with nonuniform effects, a basis that does not depend on subjective judgments.

Notes

1. K. Marx and F. Engels, *Soch.*, 2nd Edition, Vol. 20, p. 321.
2. In comparison with new construction.
3. It is assumed in the example presented here that the maximum quantity of production of individual products (and services) in the alternatives being compared does not exceed the requirements of the corresponding region for these products (or services). In the opposite case it is necessary either to reject such an alternative or to demonstrate the advisability of subsequent shipments of the surplus product to other regions. In general, we must remember that the application of the proposed scheme must either be based on well-developed data concerning the requirements for the complex's products or critically verified by the subsequent study of requirements. In the opposite case it is possible to have a choice of an alternative involving the production of a surplus of a product or with an incorrect relationship between lines of production that are and are not important for economic development.

CHAPTER 4

METHODS OF FINDING THE MAXIMUM EFFECT OF CAPITAL INVESTMENT IN A SOCIALIST ECONOMY

Calculating the effectiveness of capital investment is the most difficult and consequently the most controversial aspect of the problem of measuring projected outlays. The problem of calculating the profitability of productive capital corresponds, in the practice of economic calculation, to this question.

The effectiveness of project alternatives is already being calculated in socialist economic practice on the basis of "adjusted expenditures," and payments for capital are being introduced, but the incomplete state of the theory of this question has begun to be more sharply felt. Not only mathematical economic models but also algorithms that are practicable given the present system of economic information and computer technology are necessary for the planned calculation of norms of payment for capital investment and productive capital. Moreover, this problem is so complex and it affects so many different aspects of public life that mathematical models appear to be a too simplified representation of reality.

What is the function of payments for assets and capital investment, when we examine them in the context of optimal planning? It would seem that the simplest answer is the following: Payments for investment and capital funds are a stimulus for their most effective utilization. In this respect payments for investment are apparently similar to payments for natural resources. But this is how the matter appears only at first glance. Both investment and productive capital differ from natural resources in that the former are reproducible. This is a substantial difference. In

67

simplifying the task, we can proceed from the prescribed limit of the national economy's capital investment and seek to determine the most effective distribution of investment among different purposes. The optimality of this distribution of investment will depend on whether the overall limit of investment was correctly established, i.e., on whether the relationship between accumulation and consumption is optimal.

It follows that we can divide the problem of payments for capital investment and productive capital into two parts. First we will examine the basis for calculating these payments in problems of maximizing the overall effect of the limit of the national economy's capital investments and productive capital. Then we will investigate the connection between these payments and the planning of the optimal relationship between accumulation and consumption.

1. Initial Propositions of the Model of the Maximum Effective Balance of Capital Investment

It is well known that the opportunities for effective capital investment exceed the magnitude of existing accumulation. We could make many extremely effective capital outlays in excess of those planned, but the insufficiency of accumulation obstructs this. This is not a conjunctural, transient phenomenon. While the study of natural resources and technological inventions create sufficiently rapidly ever-new opportunities for effective investment, no matter how large national economic accumulation, a relative shortage of accumulation will prevail.

If effective investment can be undertaken on a larger scale than existing resources permit, this means that we must concentrate investment only on those projects that promise to yield an adequate effect. If accumulation is insufficient for all effective purposes, this means that it must be used only for the most effective purposes in order for the overall effect of total investment to be optimal.

The effect of investment is measured by the labor savings it yields. ". . . The productivity of a machine is measured by the degree to which it replaces human labor power."[1] No matter how varied the advantages yielded by a more capital-intensive alternative of construction in comparison with a less capital-intensive one, in the majority of cases these advantages can be reduced to, and measured by, labor savings. This possibility is created by the method of adjusting the compared project alternatives to an identical national economic effect.

The labor savings resulting from the production of different products are just as commensurable as are the outlays of labor associated with the production of different use values. This conclusion does not change when we conduct calculations in value terms. In monetary terms the labor savings that, for example, should result from investment in an electric power plant can be commensurable with the labor savings that can be obtained from the same sum of investment in a tunnel that shortens a route. In all branches and lines of production the effect of investment is measured by the same standard. But the investment itself is also measured in the same units independently of the branches into which it is directed.

Therefore, the relationship of the effect of investment to its magnitude, i.e., the effectiveness of investment, embodies the same measure in all branches and lines of production. We cannot determine how much more (or less) necessary cast iron is than are shoes, but this does not prevent us from measuring how much more (or less) effective a given sum of investment is in a metallurgical plant than in a shoe factory.

However, an important reservation is necessary here. We cannot measure the effect of the entire sum of investment in a particular project, because for this purpose it would be necessary to compare the given investment alternative with the production of the same product without any additional investment. But production without any investment is not only clearly ineffective (by virture of high labor costs), but is often technically impossible (for example, melting cast iron) and does not satisfy the qualitative requirements of a socialist economy (for example, with respect to conditions of labor). In reality the question never arises of producing a given product with or without the help of means of production. The question is that of choosing a more capital-intensive or less capital-intensive alternative of the given line of production, i.e., of expending more or less labor on the creation of capital to produce a specific output. In solving this problem there is no need to know the savings yielded by the entire sum of investment. It is altogether sufficient to determine only those additional savings in labor costs caused by the additional investment required by the more capital-intensive alternative in comparison with the less capital-intensive one of that line of production.

The minimum necessary sum of investment is determined by the production program for the national economy's final output and its distribution among branches. The task of finding the optimal effect of investment arises only for that part of it that exceeds the minimum investment necessary to fulfill the production program for final output in the planned period. The difference between the national economy's accumulation and the necessary minimum investment can be distributed in different ways among branches and construction projects without causing changes in the production program for final output. This is where the problem arises of comparing the effectiveness of various alternatives of additional investment and of finding the overall optimal effect of investment.

Briefly, this is the problem. The following are given:

(1) The production program for the national economy's final output.

(2) The minimum sum of investment necessary for fulfilling this program and its distribution among branches.

(3) The national economy's planned accumulation.

(4) Alternatives of additional investment in all construction projects necessary for fulfilling the production program for final output.[2]

The question is how to distribute additional investment among various possible purposes so that there is the greatest overall effect from all investment.

In accordance with this way of formulating the problem, the index of effectiveness of investment will be the ratio of savings in production costs resulting from additional investment to the amount of this investment.

We will denote the production costs of annual output of two project alternatives as C_1 and C_2; and investment in the same alternatives as K_1 and K_2. In so doing we will agree that the additional investment in the second alternative yields a positive effect, i.e., that

$$K_2 > K_1 \text{ and } C_2 < C_1.$$

Then the index of effectiveness of additional investment of the second alternative will be expressed as:

$$E_{2/1} = \frac{C_1 - C_2}{K_2 - K_1}. \tag{4.1}$$

This quantity shows the share of the additional investment that constitutes its annual effect. Index (4.1) can be calculated in inverse form:

$$\frac{1}{E_{2/1}} = \frac{K_2 - K_1}{C_1 - C_2}. \tag{4.2}$$

70

In this case it denotes the recoupment period, in years, of additional investment resulting from savings in production costs yielded by this investment. The second (inverse) form of the index has been preferred in planning practice, apparently on the supposition that this form corresponds more closely to the nature of a socialist economy. The difference between the two forms is inconsequential. Both indicators (4.1) and (4.2) have the same meaning but in a different form (direct and inverse). Therefore, it cannot be that one of them corresponds and the other does not correspond to the nature of a socialist economy.

In calculating the index of effectiveness of investment it is necessary to observe the fundamental rule for comparing the national economic effectiveness of project alternatives. This is the rule of identity of national economic effects of the compared alternatives. We can measure the relative effectiveness of different project alternatives only given the condition of identity of requirements and goals of economic policy that these alternatives serve. If the project alternatives requiring additional investment yield a differing national economic effect (for example, different by-products) it is necessary to adjust these alternatives to an identical effect.

We will demonstrate that the effect of additional investment, expressed in the form of an increase in output, can be measured by labor savings.

Assume that with given outlays of labor (we will denote this by C) an increase in investment from K to $(K + \Delta K)$ causes an increase in the product from Q to $(Q + \Delta Q)$. These alternatives yield national economic effects that are not identical: the first — Q, the second — $(Q + \Delta Q)$. Therefore, we cannot directly measure the relative effectiveness of outlays of labor on these alternatives. For the same reason, in expressing the effect of investment on the increase in output (ΔQ), we cannot calculate an index of effectiveness of additional investment (ΔK) that would be commensurable with the same index in producing other products. In fact, the index $\Delta Q / \Delta K$ has output in physical units as the numerator. When the output of the compared project alternatives is heterogeneous in quality, comparison of this index is impossible.

If ΔQ denotes cast iron, and $\Delta Q'$ cloth, it is not possible to determine whether $\Delta Q / \Delta K$ or $\Delta Q' / \Delta K'$ is larger.

We will adjust the above alternatives of producing Q and $(Q + \Delta Q)$ to an identical national economic effect. For this purpose we recalculate the first alternative for the same volume of

71

production as the second alternative yields, i.e., for $Q + \Delta Q$ (Table 13).

Table 13

	National economic effect	Investment	Costs of production of annual output
The first alternative (adjusted)		$K \cdot \dfrac{Q + \Delta Q}{Q}$	$C \cdot \dfrac{Q + \Delta Q}{Q}$
	$Q + \Delta Q$		
The second alternative		$K + \Delta K$	C

Now we will find the effectiveness of the second alternative's additional investment in relation to the adjusted first alternative:

$$\frac{C \cdot \dfrac{Q + \Delta Q}{Q} - C}{K + \Delta K - K \cdot \dfrac{Q + \Delta Q}{Q}} = \frac{C \cdot \dfrac{\Delta Q}{Q}}{K \left[\dfrac{\Delta K}{K} - \dfrac{\Delta Q}{Q} \right]}$$

Outlays on production are in the numerator of this index. In all branches they are homogeneous and are commensurable with each other. The dimensions of the denominator are also homogeneous in all branches. The denominator represents investment. This means that this index of effectiveness of investment can be compared not only within the limits of producing the same product but also in comparing alternatives of producing different products.

The comparability of effectiveness of investment in different branches is based on the fact that in choosing any of the investment alternatives compared in this index the final national effect of labor remains constant. Only outlays change, namely, their distribution among lines of production and the total sum of outlays. Suppose, for example, that we are comparing the effectiveness of investment in producing product A with the effectiveness of investment in producing product B. The investment alternatives are presented in Table 14.

72

Table 14

Alternatives	A Production costs of annual output, in millions of rubles	A Investment, in millions of rubles	A Effectiveness of additional investment	Alternatives	B Production costs of annual output, in millions of rubles	B Investment, in millions of rubles	B Effectiveness of additional investment
I_A	50	50	—	I_B	45	25	—
II_A	49	75	0.04	II_B	35	50	0.4

We will assume that each of the alternatives of producing A yields the same effect and that each of the alternatives of producing B also yields an identical national economic effect. This means that any combination of alternatives of A and B, with one alternative in each line of production, yields the same overall national economic effect. Consequently, comparing the effectiveness of 25 million rubles of investment in producing A with the effectiveness of the same amount of investment in producing B will involve the comparison of two combinations of alternatives with an identical national economic effect $A + B$, but with a different distribution of investment between these two lines of production.

Differences in labor outlays will be the sole consequence (effect) of differences in the distribution of investments. Moreover, outlays are commensurable.

2. A Simple Example of Finding the Overall Maximum Effect of Investment

Problem No. 1. The basic idea of finding the maximum effect of investment is very simple. We will demonstrate it with an elementary example. We will assume that 340 million rubles have been allotted to a certain trust for fulfilling a production program involving five products, A, B, C, D, and E. The outlays necessary to fulfill the prescribed program for each product are shown in Table 14a. As we see, only one alternative of additional investment exists for each project.

Alternatives	A Production costs of annual output, in millions of rubles	Investment, in millions of rubles	Alternatives	B Production costs of annual output, in millions of rubles	Investment, in millions of rubles	Alternatives	C Production costs of annual output, in millions of rubles
I_A	91	50	I_B	76	50	I_C	64
II_A	81.2	80	II_B	71	80	II_C	60.8

Each of the alternatives corresponds to a program, and alternatives with identical letters (*A, B,* etc.) are adjusted to an identical national economic effect. Accordingly, any combination of alternatives, with one alternative for producing each product, yields the same overall national economic effect.

It may be asked which possible combination of these alternatives ensures the utilization of the allotted limit of investment with the maximum overall effect.

It is very easy to solve this problem by directly choosing the more effective alternatives of additional investment.

1. Let us calculate the effectiveness of additional investment for each alternative with the greater investment (Table 15).

Table 15

Alternatives	The effectiveness of additional investment, in % of annual investment
II_A	32.7
II_B	16.3
II_C	10.7
II_D	8.3
II_E	6.7

2. We list all alternatives in order of decreasing effectiveness of investment and show the amount of additional investment required by the corresponding alternatives. At the beginning of this series we show the total amount of minimum necessary investment, i.e., the amount of investment for alternatives I_A, I_B, I_C, I_D, and I_E. We obtain Table 16.

74

D				E		
Investment, in millions of rubles	Alternatives	Production costs of annual output, in millions of rubles	Investment, in millions of rubles	Alternatives	Production costs of annual output, in millions of rubles	Investment, in millions of rubles
50	I_D	53.2	50	I_E	42.6	50
80	II_D	50.7	80	II_E	40.6	80

Table 16

Alternatives	Annual effectiveness of additional investment, in % of investment	The amount of investment utilized with given effectiveness, in millions of rubles
I_A, I_B, I_C, I_D, I_E	∞ *	250
II_A	32.7	30
II_B	16.3	30
II_C	10.7	30
II_D	8.3	30
II_E	6.7	30

{ 340 (braces grouping the five 30-value lines)

*We provisionally show the effectiveness of minimum necessary investment as being infinitely large. The infinity sign here means only that without the given investment the production cannot be fulfilled.

3. We select from this table, beginning at the top, as many lines as are necessary for investment requirements to equal their limit. For example, given a limit of 340 million rubles it is necessary to select the four lines from the top.

4. From the alternatives included in this manner in the sum of investment, we will accept for each line of production the alternative with the largest investment. With a limit of 340 million rubles we must accept alternatives II_A, II_B, II_C, II_D, and I_E. The meaning of this rule lies in the fact that in Table 16 the alternatives with the largest investments relate not to the total sum of investment but emerge only as additional investment above the minimum necessary sum of outlays. Moreover, the larger investment sums include not only the additional investments (30 million rubles) but also their necessary minimum amounts. This means that the accepted alternatives II_A, II_B, and II_C exclude the realization of alternatives I_A, I_B, and I_C.

75

The balance of accumulation and investment compiled in this manner can be called the maximum effective or optimal one, because variants II_A, II_B, II_C, I_D, and I_E yield the maximum effective utilization of the limited amount of investment funds. In other words, these alternatives ensure obtaining planned output with the least production costs among all possible combinations of those alternatives within the bounds of the same limited investment funds.

3. A More Complicated Case
of Finding the Overall
Maximum Effect of Investment

Problem No. 2. We will now assume that the limit of funds is increased to 410 million rubles and that for each project there exists not one but several alternatives of additional investment (Table 17).

Table

	A			B			C
Alternatives	Production costs of annual output, in millions of rubles	Investment, in millions of rubles	Alternatives	Production costs of annual output, in millions of rubles	Investment, in millions of rubles	Alternatives	Production costs of annual output, in millions of rubles
I_A	91	50	I_B	76	50	I_C	64
II_A	90	60	II_B	72.8	70	II_C	63.5
III_A	88	70	III_B	71	80	III_C	62.9
IV_A	81.2	80	IV_B	70	100	IV_C	60.8
V_A	80	100				V_C	60

Here the solution is complicated by the problem of choosing a base for calculating indicators of the effectiveness of investment. Should we accept a constant base, i.e., an alternative with the least investment, or a variable one, i.e., an alternative with the next smallest investment? In the first case calculation will show us the effectiveness of the entire sum of additional investment, but in the second case calculation will give us only the effectiveness of the upper portion of additional investment.

It would seem that uniformity in the principle of constructing a series requires application of a single base for calculating the effectiveness of investment. But in fact such a solution is wrong. In reality, a constant base is suitable only under conditions of continuously growing effectiveness of successive investments. In this case either technological impossibility or a negative effectiveness of further investment must set in following the maximum effective outlays on investment. A variable base is correct only under conditions of continuously decreasing effectiveness of successive investments.

Let us demonstrate these propositions.

1. When each successive sum of investment for producing a given output is more effective than the preceding sum, the effectiveness of the entire sum of additional investment above its minimum will always be lower than the effectiveness of the upper portion of investment. Nevertheless, it is not possible to carry out only one "upper layer" of investments and not make all the preceding ones. This is as impossible as filling only the upper half of a glass and not filling the lower half. Accordingly, given the growing effectiveness of successive investment, the indicators must be calculated on a constant base. We will demonstrate the incorrectness in this case of calculations resting on a variable base.

17

Investment, in millions of rubles	D			E		
	Alternatives	Production costs of annual output, in millions of rubles	Investment, in millions of rubles	Alternatives	Production costs of annual output, in millions of rubles	Investment, in millions of rubles
50	I_D	53.2	50	I_E	42.6	50
60	II_D	50.7	80	II_E	40.6	80
70	III_D	50	100	III_E	40	100
80						
100						

We will use for this purpose data from Table 17, In the table alternative IV_C has an investment effectiveness (E) in relation to variant III_C equal to

$$\frac{62.9 - 60.8}{80 - 70} = 21\% \text{ per year,}$$

and in relation to alternative I_C equal to

$$\frac{64 - 60.8}{80 - 50} = 10.7\% \text{ per year.}$$

But alternative III_B has an investment effectiveness in relation to variant II_B equal to

$$\frac{72.8 - 71}{80 - 70} = 18\% \text{ per year,}$$

and in relation to variant I_B equal to

$$\frac{76 - 71}{80 - 50} = 16.7\% \text{ per year.}$$

In calculating investment effectiveness on a variable base, i.e., on the base of the alternative with the next smallest investment, alternative IV_C falls into a higher place than alternatives IV_B and III_B.

If the limit of investment funds allows us, in the course of selecting the most effective alternatives, to accept alternatives with effectiveness not lower than 20%, then with chain indicators of investment effectiveness alternative IV_A will, and alternative III_B will not, be among the alternatives selected (since $E_{IV_C/III_C} > 20\%$, and $E_{III_B/II_B} < 20\%$). Moreover, to implement alternative IV_C it will be necessary to spend not only the "upper layer" of investment, $80 - 70 = 10$, but also all "previous layers" of investment with lower effectiveness than for the "upper layer." [3] As a result, the effectiveness of *all* additional investment as a whole for alternative IV_C will not only be lower than 20% but also lower than the investment effectiveness of variant III_B:

$$E_{IV_C/I_C} = 10.7\% \text{ per year,}$$

$$E_{III_B/I_B} = 16.7\% \text{ per year.}$$

2. When each subsequent sum of investment in producing the given output is less effective than the previous one, the effectiveness of the entire sum of additional investment will always be higher than that of the "upper layer" of investment. Accordingly, in the given case it is not possible to determine from the effectiveness of the entire sum of additional investment whether that of the "upper layer" of investment is sufficient. Moreover, we can reject the "upper layer" of investment without rejecting the "lower layers" (in the same way as the lower half of a glass can be filled without filling the upper half).

Therefore, the calculating of investment effectiveness on a constant base would be incorrect in the given case. It would lead to undertaking a less effective investment and rejection of the more effective one. For example, it is apparent from the data of Table 17 that E_{V_A / I_A} is equal to 22% per year whereas E_{V_A / IV_A} is only 6% per year.

If we judge the investment effectiveness of alternative V_A according to the first of these indicators (calculated on a constant base), this alternative will be ahead of alternatives III_B, IV_C, II_D, and II_E, which, if calculation has been done on a constant base, have lower indicators of investment effectiveness but at the same time have considerably greater effectiveness of the "upper layer" of investment.

Thus, with decreasing effectiveness of successive investments the indicators of effectiveness must be calculated by the chain method for each sufficiently "thin layer" of investment. "Thinness of the layer" of investment in the given case is necessary so that all possibilities of comparatively more effective investment can be most fully used, yet without permitting concealment of investments of low effectiveness by means of combining them into one sum (into one "layer") with more effective investments.

In practice the effectiveness of successive investments (in the same project) can grow at certain times and decline at other times. In the transition from alternatives that are low with respect to the level of technology to those that are technologically advanced the effectiveness of successive investments often grows. In comparison of alternatives that are identical in level of technology the effectiveness of successive investments usually declines. Under such conditions how are we to calculate its indicators?

Only one conclusion follows from what has been said – this must be done by alternating both bases. For sectors with growing effectiveness of successive investments these indicators must be calculated on the base of the alternative from which growth in the effectiveness of successive investments begins. For sectors with declining effectiveness of successive investments the effectiveness must be measured by the chain method, i.e., on the base of the alternative with the next smallest investment.

4. Alternatives Whose Effectiveness Can Be as High as Desired but Which Can Never Enter into the Maximum Effective Balance of Investment

However, this conclusion immediately gives rise to doubt. Can indicators calculated on various bases be combined into one declining series for selection of that portion of the more effective investments that is contained in the overall limit of accumulation?

This question is easy to resolve when we try to construct such a series. For the sake of brevity we will form it from the alternatives of only one project, A.

Let us calculate the effectiveness indicators on constant and variable bases (Table 18).

Table 18

Alternatives	Investment, in millions of rubles	Production costs of annual output, in millions of rubles	Annual effectiveness of investment, in % of investment	
			On a constant base	By the chain method
I_A	50	91	∞	∞
II_A	60	90	10	10
III_A	70	88	15	20
IV_A	80	81.2	32.7	68
V_A	100	80	22	6

As we see, the effectiveness of investment grows over the range from variant I_A to IV_A and then declines (variant V_A). According to what we have demonstrated, for solving our problem for alternatives II_A, III_A, and IV_A, calculations are necessary on the base of alternative I_A, and for alternative V_A they are necessary by the chain method on the base of the alternative with the next smallest investment.

Let us examine what will result if we try to place these indicators (enclosed in Table 18 by rectangles) in a declining series, compiled by analogy with Table 16 (see Table 19).

Table 19

Alternative and bases	Effectiveness of investment. in % per year	Investment with given effectiveness.* in millions of rubles	Total sum of investment of the alternative, † in millions of rubles
1	2	3	4
I_A	∞	50	50
$IV_A \quad I_A$	32.7	30	80
$III_A \quad I_A$	15	20	70
$II_A \quad I_A$	10	10	60
$V_A \quad IV_A$	6	20	100

* Column 3 contains the difference between investment in the alternative to which the indicators of investment effectiveness pertain and investment in the alternative serving as the base for calculating this indicator.

†Column 4 contains the entire sum of investment in alternatives to which the indicators of investment effectiveness pertain. Thus, the second line of this column shows the investment in alternative IV_A, the third line the investment in alternative III_A, etc.

Let us assume that the limit to investment grows, beginning with a quantity for which we can implement only the alternative with minimum investment up to a quantity for which we can implement an alternative with the greatest investment.

It then turns out that whatever the possible limits to investment, alternatives III_A and II_A cannot be included in the maximum effective balance of accumulation and investment. In fact, it is apparent from column 2 of Table 19 that alternative III_A could be included in this balance only when the limit to investment will allow implementing investment both in producing A and in other lines of production, with an effectiveness on the order of 15% yearly. It is apparent from column 4 of the same table that with the expansion of the overall limit to investment it well be necessary to reduce investment in producing A, because alternative III_A requires less investment than alternative IV_A. A kind of incongruity is already apparent in the fact that, with an increase in the total limit of investment (with other conditions remaining unchanged), investment in producing A decreases.

An even greater incongruity is apparent in the rejection of highly effective additional investment alternative IV_A for the sake of less effective investment in other production units. Indeed, the transition from alternative IV_A to alternative III_A means the rejection of additional investment with an effectiveness equal to 68% per year (as Table 18 shows), while in other production units, due to expansion of the limit on accumulation, this investment can be used only with an effectiveness of the order of 15% per year.

Thus, whatever the limit on accumulation, alternative III_A cannot enter into the maximum effective balance of accumulation and investment.

Similarly, it can be demonstrated that alternative II_A must share the fate of alternative III_A With respect to indicators of investment effectiveness it is acceptable with higher limits on accumulation than alternatives III_A and IV_A, but in amount of investment it corresponds to lower limits on accumulation.

Alternative V_A is in a different position. It has the lowest index of investment effectiveness, but, given a sufficiently large accumulation, it can enter the maximum effective balance. This will become possible if the volume of accumulation permits the use of investment with an effectiveness of the order of 6% and less. Alternative V_A requires greater investment than IV_A; and, accordingly, accepting alternative V_A does not exclude, but on the contrary also includes, the implementation of all previous "layers" of investment, including investment in alternative IV_A, for an effectiveness of 6% is applicable only to the final "layer" of investment — 20 million rubles — i.e., the additional investment in alternative V_A in excess of the investment in alternative IV_A. Another "layer" of investment in alternative V_A — 30 million rubles — i.e., the additional investment in alternative IV_A in excess of the investment in alternative I_A, has the same effectiveness as the investment in alternative IV_A.

Thus, although alternatives II_A and III_A have a greater investment effectiveness than alternative V_A, nonetheless alternative V_A can be included under certain conditions in the maximum effective balance of investment, whereas alternatives II_A and III_A can never be included. These alternatives cannot be included in the maximum effective balance not because their investment effectiveness is low, but because it is lower than the effectiveness of a greater investment in the same project (alternative IV_A). The whole point is that alternatives II_A and III_A occupy an intermediate position on the scale of increasing effectiveness of successive investments. No matter how high the effectiveness of these alternatives, they cannot be included in the maximum effective balance of investment, although less effective alternatives of the same projects on the scale of declining effectiveness of successive investment (for example, alternative V_A) can be included in the maximum effective balance of investment.

Important practical conclusions follow from this. Given a declining effectiveness of successive investments, additional investment must be comparatively uniformly distributed among different kinds of production units and objectives. Given a small accumulation, additional investment is directed toward many production units but in small quantities, whereas with a large accumulation it is also directed toward many units but in large quantities.

Thus we attain the maximum effect of investment given a declining effectiveness of successive outlays.

This maximum is formed differently in the case of increasing effectiveness. Here the constraint on accumulation must lead not to choosing alternatives with small additional investments in many production units, but to selecting alternatives with the greatest effectiveness of investment in a few units, and alternatives with the necessary minimum investment in many other units. Given a uniform distribution of additional investments in the particular case, not the most effective alternatives would be realized, but rather those intermediate ones that can never enter into the maximum effective balance, namely, alternatives occupying an intermediate position on the scale of increasing effectiveness of successive investments.

Hence it follows that in periods of rapid technological progress, when the effectiveness of successive investments increases in many cases, the development of the technological level of the economy must proceed not uniformly (by gradual movement from one level to another) but instead must move abruptly, in jumps. The shortage of accumulation in the given case will be reflected not in a decrease in the height of the jump in the technological level of individual lines of production and enterprises, but by a restriction on the number of lines of production and enterprises taking these jumps. On the other hand, the average height of an individual jump will be even more significant than in a situation in which there is a large volume of accumulation, since we must limit ourselves to only the most effective investment alternatives. But of course raising the technological level of the entire national economy (with due account of enterprises that are not involved in the jump) will be all the more important the greater the volume of accumulation.

The practice of socialist reconstruction of the national economy of the USSR corresponded to this principle of distributing investments with increasing effectiveness of successive outlays. Although our construction was accomplished with a significant shortage of accumulation in comparison with the possibilities for effective investment, it was nonetheless carried out according to the last word in technology. As a result of the combined effect of the advantages of the socialist system and the transition from a very low technological level to a modern one, the effectiveness of successive investments has probably also increased in many sectors where there have been significant intervals in successive outlays.

In this case all intermediate alternatives ranging from the necessary minimum investment to alternatives with the greatest effectiveness do not correspond to the principle of the maximum effect of investment. Hence the concentration of capital investment on the most effective projects. Party resolutions contain direct instructions on this question. Thus, the XVth Congress of the VKP(b) stated in one of its resolutions that the plan for capital construction "must proceed from the greatest effectiveness of capital outlays both with respect to *periods of completion of work* and with respect to the *productive effect* of enterprises under construction. Accordingly, each year's capital outlays must provide for maximum investment in a comparatively limited number of new plants and operating enterprises selected for reconstruction."[4]

Thus, project alternatives occupying intermediate places on a scale of growth of effectiveness of successive investment do not correspond under any conditions to the overall maximum effect of investment. Accepting these alternatives reduces the overall effect of investment below that possible with the same production program for final output and with the same accumulation, and this means that it raises total production costs of this output.

Having excluded alternatives with lower investment effectiveness than those with a larger investment in the same project, we obtain a number of alternatives with indicators calculated by the chain method (Table 20).

Table 20

Alternative and base	Investment, in millions of rubles	Production costs of annual output, in millions of rubles	Annual investment effectiveness, in % of investment
I_A	50	91	∞
IV_A / I_A	80	81.2	32.7
V_A / IV_A	100	80	6

After alternatives II_A and III_A were dropped, alternative I_A became the immediate neighbor of alternative IV_A. Accordingly, the index of investment effectiveness of alternative IV_A, calculated on the base of the alternative preceding the growth of effectiveness of successive investments, is now calculated on the

84

base of the alternative with the next smallest investment. At the same time, the dropping of intermediate alternatives on the scale of increasing effectiveness of successive investments transforms every series of alternatives either into two alternatives with the smallest and the largest investments, or into a series with declining effectiveness of successive investments.

The first possibility is realized if in the original series of alternatives the effectiveness of successive investments increases until the end of the series, even if there are intermediate declines.

The second possibility occurs if in the original series of alternatives the increase in effectiveness of successive investments is replaced by its decline.

5. Solution of a More Complex Problem of Finding the Overall Maximum Effect of Investment

Let us return to the solution of our problem No. 2. We will compute indicators of investment effectiveness for the alternatives relating to the remaining lines of production *(B, C, D,* and *E),* being guided by the rules explained above.

By the chain method of calculation we obtain the following series of indicators (Table 21 up to the lower line).

We recall that the alternatives are numbered in the order of increasing investment. We note that alternatives II_B, II_C, and III_C, outlined with rectangles in the table, must be excluded as intermediate alternatives given an increase in effectiveness of successive investments.

In accordance with this we must recalculate the indicators of effectiveness of alternatives III_B and IV_C on bases I_B and I_C. We obtain

$$E_{III_B/I_B} = 16.7\%;$$
$$E_{IV_C/I_C} = 10.7\%.$$

We include these indicators in the table (under the lower line). As a result we have indicators of effectiveness of alternatives that can be included in the maximum effective balance of investment (see the indicators in Table 21 that are not enclosed in rectangles).

We will rank these investment alternatives by decreasing effectiveness (Table 22), and in so doing will show the amount of investment to which the corresponding indicators of effectiveness pertain (including data for product *A* from Table 20).

We will select from this table, beginning at the top, as many investments as are contained in the limit. To facilitate selection,

B		C	
Alternative and base	Effectiveness of investment in % per year	Alternative and base	Effectiveness of investment in % per year
II_B I_B	16	II_C I_C	3
III_B II_B	18	III_C II_C	6
IV_B III_B	5	IV_C III_C	21
		V_C IV_C	4
III_B I_B	16.7	IV_C I_C	10.7

column 4 shows the sum of investments obtained by the summation of column 3. It is apparent from column 4 that the combination of alternatives with a total sum of investment of 400 million rubles corresponds to the investment limit that is equal to 410 million rubles according to the conditions of the problem.

The combination of alternatives with the next highest amount of investment is not contained within the limit (it requires 420

Table 22

Alternatives	Investment effectiveness in % per year	Amount of investment with this effectiveness, in millions of rubles per year	Cumulative sum of investment, in millions of rubles	Total production costs (A, B, C, D, E) (for investments in column 4), in millions of rubles per year
1	2	3	4	5
$I_A, I_B, I_C,$ I_D, I_E	∞	250	250	326.8
IV_A	32.7	30	280	317.0
III_B	16.7	30	310	312.0
IV_C	10.7	30	340	308.8
II_D	8.3	30	370	306.3
II_E	6.7	30	400	304.3
V_A	6.0	20	420	303.1
IV_B	5.0	20	440	302.1
V_C	4.0	20	460	301.3
III_D	3.5	20	480	300.6
III_E	3.0	20	500	300.0

D		E	
Alternative and base	Effectiveness of investment, in % per year	Alternative and base	Effectiveness of investment, in % per year
II_D I_D	8.3	II_E / I_E	6.7
III_D II_D	3.5	III_E / II_E	3

million rubles). This means that it is not possible to compile from the alternatives of our problem the combination that would require 410 million rubles of investment and yet would be of maximum effectiveness. It is true that from the alternatives in our problem (even after excluding those that cannot enter into the maximum effective balance of investments) we can compile thirty different combinations that yield output A, B, C, D, and E with investments equal to 410 million rubles. But not one of them yields a solution to our problem.[5] Therefore, the investment limit must be decreased to 400 million rubles.

The sum of investments selected in this way will also determine those alternatives whose combination solves our problem. For this purpose we must take for each project $(A, B, C, D,$ and $E)$ the alternative that is distinguished by the largest investment in comparison with the ones that are included in the limit insofar as their additional expenditures are concerned. The use of such a method is explained by the fact that the investment in this variant is equal to the sum of its additional investment together with all preceding "layers" of investment in the same project. For example, in solving our problem the following "layers" of investment in producing A were included in the investment limit:

minimum investment in alternative I_A . . . 50 million rubles
additional investment in alternative IV_A
above the investment in alternative I_A . . . 30 million rubles

Total . . . . 80 million rubles

This is equal to the investment of alternative IV_A. By accepting for each project the alternative that is the highest of those located above the line in column 1 of Table 22, and by separating the accepted alternatives of investment from the rejected ones, we obtain a combination of alternatives that solves our problem, namely, IV_A, III_B, IV_C, II_D, and II_E.

In finding this combination we have thereby constructed an optimal balance of investment (Table 23).

Table 23

(in millions of rubles)

	Distribution of investment	
	Alternative	Investment
Total investment limit — 400	IV_A	80
	III_B	80
	IV_C	80
	II_D	80
	II_I	80
	Total	400

This balance ensures not only equality between the total sum of investment and the allowable limit but also the maximum effective use of the limit.

6. Possible Inaccuracy of the Proposed Solution

The balance we have constructed ensures the maximum effective use of the investment limit on the assumption that there are no investment alternatives for these lines of production other than those that entered into the conditions of the problem. But the overall effect of investment can be greater still if the number of alternatives with investment effectiveness exceeding the minimum effectiveness of the accepted alternatives (6.7%) is increased. The highest effectiveness indicators for each project can thus remain unchanged. The appearance of additional alternatives with an effectiveness lower than the highest but higher than the minimum effectiveness of accepted alternatives increases the overall effect of investment.

Indeed, suppose that for projects *A, B,* and *C* new alternatives appear with investments larger than the investments of alternatives IV_A, III_B, and IV_C by 10 million rubles for each, and that the effectiveness of additional investment in these alternatives is, respectively, 15, 12, and 9% per year. Then we should reject alternative II_E with an investment effectiveness of 6.7% per year, replacing it by I_E, and this 30 million rubles of additional

88

investment (the investment of alternative II_E minus the investment of alternative I_E) should be distributed among the new alternatives. In the process the overall effect of investment grows by 1.6 million rubles per year:

$$30 \times \left(\frac{15 + 12 + 9}{3} - 6.7 \right) \times \frac{1}{100}.$$

The increase in the effect of investment occurred without raising the effectiveness of the most effective alternatives, only by increasing the number of intermediate alternatives among those with declining effectiveness of successive investments. As a result, differences in the effectiveness of the final (highest) "layers" of accepted investment in different projects have also decreased. Thus, these differences in our example were in the range of 6.7 to 32.7% before the appearance of new alternatives, and after the inclusion of new alternatives they were in the range of 8.3 to 15%.

Introducing other alternatives with an effectiveness of additional investment greater than 8.3% but less than 15% will yield a further increase in the overall effect of the same investment limit (by rejecting less effective and accepting more effective additional investments).

Continuing this analysis further, we arrive at the conclusion that increasing the number of intermediate alternatives among those with a declining effectiveness of successive investment, other conditions being equal, increases the overall effect of investment, raises the minimum effectiveness of accepted alternatives, and reduces differences in the level of effectiveness of the final "layers" of investment in different lines of production (projects).[6] It follows that it is advantageous to work out additional alternatives so long as the resulting increment in the overall effect of investment exceeds the cost of working out the project alternatives.

7. The Norm of Investment Effectiveness — the Index of Conformity of Individual Investments to Their Maximum Overall Effect

The maximum effective balance of investment cannot encompass all investment alternatives, for their number is practically unlimited. Thus, in choosing the diameter of a pipeline, material for a machine part, or the thickness of walls, and in solving other similar questions, there arises the problem of comparing production costs and investment. To centralize the solution of such questions, i.e., to solve them by constructing an optimal balance of investment, is inconceivable.

89

Moreover, new investment alternatives arise daily and hourly by virtue of technological progress. It is impossible to determine their effectiveness by compiling new optimal balances.

Hence it is clear that a norm is necessary by means of which we could determine, in each separate case, whether the given investment corresponds to the maximum overall effect of investment in the national economy and whether the given investment can be included in the optimal balance of investment. This norm arises directly from the optimal balance. Let us examine the properties that characterize the alternatives included in the optimal balance of investment.

It is apparent from Table 22 that the alternatives included in the optimal balance are distinguished by two properties:

(1) the effectiveness of each of the accepted investment alternatives is greater than that of each of the rejected alternatives, and greater than, or equal to, the minimum effectiveness of accepted alternatives;

(2) investment requirements for all selected alternatives are less than, or equal to, the limit.

Let us examine how we can find the alternatives possessing these properties.

From the first property it follows that the minimum effectiveness of accepted alternatives must be greater than the maximum effectiveness of rejected alternatives, or at least equal to it.

This means that in finding the minimum effectiveness of accepted alternatives with respect to the optimal balance, we obtain a norm on the basis of which we can judge whether the effectiveness of projected investments is high enough and whether they can be included in the optimal balance.[7]

By comparing the actual effectiveness of a number of investment alternatives with the norm we can determine which of the alternatives can be included in the optimal balance of investment. In this comparison it is necessary, first of all, to exclude alternatives occupying intermediate positions among those with increasing effectiveness of successive (additional) investment and, second, to compute effectiveness indicators for the remaining alternatives by the chain method. Then *the alternative with an investment effectiveness just larger than or equal to the norm will be the optimal one.* It is precisely this alternative that must be included in the optimal balance of investment.[8]

Let us clarify this rule. We recall that in the case of the direct selection of the most effective investments (according to Table 22) we accepted for each project the alternative with the largest investment of all those located above the line separating the accepted alternatives from the rejected ones. But the alternative with the largest investment is at the same time the one with the least effectiveness of investment of all alternatives of the same project that were placed above the boundary line. This arises from the basic rules for the direct selection of the most effective investments, namely, the rule for choosing the base for calculating the effectiveness of investment and the rule for excluding alternatives occupying intermediate places among those with an increasing effectiveness of successive investments.

The norm of investment effectiveness can also be used in another method of selecting alternatives. We will present the method explained above in mathematical form.

Let the investment in the alternatives of the same project be $K_1, K_2,..., K_m$;

Let the production costs of annual output for the same alternatives be, respectively, $C_1, C_2,..., C_m$.

We will assume that $K_1 < K_2 < ,..., < K_m$; $C_1 > C_2 >,..., > C_m$.

We will also assume that investments occupying intermediate positions among those with increasing effectiveness of successive investments do not enter into the designated alternatives. This condition will be expressed by the following inequalities:

$$\frac{C_1 - C_2}{K_2 - K_1} > \frac{C_2 - C_3}{K_3 - K_2} > \ldots > \frac{C_{m-1} - C_m}{K_m - K_{m-1}}.$$

We will call the allowable minimum of investment effectiveness the norm of investment effectiveness, denoting it by r.

Suppose that alternative f has an investment effectiveness equal to, or just larger than, the norm.

Writing this condition symbolically,

$$\frac{C_1 - C_2}{K_2 - K_1} > \frac{C_2 - C_3}{K_3 - K_2} > \ldots > \frac{C_{f-1} - C_f}{K_f - K_{f-1}} \geqslant r >$$
$$> \frac{C_f - C_{f+1}}{K_{f+1} - K_f} > \ldots > \frac{C_{m-1} - C_m}{K_m - K_{m-1}};$$

91

from which it follows that:

$$\frac{C_1 - C_2}{K_2 - K_1} > r;$$

$$\frac{C_2 - C_3}{K_3 - K_2} > r\,\frac{C_f - C_{f+1}}{K_{f+1} - K} < r;$$

$$\cdots \cdots \qquad \cdots \cdots$$

$$\frac{C_{f-1} - C_f}{K_f - K_{f-1}} \geqslant r\,\frac{C_{m-1} - C_m}{K_m - K_{m-1}} < r.$$

These inequalities will be transformed into the series of inequalities:

$$C_1 + K_1 r > C_2 + K_2 r;$$
$$C_2 + K_2 r > C_3 + K_3 r;\quad C_f + K_f r < C_{f-1} + K_{f-1} r;$$

$$\cdots \cdots \cdots \cdots \cdots \cdots \qquad \cdots \cdots \cdots \cdots \cdots \cdots$$

$$C_{f-1} + K_{f-1} r \geqslant C_f + K_f r;\quad C_{m-1} + K_{m-1} r < C_m + K_m r;$$

from which

$$C_1 + K_1 r > C_2 + K_2 r > C_3 + K_3 r > \ldots > C_{f-1} + K_{f-1} r$$

$$\geqslant \boxed{C_f + K_f r} < C_{f+1} + K_{f+1} r < \ldots < C_m + K_m r.$$

Here, of all sums of the form $C + \bar{K} r$ the sum $C_f + K_f r$ is the smallest.[9] But alternative f is the alternative with an investment effectiveness equal to, or just larger than, the norm, i.e., the alternative corresponding to the overall maximum effect of investment. Consequently, *we can replace the selection of alternatives with an effectiveness of investment equal to, or just larger than, the norm by the selection of alternatives for which the sum of production costs of annual output and the product of investment and the norm of effectiveness is the smallest.*

In other words, we can replace the determination of the optimal balance according to the minimum nonnegative difference between actual and normative effectiveness of additional investment with finding an alternative according to the formula $C + Kr = $ min. In this formula the product Kr expresses normative effect of investment K, i.e., the minimum labor savings that must be yielded by investment of amount K in order for us to be able to include it in the optimal balance. Thus, the sum $C + Kr$ is the sum of production costs and normative labor savings from projected investment.

At this point the reader may have a question. Why does the choice of the alternative according to the minimum of $C + Kr$ not require the prior exclusion of alternatives occupying intermediate places among those with increasing effectiveness of successive outlays of limited resources? The answer is simple. It is because with any economically possible values of the norm of effectiveness such variants cannot have minimum sums of the form $C + Kr$.

We can become convinced of this by means of the following reasoning. Suppose we have three alternatives for the production of a product. Outlays on these alternatives will be, respectively, K_1, K_2, and K_3 for investment; and the production costs of annual output will be C_1, C_2, and C_3.

We have

$$K_1 < K_2 < K_3, \quad \text{and} \quad C_1 > C_2 > C_3. \qquad (4.3)$$

Furthermore, the effectiveness of additional investments for alternative 3 is greater than the investment effectiveness for alternative 2:

$$\frac{C_2 - C_3}{K_3 - K_2} > \frac{C_1 - C_2}{K_2 - K_1}. \qquad (4.4)$$

This means that alternative 2 occupies an intermediate place among those with increasing effectiveness of successive investments.

It is not possible under conditions (4.3) and (4.4) for alternative 2 to have the least sum $C + Kr$, i.e., it is not possible with $r \geqslant 0$ that

$$C_2 + K_2 r < \left| \begin{array}{l} C_1 + K_1 r \\ C_3 + K_3 r \end{array} \right.$$

In actuality, these inequalities are equivalent to inequalities

$$\frac{C_2 - C_3}{K_3 - K_2} < r < \frac{C_1 - C_2}{K_2 - K_1},$$

from which

$$\frac{C_2 - C_3}{K_3 - K_2} < \frac{C_1 - C_2}{K_2 - K_1},$$

which contradicts condition (4.4).

This means that alternative 2 cannot have a minimum sum of the form $C + Kr$. This impossibility occurs for any norm effectiveness of investment except a negative one.

It is easy to see that choosing alternatives according to the minimum of the sum $C + Kr$ is simpler than choosing them according to the minimum nonnegative difference between the actual effectiveness and the norm. Certain additional rules and reservations, the neglect of which could have led to error, become superfluous. Nevertheless, the advantages that the method of least sums $(C + Kr)$ possesses are immeasurably more important than simplicity or convenience of calculation.

From a theoretical standpoint, calculating the sum $C + Kr$ is a special method of measuring labor outlays — a method directed to finding their overall minimum. In practice this measurement of outlays is the only possible one not only for constructing an optimal balance of accumulation and capital investment but also for solving a number of other important problems in planning the national economy.

8. The Need for Another Method of Finding the Maximum Effect of Investments Besides the Direct Selection of the Most Effective Investment Alternatives

The method we have presented for finding the maximum effect of investment by means of direct selection of the most effective alternatives is very simple. Nevertheless, in practice it is applicable on only a modest scale, for only in rare cases can we calculate the index of effectiveness of capital investment.

The index $(C_1 - C_2)/(K_2 - K_1)$ can be calculated only if savings in production costs $(C_1 - K_2)$ are the result only of additional investment $(K_2 - K_1)$. But, labor savings (and this means also savings in production costs) are accomplished not only by investment but also by the utilization of better natural resources (better soil, better minerals) and other relatively superior means of production. Usually, better means of production are insufficient to meet the demand for them. In this respect the better means of production are similar to investment. The volume of possible effective uses is greater than the supply of these means of production. Hence the problem arises of finding the maximum effective use of the better, but limited, means of production. This is a problem similar to that of finding the maximum effect of investment.

94

At first glance it appears that we can solve these problems separately for each kind of limited means of production. But in actuality such a solution is impossible.

It is impossible because we cannot divide the savings in production costs $(C_1 - C_2)$, which are the joint effect of several limited means of production, into a number of terms expressing the effects of expenditures of each of these means separately, for this would mean solving one equation with several unknowns.

On the other hand, with joint outlays of two or more limited means of production it is not possible to consider the savings in production costs as the effect of only one limited means, for example, investment. Otherwise, the effectiveness of those investment alternatives that presuppose the use of scarce means of production would be exaggerated because of the effect of using these means. As a result, a maximum effective balance compiled on the basis of incorrect investment indicators would require a larger amount of scarce means of production than are available. Having selected from a number of investment alternatives, arranged in order of their decreasing effectiveness, as many alternatives as are contained in the investment limit, we would obtain that balance of investment for whose realization neither better natural resources nor scarce kinds of raw materials or fuel would be lacking.

Thus, the method of direct selection of the most effective investment is applicable only when the compared alternatives require identical outlays of each scarce means of production but require different amounts of investment.

Hence it is apparent that our examples of determining the maximum effect of investment (see above, Tables 14 and 17) require an important reservation, namely, that for each project (*A, B, C, D,* and *E*) the outlays of all limited means other than investment be identical for all alternatives.

It should be noted that when we refer to other limited means we have in mind only those better means of production whose availability or production is less than the amount required or, more accurately, less than the volume of their possible effective applications. Here it is not the quality of a means of production but its limited quantity that has decisive significance.

We can become convinced of this by imagining that very rich deposits of a raw material have been discovered, deposits whose quality surpasses the best previously known scarce varieties of this raw material and which exceed in quantity all possible effective uses. Then the given kind of raw material, which is better than the previously scarce one, will not be scarce, and the previously scarce raw material will become unnecessary (ineffective). Although the new, abundant raw material will be more effective than the previous scarce one, differences in its outlays in the compared alternatives will not prevent us from finding the maximum effect of investment by the method presented here, since in constructing a maximum effective balance of investment we will not encounter a shortage of the given raw material.

Problem No. 3. Let us clarify what has been said with a simple example. Suppose that to produce three products, *A, B,* and *C,* there are the following limited means: 260 thousand rubles of investment and 40 tons per year of a scarce raw material.

The annual production program for each of these products can be fulfilled with different amounts of investment and with different expenditures of the scarce raw material. Outlays for each of the alternative ways of fulfilling the annual program for each product are shown in Table 24.

Table

	.1				*B*
Alternatives	Production costs. of annual output in thousands of rubles	Investment, in thousands of rubles	Expen- ditures of scarce raw material. in tons per year	Alternatives	Production costs of annual output in thousands of rubles
I_A	102	80	0	I_B	200
II_A	96	70	10	II_B	180
III_A	90	120	10	III_B	175

The question is how to find the combination of alternatives for which:

(1) the production program for all three products will be fulfilled;

(2) investment and expenditures of scarce raw material will not surpass the limits;

(3) there will be the greatest overall effect from using the scarce raw material and the investments (i.e., total production costs of products *A, B,* and *C* will be minimized).

Let us try to solve this problem by the same method that was used to solve the previous problem. We will determine indicators of investment effectiveness on the assumption that all savings in production costs that are promised by any of the alternatives are the effect only of investment. In other words, we assume that the effectiveness of expenditures of a scarce means of production is equal to zero. It is obvious that given this condition alternatives

I_A, I_B, and I_C drop out, since additional investment for these alternatives is accompanied not by saving but by overexpenditures of production costs of output (in comparison with alternatives II_A, II_B, and II_C).

Let us calculate the effectiveness of additional investment for alternatives III_A, III_B, and III_C:

$$E_{III_A/III_A} = \frac{96 - 90}{120 - 70} = 12\% \text{ per year;}$$

$$E_{III_B/II_B} = \frac{180 - 175}{120 - 80} = 12.5\% \text{ per year;}$$

$$E_{III_C/II_C} = \frac{100 - 95}{110 - 100} = 50\% \text{ per year.}$$

Let us set up Table 25 to select the most effective alternatives.

24

Investment, in thousands of rubles	Expenditures of scarce raw material, in tons per year	Alternatives	Production costs of annual output, in thousands of rubles	Investment, in thousands of rubles	Expenditures of scarce raw material, in tons per year
		C			
100	0	I_C	130	110	0
80	20	II_C	100	100	20·
120	20	III_C	95	110	30

Table 25

Alternative and base	Effectiveness of investment, in % per year	Investment with this effectiveness, in thousands of rubles
II_A, II_B, II_C	∞	250
III_C / II_C	50	10
III_B / II_B	12.5	40
III_A / II_A	12	50

97

It is obvious that alternatives II_A, II_B, and III_C are within the investment limits. But the requirements for the scarce raw material necessary for this combination of alternatives is not contained within the limit for this raw material. It constitutes $(10 + 20 + 30)$ = 60 tons per year with a limit of 40 tons per year.

We arrive at a similar result in solving this problem by finding the maximum effectiveness of utilization of the scarce raw material if, in calculating indicators of this effectiveness, we attribute to the scarce raw material all the savings in production costs promised by the given alternative in comparison with another one.

The indicators of the effectiveness of the scarce raw material represent the ratio of savings in production costs resulting from the application of this raw material to its outlays (expressed in natural units). Taking investment effectiveness as zero, we obtain such indicators of effectiveness of the scarce raw material (according to the condition of problem 3).

Alternatives III_A and III_B have an infinitely greater effectiveness of utilization of the scarce raw material relative to alternatives II_A and II_B. Savings in production costs are obtained without additional expenditures of the scarce raw material. Accordingly, alternatives II_A and II_B drop out.

The effectiveness of expenditures of the scarce raw material is expressed for the remaining alternatives by the following quantities (in thousands of rubles per ton):

$$E_{III_A/I_A} = \frac{102 - 90}{10 - 0} = 1.2;$$

$$E_{III_B/I_B} = \frac{200 - 175}{20 - 0} = 1.25;$$

$$E_{III_C/I_C} = \frac{130 - 100}{20 - 0} = 1.5;$$

$$E_{III_C/II_C} = \frac{100 - 95}{30 - 20} = 0.5.$$

We set up a table to select the most effective alternatives (Table 26).

Table 26

Alternative and base	Effectiveness of outlays of the scarce raw material, in thousands of rubles per ton.	Amount of the scarce raw material that can be expended with this effectiveness, in tons per year
$I_A \cdot I_B \cdot I_C$		0
II_C / I_C	1.5	20
III_B / I_B	1.25	20
III_A / I_A	1.2	10
III_C / II_C	0.5	10

The combination of alternatives I_A, III_B, and II_C satisfies the constraint on the scarce raw material. But these alternatives use more than the limited investment funds. Investment in the given case is $(80 + 120 + 100) = 300$ thousand rubles, with a limit of 260 thousand rubles.

Thus, both attempts to solve the problem proved unsuccessful. The reason for the lack of success in both cases is the same. All the savings in production costs were considered to be the effect of only one of two limited means. Indeed, according to the conditions of the problem, both the investment and the outlays of the scarce raw material yield savings in production costs. This is apparent from Table 24. Thus, additional investment in alternative III_A in comparison with alternative II_A is accompanied by savings in production costs with unchanged expenditures of the scarce raw material. On the other hand, expenditures of the scarce raw material in alternative II_A are accompanied by savings in production costs, in spite of a decrease in investment in comparison with alternative I_A. Similar relationships can be seen in comparing alternatives II_B and III_B, I_B and II_B, and III_C and I_C.

Yet both investment and the scarce raw material are limited. There are less of them than required for all labor saving applications (within the limits of the prescribed program for producing products *A, B,* and *C*) Consequently, both capital investment and the scarce raw material must be used in the maximum effective manner, i.e., so that there is the greatest overall effect from their utilization.

Hence the error is clear in the attempts presented above to solve problem No. 3. We solved it by finding the maximum effect stemming from the use of one kind of limited means of production, although the problem is that of finding *the maximum overall effect of the utilization of two kinds of limited means of production.*

But for solving such a problem the method presented above is unsuitable. Indeed, direct selection of the most effective alternatives is based on comparing effectiveness indicators for the application of a limited means of production. In this case of joint expenditures of two (or more) limited means of production the savings in production costs expected from their use are the combined effect of several heterogeneous means of production.

But we cannot calculate the index of effectiveness of outlays of several heterogeneous means of production. For this it would be necessary to calculate the ratio of savings in production costs resulting from the joint expenditure of different means of production to the sum of the expended means of production. If these are heterogeneous their summation is impossible. It is impossible to add rubles of investment to tons of copper or hectares of land. In actuality, the joint outlay of several limited means of production is a typical case. Therefore, as a rule the calculation of indicators of investment effectiveness contains, to a larger or smaller degree, the same error that occurred when we calculated these indicators according to the data of Table 24 (for Table 25) and assumed that the effectiveness of the scarce raw material was equal to zero.

Thus the problem of finding the maximum effect of investment for the national economy cannot be solved apart from the more general problem of finding the maximum effect of all limited means of production. Obviously, this is a different problem from the one we have been working on until now. We sought the maximum effect only of investment. Now a broader problem confronts us, that of finding the maximum effective use of several limited types of means of production.

Nor is this all. The problem of finding the overall maximum effect of limited means of production is, in turn, part of the problem of maximum effective utilization of all means of production in general.

Indeed, strictly speaking those means of production are limited whose possibility for effective application exceeds their availability (or production). This applies to all means of production that are better than the poorest of those of a given kind that are necessary to meet requirements. Each means of production whose use produces output with smaller outlays than with the use of the poorest necessary means of production will be limited. Its application will result in less use of labor, and the possibilities of its effective applications (i.e., labor-economizing ones) will be less than its availability. If this were not the case there would be no need to use less effective means of production.

100

Thus, the composition of limited means of production is extremely broad. It includes all usable natural resources except the poorest ones, and a multitude of reproducible means of production whose availability is restricted by the limits of accumulation. But in finding the maximum effective use of limited means of production we must also take into account the application of the poorest required means of production, for the comparative effectiveness of possible applications of limited means depends on the quality of the poorest required means.

Consequently, the maximum effective balances of limited means of production can be constructed only by introducing into these balances "nonscarce" means of production. Thus, the problem of the maximum effectiveness of investment has led us to a much more general problem, which goes beyond the limits of this chapter. However, even within the limits of the premises of this chapter (the assumption that only one kind of means is limited — investment), we can substantiate in the simplest way the method of constructing optimal balances that is appropriate for any number of limited means.

9. Potentially Optimal Combinations of Alternatives

We have examined the norm of investment effectiveness as a criterion for introducing small additions into the optimal balance of investment. However, this norm can be used for constructing an optimal balance as a whole. In fact, if we could identify, by some method, a norm of investment effectiveness the entire problem would be immediately solved. It would then be necessary to select for each project an alternative that has either an investment effectiveness equal to or just larger than the norm or one that minimizes the sum $C + Kr$. The question is only how to find this norm.

We saw that the norm arises from the optimal balance of investment. Hence we can arrive at the conclusion (as yet a hypothetical one) that any method of determining the norm of investment effectiveness is at the same time a method of constructing an optimal balance of investment.

The direct selection of the most effective investment alternatives is not the only method, and even (as we will see below) not the most suitable one. It is only the simplest and most comprehensible one. Taking it as the point of departure, it is easier to explain a different method of constructing optimal balances that, although more complex, corresponds to the conditions of the modern economy.

This more complex method is based on the property of the norm of investment effectiveness as the lower limit of the effectiveness of accepted alternatives. This property of the norm is obvious in its use in the formula

$$\frac{C_1 - C_2}{K_2 - K_1} - r = \min \geqslant 0$$

or (by using the recoupment period) in the formula

$$\frac{1}{r} - \frac{K_2 - K_1}{C_1 - C_2} = \min \geqslant 0.$$

It is obvious that if the investment selected satisfies the conditions of these formulas its effectiveness will not be lower than the norm.

But the effectiveness norm has the same property when it is used according to the formula $C + Kr = \min$. Hence it follows that given any nonnegative norms of investment effectiveness, alternatives selected on its basis form a combination for which investment, as a whole, yields the greatest effect (the greatest labor economies) among all possible applications of the same total sum of investment for producing the same output.

It is true that the magnitude of the norm of effectiveness influences the sum of investment selected and consequently its overall effect. With a high norm of effectiveness both the total sum of selected investment and its overall effect will be less than with a low norm. But with any nonnegative norm of effectiveness the most effective combination alternatives can be selected in comparison with all other possible combinations of them with the same (or a smaller) total sum of investment.

Therefore, combinations of alternatives formed by selecting them on the basis of any nonnegative norm of investment effectiveness can be called potentially optimal alternatives.

Such combinations can be optimal ones if the amount of investment that is required for them is equal to the investment limit. Hence it follows that the optimal balance of investment can be established by setting up several potentially optimal combinations on the basis of experimental norms of effectiveness. The relationship between required investment and the limit should be the criterion in these trials. If the required investment exceeds the limit established, the experimental norm of effectiveness must be raised. If the required investment is substantially less than the limit, the norm of their effectiveness must be reduced. The potentially optimal combination for which the required investment is equal to the limit will become the expenditure part of the optimal balance of accumulation and investment.

Each potentially optimal combination is distinguished by the following properties:

(1) it has the lowest production costs of all combinations that require equal (or less) investment;

(2) it requires the least investment of all combinations with equal (or lower) production costs for the same output.

Let us prove this in the simplest case of producing two products (1 and 2).

Let us assume that, having set the norm of investment effectiveness ($r > 0$), we selected alternatives of producing two products with minimum sums of the form $C + Kr$:

$$C_1' + K_1'r = \min;$$

$$C_2' + K_2'r = \min,$$

where subscripts 1 and 2 denote the products, and the primes signify the production costs of annual output and the investment required to produce it according to the selected alternatives.

We will now replace alternatives marked with a prime in this combination by two other alternatives picked so that the total sum of required investment does not increase:

$$K_1'' + K_2'' \leqslant K_1' + K_2', \tag{4.5}$$

where K_1'' and K_2'' are investments in alternatives of the changed combination.

Thus total outlays (of the form $C + Kr$) will grow (or at least remain constant):

$$C_1'' + K_1''r + C_2'' + K_2''r \geqslant C_1' + K_1'r + C_2' + K_2'r. \tag{4.6}$$

This increase in total outlays (with a given r) is possible only through an increase in total production costs. Indeed, multiplying both parts of inequality (4.5) by r (a positive quantity), we obtain:

$$K_1''r + K_2''r \leqslant K_1'r + K_2'r. \tag{4.7}$$

Subtracting this inequality from inequality (4.6) so that from the smaller part of inequality (4.6) we subtract the larger part of inequality (4.7); and from the larger part of inequality (4.6) we subtract the smaller part of inequality (4.7), we have; :

$$C_1'' + C_2'' \geqslant C_1' + C_2'.$$

Thus it is demonstrated that potentially optimal combinations have the lowest production costs of output of all possible combinations requiring the same (or smaller) sums of investment.

Let us now replace the selected alternatives by others so that overall production costs of both products do not increase (we will denote the production costs of the changed combination of alternatives by C_1''' and C_2'''):

$$C_1''' + C_2''' \leqslant C_1' + C_2'. \tag{4.8}$$

Thus total outlays of the form $C + Kr$ will increase (or at least will remain the same):

$$C_1''' + K_1'''r + C_2''' + K_2'''r \geqslant C_1' + K_1'r + C_2' + K_2'r. \tag{4.9}$$

With a given r this increase in total outlays is possible only through an increase in the total amount of investment in producing both products.

Indeed, subtracting inequality (4.8) from inequality (4.9) we obtain

$$K_1'''r + K_2'''r \geqslant K_1'r + K_2'r.$$

Dividing both parts of this inequality by r ($r > 0$), we obtain

$$K_1''' + K_2''' \geqslant K_1' + K_2'.$$

Thus it has been proved that potentially optimal combinations require the least investment of all possible combinations of alternatives with the same (or smaller) overall production costs of the same output.

Thus the formation of potentially optimal combinations of alternatives of investment can be used to solve two problems:

(1) problems relating to the overall maximum effect of using a certain investment limit (or, what amounts to the same thing, problems relating to the overall minimum production costs of the given output);

(2) problems relating to the overall minimum investment (with a prescribed limit of overall production costs of output).

The economic meaning of these problems is different. The problem relating to a minimum of capital investment is based on the implicit assumption that the economy strives to reduce to a minimum not the working time (the amount of labor) necessary for producing the required output, but the time necessary for its production and circulation.

Indeed, there is a relation between the production costs of output and the capital necessary for its production and circulation, namely, $K = C\bar{t}$, where K is capital, C is production costs of annual output, and $\bar{t}$ is the average period of production and circulation of capital, weighed according to the amount of outlays. Hence it follows that the problem relating to a minimum of K with limited C is a problem relating to a minimum of $\bar{t}$.

As will be seen below, the existence of potentially optimal combinations of alternatives can be used to construct optimal balances not only for investment but also for any means of production (material balances). This method of optimal balancing does not have the clarity of the direct selection of the most effective alternatives. In forming experimental, potentially optimal combinations of alternatives, we advance gropingly, so to speak, toward the goal.

However, in forming potentially optimal combinations we do not have to measure the effectiveness of investment. Selecting alternatives according to the formula $C + Kr = $ min involves selection according to minimum labor outlays. *Measuring the effectiveness of investment is replaced by measuring labor outlays.* That investment is considered most effective for which outlays of labor on output are minimized. This form of comparing alternatives (according to labor outlays) corresponds more to the nature of the problem of investment effectiveness than comparing indicators of investment effectiveness, i.e., of actual with normative ones. The effect of investment is measured by labor economies, and the sum $C + Kr$ expresses labor outlays measured by a method that facilitates finding their overall minimum. A demonstration of this statement constitutes the content of the following chapter.

10. Why the Norm of Investment Effectiveness Cannot Be the Average Level of Its Effectiveness

The necessity of establishing a norm of investment effectiveness has been widely recognized. This recognition is expressed in the "Recommendations of the All-Union Scientific-Technical Conference on Problems of Determining the Economic Effectiveness of Capital Investments and New Technology in the National Economy of the USSR." In Section 13 of the "Recommendations" we read: "In calculating effectiveness for the purpose of choosing the most suitable alternatives of capital investment it is necessary to compare the recoupment periods obtained (or the reciprocal — the coefficients of effectiveness) with the normative values of these indicators. These normative indicators should be established for the national economy as a whole and for branches in order to attain the greatest effect from capital investment on the scale of the entire national economy. The maximum allowable (normative) recoupment periods for choosing alternatives of capital investment and new technology should be determined by proceeding from the replacement of one

105

kind of technology by another, newer kind of technology, based on the amount of capital investment allotted to the given branch."[10]

This is a correct definition of the purpose the norm of investment effectiveness must serve ("to attain the greatest effect from capital investment on the scale of the entire national economy"), and also of the value of this norm as a marginal allowable quantity, and the basic conditions for defining its dimensions. The question of the role of branch effectiveness norms (recoupment periods) remains a controversial one. It is not clear how to justify them from the standpoint of attaining the maximum effect from investment on the scale of the entire national economy. However, they can be useful at least as stages on the way to determining national economic norms.

Not all Soviet economists agree with the definition of the norm of effectiveness as a minimum standard (and, correspondingly, of the recoupment period norm as a maximum allowable standard). Some investigators assume that the norm of investment effectiveness should be not a minimum but an average standard, namely, the average level of investment effectiveness. Such a viewpoint has been expressed by Academician S. G. Strumilin, [11] L. A. Vaag,[12] and others.

Adherents of this viewpoint evidently ignore the fact that the norm of investment effectiveness cannot be an average standard. Given any method of comparing production costs and investment by using effectiveness norms, only those investment alternatives whose effectiveness is not lower than the norm will always be the most advantageous. These results will follow whether we use formula

$$\frac{C_1 - C_2}{K_2 - K_1} - r = \min \geqslant 0,$$

or formula $C + Kr = \min.$[13]

This means that equating the norm of investment effectiveness to its average effectiveness leads to the equality of the minimum effectiveness of planned investment and its average effectiveness.

Equality of the minimum investment effectiveness and the average effectiveness is possible only under the condition that average effectiveness pertains to a different set of investments than does the minimum effectiveness. Average effectiveness can pertain to all possible future investment. This is apparently the sense in which Academician S. G. Strumilin treats the average level of effectiveness. Average effectiveness can also refer to investment realized in the past, expressing the average profitability of productive capital. Such a viewpoint has been expressed by L. A. Vaag and others.

However, neither of these concepts of the average as the norm of investment effectiveness gives us a suitable instrument for compiling optimal balances of investment. The average effectiveness of all possible investment does not at all guarantee that an investment plan constructed on its basis will be within the investment limit. Such an average could serve only as a first approximation in the search for a norm of investment effectiveness. Thus, having become convinced that the investment plan constructed on its basis does not comply with the limit (the accumulation plan), we would have to establish another norm. If after trying several experimental norms we succeeded in equating the investment plan and the accumulation plan, the derived norm of investment effectiveness would not in any case be the average effectiveness of planned investment. It would be its minimum effectiveness. Therefore, it is hardly worthwhile (even as a first approximation) to proceed from the average effectiveness of possible investment as the norm of its effectiveness.

Use of the average profitability of productive capital as the norm of investment effectiveness leads to different results. Choosing new investment alternatives on the basis of the average effectiveness of past investments is equivalent to raising the lower limit of investment effectiveness. The average effectiveness of investment in each previous period becomes the lower limit of investment effectiveness in the following period. This is equivalent to the systematic narrowing of possibilities for the growth of labor productivity. There is no doubt that the defenders of the average norm of profitability of capital as the norm of investment effectiveness do not foresee such consequences. Yet these consequences are unavoidable as soon as the average effectiveness of past investment is used for selecting future investment with an effectiveness no lower than this norm. But such a selection is dictated by the formula $C + Kr_{cp} = min$, which the defenders of the average as the norm of effectiveness recommend.[14]

However, in considering the norm of effectiveness as the minimum allowable standard we must be somewhat more precise.

First of all, it would be incorrect to calculate this quantity from statistical data on the actual effectiveness of investment. For a nonoptimal balance of investments the minimum effectiveness of accepted alternatives will be lower than in an optimal one, and also lower than the maximum effectiveness of rejected investment alternatives. This means that in asserting that the norm of investment effectiveness is equal to the minimum effectiveness of accepted alternatives we still do not provide a complete definition of this norm. There can be as many such minima as there can be different sets of selected uses of investment.

But when the accepted uses ensure an overall maximum effect of investments, then:

(1) the minimum effectiveness of accepted alternatives will be a maximum;

(2) the maximum effectiveness of rejected alternatives will be a minimum;

(3) the first quantity will be greater than, or equal to, the second.

Thus, the norm of investment effectiveness is a limiting quantity of a special kind. This is the saddle point — the maximin or the minimax.

11. Conclusions

We shall sum up this chapter. The limited amount of accumulation poses the problem of its most effective use. When the volume of accumulation is insufficient to use all the labor - economizing possibilities of capital investment, it is necessary to select those investments for which, in the first place, the production program for final output will be fulfilled and, in the second place, there will be the greatest overall effect of all capital investment. This requirement arises from the principles of economizing on labor.

However, it is not possible to solve this problem in isolation from the problem of the best utilization of all means of production. It is possible to form an optimal (maximum effective) balance of accumulation and investment without considering its connection with the maximum effective balances of all means of production. *The optimal balance of capital investment can be formed only as a part of the system of optimal balances of means of production.*

An optimal balance of accumulation and investment drawn up by the method of direct selection will be impracticable to the extent that there is a shortage of the best means of production, since not only investment but also many means of production are limited. The principle of economizing on labor requires the maximum effective use not only of investment but of all generally limited means of production. Consequently, we must seek not the maximum effect of overall investment, but the maximum overall effect from the use of investment and limited means of production.

But this is not all. The dividing line between means of production that are relatively better (limited) and those that are not scarce, but are still suitable for use as means of production, can be found only by constructing maximum effective balances of all means of production. Thus it follows that the best use of capital investment can be found only by drawing up an entire system of maximum effective material balances and a balance of investment. This means that there is no special problem of effectiveness of capital investment that can be posed and solved in isolation from the more general problem of the most effective use of all means of production.

This is the first result of this chapter, a negative result. Nevertheless, it is an important result because in the literature and in practice the problem of effectiveness of capital investment is posed in isolation from the problem of the greatest overall effect of the use of all means of production.

However, this negative result also has its positive side. Having become convinced of the impossibility of solving the problem of effectiveness of capital investment in isolation from the broader problem, we have also determined not only the essence of this problem but also the fundamental means of solving it.

The essence of the problem, part of which is the problem of effectiveness of capital investment, consists of finding the overall minimum outlays of labor required to produce the given output. The method of solving it requires the construction of a system of optimal balances of means of production (also including a balance of capital investment).

This system of balances cannot be constructed by the method of direct selection of the effective alternatives of application of each kind of means of production taken separately. For when there are joint outlays of several heterogeneous means of production to manufacture a product, there is no possibility of determining the savings of labor caused by each of them.

Nevertheless, the direct selection of the most effective applications of a limited means can be replaced by selection according to minimum outlays if we include in total outlays a normative labor saving from the use of the given means. We studied this possibility for the case when only one kind of means was limited. We established that the norm of effectiveness of a given limited means can be found by drawing up several experimental balances. The outlay part of each of these balances represents requirements for the given means for all of those uses that yield planned output with minimum costs of reproduction

109

and the normative labor saving from using the given means.

If the norm of effectiveness is correctly determined, the balance works out without a shortage or surplus of limited means. If the norm is set too low, a shortage of means arises. In finding the correct value of the norm of effectiveness we also determine that combination of alternatives for which final output corresponds to the assignment; the limited means are used with maximum overall effect, and costs of reproducing all final output are minimized.

Thus, when only one kind of means is limited, the direct selection of its most effective uses can be replaced by selection according to minimum outlays measured in a particular manner.

To sum up, Chapter 4 has posed two questions for us:

1. What is the economic meaning of measuring outlays according to the formula $C + K_r$?

2. Can this method of measuring outlays be applied in actual practice, and can we use it as a basis for constructing a system of optimal balances of all resources, and an optimal plan for developing the national economy?

Notes

1. K. Marx and F. Engels, *Soch.*, 2nd Edition, Vol., 23, p. 402.

2. Final output of the national economy in a particular period consists of objects of consumption (individual and social), circulating capital, and that part of the means of production that is intended for subsequent expansion of production (in later periods). Strictly speaking, these means of production are not themselves the final goal of production. This is clear as soon as we look beyond the limits of the planned period. However, we assume a condition of constant growth of production. The planned period is always limited by a definite interval of time. Therefore, no matter how far into the future the plan extends, and no matter how broadly we extend the limits of the planned period, some means of production whose purpose will still not have been determined will remain in the composition of output of this period. Therefore, although means of production are not an end in themselves, a certain part of the means of production is included in the composition of the planned final output — namely, the part that is intended for growth of consumption beyond the limits of the planned period.

3. Thus, $E_{IIIC/IIC} = (63.5 - 62.9) / (70 - 60) = 6\%$ per year, and $E_{IIC/IC} = (64 - 63.5) / (60 - 50) = 5\%$ per year.

4. *KPSS v rezoliutsiiakh i resheniiakh s'ezdov, konferentsii i plenumov TsK*, 7th edition, State Political Literature Publishing House, 1953. Part II, pp. 458-459.

5. Twenty-eight combinations (with an investment of 410 million rubles) yield output with a higher production cost than the combination found above, which requires only 400 million rubles of investment. One of the combinations (with an investment of 410 million rubles) does not yield any savings in production costs in comparison with the combination found above, which requires less investment. Finally, one combination with an investment of 410 million rubles yields some savings in production costs in comparison with the combination that we found. However, the effectiveness of additional investment in the best of the combinations with an investment of 410 million rubles is much lower than the lower limit of effectiveness of alternatives accepted in our combination. In fact, the best of the combinations with 410 million-rubles of investment is a combination of variants V_A, IV_B, IV_C, II_D, and I_E. The production costs of output of this combination amount to 304.1 million rubles. Hence the effectiveness of additional investment in this combination, calculated on the base of our combination, is equal to 2% per year [$(304.3 - 304.1)$: $(410 - 400)$], which is three times lower than the lower limit of effectiveness of the accepted alternatives (6.7% per year) of our combination.

6. The complete equality of effectiveness of the higher layers of investment in all projects is conceivable only under those unreal conditions in which the effectiveness of successive investments is a continuous function of their size, and if the number of alternatives of successive investments in each project is infinitely large.

7. The maximum effectiveness of rejected alternatives could also serve as such a norm. However, in the given example this maximum is not a completely clear criterion of the sufficiency of the effect. It demonstrates that investment with greater effectiveness can be included in the optimal balance, but it does not indicate how much greater. In the actual optimal balance, given the presence of a large number of investment alternatives, the maximum effectiveness of rejected alternatives practically coincides with the minimum effectiveness of accepted alternatives. It is clear that the norm of investment effectiveness determined from the optimal balance will be suitable for introducing only small changes in the optimal balance of investment. The norm of effectiveness can also change when there are large changes in the balance.

8. It is wrong to consider the alternative with the greater effectiveness of investment as the optimal one. It is likewise inaccurate to consider the alternative with an effectiveness surpassing the norm as the optimal one, for there can be several such alternatives.

9. The equality $C_{f-1} + K_{f-1}r = C_f + K_f r$ means that additional investment $K_f - K_{f-1}$ has only the minimum allowable effectiveness.

10. *Voprosy ekonomiki,* 1958, No. 9, p. 157.

11. See S. G. Strumilin, *Ob ekonomicheskoi effektivnosti novoi tekhniki,* Moscow, Academy of Sciences of the USSR, All-Union Council of Scientific and Technical Societies, 1958, pp. 14-15.

12. L. A. Vaag, *Obshchie voprosy otsenki ekonomicheskoi effektivnosti kapitalnykh vlozhenii,* Moscow, Academy of Sciences of the USSR, All-Union Council of Scientific and Technical Societies, 1958, p. 36.

13. The method of comparing alternatives recommended by Academician S. G. Strumilin does not formally coincide with any of these methods. It can be represented in the form of the following inequality: $(C_0 - C_1) + (K_2 - K_1)r_{cp} < C_0 - C_2$, where C_0, C_1 and C_2 are the production costs of normal output and output according to two investment alternatives; K_1 and K_2 are investments, and r_{cp} is the average norm of their effectiveness. This inequality can be simplified, however, to $C_1 + K_1 r_{cp} > C_2 + K_2 r_{cp}$. Thus, the method recommended by Academician S. G. Strumilin for comparing alternatives is essentially equivalent to the formula $C + K r_{cp}$ = min.

14. See L. A. Vaag, *op. cit.,* pp. 9, 36-37, and others.

CHAPTER 5

PRINCIPLES OF MEASURING COSTS

Measuring the labor costs of a product by a labor involved in its production is not the only method of measurement. It is only an elementary method of measuring costs by means of elementary mathematics. Other procedures for measuring costs, namely, procedures involving the mathematics of variable quantities, are also possible and, under certain conditions, are necessary.

The measurement of costs is subject to economic laws, both to general and specific laws of each stage of development. These laws, as well as others, direct the measurement of costs to the solution of certain extremal problems.[1] Thus, the general law of the economy of labor requires a measurement of labor costs that would make it possible to find their minimum. The specific law of surplus value subordinates the measurement of costs under capitalism to the task of maximizing profit. In this process, the law of the economy of labor is realized insofar as this is compatible with the maximization of capitalist profit.

The specific economic laws of socialism — the basic law, the law of continuous growth of labor productivity, and the law of the planned development of the national economy — direct the measurement of costs to the attainment of the greatest possible rate of growth of labor productivity.

The extremal character of those problems whose solution helps to measure costs requires (under certain conditions) the use of procedures for measuring labor costs other than the simple calculation of outlays on production. The necessity of using other procedures does not depend on the value form of expressing labor costs. There are certain general principles of measuring costs in a highly developed social economy that encompass the law of value as well as labor accounting.

The special features of measuring outlays of labor that are characteristic of a particular economic system can be made apparent only by studying the general principles of this measurement. Accordingly, at first we will ignore value. We will assume that we have already made the transition to measuring costs in terms of labor time. Then we will return again to value measurement. This sequence of investigation will enable us to specify both the general laws of measurement of costs and the specific peculiarities of this measurement that are inherent in different types of production relations.

Many economists implicitly share the view that the measurement of costs does not require higher mathematics. Usually the thought does not even arise that the measurement of costs for the purpose of finding their minimum must be done differently than in a situation in which this problem does not exist. In finding minimum costs for a particular product it is considered quite sufficient to calculate its costs of production according to different alternatives and to compare the results. However, this problem can be solved in this way only at the lower stages of economic development, stages no higher than the conditions of simple commodity production. Under simple commodity production the objects exchanged were almost completely the product of the individual labor of peasants or craftsmen. "What did they expend in the making of these objects? Labor, and only labor. In replacing implements of labor, in producing raw material, and in processing it they expended only their own labor power. Accordingly, could they have exchanged these products of theirs for the products of other producers otherwise than in proportion to the labor expended?" [2]

Under such conditions the determination of the least labor-intensive processes of producing each product was possible by directly comparing the outlays of labor required. It is not possible to solve the problem of minimum costs under socialism in this way. The problem itself has fundamentally changed. Instead of a problem relating to the minimum amount of labor required to produce each individual product, we have the problem of finding overall minimum costs. It arose not only by virtue of the conscious priority of general interests over private ones, and of overall minimum costs over particular minima, but also (and above all) by virtue of the objective impossibility of being guided by particular cost minima. In a socialist economy individual minima of costs of production (for each product and enterprise taken separately) are incompatible with each other. This means that each particular minimum can be attained separately, but together they are unattainable.

To illustrate this proposition we will again return to Table 17 (see pp. 76-77). Suppose that we can spend not more than 400 million rubles on all five investment projects. As is apparent from this table, it is necessary to invest 100 million rubles in each to attain for each project the alternative with the least production costs of output. Obviously, each of these alternatives is attainable if taken separately, but together they are unattainable. For this purpose 500 million rubles are required, whereas we can spend only 400 million rubles.

Every experienced planner knows that he cannot be guided by minimum production costs of output in choosing an alternative, for the investment limit, the limited nature of scarce means of production, the shortage of the best natural resources, etc., prevent the attainment of this minimum. The situation does not change if planners calculate the individual value of output instead of production costs. The possible minimum magnitudes of individual values of separate products also presuppose the use of only the best conditions of application of labor and consequently are not compatible with each other. Thus, in a socialist economy the principle of a particular minimum of outlays on production is inoperative independently of people's will. It becomes objectively unattainable.

The principle of the economy of labor under socialism can be realized only as a principle of an overall minimum of labor costs for the national economy's entire output. The primacy of the overall minimum of outlays over particular minima is an objective necessity of a socialist economy.

This means that the most effective alternative of the production of any product is not the alternative that requires the lowest costs of production of this product, but the alternative that corresponds to overall minimum costs. It is impossible to find this alternative in an elementary way (by calculating costs and comparing results). For this purpose it would be necessary to calculate the costs of production of the national economy's entire final output for all possible combinations of alternatives of producing individual products. The number of such combinations is enormous, and the overwhelming majority of combinations will always be ineffective. This way of solving the problem is extremely irrational. It requires

114

a multitude of unnecessary calculations.

1. Differential Costs

It is not at all necessary to calculate total outlays in the national economy in order to find the alternative corresponding to overall minimum costs. For this purpose it is sufficient to calculate only the increment in costs of production of the national economy's final output that is caused by the production of the given product. That alternative of producing any product that requires the smallest increment in the costs of producing all final output corresponds to the overall minimum of costs. The measurement of costs as increments of a variable quantity suggests that we call such costs the national economy's differential costs for the given product.

If the selection of an alternative of producing an individual product did not affect the costs of production of other products, then its differential costs would coincide with its costs of production. In reality, however, the selection of an alternative of producing an individual product influences the cost of producing other products. As will be demonstrated, the choice of an alternative of producing each product is usually associated with certain increments in the costs of other products. Therefore, the differential costs associated with the production of an individual product are not, as a rule, equal to its costs of production.

Differential costs for the given product can be most easily understood as the difference between the labor necessary to produce the national economy's output, including the given product, and the labor necessary to produce the same output without the given product.

However, this definition of the concept of differential costs does not reveal the method of calculating them. The essence of this method consists of calculating the labor expended in producing the given product and those increments in costs of producing other products that are connected with producing the given product.

2. Feedback Between Costs for Different Purposes

A twofold relationship exists between outlays on different products:

(1) Direct: an increase in outlays on a given product causes an increase in outlays on other products.

(2) Indirect: an increase in outlays on a given product causes a decrease in outlays on other products.

The direct connection between outlays is generally recognized. It is based on the fact that outlays on means of production are included in the costs of products made with these means.

If there were a direct connection only (larger — larger, smaller — smaller) between the costs of different products, then particular minimum outlays would be compatible with each other. In that case overall minimum costs could be found by seeking the minimum costs for each product separately.

But the existence of a feedback relationship between costs complicates matters. A project alternative requiring minimum costs for the given product can be associated with such an increment in outlays on other products that the latter will offset any savings in the costs of producing the given product.

Because of the existence of feedback effects between outlays on different products, the sum of particular values of minimum costs does not coincide with overall minimum costs for the national economy. Therefore, it is not possible to find overall minimum costs by seeking minimum costs for each product separately.

The feedback effect between costs always arises when there is a combination of the following three conditions:

(1) the interchangeability of different means of production, i.e., the capacity of different means of production to serve the same function;

(2) the unequal effectiveness of different interchangeable means of production;

(3) a shortage of the more effective means of production in comparison with requirements for them (more exactly — with the number of their effective uses).

All these conditions are necessary for the existence of a feedback effect between costs. The importance of the first two conditions is quite apparent. The third condition requires explanation.

The unequal effectiveness of means of production would not be economically significant if the most effective means of production

116

were available in quantities no smaller than are required for all purposes. But the scarcity of these means of production requires that we also use less effective means. In this process there necessarily arises a feedback effect between outlays on purposes that could use more effective means of production. For the use of better means of production (better sources of raw material or power, better machinery, etc.) for one purpose is always connected with the necessity of using poorer means of production (poorer sources of raw material or power, less-advanced machinery, etc.) for other purposes.

Therefore, the economy of labor attainable by using better but quantitatively limited means of production always involves an increase in outlays of labor for some other purposes. An economy of labor in one place is counterposed to additional labor costs in another. In this process the savings attained can be either larger or smaller than the additional outlays. Different uses of the better means of production are not equally effective. Some uses yield a larger and others a smaller economy of labor in comparison with the use for the same purposes of less effective means of production, but means of production that are necessary to meet requirements.

Let us present examples of feedback between costs.

With a given amount of accumulation in the national economy the project alternative that requires a larger investment, in comparison with another alternative of the same project, correspondingly reduces investment in other projects. The selection of alternatives with smaller investment in other projects involves such consequences as the application of less advanced machinery, rejection of expensive but effective structures (tunnels, providing a road with embankment, etc.), increasing the life of obsolete machinery, reducing intervals between cuttings of a forest, decreasing the size of parts in serial machine-building, and other similar consequences of reducing capital investment without decreasing annual output. All these consequences are connected, as a rule, with an increase in the production costs of the corresponding output.

This means that the selection of an alternative requiring greater investment in a given project lowers the production costs of this project, but raises those of other products, and precisely those in the production of which investment must be curtailed stemming from their larger outlays on the given project.

Another example is oil, a fuel of high caloric value. The number of uses in which it yields an economy of labor in comparison with

117

other kinds of fuel is much larger than its possible production. Accordingly, in choosing methods of using oil we should not be guided only by those expected savings in production costs and in investment in one particular use. Each use of oil excludes other effective uses, which could also yield savings in production costs and in investment.

This means that the choice of an alternative requiring expenditures of oil reduces production costs and capital investment at the cost of raising production costs and capital investment in other lines of production where its use is effective but is incompatible with the given use.

3. Feedback Costs and Differential Costs

In finding the project alternative corresponding to overall minimum costs for the national economy it is necessary to measure not only the costs of reproduction for different alternatives of the project but also those increments of costs for other products associated with the use of more effective means of production for the given purpose rather than for others. We will call these increments of labor costs for other products feedback costs, since they reflect the indirect relationship between costs of producing different products.

Then we can say that the differential costs of each individual product are composed of: (1) its costs of production, and (2) its feedback costs. [3]

The calculation of feedback costs is an objective necessity for a socialist economy. Hence it has an effect even if there is ignorance of the essence and correct methods of measuring these costs, even if there is a reluctance to take them into account, and even if there is criticism of this calculation.

The calculation of feedback costs influences practice above all, because the absence of this calculation would make itself known in the same convincing way that all unaccounted-for outlays make themselves known, namely, the purpose of the outlays becomes attainable by virtue of a lack of means.

However, the consequences of disregarding the calculation of feedback costs are broader than the consequences of gaps in the calculation of costs of production. If certain costs of production of a product (for example, fuel consumption) are not taken into account, then the specific objective of these outlays is unfulfilled (completely or in part). If feedback costs caused by the use of any means of production are not taken into account, then all those

118

uses of this means that yield cost savings in comparison with other forms of the same means of production will prove to be incompatible.

For a long time scientifically substantiated methods of calculating feedback costs were not available in practice. Instead of these methods, capital investment, the consumption of scarce raw materials, expenditures of scarce fuel, and other elements of production with qualities and dimensions altogether different from the feedback costs dependent on them were taken into account, together with production costs. As a result, a heterogeneous, nonadditive composition of costs was derived in which it was not even possible to raise the question of the minimum of all costs.

Of course, we can balance the total outlays of limited means with their availability without comparing production costs and outlays of limited means, i.e., without calculating feedback costs. For this purpose it is sufficient to reduce claims on the basis of some simple rule (for example, proportionally). A plan balanced in this way can be considered as provided with material resources. But it will not promote the best use of these resources. The plan will be workable, but not optimal.

It is true that in a socialist economy there is no place for such a purely mechanical curtailment of requirements for limited means. The balance of these means was constructed and is still constructed by calculating the importance of different requirements, and, to the extent possible, by calculating the effectiveness of different uses of these means. If there is a shortage of any means in comparison with requirements, its less important uses are discarded (or reduced) and more important ones are retained in the balance of this means.

In turn, the consumers of limited means must somehow or other compare the production costs of output with expenditures of limited means in choosing alternatives of their use. Without such a comparison (even if it is imprecise) it is frequently not even possible to decide approximately which alternative is most effective and, what is more important, the savings in production costs (so many rubles per year) or additional investment (so many rubles) plus additional consumption of scarce means of production (so many tons), etc.

Therefore, various methods of measurement (recoupment periods, increased prices for scarce materials, etc.) were used in practice. They were used despite the absence of a clear understanding of the essence of these methods, despite lack of

119

knowledge of methods of calculating norms of comparison, and despite the sharp criticism by some economists of procedures for measuring costs. But behind these various coefficients of comparison were concealed imperfect norms for calculating feedback costs.

Thus, the necessity for calculating feedback costs is manifested both in the need to construct balances of means with due regard for the calculation of their effective uses, and in the need to compare costs of production with outlays of limited means. Nevertheless, the necessity of measuring feedback costs is still insufficiently recognized. It is true that the economic reform opened up broad possibilities for taking account of feedback costs in prices and in economic accounting. Nevertheless, economists usually treat payments for capital and rent payments only as stimuli to achieve economies. This is a superficial conception. It does not explain why it is necessary to economize on capital and natural resources, and — most important — it does not provide a key to calculating the amount of these payments for their use.

4. The Range of Differential Feedback Costs

We will determine how extensive is the group of those means of production whose use is associated with feedback costs. For this purpose it is necessary to establish which means of production satisfy all three conditions for the existence of a feedback effect between costs.

Here we include, first of all, a multitude of nonreproducible means of production, such as parcels of land, deposits of useful minerals, flowing water available for use, etc. All the relatively better means of production of this kind will be burdened by feedback costs. Only the use of the least effective means of production that are necessary to meet requirements will not involve these costs.

There is also a multitude of reproducible means of production. These are interchangeable, but not equally effective, and their reproduction is limited by the amount of the national economy's accumulation. Each reproducible means of production can be produced separately in an amount that is required for all of its effective uses, i.e., for all uses in which it is required and yields an economy of labor in comparison with other means of production. However, the production of *all* reproducible means of production is limited by the amount of the national economy's accumulation (by the limited nature of accumulation we do not mean that it is absolutely small, but that it is smaller than the opportunities for effective investment). This scarcity of the best reproducible means of production involves an extremely wide range of feedback between labor costs for these means. All branches are encompassed by this feedback, for reproducible means of production are used in all branches, and outlays of these means depend everywhere on the same common limit, the limit of the national economy's accumulation.

Furthermore, a multitude of previously produced means of production satisfy all three conditions for the existence of feedback costs. Here we include almost all of the national economy's fixed and circulating capital. This assertion might appear paradoxical. As a rule, old means of production are inferior to new ones. They are technologically backward and worn out.

Nevertheless, the comparative effectiveness of existing old means of production and new, not yet produced, ones will appear in a different light if we seek not the overall minimum of past and impending costs, but rather the overall minimum of impending labor costs, i.e., the costs of reproduction. In the calculation of impending costs, previously produced means of production have a great advantage in comparison with new, not yet produced, ones. They do not require outlays of labor for production; they require only outlays on utilization, whereas means of production that have not yet been produced require labor for both production and utilization. Owing to this advantage, means of labor that are too obsolete to reproduce can be more effective in utilization than the most effective of the new, but not yet produced, means of labor.

This relation between the effectiveness of old and new means of labor is a normal one. Old means of labor are usually reproduced not in their previous form but in a new one. It is impossible to assume that this is a massive error of calculation. It is more likely that it is ineffective to reproduce them in their previous form.

Yet many means of labor that are too obsolete to reproduce are still used. It is improbable that there has been a universal error in calculation. On the contrary, it is more probable that by using partially obsolete means of labor, we expect — with adequate justification — to obtain output with smaller outlays of future labor than would be obtained with new, more advanced, but not yet produced machines and implements.

Hence it follows that we must strictly distinguish between obsolescence with respect to reproduction and obsolescence with respect to utilization. The former depends on the answer to the following questions: In what form should the means of production

121

be reproduced — in their previous or in a new form? What should be the new means of production? Obsolescence with respect to utilization depends on the answer to the following question: Up to what point can the old means of production be used?

Of course, the advantage of using the old means of production compensates for their defects only up to a certain point. Instruments of labor can become obsolete not only with respect to reproduction but also with respect to utilization. This will happen if the costs of reproduction of output with old instruments of labor, not counting past outlays on these instruments, will no longer correspond to the overall minimum of outlays, i.e., if the production costs of output with the old instruments of labor (without considering amortization) exceed the sum of total production costs with new instruments of labor and the feedback costs associated with investment in these instruments.[4]

But until this limit is reached almost all old means of production yield an economy of labor in reproduction in comparison with the best, but not yet produced, means of production. An exception to this applies only to those old means of production that are on the margin of obsolescence with respect to utilization. Consequently, the use of almost any old means of production for any one purpose involves an increase in future labor for other possible purposes, i.e., it involves feedback costs.

These costs must be taken into account in calculating the effectiveness of production with old means of production. Without considering these feedback costs it is impossible to determine which alternatives of utilization of old means of production are the most effective ones, i.e., correspond to the overall minimum of labor costs for fulfilling the prescribed production program.

At the same time the magnitude of feedback costs shows the degree of productive suitability (effectiveness) of the old means of production. If these costs are equal to zero, this signifies that the given means of production have attained the limit of effective utilization and, with a subsequent worsening of the indicators, must be replaced by new ones.

The vast majority of means of labor used have an effectiveness greater than zero. In other words, the vast majority of available instruments of labor make it possible to produce output with smaller outlays of future labor than is possible with better, but not yet produced, machines and implements. Consequently, from the standpoint of savings of future labor, feedback costs arise in connection with the use of the vast majority of previously produced means of production.

Thus, the principle of economizing on future outlays takes past outlays into account only to the extent of future feedback costs associated with the utilization of the product of past outlays. This conclusion is a generalization of the indisputable statement that existing means of production must be valued according to their costs of reproduction.

In such a formulation this proposition applies only to the case of identity of the old and the most effective new (but not yet produced) means of production. In this case feedback costs associated with the use of old means of production are equal to the costs of reproducing them. Raw materials and fuel can serve as the most characteristic example of such a case. Reserves of these means of production usually consist of kinds that will continue to be reproduced in the future. Therefore, feedback costs associated with the use of these reserves generally coincide with the costs of reproducing them.

No less important is another case in which the means of production are reproduced in a different form, with different properties and different designs. Precisely such a situation is typical for implements of labor. But in this case the valuation of old means of production cannot be equal either to the costs of reproducing them in the previous form or to the costs of reproducing them in a new form. For example, suppose that a new machine is cheaper and more effective than an old one. Then neither the costs of reproducing the latter nor the costs of reproducing the new machine will be suitable for purposes of valuation of the old machine. Both types of costs will be too high.

True, it can be said that the costs of reproducing old implements of labor are determined by the costs of reproducing new ones, with due regard for difference in quality. However, in order for differences in quality to be expressed in differences in costs, it is necessary to impart a broader meaning to the principle of valuation according to reproduction costs, namely, that the previously produced means of production must be included in costs in accordance with those increments of labor that are necessary for reproducing other products that are caused by the utilization of these means of production. Let us put the same thing differently. Old means of production must be valued in accordance with the savings of future labor that they yield, accepting past labor as equal to zero. These savings of future labor are nothing other than feedback costs.

Thus, valuation according to feedback costs is a general rule for

123

the valuation of produced means of production both in the case of different and in that of identical quality of old and new means of production.

Let us note yet another case of the appearance of feedback costs. The use of accumulation can be accompanied not only by those feedback costs that are caused by its limited nature but also by other, additional feedback costs.

This will occur when the reproduction of any means of production is limited to a greater extent than follows from the overall balance of the national economy's accumulation and capital investment. The use of such a means of production will be associated with additional feedback costs caused by a shortage of the given means of production that is not warranted by the limited amount of accumulation.

It is not difficult to see that feedback costs in this case are the consequence of a removable scarcity of a particular means of production. It is clear that such a case contradicts the principle of economy of labor, for feedback costs are a reflection of unused possibilities for economizing on labor. This means that they must be reduced, i.e., that every available opportunity for economizing on labor be used. Nevertheless, in current planning, a scarcity of certain reproducible means of production can be both the legacy of disproportions in the past as well as the result of sudden change in the production program.

Production cannot instantaneously eliminate inherited disproportions, and it cannot instantaneously adapt itself to sudden changes in the production program. In these cases a scarcity of certain reproducible means of production will be a temporarily unavoidable phenomenon. Accordingly, we must take account of it in the plan beforehand, and also its consequences — additional feedback costs.

Consequently, reproducible means of production can be accompanied in certain cases by two kinds of feedback costs: first, by feedback costs caused by capital investment and, second, by feedback costs caused by a temporary shortage of production of the given means of production.

Thus, the use of the vast majority of means of production is associated with feedback costs. These costs are based on the sufficiently obvious fact that neither the better natural resources, nor the better items of previously produced means of production, nor planned accumulation are available in sufficient quantity to realize the best conditions of production in all existing and projected enterprises. The range of feedback costs reflects the no less obvious fact that for each kind of means of production there are many means that are more effective than the poorest of those required for fulfilling the program.

Feedback costs are not a rare exception but a general rule. On the contrary, their absence is an exception. Accordingly, we can say without stretching the point that in finding the plan alternative corresponding to the overall minimum of labor costs we must seek the alternative requiring the lowest sum of reproduction costs and feedback costs, i.e., the lowest differential costs. For some means of production the feedback costs will be equal to zero.

5. The Measurement of Differential Costs as an Application of the Mathematics of Variable Quantities to the Calculation of Costs

Differential costs are distinguished by important special features arising from the fact that they can be used to solve an extremal problem, that of finding minimum outlays.

The first special feature is that the measurement of costs must be a measurement of their movement, i.e., a measurement of the increments of outlays of social labor associated with the production of each product.

The second special feature is that the measurement of costs must take into account their interrelationships in the national economy.

As we saw earlier, differential costs encompass feedback costs. But feedback costs can be measured only if we treat outlays on each product not as part of, but as an increment in, the labor necessary to produce society's total output. Only by comparing outlays on the entire social product before and after introducing the given output can we discern those increments in the costs of producing other products that are caused by the given product. A different method, that of regarding outlays on specific output as a part of outlays on the entire social product, does not enable us to detect feedback costs.

Accordingly, the first condition for measuring differential costs is to measure costs as increments of a variable magnitude rather than as parts of a constant magnitude. Only such a method of measuring costs will reflect their movement in the production process.

But this is not all. We can measure outlays as increments in costs of production in those sectors of the national economy engaged in the production of the given product and the means of production for it. In this case we would be ignoring those increments in other sectors of the national economy that are caused by producing the given product, i.e., feedback costs. Accordingly, the second necessary condition for measuring differential costs is that of calculating the interrelationships of costs in all sectors of the national economy. For this purpose it is necessary to measure outlays on each individual product as increments in outlays on the national economy's total output.

Hence it is clear that the measurement of differential costs is an application of dialectics to the measurement of labor costs. Finding the maximum or minimum of a variable quantity is one of the specific tasks of the mathematics of variables, which, according to Engel's definition, "is in essence nothing else than the application of dialectics to mathematical relationships."[5] "The relation of the mathematics of variable quantities to the mathematics of constant quantities is generally the same as the relation of dialectical thought to that of metaphysical thought."[6]

6. The Measurement of Differential Costs When Only One Kind of Resource of Production Is Scarce

If only one kind of resource is scarce, then the optimal balance of these resources can be constructed by directly selecting the most effective alternatives (see Chapter 4). Measuring differential costs is not necessary in this case. But it is easiest of all to illustrate the essence of differential costs precisely with this example.

How do we measure differential costs? How do we measure the increments in costs for the national economy's total final output? For this purpose we must know precisely which of the other possible uses of a limited resource will be excluded by its use for the given purpose.

At first glance a definite solution of this problem appears impossible. Depending on the procedure for distributing a scarce resource, its use for each purpose can exclude other uses that differ in effectiveness. But this indeterminateness vanishes if we subordinate the distribution of a scarce resource to the law of economy of labor. Then the formulated question yields a definite solution. Then in calculating differential costs we must assume that each use of a scarce resource excludes another use whose effectiveness is equal to the norm necessary for constructing an optimal balance of the scarce resource.

Consequently, the norm of effectiveness of a scarce resource is likewise the norm for calculating feedback costs. It expresses not only the minimum effectiveness of those alternatives of use of the resource that must be accepted but also the maximum effectiveness of alternatives that must be rejected. This means that it expresses the maximum feedback costs associated with the use of a unit of a scarce resource.

Thus, in comparing investment alternatives according to the formula

$$\frac{C_1 - C_2}{K_2 - K_1} - r = \min \geqslant 0$$

r expresses the norm of investment effectiveness, and in comparing investment alternatives according to formula

$$C + Kr = \min$$

r expresses the norm of feedback costs associated with one ruble of investment. Correspondingly, Kr expresses feedback costs caused by investment K, ánd sum $C + Kr$ expresses differential costs.

The cost of producing the national economy's entire final output will increase precisely by the sum $C + Kr$ if we increase it by a certain product requiring costs of production $= C$ and investment $= K$. (In so doing, it is assumed that the given product constitutes a comparatively small increment in the national economy's output.)

We will demonstrate the construction of the optimal balance of investment by calculating differential costs for Problem No. 2 (see pp. 76-79) as an example. Since in this chapter we at first ignore the value form of costs, we will change the unit of measurement of costs in Problem No. 2. We will assume that in the headings of Table 17 "man-hours" appears in place of "rubles." Then, given an investment limit equal to 400 million man-hours, the norm of investment effectiveness will be 0.067 man-hours per year for one man-hour of investment. The conditions for calculating differential costs are shown in Table 27.

We can draw the following conclusions from this table:

1. The minima of differential costs are found in those alternatives that are included in the optimal balance of investment formed by direct selection (IV_A, III_B, IV_C, V_B, II_D) (see page 87).

For production of E the minimum of differential costs fell

Table 27

1	2	3	4	5
				6
1_A	91	50	3.3	94.3
II_A	90	60	4.0	94.0
III_A	88	70	4.7	92.7
IV_A	81.2	80	5.3	86.5
V_A	80	100	6.7	86.7
1_B	76	50	3.3	79.3
II_B	72.8	70	4.7	77.3
III_B	71	80	5.3	76.3
IV_B	70	100	6.7	76.7
1_C	64	50	3.3	67.3
II_C	63.5	60	4.0	67.5
III_C	62.9	70	4.7	67.6
IV_C	60.8	80	5.3	66.1
V_C	60	100	6.7	66.7
1_D	53.2	50	3.3	56.5
II_D	50.7	80	5.3	56.0
III_D	50	100	6.7	56.7
1_E	42.6	50	3.3	45.9
II_E	40.6	80	5.3	45.9
III_E	40	100	6.7	46.7

Key: 1. Number of alternative
2. Costs of reproduction of output, in millions of man-hours per year
3. Investment of labor in productive capital, in millions of man-hours
4. Feedback costs
5. Differential costs
6. Millions of man-hours per year

Note: Column 5 is the sum of columns 2 and 4.

outside alternative II_E, since the effectiveness of additional investment in alternative II_E was equal to the norm of effectiveness. The investment limit allows us to accept alternative II_E, which is preferred on the grounds of costs of production.

2. The minima of differential costs are compatible with each other because overall investment in the alternatives to which they belong does not exceed the limit.

3. Finally, the table convinces us that a relative increase of production of any product compared with the optimal plan causes

128

an increment in costs of reproduction of *total* output that is equal to differential costs.

According to Table 27 the differential costs associated with producing A (alternative IV_A) are 86.5 million man-hours per year. Let us assume that the production plan for A is increased by 3/8 with the same overall investment limit. Differential costs for this additional output will be

$$86.5 \cdot \frac{3}{8} = 32.4 \text{ million man-hours per year.}$$

(This calculation is based on the assumption that an increase in the production of A by 3/8 will cause *proportional* increase both in costs of production and in investment in A.)

Let us now examine by how much the costs of producing all five products *(A, B, C, D, E)* will increase.

An increase in the production plan for A by 3/8 will require 30 million man-hours of investment. As a consequence, it will be necessary to reduce investment in the production of E correspondingly, since this investment is least effective. Instead of alternative II_E we will have to accept alternative I_D, investment in which is less by 30 million man-hours. Then the corrected optimal balance of investment will consist of alternatives IV_A, III_B, IV_C, II_D and I_E. Total costs of production of annual output according to these alternatives will be:

$(81.2 \times 1 1/8) + 71 + 60.8 + 50.7 + 42.6 = 336.7$ million man-hours.

Costs of production of annual output for the same units before the increase in production of A were:

$81.2 + 71 + 60.8 + 50.7 + 40.6 = 304.3$ million man-hours.

By comparing costs of production of total output before and after the increase in the production plan for A we find that the increase in costs caused by increasing production of A by 3/8 is:

Costs of production $\boxed{A, B, C, D, E}$ + 3/8 A = 336.7 million man-hours

Costs of production $\boxed{A, B, C, D, E}$ = 304.3 million man-hours

difference   = 32.4 million man-hours.

But this increment represents differential costs for 3/8 of A.

Thus, the calculating of differential costs on the basis of the costs of production of total final output yielded the same result as calculation according to the formula $C + Kr$.

Let us illustrate with this example certain peculiarities of differential costs.

1. Under optimal planning differential costs express the increment in the minimum costs of producing the prescribed output attainable with the best use of existing resources. Thus, in our example the differential costs for 3/8 of A were calculated in comparison with the minimum costs of producing the five products that were possible with the given investment limit.

2. It is not difficult to see that if we had increased the production of product A by more than 3/8, calculation according to formula $C + Kr$ would yield a somewhat smaller result than calculation of the increment in costs of production of all five products. For, in order to increase production of A, let us say by 3/4, it would be necessary to reduce investment with an effectiveness higher than the norm, i.e., to replace alternative II_D by alternative I_D. This means that the calculation of differential costs on the basis of norms of effectiveness is intended for calculating the costs of output forming a small share of the total social product. But in this connection the calculation of differential costs on the basis of norms of effectiveness permits us to seek an overall minimum of costs of production according to minimum values of differential costs for each small part of the social product separately, i.e., according to their particular minima. This property of differential costs is extremely valuable from the standpoint of organizing the management of a socialist economy.

3. It is also not difficult to see that the calculating of differential costs can best serve the law of economy of labor if it is used not to alter already fulfilled decisions (alternatives), but to discover the best of the possible (but not yet fulfilled) alternatives. Indeed, let us change our example and assume that the production of A is increased by 3/8 after the investment limit has already been distributed and the production of E has already been carried out according to alternative II_E. Then it would be difficult, or more likely impossible, to replace the implemented alternative II_E by alternative I_E. An unlimited opportunity to replace some alternatives by others for each producing unit is conceivable only under the condition that as yet unaccomplished alternatives, i.e., planned alternatives, are compared. But if this is so, then differential costs will reflect the comparison of possible rather than actual costs of production of the national economy's total final output. Thus, in our example the costs of production of A, B, C, D, $E + 3/8A$ are compared with the costs of production

130

according to another plan alternative — according to the production of A, B, C, D, and, E. The result is that the production of the additional $3/8A$ requires from the national economy 32.4 million rubles per year of additional costs of production in comparison with another possibility — the production of A, B, C, D, and E. But if this other possibility had already been implemented, this calculation could prove to be unrealistic.

4. Differential costs have a characteristic that must inevitably hinder those who are not accustomed to dialectics in quantitiative analysis. We refer to the fact that when differential costs for different products are added, they result in double counting of the same costs of production. The sum of differential costs for all individual parts of the social product is greater than the costs of production for the whole — by the sum of feedback costs. This inequality contradicts the requirement that the sum of outlays on all individual parts of the social product be equal to the costs of production of the whole.

However, when we are dealing with differential costs it is not their absolute but their relative magnitude that is important for us. They are necessary for purposes of comparing alternatives. Therefore, the difference between the sum of differential costs and the sum of costs of production can be eliminated by an appropriate change in the units of measurement of differential costs. For example, if the entire sum of differential costs is $1/3$ larger than the sum of costs of production, then to restore equality between these sums it is sufficient to set one man-hour of differential costs as equal to $3/4$ of an hour. The relationships between differential costs of different alternatives do not change, and the minimum of costs is not altered with a change in the unit of measurement. But if this is the case, then it is possible for the prices of means of production to be proportional to differential costs, and for the entire sum of prices of final output to be equal to its value. This possibility is embodied in a certain peculiarity of production costs, namely, that outlays of living labor on each product are taken into account only to the extent of wages, without the value of the surplus product created by this labor's being included.

As an example we will calculate adjusted differential costs for the data in Table 28.

Table 28

1	2	3	4
		5	
IV_A	81.2	86.5	79.6
III_B	71.0	76.3	70.3
IV_C	60.8	66.1	60.8
II_D	50.7	56.0	51.6
II_E	40.6	45.9	42.2
	304.3	330.8	304.5

Key: 1.   Number of the alternatives in the optimal balance
2.   Costs of production
3.   Differential costs
4.   Differential costs adjusted to overall equality with costs of production
5.   Millions of man-hours per year

In this table the total sum of adjusted differential costs is equal to the total sum of costs of production:

$$304.5 \approx 304.3$$

Thereby differential costs become a transformed form of costs of production. This equality is attained by multiplying differential costs (for each alternative) by $304/331 \approx 0.92$. Thus, each man-hour of differential costs is equated to 0.92 man-hour of costs of production. The relations between differential costs for the different alternatives do not change as a result of this recalculation. Therefore, the adjusted differential costs for individual products deviate for the most part from costs of production. These deviations are caused by differences in the ratios of investment to costs of production, i.e., by differences in K/C, where K is investment and C is costs of production. When this ratio is equal to the average for all lines of production

$$\left(\frac{\Sigma K}{\Sigma C} \right)$$

adjusted differential costs are equal to costs of production (alternative IV_C). When $K/C < \Sigma K/ \Sigma C$, adjusted differential costs are less than costs of production (alternatives IV_A and III_B). When $K/C > \Sigma K/\Sigma C$, adjusted differential costs are greater than costs of production (alternatives II_D and II_E).[7]

We will illustrate this with the data of Problem No. 2 (Table 29).

Table 29

Number of alternative	K	C	$\dfrac{K}{C}$	$\dfrac{K}{c} : \dfrac{\Sigma K}{\Sigma C}$	$(C+Kr)\dfrac{\Sigma C}{\Sigma(C+Kr)}$	Ratio of adjusted differential costs to costs of production
1	2	3	4	5	6	7=6:3
IV_A	80	81.2	0.98	0.75	79.6	0.98
III_B	80	71.0	1.13	0.86	70.2	9.99
IV_C	80	60.8	1.32	1.00	60.8	1.00
II_D	80	50.7	1.58	1.20	51.6	1.02
II_E	80	40.6	1.97	1.50	42.2	1.04
$\Sigma K = 400$		$304.3 = \Sigma C$	$\dfrac{\Sigma K}{\Sigma C}=1.32$			

7. The Measurement of Differential Costs When Many Means of Production Are Scarce

The example we have examined demonstrated that we can find the alternatives corresponding to the overall minimum of costs of production by calculating differential costs. But we still have not proved that measuring differential costs is necessary for this purpose. It would be simpler to solve the problem examined by directly selecting the most effective uses of a scarce kind of resource.

However, direct selection of the most effective alternatives is applicable only when one kind of resource is scarce. If two or more different means of production are scarce, direct selection cannot be used. The latter presupposes the calculation of indicators of effectiveness of utilization of each means. Moreover, in the case of joint outlays of two or more scarce means, the labor saving yielded by one production alternative in comparison with others is a joint and indivisible effect of several scarce means (for example, capital investment, oil, copper, tin, etc.). Accordingly, it is impossible to calculate those indicators of effectiveness of each of the scarce means that are necessary for the direct selection of their most effective uses. In other words, if we have several conditions that limit overall minimum costs, such as limits on accumulation, limited reserves of different natural resources, etc., we cannot look for a relative minimum of costs under each of these conditions separately. We must search for minimum costs by taking account of all the limitations.

The measurement of differential costs is possible with any

number of limited means, for the calculation and comparison of actual effectiveness of each of the expended means. Only norms of their effectiveness are necessary. For example, the calculation and comparison of differential costs according to the formula $C + Kr =$ min did not require the determination of the effectiveness of the corresponding investments.

But we can generalize the formula $C + Kr$, extending it to cases of joint outlays of any number of different resources.

Indeed, suppose we have limited means. Outlays of these for the national economy's annual final output will be $q_1, q_2, \ldots, q_m$, and their norms of effectiveness (we will assume that we know them) are equal, respectively, to $r_1, r_2, \ldots, r_m$. Then that alternative of each project for which $c + q_1 r_1 + \ldots + q_m r_m = $ min or, more briefly, $c + \sum_{h=1}^{m} q_h r_h = $ min $(h=1, 2, \ldots, m)$ will correspond to the overall maximum of the total effect from using all means of production (i.e., to the overall minimum costs of production expenditures). This is the general formula for differential costs[8] and is the rule for choosing alternatives by its use. It shows that, knowing the norms of effectiveness for each limited means, we can calculate differential costs for any number of jointly expended means. For this purpose we must:

(1) multiply the consumption of each means by the corresponding norm;

(2) add these products;

(3) add the sum of feedback costs obtained in this way to the costs of production of the given output.

The question is only how to determine the norms of effectiveness.

Differential costs have a remarkable property that makes it possible to determine the desired norms. For any nonnegative norms of effectiveness, alternatives requiring the least differential costs form a potentially optimal combination of alternatives. Even with incorrect norms of effectiveness, alternatives requiring the least differential costs still correspond to that general minimum of costs that can be attained within the limits of the means of production and the amount of investment required for the given alternatives.[9]

We have already demonstrated this for the case in which only one kind of means was scarce and the final output consisted of only two products (see page 103):

We will now demonstrate this for the case, corresponding to reality, in which a number of means are scarce and the final output consists of a number of different products.

If we select the alternative for the production of each final product that requires the least differential costs, then for any norms of effectiveness that combination of plan (project) alternatives will be formed that:

(1) is intended for the prescribed production program;

(2) is characterized by the least overall sum of differential costs (for the entire program).

But differential costs consist of two different terms — costs of production and feedback costs. We will examine which of these two terms determines the minimum overall sum of differential costs (for all of the national economy's final output).

With given norms of effectiveness and constant total amounts of each means, the total sum of all feedback costs calculated according to the norms will be a constant quantity, independent of any changes in the purposes of the limited means.

But the total sum of costs of production depends on how the means of production are used, since different applications of each yield different savings.

Consequently, the minimum overall sum of differential costs is determined by the minimum total sum of costs of production of the final product.

More precisely, the combination of alternatives for which the sum of differential costs is minimal will have the lowest costs of production of the final product among all the possible combinations of alternatives for which the amounts of each of the means of production required at the beginning of the planned period are the same as those necessary for the given combination of alternatives.

This conclusion holds for any nonnegative norms of effectiveness. But an overall minimum of costs of production that is feasible with the actual availability of means is attained only with a specific system of these norms. We can find this system of norms by setting up experimental balances of means of production with different experimental values of norms of effectiveness. The values of the norms for which the balances of all means of production will be equilibrated will yield a solution of the problem.

The most complete utilization of all relatively better means, such as the maximum economy of labor, i.e., the general minimum of costs of production for the prescribed output, must be the criterion in these trials (experiments). Such a situation is attained when:

135

(1) the individual minima of differential costs are consistent;

(2) all the relatively better means are completely used.

The first condition signifies that the total requirements for each means for alternatives having the lowest differential costs do exceed its supply.

The second condition signifies that all means whose norms of effectiveness are greater than zero are completely used. The means of production whose norms of effectiveness are equal to zero may be used partially or even not at all.

If the norms of effectiveness are low, the total requirements for the corresponding resources will exceed their availability. Particular minima of differential costs will be inconsistent with each other because of a shortage of the better resources. If the norms of effectiveness are too high, requirements for the corresponding means will be less than the amount available, which will signify a combination of alternatives for which greater outlays of labor will be required for the same program than is necessary, given the complete utilization of all better means.

For the sake of clarity we will solve Problem No. 3, presented in Table 24 (see Chapter 4, pp. 96-98), by this method.

Since we are ignoring the law of value for the present, we will replace the monetary unit of measurement of costs under the conditions of this problem by the man-hour unit. Then Table 24 must be replaced by Table 30.

Table 30

Number of alternative	Cost of production of annual output, in in thousands of man-hours per year	Investment, in thousands of man-hours	Outlay of scarce raw material, in tons per year
I_A	102	80	0
II_A	96	70	10
III_A	90	120	10
I_B	200	100	0
II_B	180	80	20
III_B	175	120	20
I_C	130	110	0
II_C	100	100	20
III_C	95	110	30

As a first approximation the following norms of effectiveness are selected: for investment − 0.1 man-hours per year per man-hour of investment, and for scarce raw materials − 2.0 thousand man-hours per ton. We calculate experimental differential costs according to these norms, and show the minima in boldface numbers (Table 31).

Table 31

Number of alternative	Differential costs	Number of alternative	Differential costs	Number of alternative	Differential costs
I_A	110	I_B	210	I_C	141
II_A	123	II_B	228	II_C	150
III_A	122	III_B	227	III_C	166

The requirements for investment and scarce raw materials for alternatives with least sums (I_A, I_B, I_C) are 290,000 man-hours of investment and zero tons per year of scarce raw materials.

By comparing these quantities with the limits (260,000 man-hours and 40 tons) we see that the norms of effectiveness we have accepted are incorrect. We must raise the norm of effectiveness of investment and reduce the norm of effectiveness of scarce raw materials. As a second approximation we set an investment norm of 0.2 man-hours per year per man-hour of investment, and for the scarce raw material a norm of 1,000 man-hours per ton.

We calculate differential costs according to these norms (Table 32).

Table 32
(in thousands of man-hours per year)

Number of alternative	Differential costs	Number of alternative	Differential costs	Number of alternative	Differential costs
I_A	118	I_B	220	I_C	152
II_A	120	II_B	216	II_C	140
III_A	124	III_B	219	III_C	147

The requirements for limited means for alternatives with the lowest differential costs are now 260,000 man-hours of investment and 40 tons per year of scarce raw materials, which correspond to the limits.

Thus, the optimal balances of investment and scarce raw materials are obtained with the following combination of alternatives: I_A, II_B, II_C.

We must emphasize that this yields the maximum total effect of investment and the scarce raw material taken together. What we find by using this method is not the maximum effect of investment and not the maximum effect of the use of the scarce raw material, but the maximum effect of the use of all limited means.

It is not difficult to see that precisely this maximum corresponds to the principle of economy of labor, for this maximum signifies the overall maximum of economies of costs of production for all prescribed output, i.e., the overall minimum of outlays on its production. In our example the alternatives I_A, II_B and II_C ensure the production of A, B, and C in the prescribed amounts with the least total costs of production among all those combinations of alternatives in Table 30 that fall within the limits of investment and scarce raw materials.

8. Actual Costs of Production and Mathematical Methods of Minimizing Them

All that has been said leads to the conclusion that feedback costs are auxiliary magnitudes serving as a means of finding the overall minimum of actual production costs — of the labor required in production. Calculating actual production costs for each product is insufficient for the main purpose it must serve, that of finding their minimum. Because of the scarcity of the better conditions for the application of labor, individual minima of actual costs are inconsistent with each other. But by adding to the actual costs auxiliary quantities — feedback costs — we can obtain via the minimizing of these sums the overall minimum of actual costs of reproduction. The calculation of feedback costs helps us solve the problem of minimizing actual costs of production as if there were no limitations on resources and as if the better resources were sufficient for all effective uses. This remarkable property of feedback costs disturbs certain economists very much. It seems strange that in finding the most economical alternatives we must calculate not the value of output but a transformed value. The question necessarily arises as to whether there is a mathematical error here. Therefore, we will demonstrate by the use of a simple economic model the role of norms of effectiveness of resources and the calculation of feedback costs.

The mathematics of variable quantities distinguishes between problems of an unconditional and a conditional extremum. The extremum of a quantity that depends on independent variables is called an unconditional extremum. If the variables determining the quantity whose minimum (or maximum) we are seeking are connected by certain relations, then we are confronted with a problem of a conditional extremum. The problem of finding minimum costs of production is precisely this kind of problem. It must be solved with constraints on resources.

From a mathematical standpoint, norms of effectiveness of material resources are auxiliary multipliers that can be used to find a conditional extremum as if the limiting conditions were removed, and as if we were finding an unconditional extremum. With respect to the problem of mimimum costs this means that by using norms of effectiveness we overcome the incompatibility of particular minima of costs. Particular minima of differential costs become compatible and apply to alternatives corresponding to the overall minimum of costs of production.

Let us first examine the role of these multipliers in the classic method of finding a conditional extremum — the Lagrange method — and then demonstrate the transition from this method to the use of the same multipliers for measuring differential costs.

The initial data include m different conditions for the application of labor, i.e., means of production and investment. We will designate the availability of each of these at the beginning of the planned period by Q_h where $h = 1, 2, \ldots, m$.

In order not to increase the number of different symbols we will agree that Q_h encompasses all material resources available at the beginning of the planned period, namely:

(1) reproducible objects of labor;
(2) reproducible implements of labor;
(3) natural resources;
(4) planned capital investment.[10]

The planned period is sufficiently long to encompass the time during which capital investment will be transformed into productive capital and will be used.

139

The production program for final output consists of the production of n different products materially embodied in the national income. We will denote outlays of labor (in natural or monetary units) on each of them by c_i, where $i = 1, 2, \ldots, n$.

We will denote outlays of the hth means of production on the ith product as q_{hi}.

c_i has different values depending on the means of production used, i.e.,

$$c_i = f_i (q_{1i}, q_{2i}, \ldots, q_{mi}) \ (h = 1, \ldots, m; \ i = 1, \ldots, n).$$

All these functions have continuous partial derivatives with respect to q_{hi}.

It is necessary to find that distribution of means of production and investment among different purposes (i.e., those q_{hi}) for which $\sum_{i=1}^{n} c_i = \min$ under the condition that the use of each means of production is equal to its supply:

$$\sum_{i=1}^{n} q_{hi} - Q_h = 0. \tag{5.1}$$

Adding to the function whose minimum we are seeking $(\sum_{i=1}^{n} c_i)$, conditions (5.1), multiplied by certain (as yet unknown) multipliers λ_h, we will obtain the more complex function

$$\Phi = \sum_{i=1}^{n} c_i + \sum_{h=1}^{m} \lambda_h \left(\sum_{i=1}^{n} q_{hi} - Q_h \right).$$

When conditions (5.1) hold, this function is equal to $\sum_{i=1}^{n} c_i$. However, we can seek the minimum of this function as if conditions (5.1) were not present. By equating to zero the partial derivatives of the first order with respect to q_{hi} in this function (considering λ_h as constants), we will obtain mn equations of the form:

$$\frac{\partial \Phi}{\partial q_{hi}} = \frac{\partial}{\partial q_{hi}} \left(c_i + \sum_{h=1}^{m} \lambda_h q_{hi} = 0 \right). \tag{5.2}$$

We obtain, together with the m conditions (5.1) expressing the requirement of equality of outlays of each means of production to its availability, $nm + m$ equations, the solution of which yields the nm unknown q_{hi} and the m multipliers λ_h.

This is the way of finding minimum costs by the Lagrange method. This method is not applicable in practice. However, we

140

can build a bridge from it to the calculation of differential costs as an instrument of optimal planning.

Indeed, multipliers λ_h not only enable us to solve the problem as if conditions (5.1) were absent but, in addition, they eliminate that incompatibility of particular minima of costs (c_i) that emerges as a consequence of these conditions. For this purpose let us examine the relations between finite quantities that correspond to equations (5.2).

As we know, equality of the first derivative to zero is the necessary condition for the extremal value of the function.

This means that equalities (5.2) can supposedly be replaced by the relations:

$$c_i + \sum_{h=1}^{m} q_{hi}\lambda_h = \text{extremum}. \tag{5.3}$$

Let us check this proposition.

Summing expression (5.3) over i, we obtain

$$\sum_{i=1}^{n} c_i + \sum_{i=1}^{n} \sum_{h=1}^{m} \lambda_h q_{hi}. \tag{5.4}$$

In this expression the double summation is constant (with given λ_h), and does not depend on the distribution of Q_h according to different purposes:

$$\sum_{i=1}^{n} \sum_{h=1}^{m} \lambda_h q_{hi} = \sum_{h=1}^{m} \sum_{i=1}^{n} \lambda_h q_{hi} = \sum_{h=1}^{m} \lambda_h \sum_{i=1}^{n} q_{hi} = \sum_{h=1}^{m} \lambda_h Q_h = \text{const}.$$

This means that if sum (5.4) is a minimum, then also

$$\sum_{i=1}^{n} c_i = \text{min}.$$

Thus, solving our problem by the Lagrange method gives us those multipliers for the means of production for which the following relations are jointly realized:

$$S_i = c_i + \sum_{h=1}^{m} q_{hi}\lambda_h = \text{min} \tag{5.5}$$

and

$$\sum_{i=1}^{n} q_{hi} = Q_h. \tag{5.6}$$

This means that particular minima of S_i are compatible. But S_i expresses nothing else than differential costs of the ith product. This means that the Lagrange method gives us the multipliers that are necessary for calculating differential costs, namely the λ_h in our formula for differential costs.

It follows from relations (5.5) and (5.6):

(1) that finding multipliers λ_h solves the problem. Knowing their values we can determine all the desired alternatives of use of means of production according to the minimum of S_i;

(2) that the value of the multipliers can be found by approximations. With incorrect values of the multipliers alternatives of the plan satisfying condition (5.5) will not satisfy condition (5.6). We will express the same thing in other words. If, for given values of the multipliers, requirements for each means of production are not equal to its supply, this means that the multipliers are incorrect.

However, this model of optimal balances has the defect of introducing into the initial conditions of the problem certain unknowns.

Indeed, in this model the scarcity of available means of production is expressed by equalities (5.6). This means that the amount of utilized means of production must be determined before the solution of the problem. This is easy to do for the best means of production. They must be completely used. But requirements for those means of production whose norms of effectiveness must be equal to zero (or close to it) can be determined only by constructing systems of optimal balances. Only after constructing optimal balances can all available means of production be clearly divided into those that are appropriate and those that are not appropriate for use. This means that condition (5.6) includes the solution of one of the problems of the system of optimal balances. Therefore, the solution of the problem based on this condition can prove to be not the optimal one if certain norms of effectiveness (λ_h) are negative.

Consequently, the equality of requirements for each means of production and its supply must be replaced by an inequality expressing the fact that requirements for each means of production must not exceed its supply:

$$\sum_{i=1}^{n} q_{hi} \leqslant Q_h. \tag{5.7}$$

Such an expression of the constraints of the problem is more correct than the equality. It does not anticipate the solution of the problem and pertains both to those means of production for which the norms of effectiveness are greater than zero and to means of production with norms of effectiveness of zero:

$$\text{if} \quad \sum_{i=1}^{n} q_{hi} = Q_h, \quad \text{then} \quad \lambda_h > 0,$$

$$\text{if} \quad \sum_{i=1}^{n} q_{hi} < Q_h, \quad \text{then} \quad \lambda_h = 0.$$

142

If we add to conditions (5.5) and (5.7) the requirement that λ_h and q_{hi} be nonnegative, we obtain the method that was substantiated in general form by Academician L.V. Kantorovich and called the method of resolving multipliers. [11]

Now we can demonstrate very briefly the role of conditions (5.1) and (5.7) that create the greatest difficulties in measuring costs, in particular, in using the law of value under socialism.

Conditions (5.1) and (5.7) lead:

(a) either to replacing the function whose minimum we are seeking (costs of production of final output $\sum\limits_{i=1}^{n} c_i$), by the more

complex function $\Phi = \sum\limits_{i=1}^{n} c_i + \sum\limits_{h=1}^{m} \lambda_h \left(\sum\limits_{i=1}^{n} q_{hi} - Q_h \right),$

(b) or to replacing costs of production of individual products (c_i) by more complex differential costs:

$$S_i = c_i + \sum\limits_{h=1}^{m} \lambda_h q_{hi}. \tag{5.8}$$

The first complication arises in the solution of the problem by calculus of infinitely small quantities, and the second complication arises in the use only of finite quantities. In both cases the complication of costs allows us to solve the problem for their minimum as if limiting conditions (5.1) or (5.7) were removed.

In practice only the second method of solution is available. Consequently, measuring costs for each product in the complicated form – in the form of differential costs – is necessary to attain the greatest labor saving.

9. The Problem of Measuring
Costs Under Communism

The problem of measuring costs under communism is not just of theoretical interest. Its investigation has more important practical value for a socialist economy than does the study of capitalist practice in this kind of measurement. The key to the correct solution of problems of the law of value under socialism must be sought not in the forms of manifestation of value inherent in lower forms of production relations. We must not derive higher forms from lower ones; on the contrary, lower ones can be better understood on the basis of knowledge of higher forms.

"The anatomy of man is the key to the anatomy of the ape. On the other hand, hints of the higher in the lower forms of animals

143

can be understood only if this higher form itself is already known. Bourgeois economic structure thus gives us a key to that of antiquity, and so on."[12]

Hence we have the right to conclude that the hypothesis concerning the laws of measurement of costs under communism is capable of illuminating the laws of their measurement under socialism and of illuminating the direction and final point of development of the law of value in a socialist economy. Investigation of the operation of the law of value under socialism can in turn reveal those "hints of the higher" in the lower, in the capitalist form of value, that can be understood only if this higher one is already known.

Let us try to look into the future. We will imagine a communist society with a much higher level of technology, planning, and organization of the national economy than that which we have already achieved. There can hardly be any doubt that in a communist society the measurement of costs will involve extremal problems to a greater degree than ever before.

We will assume that costs will be calculated in working time, and we will examine which methods of measuring them are necessary to find the minimum of labor costs for final output with a given composition and volume for the prescribed volume of accumulation. The hypothesis of the measurement of costs in working time allows us to examine differential labor costs in their direct form, freed from the value framework.

But will those conditions that make it necessary to measure *differential* costs exist under communism?

In all probability, yes. The necessity of calculating feedback costs and differential costs arises in consequence of differences in the conditions of application of labor and in the effectiveness of utilized means of production. These differences, obviously, will remain even under communism.

In the first place, differences in the effectiveness of the natural resources used will remain. Furthermore, they can even grow, if technological progress permits the effective utilization of those natural resources that at present have no economic value.

In the second place, differences will remain in the effectiveness of utilized reproducible implements of labor. Technological progress cannot eliminate these differences. Rather, it gives rise to them. Differences in the effectiveness of the fixed capital used could vanish only in the case of the cessation of technological progress. Under communism we can expect still higher rates of technological progress than at present. Accordingly, under

144

communism implements of labor for one and the same purpose, but with different designs and nonuniform effectiveness, will be used simultaneously. Too frequent, let us say daily, changes in the implements of labor would be connected with excessive surplus labor; and the share of surplus labor cannot be unlimited.

Hence it follows that even under communism the incompatibility of individual minima of costs of production will continue to exist. If this is so, then the calculation of differential costs can be a useful tool in planning the national economy.

We will demonstrate the role of calculating differential costs in constructing the plan, ensuring minimum outlays on the production of the prescribed final output. In this problem current labor, i.e., the living labor that society has available, is the quantity to be minimized. Thereby past labor is equated to zero, and the means of production produced by it enter into the analysis of costs according to these savings of current labor that their use yields, i.e., according to feedback costs.

For society as a whole past labor at each given moment (for example, at the beginning of the planned period) is a constant quantity. It is as impossible to change it as it is impossible to change the entire past. Current (living) labor is a variable quantity. It can be larger or smaller depending on how the final output prescribed by the plan will be produced. Consequently, for society as a whole, the minimum of all labor costs (past and living) involved in producing the prescribed output is determined by the minimum outlays of living labor. The minimum of the sum of constant and variable quantities is determined by the minimum of the variable quantity.

Thus, the law of the economy of labor is, in the final analysis, the law of the economy of living labor, the law of the growth of its productivity.

Equating past labor to zero in a communist economy is based on the same property of past labor that justifies equating past capital to zero in a capitalist economy (for example, in calculating rates of surplus value), i.e., the property that past labor is a constant quantity. [13] In a communist economy there is no capital, and accordingly there is no division of it into constant and variable; but the division of labor costs into two parts — constant and variable (past and current outlays) — remains.

However, past labor is a constant quantity (at each given moment) only for society as a whole. For any part of the national economy, outlays of past labor are a variable quantity. Thus, an individual sector of the national economy can use more or less past labor stemming from changes in its outlays in other sectors. Accordingly, in analyzing outlays on each product, material outlays enter together with living labor. Setting past labor outlays as zero does not at all mean that the products of these outlays must be considered as free goods that do not cost labor. It means only that products of past labor enter into the calculation of costs not according to past, but according to current outlays, i.e., to the extent that their use economizes on society's living labor. In this process the measurement of outlays of products of past labor must be subordinated to finding that utilization of the results of past labor that would yield the greatest economy of living labor.

The objective necessity of precisely such a measurement of outlays of products of past labor appeared even under capitalism in the decisive importance of reproduction costs, in the existence of obsolescence. It is well known that if means of production are reproduced in their previous form their value is determined by the labor time necessary for their reproduction. If they are reproduced in a different form, outlays of labor on them are determined by the savings in current labor yielded by use of the given means of production, treating past outlays as equal to zero in this process. From this standpoint, the determination of the value of goods by the costs of reproducing them is a particular case of calculating conditions of application of labor according to the savings in current labor that the use of these conditions can yield.[14]

Let us now imagine the basic features of the construction of an optimal plan and, in this connection, of the measurement of differential costs under communism.

The initial data are:

(1) the amount of each means of production (reproducible and nonreproducible), available at the beginning of the planning period. We will denote them by Q, with an index referring to the number of the means of production, for example, Q_h, where $h = 1, 2, \ldots, m$ (we will call these means of production the *available* ones);

(2) planned accumulation in the course of the same period, i.e., labor outlays allotted for the creation of new productive capital. We will denote them by A;

(3) the production program for final output, during the planning period[15] consisting of final products;

(4) outlays of each of m means of production, available at the beginning of the planning period, for the annual production of each of n final products. We will denote these outlays by q, with two indices showing the number of the means of production and

146

the number of the final product for which this means is used. Thus, outlays of the hth means of production on the ith product will be expressed by q_{hi} $(h = 1, 2, . . ., m)$ and $(i = 1,2, . . ., n)$.

(5) We will denote current outlays of social labor on the annual production of each final product by c, with an index for the number of the final product. Thus, outlays of labor for producing the ith product will be expressed by c_i.

(6) We will denote one-time investments necessary for producing each final product by k_i, where i is the number of the final product.

Each final product can be produced by different methods. Accordingly, c_i, q_{hi}, and k_i have different values depending on the method of producing the ith final product.

The question is how to find those alternatives of the production of each final product for which the entire program of final output can be fulfilled with the least outlays of current labor, i.e., for which $\sum_{i=1}^{n} c_i = \min$.

Method of Solution

1. We eliminate the incompatibility of the national economic effects for those plan (project) alternatives of individual objects of outlays in which this incompatibility occurs.[16]

2. We set experimental norms of effectiveness for each kind of available means of production and for investment. We will denote them by r with an index for the number of the means of production (for example, r_h), and we will denote the norm of effectiveness of investment as r_k. The norms of effectiveness for those available means of production that can be assumed to be the worst of the required ones we will take as equal to zero. This means that the given means of production (a parcel of land, an old machine, etc.) do not yield an economy of labor in comparison with any of the required means of production. The norms of effectiveness for the remaining (relatively better) means of production must be greater than zero.

3. For each alternative of producing each final product we calculate differential costs S_i according to formula (for the ith product):

$$S_i = c_i + k_i r_k + \sum_{h=1}^{m} q_{hi} r_h. \qquad (5.9)$$

4. We choose an alternative with the least differential costs (5.9)

147

for production of each final product. We obtain a potentially optimal combination of alternatives. This means that it yields a final output with the least costs of production $(\sum_{i=1}^{n} c_i)$ of all possible combinations of alternatives of that output, using the amount of each means of p r o d u c t i o n $(\sum_{i=1}^{n} q_{hi})$ and the amount of investment $(\sum_{i=1}^{n} k_i)$, needed for each combination of alternatives.

5. We calculate the requirement for each available means of production and for investment for all alternatives selected in this way.

6. We compare the results of these calculations with the availability of means of production and with the planned investment limit. If there is a divergence of requirements from the limit we correct the experimental norms of effectiveness of the corresponding means. If requirements are larger than availability or the limit, then the norm of effectiveness is, as a rule, increased. If requirements are lower than the limit, then the norm of effectiveness is, as a rule, reduced.

In connection with the correction of the norms of effectiveness, the supply part of the balances of the corresponding means of production is likewise corrected. In some cases we reject those means of production with zero norms of effectiveness that (even with a zero norm) were not included in any of the alternatives with differential costs. In other cases additional means of production, the best of the previously rejected ones, are included. Zero norms of effectiveness or even positive ones are given to the means of production again included in the balance. In this process, all the relatively better means of production with a norm of effectiveness greater than zero must be fully used.

7. We calculate differential costs according to the corrected norms, and we repeat operations 3, 4, and 5 as long as the requirements for each means of production with a norm of effectiveness greater than zero, and for investment, are not equal to their availability and limit. In so doing we derive a plan that is feasible within the limits of the planned sum of accumulation and the available means of production, and that, furthermore, ensures the attainment of minimum outlays of labor on the prescribed program of final output.[17]

The effective requirement for those means of production for which $r_h = 0$ can be less than their supply. All those natural resources and previously produced means of labor, which even

148

with a zero norm of effectiveness are not included in any of the alternatives with the least differential costs, must remain beyond the limits of the balances.

We will denote those norms of effectiveness for which a balance of requirements is attained in each available means of production and in investment by $\hat{r}_h$ and $\hat{r}_k$.

Thus, we obtain m material balances of the form

$$\sum_{i=1}^{n} \hat{q}_{hi} \leqslant Q_h \tag{5.10}$$

and a balance of investment,

$$\sum_{i=1}^{n} \hat{k}_i = A. \tag{5.11}$$

We designate with the $\wedge$ sign the fact that given values $q_{hi,}$ k_i (and also c_i and S_i) pertain to alternatives satisfying conditions (5.9), (5.10), and (5.11), or to those alternatives of producing the ith product that are distinguished by the least differential costs with final values of the norms of effectiveness, i.e., with $\hat{r}_h$ and $\hat{r}_k$

Finding these alternatives solves the problem.

Thus, the norms of effectiveness are determined by the balance method in connection with the construction of a system of optimal balances of available means of production and investment. That potential by optimal combination is sought in which the total requirement for each of the available means of production and for investment will not exceed their planned supply and limits.

The balances of means of production and of investment constructed in this way will determine those alternatives of producing n final products for which outlays of current labor in producing all these products will be the least. In addition, the kinds, types, and amounts of those means of production which it is necessary to produce in the planning period in order to fulfill the program for final output are determined. Just as at the plant the production of semifinished products is determined by the program for producing marketed output and by indicators of the effectiveness of different industrial processes, so in the national economy the program for producing means of production is derived from the program for final output and from the outlays necessary to accomplish it by one means or another.[18]

We have essentially already given the proof of the effectiveness of this method, first in words (page 135) and then very briefly in a mathematical proof of the connection of this method with the

149

Lagrange method (pp. 140 - 143). The basic proof of the effectiveness of the method in the simplest case was given as the substantiation of the first property of the potentially optimal combinations of alternatives of investment (see Chapter 4). This method of constructing an optimal plan is nothing else than an approximation to the optimal plan by means of successive constructions of a series of potentially optimal combinations.

We need only to extend this proof to the case of the production of n final products with the use of m available means of production, in addition to investment.

1. We will prove, first, that with any other uses of the same available means of production and of the same amount of investment than the ones accepted according to balances (5.10) and (5.11), the costs of producing final output will be greater than $\sum\limits_{i=1}^{n} c_i$.

The values of outlays pertaining to other balances, besides (5.10) and (5.11), we will denote by the same symbols but without the $\wedge$ sign. We must prove that

$$\sum_{i=1}^{n} \hat{c}_i < \sum_{i=1}^{n} c_i.$$

We will take for some final products production alternatives other than those given by balances (5.10) and (5.11). For example, we will take other designs of machinery producing raw materials for certain final products, but in so doing we will select the new alternatives so that requirements for each available means of production and for accumulation for the new combination of alternatives is equal to the corresponding requirements for the previous combination of alternatives:

$$\sum_{i=1}^{n} q_{hi} = \sum_{i=1}^{n} \hat{q}_{hi}; \quad \sum_{i=1}^{n} k_i = \sum_{i=1}^{n} \hat{k}_i. \tag{5.12}$$

Those alternatives, which for the same system of norms of effectiveness $r_h = \hat{r}_h$ and $r_k = \hat{r}_k$ will require larger sums S_i (larger experimental differential costs) than the excluded alternatives, appear without fail in this rearrangement of the purposes of available means of production and of investment. For the alternatives accepted before the rearrangement have least sums S_i.

Consequently, the sum of differential costs for all of the national economy's final output will increase:

$$\sum_{i=1}^{n} S_i > \sum_{i=1}^{n} \hat{S}_i. \tag{5.13}$$

150

But in this process the total sum of normative feedback costs for all final output will not change. For in the course of the indicated changes in the purposes of means of production and of investment the following will remain unchanged:

(a) the amount of each of the available means of production;
(b) accumulation in the national economy;
(c) the norms of effectiveness of means of production and investment.

This conclusion can be expressed as follows in symbols. We will expand the inequality (5.13). For this we sum over i (1 to n) the inequalities of the form:

$$c_i + k_i \hat{r}_k + \sum_{h=1}^{m} q_{hi} \hat{r}_h > \hat{c}_i + \hat{k}_i \hat{r}_k + \sum_{h=1}^{m} \hat{q}_{hi} \hat{r}_h.$$

We obtain the following results:

$$\sum_{i=1}^{n} c_i + \sum_{i=1}^{n} k_i \hat{r}_k + \sum_{i=1}^{n} \sum_{h=1}^{m} q_{hi} \hat{r}_h > \sum_{i=1}^{n} \hat{c}_i + \sum_{i=1}^{n} \hat{k}_i \hat{r}_k + \sum_{i=1}^{n} \sum_{h=1}^{m} \hat{q}_{hi} \hat{r}_h. \qquad (5.14)$$

But it immediately follows from condition (5.12) that

$$\sum_{i=1}^{n} k_i \hat{r}_k = \sum_{i=1}^{n} \hat{k}_i \hat{r}_k, \qquad (5.15)$$

$$\sum_{i=1}^{n} q_{hi} \hat{r}_h = \sum_{i=1}^{n} \hat{q}_{hi} \hat{r}_h. \qquad (5.16)$$

We sum the equality (5.16) over h (from 1 to m):

$$\sum_{h=1}^{m} \sum_{i=1}^{n} q_{hi} \hat{r}_h = \sum_{h=1}^{m} \sum_{i=1}^{n} \hat{q}_{hi} \hat{r}_h. \qquad (5.17)$$

Adding equalities (5.15) and (5.16), we obtain the total sum of feedback costs, on the right side according to alternatives that entered into balances (5.10) and (5.11), and on the left side according to other alternatives of use of the same available means of production and the same accumulation. But if the feedback costs remain unchanged when there is an increase in differential costs, this increase occurs because of the costs of production.

In symbols, subtracting equalities (5.15) and (5.17) from inequality (5.14) we have:

$$\sum_{i=1}^{n} c_i > \sum_{i=1}^{n} \hat{c}_i.$$

This is what we had to prove.

2. It remains for us to prove that introducing other available means of production from among those that were not included in

the optimal balances (5.10) and (5.11) would increase the costs of producing final output (provided that accumulation does not increase).

Let us recall that the norms of effectiveness for each of the available means of production must begin from zero and that all means of production whose norms of effectiveness are higher than zero must be fully used. Hence it follows that only those available means of production remain outside the balances that, even with a zero norm of effectiveness, are not included in any of the alternatives with the least sum S_i.

Therefore, the introduction into the balances constructed in this manner of any of the available means of production that were not included will, at the very least, not reduce the costs of reproducing final output.

To sum up, we have demonstrated that the problem of maximizing labor productivity under communism can be solved by means of measuring differential costs. Balances of means of production constructed by the method explained here and balance of accumulation ensure the production of the national economy's prescribed final output with the lowest expenditures of labor among all those that are possible by using available natural resources and previously produced means of production and planned output.

If outlays are so small that it would be advisable to increase the production program, the latter can be reexamined. Then, by finding minimum costs for the new production program for final output, we can determine the optimal production program with due regard for both requirements and possible outlays.

However, the economics of communism will be subordinate not only to the law of economy of labor but also to other laws. The question is asked whether the measurement of differential costs corresponds to other economic laws of communism.

A communist economy presupposes an extremely high level of both centralization and democratization of management of the economy, i.e., the full development of both aspects of democratic centralism. The Party Program states: "All production units, all self-governing associations will be harmoniously combined into a common economy organized according to plan and in a single rhythm of social labor. . . . Organs of planning and calculation, and of guiding the economy and cultural development, which are now state organs, will lose their political character and will become bodies of social self-government."[19]

The full development of democratic centralism is possible only on the basis of combining direct and indirect centralization. Under communism, norms of effectiveness of resources will be used as means of management (managing variable systems).

Thus, the measurement of differential costs corresponds not only to the law of economy of labor, but also to the law of development according to plan, to democratization of economic management, and to an increase in the role of the national masses. There are no other methods of measuring costs that could simultaneously serve these laws. We can therefore assume that the measurement of differential costs will be an objective necessity in a communist economy.

Our scheme (model) of optimal planning under communism is highly simplified. It is not intended for developing algorithms for plan calculations and does not provide measures that ensure sufficiently rapid convergence of iterations (repeated calculations of the plan and of norms of effectiveness). Its purpose is to establish the most general features of the measurement of costs in a communist economy, features that stem from the most important economic laws of communism. In so doing, we have assumed that methods of planned work will be used that have already been tested in practice, namely, the balance method of planning and the method of successive approximations. Adding to these methods the methods of optimization and methods of solving extremal plan problems, we have derived a very general scheme for the application of calculations of differential costs in the construction of the plan, which minimizes outlays of labor on the prescribed final output.

Planning the national economy is possible only with sufficiently consolidated indicators. Therefore, the number of final products in our scheme (n) and the number of different kinds of resources (m) must not be too large. In the opposite case calculations could not be carried out even on the most advanced electronic computers. There arises the problem of "disaggregation" of consolidated norms of effectiveness of resources (r_h) and in connection with this the problem of specifying the plan for distribution of resources according to purposes. Methods of disaggregation have been little developed, and in practice we are forced to make use of provisional methods. In optimal planning the disaggregation of indicators is connected with the construction of optimal plans for corresponding sectors of the national economy, for branches, regions, enterprises, and shops. In particular, the problem of finding an overall minimum of outlays in disaggregating the results of its national economic solution

153

naturally changes into a series of subproblems relating to a minimum of outlays for individual sectors of the national economy. In this process its formulation is similar to the formulation of the overall problem (see page 146), with the difference that the results of the solution of the overall problem serve as its initial data. While in the national economic plan the program for production and resources is distributed among the branches, the plans of the branches are formed by proceeding from branch programs and limits of resources. The plans of the branches are constructed by the same method as the national economy's plan. Intrabranch norms of effectiveness of resources found in this manner may not coincide with each other and with the norms of the national economic plan. These divergences occur in consequence of errors in consolidation (aggregation). Thus, in distributing resources among branches, outlays of labor on a branch's final output (c_i) and outlays of means of production (q_{hi}) pertain to groups of different products. Calculated according to consolidated norms, they necessarily deviate from the results of more detailed calculations for enterprises. Divergences between branch norms of effectiveness of the same resource indicate that this resource is not optimally distributed. At the same time these divergences indicate the direction of the error in the distribution of a resource.

For example, suppose that the norms of effectiveness of investment and scarce raw materials in branch No. 1 are equal to 0.1 of investment per year and to 2,000 rubles per ton, and in branch No. 2 to 0.2 of investment per year and 1,000 rubles per ton, respectively. The divergence of norms shows that, within the limits of these two branches, the distribution of investment and scarce raw materials does not correspond to the overall minimum of outlays on the output of both branches. Branch No. 1 receives too much investment and too little of scarce raw materials in comparison with branch No. 2. In branch No. 1 part of the investment is used with less effectiveness than would be possible in branch No. 2. Accordingly, some increase in the investment limit of branch No. 2 by decreasing it for branch No. 1 would increase the overall effect of investment for these two branches. On the other hand, a certain amount of scarce raw materials can be used in branch No. 1 with greater effectiveness than in branch No. 2. Accordingly, some increase in the limit of these raw materials for branch No. 1 at the expense of branch No. 2 would increase the effect of the use of scarce raw materials in these two branches.

After such a redistribution of resources between branches it is necessary to calculate new alternatives of branch plans and norms of effectiveness of resources on the basis of new branch limits. By repeating similar calculations (iterations) we can obtain a sufficient drawing together of branch norms of effectiveness of resources, which will be a sign of conformity of branch plans to the national minimum of labor costs.

In a similar way we can solve the problem of the optimal distribution of resources among enterprises of the branch. Discrepancies of plant norms of effectiveness of resources will indicate errors in this distribution and the nature of the corrections required.

Consequently, disaggregation of indicators in optimal planning involves the division of the problem of an optimum relating to a large subdivision into a series of subproblems for parts of this subdivision. As far as we can foresee, the comparison of local norms of effectiveness of resources is not just a possible but a necessary means for approaching the overall optimum. Only this route corresponds to the development of democratic centralism in a communist economy.[20]

10. Laws and Tendencies in the Development of the Measurement of Costs in a Socialist Economy

The study of the laws of measurement of labor costs under communism illuminates the direction of development of measurement of costs under the conditions of socialism, for there is much in common between socialism and communism. They are two phases of the same social system.

However, under socialism the law of value and the law of distribution according to labor still operate. The question is what particular features of the measurement of costs are affected by the operation of these laws.

Let us begin with the law of value. It operates together with the action of other specific economic laws of socialism, namely, the basic economic law, the law of continuous growth of labor productivity, the law of development of the national economy according to plan, and others. The systematic deviations of prices and calculations of costs from values are explained by the subordination of the law of value under socialism to the same general extremal problems that will be inherent in a communist economy.[21] Accordingly, the above scheme of the construction of optimal balances of means of production under communism also pertains to socialism. However, by virtue of the operation of the law of value the expression of costs in working time in this scheme must be replaced by the corresponding value magnitudes.

Thus, outlays of living labor (c_i) must be expressed by the sum of wages that must be paid to produce the ith final products at all enterprises participating in its creation. In this process the norms of effectiveness will have different specific meanings depending on the means of production to which they apply:

1. For reproducible objects of labor (available at the beginning of the planned period) these norms will express their prices, formed with due consideration of feedback costs.

2. For previously produced implements of labor — buildings, installations, and equipment — the norms of effectiveness must appear in the form of payments for capital, calculated according to their effectiveness, i.e., with adjustment for obsolescence.

3. For natural resources — differential rent.

4. For investments — the normative effectiveness (for credit financing — payments for credit).

The value expression of differential costs can be called full production costs. This is a transformed form of value, just as differential costs are a transformed form of costs of production.[22]

Full production costs of the same product, produced under different conditions of application of labor, tend toward equalization, since the inclusion in these costs of normative net income differentiated according to the quality of the means of production places different enterprises in economically identical conditions of application of labor.

In order for the full production costs of the national economy's total final output to be equal to the value of this output, it is necessary that wages be less than the value of the created product by $\alpha\%$, where

$$\alpha = \left(1 - \frac{\sum\limits_{i=1}^{n} c_i}{\sum\limits_{i=1}^{n} s_i} \right) \cdot 100.$$

Obviously, this process does not essentially differ in any way from the adjustment of differential costs to equality with the overall costs of production of total final output (see page 131 *et seq.*)

Just as norms of effectiveness can be used for indirect centralization of management of a communist economy, so their value expression can be the basis for the best organization of economic calculation. In being guided by the minimum of full

156

production costs, each enterprise will follow the principle of the maximum overall economies of labor.

As under communism, the sum of orders of users of means of production must be balanced with the planned supply of these means. For norms of effectiveness (prices, payments for capital, differential rent, and the norm of investment effectiveness) are established so that the effective requirements for each means of production do not exceed its planned supply.

Hence an important conclusion follows both for the theory and the practice of the utilization of the law of value.

The equality between the demand for means of production and their supply is a necessary element of the law of value under socialism. Without this the law of value cannot fully perform the function of minimizing labor costs. The equality between the demand for means of production and their planned supply is a value form of the general law of establishing norms of feedback costs. This is a law that will be most accurately implemented under communism, with the norms of effectiveness being established by the balance method.

However, the calculation of full production costs is only gradually being established in the socialist economy. This is understandable. Their calculation presupposes the development of a system of norms of effectiveness of resources. But neither methods of optimal planning nor the technological means (electronic computers) for calculating this system of norms have been sufficiently prepared for this development. Finally, even economists are insufficiently prepared for these calculations. More than a quarter of a century of discussions was necessary in order to legalize the practice of using norms of effectiveness of capital investment (the recoupment period). In this way the very simple formula for differential costs – adjusted costs – was recognized. But this formula is already inadequate. Tasks established by the Program of the CPSU and the 1965 economic reform require the full accounting of differential costs, and consequently also the development of this formula.

Indeed, the formula for adjusted costs would be sufficient only if capital investment were the only limited factor in the national economy. But in reality not only capital investment but also the better natural resources are limited. Accordingly, calculation of the effectiveness of use of natural resources will be required together with calculation of investment effectiveness. This means that it is necessary to introduce into the formula for differential costs, besides a norm of investment effectiveness, norms of

157

effectiveness of natural resources, i.e., rates of differential rent for the optimal plan. Then a more general formula for differential costs will be obtained:

$$c_i + k_i r_k + \sum_{g=1}^{m} q_{gi} r_g, \tag{5.18}$$

where q_{gi} is the amount of the gth natural resource used for producing the ith product, and r_g is the norm of effectiveness of use of the gth resource.

Calculating costs according to formula (5.18) also corresponds to the requirement of the Program of the CPSU that prices cover costs of production, costs of circulation, and a certain profit to each normally operating enterprise. This means that prices must cover costs of production and circulation of those enterprises that operate under the least favorable natural conditions, provided these enterprises are using the natural resources allotted to them sufficiently effectively and that they operate normally.

Finally, the use of formula (5.18) is also dictated by the principle of distribution according to labor and by the principle of the workers' material interest in its results.

As we know, the principle of distribution according to labor is that "each individual producer receives back from society, after all deductions, exactly as much as he himself gives to it." It is obvious that equal payment for equal labor can be attained only when the result of each individual producer's labor is determined under equal economic conditions. Accordingly, in measuring what each producer himself gives to society it is necessary to adjust indicators of the results of labor to equal conditions of its application. The Party Program, in posing the problem of improving methods of payments according to labor on the collective farms, indicates precisely this means for its solution. "It is necessary to ensure the creation of increasingly equal economic conditions for raising the incomes of collective farms located in unequal natural-economic conditions in different areas, and also within areas, in order to realize more consistently the principle of equal payment for equal labor in the entire collective farm system."[23]

Adjustment to equal natural conditions of application of labor is conceivable on different levels. It can involve average conditions; it can involve the least favorable conditions of those necessary in the optimal plan; and, finally, it can involve any intermediate level. (Adjustment to better conditions is possible only by redistributing to agriculture part of the net product created in industry.) Adjustment to average conditions presupposes equality of prices and average costs, the extraction of part of the differential rent, and covering the losses of enterprises located where conditions are worse than average. In such a system the prices of products produced with the use of natural resources do not indicate the upper limit of costs allowable in the optimal plan.

A system of adjustment to the least favorable conditions of application of labor, but conditions that are necessary in the optimal plan, is more advisable. It is true that this system assumes a sufficiently high level of labor productivity and earning capacity of collective farms. But this problem must be solved in the course of the next few years. "By its organizational work and measures of economic policy the Party, in the next few years, will see to it that the lagging of economically weak collective farms is completely overcome and that all collective farms are transformed into economically powerful ones with high incomes."[24] Hence it follows that even in the near future the calculation and absorption into the income of society of differential rent will make it possible to place all collective farms in equal natural-economic conditions. Then the formula for the collective farms' production costs will take the form of (5.18).

It is clear that formula (5.18) will be useful for regulating distribution according to labor not only in agriculture but also in extractive industries.

Finally, those previously produced means of production that it is already inefficient to reproduce (i.e., those too obsolete for reproduction) are in a sense limited (fixed). Means that are too obsolete to reproduce do not suddenly become too obsolete to use. Ordinarily they can be effectively used for a certain time, namely, for as long as their use yields savings in reproduction costs of the corresponding output. Obsolete means of production can yield savings only under the condition that in calculating reproduction costs their value is equated to zero.[25] Such a procedure is logical. It signifies that these means do not require reproduction costs since they are not being reproduced. Accordingly, they must be reckoned in costs not according to their reproduction costs, but according to the normative economy of labor resulting from their application in the optimal plan. This means that the use of obsolete means of production must be included in the reckoning of costs not in the form of quantity c_i, which reflects labor in reproduction, but in the form of a special term calculated by means of multipliers — norms of effectiveness.

159

These norms are similar to norms of effectiveness of investment and natural resources, but with the difference that norms of effectiveness of investment and natural resources deflect prices above value, whereas norms of effectiveness of obsolete means of production deflect their prices below value, i.e., they determine the degree of obsolescence.

By taking account of the obsolescence of means of production we obtain a more general formula for differential costs:

$$c_i + k_{ir_K} + \sum_{g=1}^{m} q_{gi}r_g + \sum_{f=1}^{l} q_{fi}r_f, \qquad (5.19)$$

where q_{fi} is the amount of the fth previously produced means of production used in producing the ith product, and r_f is the norm of effectiveness of application of the fth means of production in the optimal plan.

For obsolete objects of labor, r_f will be their price. For obsolete instruments of labor, r_f will express the normative effect (economy of labor) of their use during a unit of time, i.e., a norm of their profitability in the optimal plan.[26] Means of production that are not too obsolete for reproduction enter into formula (5.19) according to their full reproduction costs in the plan period (i.e., the corresponding r_f will be equal to these production costs).

The further development of formula (5.19) consists of extending it to temporary prices of new technology. For instruments of new technology r_f must be higher than the wholesale prices of previously developed analogous output — with due regard for the higher effectiveness of new technology. Taking account, in the prices of new technological means, of their economic advantages for users is advisable not only for the purpose of finding the most effective application of this technology but also for developing its production. Temporarily increased prices for new technological means accelerate their assimilation.

Thus, the formula for adjusted costs ($c_i + k_i r_k$), used in practice, is a particular case of a more general formula (5.19). Whereas the formula for adjusted costs is designed to attain the most effective use of capital investment, the formula (5.19) is designed to attain the most effective use of all of the national economy's resources.[27] According to the Program of the Communist Party of the Soviet Union, "primary attention in all links of planning and managing the economy must be concentrated on the most rational and effective use of material, labor, financial, and natural resources, and on the elimination of excessive costs and losses."[28]

160

Accordingly, in time, a change in our practice to the calculation of costs according to formula (5.19) is unavoidable. This formula corresponds to the task on which primary intention must be concentrated in all links of planning and managing the economy. But the necessary conditions must be created for this change. The calculation of costs according to formula (5.19) presupposes the prior development of a system of norms of effectiveness (profitability) of all material resources:

(1) capital investment,

(2) natural resources (differential rent),

(3) productive capital — according to its specific forms: (a) capital too obsolete to reproduce; (b) instruments of new technology.[29]

In connection with the 1965 economic reform this task has become a realistic one, even an immediate one.

11. The Measurement of Differential Costs in a Capitalist Economy

The reader has surely already noticed that norms of effectiveness $(r_h$ and $r_k)$ are similar in their mathematical form to the average rate of profit and ground rent, and that differential costs are similar to the price of production. Of course, these similarities are not accidental. They are explained by the fact that a feedback between outlays on different products also exists in a capitalist economy and is spontaneously taken into account.

Each capitalist strives to minimize his costs. He is not concerned about the overall minimum. But particular minima of capitalist costs of production are incompatible (by virtue of scarcity of the best natural resources and accumulation). The incompatibility of particular minima of costs of production is expressed in the impossibility of having supply meet the demand for the best means of production when prices are equal to costs of production. When competition exists, the shortage of the best means of production raises their prices to the level at which particular minima of costs of production become compatible (otherwise the competition of demand would raise prices of the best means of production still higher).[30]

Competition equalizes rates of profit and transforms value into the price of production. Thereby a norm of feedback costs associated with capital investment is formed. Competition equates different individual prices of production to a common price of production. In this process capitalist "norms of effectiveness" of the relatively better natural resources or of the more productive

161

capital investments in the utilization of these resources are formed.

Thus, capitalist reckoning of feedback costs occurs as a result of a general striving for profits and the existence of competition. Thereby an important social function, the measurement of differential costs, is spontaneously and very roughly fulfilled. But the results of its fulfillment, savings in the value of the total social product, benefit the capitalists. "Each individual sphere of capital and each individual capitalist has the same interest in the productivity of the social labor employed by the total capital, because two circumstances depend upon this. In the first place, there is the mass of use values in which the average profit is expressed. This is doubly important, since profit serves both as the fund for accumulation of new capital and the fund of revenue intended for consumption. In the second place, there is the value of all advanced capital (constant and variable) that, with a given quantity of surplus value or profit for the entire class of capitalists, determines the rate for profit, or profit for a specific amount of capital."[31]

Taking account of feedback costs is doubly profitable for capitalists. By lowering the total value of goods it raises both the rate of profit and the mass of use values in which profit is expressed.

Thus, the similarity between the general rate of profit and ground rent to norms of effectiveness is explained by the fact that they all serve to measure feedback costs. However, although the role of norms of effectiveness is exhausted by this, profit and ground rent fulfill this function only "pluralistically." Profit and ground rent are not only forms of measurement of costs but also regulators of production and forms of distribution. Private ownership of means of production makes it possible to appropriate the entire effect of the utilization of relatively better means of production and even more than this (we recall absolute ground rent).

The general rate of profit is the regulator of capitalist production. Norms of effectiveness are the controlling norms of a planned system. They act on the proportions between lines of production only indirectly, as factors determining the magnitude of certain parts of outlays on individual products.

Finally, capitalist calculation of feedback costs cannot reduce the value of the final output to a minimum.

Indeed, in order to attain minimum costs we must first discover them. But in a capitalist economy costs are incurred before their overall minimum is found. The market verifies the correctness of already realized costs, not of prospective ones. The correctness of norms of feedback costs is tested in this case by comparing not planned alternatives but already realized ones.

An unsuccessful combination of plan alternatives can be rapidly replaced by another one without any losses. But an unsuccessful combination of already *realized* alternatives cannot be rapidly replaced by another one. When the period of wear and tear of means of labor is long, the time needed to correct mistakes is measured in years. During this period the initial conditions change. This means that the norms of effectiveness must no longer be adapted to previous conditions but to new ones. New mistakes arise in choosing production alternatives. While they are being corrected the initial conditions again change, and so on. As a result, alternatives are always being implemented that do not correspond in one way or another to overall minimum costs.

Thus, the capitalist reckoning of feedback costs is inherently contradictory. In its mathematical form it is designed to find overall minimum costs, but in its economic content it excludes the possibility of finding this minimum.

Deviations of prices of production from values produce the surface impression that they distort the measurement of outlays of labor. In point of fact these deviations bring prices closer to precisely those outlays of social labor that the production of each individual product costs, if we measure outlays on each product dynamically and in their interrelationships.

Concerning a price that includes costs of production and an average profit, Marx wrote: "We call it the price of production . . . for it is a necessary condition for the supply and reproduction of goods in each individual sphere of production."[32] But the differential costs are the social condition for the reproduction of every individual commodity. It is precisely these costs that express the increment of labor involved in the production of the final social product that is associated with the production of the given commodity.

Hence it follows that the price of production is based not just on capitalist competition but also on another, firmer basis. Marx first pointed to the existence of this basis.

The generally accepted concept of the price of production is based only on its single characteristic as the transformed form of commodity value, in which the commodity emerges in the process of competition. But Marx gave the price of production another characteristic, one reflecting another aspect of this category. In his view the price of production has a material basis: "All capital — means of labor as well as materials of production and labor — materially serves as the creator of the product."[33]

It is true that this second characteristic of the price of production is not complete. But it does not follow that it can be discarded. On the contrary, only by proceeding from both characteristics of the price of production given by Marx can we correctly understand its essence and role in a capitalist economy. Both characteristics can be connected with each other. We will try to do this.

The price of production is formed by the action of competition. But under competition the objective conditions of the social economy are somehow or other taken into account, and accordingly it leads to socially important results.

The first social condition considered is that "all capital — means of labor as well as materials of production and labor — materially serves as the creator of the product." This fact is apparent to every capitalist and is directly considered under competition. "The capitalist *expects* identical profit on all portions of capital advanced by him."[34]

Another phenomenon is connected with this fact, namely, that the limited amount of accumulation in the national economy is extended to all invested capital, not just to its variable part, as a result of which all parts of capital equally involve feedback costs.

This fact is not apparent to capitalists. But it is linked with the first one. Therefore, by taking into consideration the first fact, competition thereby necessarily takes account of the second one.

In fact, from the standpoint of the capitalist any ruble of invested capital must bring identical profit. From the standpoint of society any ruble of investment, taken separately, equally involves feedback costs to the extent of the minimum effectiveness of accepted investment alternatives.

By taking into account the fact that for production all capital is materially necessary, the capitalist thereby takes into account the fact that all of capital investment involves feedback costs and not just its variable part.

Finally, competition among capitalists leads to the formation of a general rate of profit, which in its magnitude roughly (i.e., only in its tendency) reflects feedback costs caused by the investment of each ruble of capital. In fact, competition among capitalists reduces prices of production to a minimum. As a result, the general rate of profit necessarily becomes the minimum acceptable rate, not the average one.[35]

164

This proposition conflicts with the generally accepted interpretation of the price of production. But this conflict is explained by the incompleteness, indicated above, of the characteristics of the basis of the price of production contained in the generally accepted interpretation.

We find the following observation in Marx: "Particular rates of profit in different spheres of production are by themselves more or less indefinite; but to the extent that they appear, not their uniformity but their difference appears. The general rate of profit itself emerges only as the lowest limit of profit, not as an empirical, directly reproducible form of the actual rate of profit."[36]

This statement is a necessary part of the concept of the price of production.

True, Marx investigated the formation of the general rate of profit by proceeding from the fact that this rate is equal to $m:K$, i.e., to the average rate (m is the entire sum of surplus value, and K is the entire social capital). The fundamental results of this investigation (deviations of prices of production from values, the relationship of these deviations to the organic composition of capital) retain their force when the general rate of profit is not an average but a minimum quantity.[37] Only the equality of the general rate of profit and the average (m/k) is discarded. But this equality assumes that the entire surplus value (including the additional profit from the use of better natural resources) will be divided only among the capitalists who are extracting it. When the general rate of profit is its lower limit, a part of the surplus value remains for the formation of ground rent.

This means that the determination of the general rate of profit as a minimum quantity is internally connected with the whole system of Volume III of *Das Kapital*. Accordingly, we cannot consider it only as a random remark of Marx's. On the contrary, the equality of the general rate of profit and the average one must be considered as a "first approximation" in investigating the formation of prices of production developed for the simplest hypothetical case.

From what has been said it follows that exchange according to prices of production corresponds to a higher degree of development of an economy and can more completely realize the principle of economy of labor than exchange of goods according to their value. The price of production strengthens the measuring function of the law of value, strengthens its subordination to the law of economy of labor, and also strengthens the social character of the law of value. The price of production is that form of value

165

whose social function is already beyond the power of capitalism and which has probably outgrown the limits of the law of value. A capitalist framework for the price of production is in conflict with its potential social function. A social function presumes planning, but the capitalist framework excludes it.

The price of production is the historically first, still extremely incomplete, form of expression of differential costs under conditions in which they differ from average costs. The development of the potential function of the price of production — finding the overall minimum of outlays — is possible only beyond the limits of the capitalist system. Only in a collective economy can we completely utilize all those possibilities for economy of labor that are embedded in the measurement of differential costs.

In the capitalist economy, however, progress in the calculation of differential costs has been replaced by retrogression. The growth of capitalist monopolies has limited and distorted the operation of competition, the operation of that force which transforms value into prices of production and creates cost savings.

The study of the principles of measurement of costs under communism and socialism helped us to understand those "hints of the higher form" in prices of production that were difficult to explain without knowledge of the principles of measurement of costs in a higher social system. Those elements of Marx's thought concerning prices of production that previously had seemed unconnected with the whole emerged more clearly.

Finally, it turned out that the deviation of prices of production from values does not worsen the measurement of labor costs for each product, but improves it. Thereby the gulf between the theory of value and the history of the measurement of costs is eliminated, that "strange regularity" of which we spoke at the beginning of the book.

12. Labor and the Conditions of Its Application

Quantitative analysis is inconceivable without qualitative analysis. The application of mathematics to economics (as in any other sphere) is fruitful only on condition that mathematical models correctly reflect the essential features and interrelationships of reality. The definition of costs is of the greatest importance in this matter. It is on this question, as a focal point, that the divergences between Marxist-Leninist political economy and bourgeois economic science are concentrated. This is

166

natural. The solution of the most important questions of political economy is connected with the definition of the concept of costs.

Defining costs in terms of labor was not easily achieved by economic science. This definition does not rest on "the surface of phenomena." At first glance the facts indicate that labor is not the sole element in costs, that costs also include the utilization of scarce resources of production, namely, natural resources and capital investment. Not only capitalist practice but, what is particularly important for us, socialist practice also suggests this. We economize not only on labor but also on production time and the better natural resources. Payments for capital and rent payments for the use of natural resources are being introduced.

The economic content of these indicators of costs can be disclosed only on the basis of an economic model that takes into account the most important economic laws. In models reflecting the law of economy of labor, overall outlays of social labor are the minimized objective function, and material resources enter into the constraints. In this way actual costs are clearly distinguished from the means of their minimization – norms of effectiveness of utilization of scarce material resources. These norms are expressed in the unit of measurement of the objective function. The results of labor must also be expressed in this unit. Otherwise they will be incommensurable with costs. Thus, the model of the operation of the law of economy of labor leads to the conclusion that it is necessary to calculate costs according to the formula: labor plus the means of its minimization.

This division of quantities is not applied in formulas for costs used in practice. Furthermore, the value form conceals the difference between labor and the conditions of its application, since labor enters into the reckoning of costs also multiplied by certain value multipliers – wage rates that establish the comparability of different types of labor. In this form the formula for costs can correspond to different economic models with different objective functions and limitations. From a mathematical standpoint there is no basis for dividing multipliers (prices and rates) into two different classes consisting of multipliers used in the case of reckoning limitations of resources and of multipliers used for the commensuration of different kinds of labor. Therefore, mathematically it is not only possible, but it is even convenient, to regard all prices and rates (including wage rates) as auxiliary multipliers and, in conformity with this, to include labor costs not in the objective function but in the composition of the limitations. Then the formula for full production costs can be

167

written as the sum of the products of coefficients of utilized resources and auxiliary multipliers. At first glance this interpretation of the formula for full production costs may seem acceptable. Not only are certain conditions of application of labor limited, but labor itself is limited. However, and this is the essence of the matter, *labor is limited differently than the conditions of its application. People strive to reduce labor costs, but they seek the maximum utilization of the conditions of its application.* The law of economy of labor, one of the most general economic laws, is an expression of this. Accordingly, in a mathematical-economic model labor costs must enter not into the limitations but into the minimized objective function. Correspondingly, wage rates must not be regarded as auxiliary multipliers.

Scarce means of the social economy are not special forms of real costs of production, but are those conditions of the application of labor whose limited nature gives rise to a feedback connection between labor costs (speaking mathematically, which impart a conditional character to the problem of minimizing costs). In a mathematical model of the social economy the difference between real costs and the conditions of their application is expressed in a difference between the minimized objective function and those limitations (equations or inequalities) that must be observed in finding the indicated minimum.

What has been said permits us to renew the criticism of the theory of costs of production as the sum of the prices of the "services" of three factors of production – labor, capital, and land. This theory is characteristic of the mathematical school of bourgeois economic science. It has been repeatedly criticized in Marxist literature, but the previous criticism of this theory is now inadequate. It is inadequate because it proceeded from the conviction that only the costs of production of a product could be included in the formula for costs. (The idea that auxiliary magnitudes – means of minimizing actual costs – can and must be considered in the formula for costs had not yet arisen.) From such positions the calculation of costs in a socialist economy according to the formula for full production costs or even for that of adjusted costs is equivalent to acknowledging that costs do not consist only of labor.

But in actual practice the formula for full production costs is already used, although in an abridged form. If we continue to adhere to previous positions this fact must be recognized as a deviation from Marxism. Some Soviet economists have reached precisely this conclusion. Proceeding from other positions,

168

bourgeois commentators on the Soviet theory and practice of measurement of the effectiveness of capital investment arrive at a similar conclusion.[38]

After what has been said above, it is not difficult to see that this is a fallacy. Calculating costs according to the formula for full production costs necessarily follows from the law of the economy of labor operating with limited material resources and the organization of a socialist economy on the principles of democratic centralism. But the formula for full production costs cannot demonstrate precisely this by itself. It retains the same form with different objective functions and limitations of the economic model. It remains the same both in the case in which the economic model reflects the law of economy of labor and in the case in which the sum of prices of the "services" of the three factors of production is minimized in the model.

Moreover, the question of the role of the law of economy of labor lies at the root of many differences between Marxist and bourgeois economic science. The theory of labor costs of production and the labor theory of value arise from the law of economy of labor. The law of economy of labor determines the minimized objective function of the economic model, the economic content and the unit of measurement of all auxiliary multipliers, and, likewise, the unit of measurement of results. Economic models of general equilibrium, in which costs of production represent the sum of prices of the factors of production, do not reflect the law of economy of labor, and therefore do not reflect the law of labor value. Consequently, the model reflecting these laws differs from models of general equilibrium in the most essential premises, even if identical mathematical means are used.[39]

The fundamental defect of the theory of costs of production and of systems of general equilibrium consists of neglecting the profound difference between subjects and objects of the social economy, and between the powers of subjects of the economy and its means. It is true that in antagonistic societies labor power is regarded by the ruling classes as the object of their management. Consequently, it seems to economists — who express the viewpoint of these classes — that labor is only one of the forms of costs.

Labor is limited in a different, higher sense of the word than capital investment or natural resources. People strive to reduce outlays of labor to a minimum and to make maximum use of the conditions of its application. This is understandable. For growth in the material well-being and culture of a society presupposes maximum utilization of means of production and, in particular, of natural resources, with a reduction in the working day.

In a mathematical model of the social economy the difference between outlays and the conditions of their application is expressed by the difference between the minimized quantity and those limitations (equations or inequalities) that must be observed in finding the indicated minimum. In this way mathematics makes it possible to formulate precisely the difference between the limited nature of labor and the limited nature of the conditions of its application. In models of a social economy, labor costs are the minimized objective function (thereby the law of economy of labor is expressed), and conditions of the application of labor are those limitations that must be observed in minimizing the objective function. It is natural that in such a model a unit of labor can serve as the unit of measurement, but only because in it costs also consist only of labor. Even such a static model, in which labor costs are minimized, is formed in a direction diametrically opposed to the construction of systems of general equilibrium, i.e., it proceeds not from prices (or utility) of consumer goods to prices of factors of production, but from labor costs to prices of consumer goods.

But the cognitive force of models that reflect the law of economy of labor and the law of value is fully revealed only upon investigating the development of an economy. It is then clearly observed that people strive to decrease outlays of labor and to make maximum use of the conditions of its application. The working day is shortened, and capital investments and the development of natural resources are expanded.

But this is not all. As we have already said, the law of economy of labor explains not only quantitative relationships within each mode of production (for example, exchange relationships) but also qualitative changes in the economic system. This law lies at the basis of the development of productive forces, and it reestablishes the disrupted conformity of production relations to the state of productive forces.

Let us summarize. The theory of costs of production and the models of general equilibrium that do not reflect the law of economy of labor ignore the main economic factor both in static and, especially, in dynamic terms. Accordingly, models reflecting the law of economy of labor differ substantially from models of economic equilibrium — moreover, in the most important respect. In form these models can be similar to models of economic equilibrium. But the content of a model is determined by its presuppositions, not by mathematical means.

Notes

1. In mathematics, problems of finding the largest or smallest value of any variable quantity are called extremal problems (from the Latin *extremum* − extreme).

2. K. Marx and F. Engels, *Soch.*, 2nd Edition, Vol. 25, Part II, p. 472.

3. The term "feedback" is also used in economics in a different sense, namely, to denote the fact that the output of goods (for example, steel) is used as an input in the production of the same output. This form of feedback must be taken into account in measuring costs of production. A feedback of this type is taken into account either by successive approximations or by solution of a system of linear equations. Feedback costs (in our sense) are determined with the aid of norms of effectiveness of use of relatively better means of production. Academician L. V. Kantorovich calls these costs "indirect costs." The term "indirect costs" has long been used in economics, but in quite another sense. Therefore, its use to denote feedback costs is hardly advisable. Misunderstandings are possible.

4. Here we give an abbreviated formula for the limits of use of old means of labor. Besides the elements indicated in it, it is also necessary to take account of feedback costs caused by the use of nonreproducible means of production.

5. K. Marx and F. Engels, *op.cit.*, Vol. 20, p. 138.

6. *Ibid.*, p. 125.

7. In general form what has been said is expressed by transformation of the following inequality:
$$(C + Kr)\frac{\Sigma C}{\Sigma (C + Kr)} \gtrless C.$$

The left side expresses adjusted differential costs, and the right side expresses costs of production. Hence (keeping in mind that $r > 0$):
$$\frac{K}{C} \gtrless \frac{\Sigma K}{\Sigma C}.$$

8. In this formula all products qr have the same dimension − the same one in which costs of production c are measured.

In fact, the norm of effectiveness of any means has the dimension man-hours per unit of means of production. Consumption of a means of production (q) is expressed either in natural units of measurement, or it has a more complex dimension − a unit of measurement of means per year. The choice of a unit of measurement of means is obviously related to the unit of measurement of costs of production (c). If q pertains to a unit of output, costs of production must be expressed in man-hours per unit of output. If q pertains to the annual production of output, costs of production must also pertain to annual production. In the first case all products qr will be expressed in man-hours:

$$\frac{\text{man-hours}}{\text{unit of means}} \cdot \text{amount of means} = \text{man-hours}.$$

In the second case all products qr will have the dimension

$$\frac{\text{man-hours}}{\text{year}} : \frac{\text{man-hours}}{\text{year}} \cdot \frac{\text{amount of means}}{\text{year}} = \frac{\text{man-hours}}{\text{year}}.$$

This means that in both cases we can total all products of the form qr and add them to the costs of production (c).

9. What has been said is correct for any values of the norms of effectiveness provided these values are not less than zero. Negative norms of effectiveness contradict the principle of economy of labor. They signify that the given means of production can be used even in cases in which this use is associated with excessive costs in comparison with alternatives providing for the use of scarce means of production.

10. It is advisable to express the availability of implements of labor in units of their possible use − machine tool-hours, etc. Capital investment, correspondingly, can be more accurately expressed in units of their combinations during the planning period.

11. See the works of L. V. Kantorovich, *Matematicheskie metody organizatsii i*

planirovaniia proizvodstva, Leningrad State University Publishing House, 1939; "Concerning One Effective Method of Solving Certain Categories of External Problems," *Doklady AN SSSR,* Vol. 28, No. 3, 1940.

12. K. Marx and F. Engels, *op.cit.,* Vol. 12, p. 731.

13. *Ibid.,* Vol. 23, p. 226.

14. What has been said makes it possible to eliminate the apparent contradiction in the generally accepted interpretation of labor productivity.

On the one hand, it is asserted that only living labor is productive. Hence it would seem to follow that we can speak only of the productivity of living labor.

On the other hand, it is asserted that labor productivity increases with savings of labor, including here savings both of living and of embodied labor on the scale of the entire society. It follows that not only living but also embodied labor is productive.

The contradiction between these statements disappears when expenditures of products of embodied labor are measured by the savings of living labor that are yielded by use of these products, i.e., by feedback costs.

15. Objects of consumption (individual and social) and that part of the means of production intended for expanding production beyond the limits of the planning period represent the final output of the period.

16. For this see Chapter 3.

17. We assume here that the planned limit of investment is correctly determined. The question of planning the volume of accumulation will be examined in the following chapter.

18. Not the entire composition of the production of means of production is determined in this way, but only the composition of those parts that are necessary for fulfilling the final output program. A certain part of the production of means of production is included in the final output program of the national economic plan.

19. *Program of the Communist Party of the Soviet Union,* State Political Literature Publishing House, 1961, pp. 64, 109.

20. In the article "Methods of Finding the Maximum Effect of Capital Investment in the Socialist Economy" *(Trudy Leningradskogo finansovo-ekonomicheskogo instituta,* No. III, Leningrad, 1947), we underestimated the role of the comparison of local norms of effectiveness of resources in finding the national economic optimum. We wrote that branch, plant, and other norms of effectiveness considerably facilitate the task of finding the national economic minimum of outlays and are useful in constructing and correcting balances of means of production and of investment (pp. 154-155). In reality, it is not possible to do without local norms of effectiveness in optimal planning.

21. Deviations of prices and cost calculations from values have often been explained by the policy of the Soviet state. This answer is correct, but it is inadequate. It is only the beginning of an answer. The policy of the socialist state is not arbitrary; it is formed on the basis of knowledge of the economic laws of socialism, including the law of value.

22. In our studies in 1958-1959 we call full production costs "national economic" production costs. Subsequently we became convinced that the term "national economic" in reference to production costs was inappropriate.

23. *Program of the Communist Party of the Soviet Union,* State Political Literature Publishing House, 1961, p. 82.

24. *Ibid.,* pp. 82-83.

25. See above, p. 126.

26. On the basis of the norm of effectiveness of an obsolete means of labor we can determine its valuation with due regard for obsolescence.

27. We recall that the problem of the most effective use of capital investment can be solved only as part of the problem of the most effective use of all means of production.

28. *Program of the Communist Party of the Soviet Union,* State Political Literature Publishing House, 1961, pp. 85-86.

29. New technological means that have been developed and applied are valued according to the full production costs of reproducing them, and the norm of effectiveness of their use is equal to the norm of effectiveness of investment (this equality signifies the absence of obsolescence).

30. In our national economy the incompatibility of particular minima of costs may not bring about these consequences, since prices of means of production are established not by the market but by the state. Accordingly, the incompatibility of particular minima of costs is experienced directly (not through prices) in the form of a scarcity of relatively better means of production. This scarcity, in turn stimulates the reckoning of feedback costs, for example, the establishment of higher prices for scarce materials.

31. K. Marx and F. Engels, *op.cit.*, Vol. 25, Part I, p. 216.

32. *Ibid.*, p. 217.

33. *Ibid.*, p. 43.

34. T. Malthus, *Principles of Political Economy*, London 1836, p. 268; cited in K. Marx and F. Engels, *op.cit.*, Vol. 25, Part I, p. 43.

35. We already proved that selecting alternatives according to the formula $C + Kr =$ min always leads to Kr's being the lower limit of effectiveness of accepted alternatives. In this proof we will change the meaning of the symbols. Let C be capitalists' costs of production, K — capital, and r — the general rate of profit. Then $C + Kr$ will express the price of production, and the proof will lead to the conclusion that the general rate of profit is always its lower limit.

36. K. Marx and F. Engels, *op.cit.*, Vol. 25, Part I, p. 403.

37. As we have seen, adjusted differential costs deviate from costs of production depending on the relation between costs of production and investment. These deviations are analogous to deviations of the price of production from value. Here the norm of effectiveness of investment is not an average quantity but a minimum one.

38. See Iu. Sukhotin, "Foreign Economists on Soviet Studies of the Effectiveness of Capital Investment," *Voprosy ekonomiki*, 1961, No. 9.

39. "It appears to us that discussions of various economic concepts would be more fruitful if they were shifted to the level of discussions of models on which the corresponding terms rest." See L. V. Kantorovich and V.L. Makarov, "Optimal Models of Long-Run Planning," in *Primenenie matematiki v ekonomicheskikh issledovaniiakh*, Vol. 3, Moscow, Mysl' Publishing House, 1965, p. 82.

CHAPTER 6

THE PROBLEM OF THE MAXIMUM
GROWTH OF LABOR PRODUCTIVITY
(The Time Factor in Economic Calculations)

Up to this point we have accepted the limit of capital investment for the national economy as being given. We have simplified the problem with such an assumption and have put off the solution of more difficult questions. Now we must raise them. If the investment limit is taken as given, the determination of the norm of investment effectiveness will differ in no way from the determination of differential rent. Thereby the difference between the limited nature of accumulation and the limited nature of natural resources disappears. This difference is an important one. It was already noted in Chapter 4. The norms of effectiveness of natural resources begin at zero, but the norm of effectiveness of capital investment must necessarily be larger than zero. What obstructs equating it with zero? Perhaps the norm of effectiveness of investment represents not only feedback costs (i.e., a means of minimizing actual costs of production) but, in addition, certain real outlays. Of what do they consist?

Taking the volume of accumulation as given, we have examined the dependence of the norm of effectiveness of investment on the volume of accumulation. But doesn't the norm of effectiveness of investment in turn influence the volume of optimal accumulation?

In assuming that the investment limit can be distributed differently among a multitude of possible purposes we came to the conclusion that the norm of effectiveness of investment must be the same for all possible purposes. But can the norms of effectiveness of those specific means of production in which investment is embodied be identical?

If we begin to treat the availability of every specific means of

174

production as a special limitation, it will be necessary to introduce as many norms of effectiveness as there are different limitations. On which factor are limitations reflected in the investment limit?

These questions appear as soon as we reject the simplifying assumption that the investment limit is given. This simplification permitted us to restrict the problem of minimizing costs to one period of time. By including the volume of accumulation among the unknowns of the problem we must look for the optimal development path. The criterion of the optimum in this case will be different from that in the previous problem.

1. The Role of Qualitative Analysis in Planning the Optimal Development Path of the Economy

A socialist economy must be guided not only by the interests of the near future, but also by more long-term interests, and even by the interests of future generations.

In this lies one of the advantages of the socialist system and one of the reasons for its vitality.

This farsighted concern about the future is manifested both in the careful use of natural resources and in high rates of accumulation.

This same concern about the future must be the guiding principle in solving specific planning problems.

As applied to the principle of economy of labor this means that we must consider as the more effective alternative not the one that promises short-term cost economies, but the alternative that corresponds to the long-term maximum growth of labor productivity.

How do we find this alternative?

Here we must rely, above all, on the qualitative analysis of the influence of different paths of economic development on labor productivity.

An example of such farsighted qualitative analysis was the Leninist idea of the victory of socialism as a necessary condition for preserving the independence of our homeland. The First World War demonstrated that the liquidation of economic backwardness was a life-and-death question for our country. Within a capitalist framework, burdened by powerful remnants of serfdom, the backwardness of Russia not only did not decrease with time but even grew.

Only a new, more advanced mode of production in which high rates of growth of labor productivity were inherent — namely, only socialism — could liquidate the age-old backwardness of Russia.

The central idea of the First Five-Year Plan had such a farsighted aim. This was the idea of the necessary systematic raising of the relative importance of the socialist economic sector. By ensuring the systematic increase in the relative importance of the socialist sector, the First Five-Year Plan created the basis for higher rates of growth of labor productivity in the following five-year plans.

The tasks of liquidating the considerable differences between physical and intellectual labor and between the city and the village were also closely connected with the problem of maximizing the growth of labor productivity. In fact, raising the cultural and technical level of workers in physical labor to the level of engineering and technical personnel and equipping agriculture with the most advanced technology not only directly influence labor productivity but also create the conditions for the broadest extension of technological creativity and for attaining on this basis higher rates of growth of labor productivity in the future.

Thus, the problem of optimal paths of economic development is solved, above all, by the qualitative analysis of the regularities of development of a socialist economy.

However, this problem also has a quantitative aspect.

Given an identity of the national economic effect, different plan (project) alternatives of implementing it differ only in costs. Costs can and must be measured. This means that in these cases the comparative effectiveness of plan (project) alternatives can be determined by calculation.

The question is how we find, among the alternatives that are identical in their national economic effect, the alternative that corresponds to the optimal development path, or, more specifically, to the overall maximum of the rate of growth of labor productivity.

2. What Is the "Time Factor" in Economics?

In our consideration of the maximum effect of investment we implicitly related investment in different alternatives to one moment of time. But in actuality construction periods can differ greatly both in overall duration and in the distribution of individual outlays over time. How do we measure the economic consequences of construction periods?

This question is usually posed separately from the

determination of the effectiveness of investment. But, in taking account of investment, we essentially also take account, as a special indicator of outlays, of the time between an outlay of labor and the appearance of its product, i.e., the period of production and circulation. Obviously, the construction time is included in the production time. This means that the limited nature of capital investment reflects the elementary fact that the production time must be limited. In the opposite case the aim of production — consumption — is unattainable. If the prolongation of the production time did not bring any advantage, then obviously we would have had to use only those methods of production for which the production time is a minimum. In reality, methods of production with a long production time often require smaller labor costs. A relationship such that the production time is a factor of production often exists between production time and the productivity of social labor. In this way, although the term "time factor" is not accurate and is not one used in the literature, it still accurately encompasses the most important aspect of the problem.

What are the real factors in the growth of labor productivity that increase production time? Above all, the use of durable instruments of labor. Labor expended on producing instruments of labor is distinct from labor using these instruments, and this means from the arrival of the finished product, by a series of gradually increasing intervals of time. Thus, if a hydroelectric power-plant dam lasts one hundred years, the time between the labor expended directly on building it and the labor involved in using the dam for producing electric power will amount to from several months (for the first quantities of electric power produced by the plant) to one hundred years (for electric power produced in the last months of the dam's life).

The use of instruments of labor is the most important, but not the sole factor in the growth of labor productivity that entails an increase in production time. Certain reserves of objects of labor are necessary for the normal course of production. Accordingly, maintaining unfinished production and reserves of finished products at a specific level prevents losses and thereby supports or even raises labor productivity. [1]

Thus, the problem arises of comparing the postponement of consumption with the future growth of labor productivity, and this means also of well-being. In such a formulation this problem is obviously insoluble. Production time is not an outlay. It is a characteristic of the national economic effect of outlays of labor.

177

Accordingly, although working time and production time are measured, it would seem, in the same units, they are nevertheless incommensurable with each other.

Marx did not investigate methods of calculating the time factor under communism. But he repeatedly noted the necessity for this calculation. Thus, concerning the question of long-term capital investment he wrote: "If we imagine not a capitalist society but a communist one, then first of all monetary capital becomes completely superfluous, and consequently all that disguising of transactions that arises because of it also becomes superfluous. It becomes simply a matter of society's calculating beforehand how much labor, means of production, and vital means it can expend without any harm to those branches of production — such as the construction of railroads — that do not yield means of production or vital means for a comparatively long period, a year or more, and, in general, during this period do not yield any useful effect but, of course, absorb from all finished production labor, means of production, and vital means." [2]

3. Indicators Necessary for Calculating the Time Factor

What indicators are needed in a socialist society in order to calculate how much labor, means of production, and means of subsistence the society can spend, without any loss, on those kinds of production that will not yield a useful effect for a long time?

At first glance, we must, for this purpose, first of all determine the social production and circulation time for the given product. But it is not difficult to see that the loss from excessive production time depends not only on its duration but also on those labor outlays that are separated by this time from the appearance of their product in consumption. This loss is greater the greater are those labor outlays that for a long time do not yield a finished product. This means that production time, weighed according to labor, must be the initial indicator in the calculating of the time factor. Because labor outlays on a product do not occur instantaneously, but are extended over time, we must weigh each segment of production time separately.

We will denote the time separating each labor outlay expended at different times for producing q units of output from the moment of the availability of that output for consumption by t_i, and we will denote the size of successive labor outlays at different times for producing the given output by c_i ($i = 1, 2, \ldots, n$). Then

178

the weighted production and circulation time will be expressed by the sum of products of $\sum_{i=1}^{n} c_i t_i$.

It is not difficult to see that before us is the formula for the input of labor necessary to create capital for producing q units of output in that unit of time in which t_i is expressed.

Indeed, for reproducing output in the amount of q units in a unit of time we must expend labor before the appearance of the first unit of output not only for output arriving in the first unit of time (calculated from the beginning of delivery for use) but also for output arriving in subsequent units of time. In this way each outlay of labor undertaken before the beginning of the delivery of output leaves a material trace, namely, incomplete and complete means of production, and also reserves of finished products not yet delivered to the user. Consequently, before the beginning of delivery of output, each part of the overall outlays of labor undertaken at different times for q units of output must be repeated all the more often as the time separating it from the arrival of the output is longer. Thus, an outlay of labor incurred during t_1 units of time before the arrival of the product will be repeated t_1 times until the moment of its arrival, and an outlay of labor incurred during t_2 units of time will be repeated t_2 times, etc. As a result a reserve (a fund) will be formed at the beginning of the arrival of output. The value of this reserve reflects each expenditure of working time on the output as many times as the units of time separate this expenditure from the arrival of the product. Thus, at the beginning of the arrival of output the funds will amount to

$$\sum_{i=1}^{n} c_i t_i \quad \text{man-hours.}$$

After the beginning of the arrival of output the fund will cease to grow, but it will not decrease for a long time. Output, equal in outlays of labor to $\sum_{i=1}^{n} c_i t_i$

will be forthcoming in each unit of time, but during the same period the same expenditure of labor on reproduction would again fill up the fund.[3]

Thus, the value of productive capital is the materialized production time, weighted according to outlays of labor. The weighted production time is taken account of precisely in this materialized form in planning and project practice. But this form is deceptive to a certain extent. Its scale does not at all contain units of production time. The value of capital is measured in rubles or in man-hours. But the weighted production time must be measured in ruble-years (or in man-hour-years). Thus, calculating the time factor on the basis of investment can create a false impression, as though the matter concerned simply expenditures of past labor on output and not the indicator necessary for calculating the *time factor*. In accordance with this, the comparison of investment and production costs is represented as "a comparison of expenditures of past labor embodied in fixed capital, raw and other materials, with expenditures of living labor."[4] If this were actually the case, the problem of commensuration would not exist. Expenditures of past and living labor on output are commensurable with each other, and they can be totaled. But the addition of investment and production costs of output is hindered by their scales.

The calculation of the time factor in planning and designing individual elements of the national economy (enterprises, shops, machines, their assemblies and parts, etc.) emerges as a problem of comparing indicators relating to different times. It is necessary to compare one-time outlays, made once and for all, with current outlays that are repeated indefinitely. Such a comparison is possible only after adjusting the compared quantities to the same scale, which presupposes the use of a certain dimensional multiplier. For example, in order to adjust one-time expenditures to current outlays we must multiply them by a multiplier expressed in units of one over time. One the other hand, in order to correct current outlays to one-time expenditures, we must multiply them by a multiplier expressed in a unit of time. This is a formal conclusion. It says nothing about the economic meaning of this multiplier and how to determine its size. It asserts only that such a multiplier is necessary for calculating how much living and past labor can be expended on those objectives that are distinguished by a long production time.

Many vain efforts have been expended on seeking other means of calculating the time factor without a special multiplier. These searches have substantially delayed the development of methods of planned determination of this multiplier.

4. The Adjustment of Costs and the Product to the Same Time as the Basis for Calculating the Time Factor

In order to find a multiplier for calculating the time factor, let us return to the proposition that production time is not a cost, but is a characteristic of the effect of labor outlays. As we demonstrated in Chapter 3, identity of the national economic effect of compared alternatives is a necessary condition for comparing the national economic effect of outlays. Inequality of production time violates the identity of the effect, even if in all other respects the effects of compared alternatives are identical. Consequently, by logical reasoning, to compare the effectiveness of project alternatives differing in the length of production time, it is necessary to adjust their effect and costs to the same time. But this is the logic of national economic practice. Costs and the product are always adjusted to the same time by means of the daily comparison of the supply and demand for objects of consumption. In so doing, the wages of a given period, which are the costs of production of future goods, are expended in purchasing commodities, the results of past labor.

Wages are usually paid and expended long before the completion of the production time of those products on which the labor paid with these wages was expended. Accordingly, the prices of consumer goods reflect not only the labor expended on them but also that surplus labor for expanding production that is caused by the length of the production time. Accumulation enters into prices.

The result is a synchronous commensuration of costs and the product, in which the time between the outlay of labor and the receipt of output becomes practically equal to zero and disappears from the calculation.

Thus, together with the usual measurement of labor expended in the course of the production of any product, which we can call asynchronous measurement, we can and must apply (and in practice we do apply) another, synchronous measurement of labor costs and of labor productivity.

The term "asynchronous measurement" indicates that outlays of labor undertaken at different times are added and are compared with their effects, which appear at different times. Asynchronous measurement fulfills extremely important tasks. However, it does not take account of the distribution of labor costs during the period of production. For example, if outlays per unit of output in alternative No. 1 were two man-hours three years before the moment of delivery of output and one man-hour one month before delivery, and in alternative No. 2 they were one man-hour three years before delivery and two man-hours one month before, then, with asynchronous measurement, outlays in both cases will be equal to three man-hours. But the length of the production period is not a matter of indifference for the national economy. Other conditions being equal, the longer the production time and the larger the outlays of labor that do not yield output for a long time, the larger are the outlays of labor per unit of final output delivered during the same period. Asynchronous measurement does not take account of these consequences. A different method of measuring outlays of labor on a product is necessary here, namely, the comparison of labor expended in a given segment of time for reproducing some output with the output that appears simultaneously for consumption. This measurement of the outlay of labor and of its productivity may be called synchronous measurement.

The synchronous measurement of outlays on a product is much more complicated than asynchronous measurement. However, we cannot do without it. This is the only method of comparing working time and the economic consequences of production time. Labor and production time are not directly commensurable. But labor and the national economic consequences of the length of production time are commensurable, because these consequences consist of additional outlays of labor per unit of output synchronous with it.

The synchronous measurement of labor expenditures not only exists in practice but is not a novelty even in theory. Marx's concept of surplus labor as such (in contrast to its form) is based on the synchronous comparison of labor and the consumed product.

Marx defines surplus labor in general as labor "beyond the extent of given requirements."[5] There is no doubt that here the matter concerns requirements in that segment of time to which the labor refers, i.e., requirements synchronous with labor. This is apparent from the fact that Marx considers the expansion of production as one of the foundations of surplus labor. "A certain amount of surplus labor is required for an insurance fund against various kinds of contingencies in order to ensure the necessary progressive expansion — corresponding to the development of needs and to the growth of the population — of the process of reproduction, which from the capitalist standpoint is called accumulation."[6]

But accumulation can be regarded as surplus labor only with the synchronous comparison of labor and requirements. If we compare outlays of labor with its future product, labor expenditures for the expansion of production also must be related only to their future product. Then we would have to take account of the time factor in its direct form, which is not commensurable with outlays.

The synchronous comparison of labor and its effect permits us to calculate the consequences of production time in expenditures of (surplus) labor and, on this basis, to calculate accurately how much labor, means of production, and means of subsistence society can use, without any harm to itself, on those lines of production that do not yield any effect for a long time. [7]

5. The Basic Functions of Synchronous Comparison of Costs and the Product

It would be an error to suppose that losses from excessive investment must be expressed only in an acute shortage of consumer goods or of manpower. These losses may also consist of unnecessary labor expenditures per unit of output produced at the same time (i.e., simultaneously with the expenditures) in comparison with ones possible with smaller investment. Production is always reproduction. With reproduction the gap in time between the labor expenditure and the receipt of the output exists only during the first period of production of the new product. Subsequently the product appears simultaneously with the expenditure of labor on its reproduction. The gap in time between labor and consumption has vanished. But the production time, of course, has not vanished. Only its economic consequences have changed. Instead of a gap between labor and consumption it causes only one or another relationship between labor and simultaneous consumption. It is precisely here that we find the economic consequences of production time for the national economy as a whole. Outlays of labor and consumption are always synchronous here.

The synchronous nature of labor and consumption in the public economy makes it possible to compare labor and the economic consequences of the length of production time. For these consequences consist of additional outlays of labor per unit of output synchronous with this labor.

Thus, by comparing labor with the consumed product synchronous with it we find it possible to combine in one indicator both the labor expended on the production of the item and the consequences of the length of production time.

Investments are the initial data for synchronous measurement. Knowing investment and the coefficient of increase in production, we can calculate the labor costs necessary to produce additional output in a unit of time. By adding this quantity to outlays on the simple reproduction of the same output, we obtain the labor costs of producing output synchronous with these outlays. However, this method of calculation is applicable to the national economy as a whole, but not to the production of individual products.

Only in the national economy as a whole are consumption and labor costs always synchronous. Moreover, the production time for any individual product always influences the synchronous productivity of all social labor. For workers employed (directly or indirectly) in the production of electric power, for example, demand not only and not so much electric power as other products. Accordingly, it would be incorrect to calculate outlays on an individual product by adding production costs to the product of capital investment per unit of output and the coefficient of annual increase in production of output of a given kind, as Z. F. Chukhanov recommends.[8] The synchronous comparison of costs and the product is applicable only to the entire national economy, and the main question solved by this comparison is the planning of the volume of the national economy's accumulation. The synchronous comparison of costs and the product consists of drawing up a balance of what the given alternative of accumulation takes away from the national economy and brings to it in return. We can see this in a simple example. Let us compare three alternatives of producing consumer goods of a given volume and composition. The indicators of these alternatives are presented in Table 33 (for the sake of clarity we will abstract from their value form).

Table 33

Number of alternative	Productive capital, in billions of man-hours	Labor costs of producing annual output, in billions of man-hours per year
I	50	50
II	55	48
III	75	47

We will further assume that the production of this output must increase annually at a rate of 10%. Then, after providing the national economy with capital according to one of the three alternatives indicated, synchronous outlays of labor on the entire annual program of consumer goods will amount to (in billions of man-hours per year):

184

according to alternative I $50 + \boxed{50 \cdot 0.1} = 55;$

according to alternative II $48 + \boxed{55 \cdot 0.1} = 53.5;$

according to alternative III $47 + \boxed{75 \cdot 0.1} = 54.5.$

The products shown in the boxes represent a calculation of that part of synchronous labor costs that is necessary for expanding production in the following year by 10%.

The scale of these products is different from that for investment. Investment is expressed in rubles (or in man-hours), and the product of investment and the coefficient of its annual growth will be expressed in rubles per year (or in man-hours per year). The difference between the scales of investment and the labor cost of the output created with its aid is thereby removed. Both terms of the costs of reproduction, labor expended on producing the product and the labor involved in accumulation, will be expressed in man-hours per year.

Let us examine the results of our calculation.

Alternative III requires smaller outlays of labor expended in producing the product than alternative II. But if we compare the product with the labor expenditures synchronous with it, it turns out that alternative III requires unnecessary outlays of labor. In this case the additional labor costs required by alternative III in comparison with alternative II will not be recouped as long as the coefficient of annual growth of production does not fall below 0.05. If this never happens the unnecessary synchronous labor costs required by alternative III will never be recouped.

This will involve a loss to the national economy caused by implementing the excessively "capital-intensive" alternative III.

But this is not all. The calculation presented here of synchronous outlays of labor pertains only to the period in which all production will be provided with capital according to one of the alternatives. Under these conditions the effect of previous investment of the same type (i.e., according to the same alternative) stands opposed to additional labor for subsequent expansion of production. However, as long as all production is not reequipped with more effective capital, synchronous outlays of labor will be higher than in the calculation presented here. It will be necessary to undertake new investment before the completion of reequipping, without obtaining the full effect of this investment. Consequently, the entire loss from implementing alternative III will be even higher than is indicated in the calculation presented above.

It is not difficult to see from this calculation that loss can be caused not only by excessive but also by insufficient accumulation. In fact, the least capital-intensive alternative, I, requires the highest synchronous labor costs.

We will now demonstrate that the synchronous comparison of costs and the product strikes a balance between what accumulation takes from the national economy and what it gives to it.

Alternative II requires smaller synchronous outlays on the prescribed program than alternative I because the additional investment required by alternative II (in comparison with alternative I) yields a greater effect than the additional accumulation that would be necessary with the subsequent expansion of production at the prescribed rate according to alternative I. The additional investment in alternative II amounts to 5 billion man-hours. The effect of this investment $(50 - 48)$ is equal to 2 billion man-hours per year. Additional accumulation for alternative II in comparison with alternative I in the expansion of production by 10% per year amounts to 0.5 billion man-hours per year. Hence the excess of the effect of investment over additional accumulation is equal to 1.5 billion man-hours per year.

The difference between synchronous outlays of labor in alternatives I and II, i.e., $55 - 53.5 = 1.5$ billion man-hours per year, is equal to this quantity.

On the other hand, alternative III requires larger synchronous outlays on the prescribed program than alternative II, for the additional investment required by alternative III (in comparison with alternative II) yields a smaller effect than does the additional accumulation that would be necessary with the subsequent expansion of production at the prescribed rate according to alternative III. Additional investment in alternative III amounts to 20 billion man-hours. The effect of this investment $(48 - 47)$ is equal to a billion man-hours per year. Additional accumulation for alternative III in comparison with alternative II in expanding production by 10% per year amounts to 2 billion man-hours per year. Hence the smaller effect of investment in comparison with additional accumulation is equal to a billion man-hours per year. The difference between synchronous labor costs in alternatives III and II, i.e., $54.5 - 53.5 = 1$ billion man-hours per year, is equal to this quantity.

Thus, synchronous measurement involves a comparison of the effect of preceding investment and the accumulation necessary for the subsequent expansion of production. Such a comparison is extremely important for choosing the volume and composition of accumulation.

Finally, the last and most general conclusion to be drawn from our example is that *the national economy's optimal accumulation is determined according to the minimum value of the entire consumed product.* Synchronous labor costs are nothing but the substance of value of the consumption fund, i.e., the sum of outlays of labor on its simple reproduction plus the surplus labor for expanding reproduction.

6. Calculation of the Time Factor in Determining the Effectiveness of Outlays on the Production of Individual Products

The example presented of the synchronous measurement of the effectiveness of social labor is highly simplified. It reflects only one aspect of the problem. In particular, we have not considered how to take account of the time factor in planning the production of individual products. As we noted earlier, the synchronous comparison of costs and the product is not applicable to individual lines of production.

At the same time, the calculation of the time factor in individual lines of production is part of the synchronous measurement of the effectiveness of all social labor. The prolongation or reduction of the production time for each individual product influences the synchronous productivity of all labor expenditures in the national economy. Hence it follows that the synchronous measurement of outlays on an individual product consists of determining the degree of conformity of one or another alternative of its production to the overall maximum effect associated with the national economy's optimal volume of accumulation.

Indeed, if the product in our example encompasses all means of consumption, then for each alternative of the volume of investment in producing it (for example, $m = 100$ billion man-hours) there can correspond an innumerable multitude of alternatives of distribution of this investment among different lines of production (without any change in the general program for producing consumer goods). Of course, different alternatives of distribution of investment are not equally effective. With given investment one of these alternatives requires greater costs of reproduction and others require smaller ones. Obviously, to find the overall minimum of synchronous costs we must take not any one of these alternatives of distribution of investment, but that one which requires the least costs with a given volume of investment. This is fulfilled by solving the problem for a maximum effect of given investment (see Chapter 4).

Thus, in our example of synchronous measurement each alternative of the volume of investment must be the most effective one among all other possiblilities of utilizing the same sum of investment with the same general program for producing consumer goods. If we were to reject the prior solution of the problem of the maximum effect of investment and picked alternatives I, II, and III with a different distribution of each limit of investment among individual projects, we could not find a minimum of synchronous outlays on the entire production program. It could then appear that alternative III was worse than alternative II only because the distribution of investment among projects was less rational in alternative III than in alternative II.

But, as we showed in Chapters 4 and 5, the maximum overall effect of investment is achieved with that distribution of its fixed sum among construction projects for which the program for producing final output is fulfilled with minimum differential costs.

With a given program the norm of investment effectiveness depends on the general investment limit. Accordingly, for each of the alternatives in our example there is a corresponding value for this norm. Thus, for alternative I $r_1 \geqslant 0.4$, for alternative II $0.4 \geqslant r_2 \geqslant 0.05$, and for alternative III $0 \leqslant r_3 \leqslant 0.05$.(This is apparent from the fact that the effectiveness of additional investment in alternative II amounts to 0.4 per year and for alternative III in comparison with alternative II it amounts to 0.05 per year.)

As we showed earlier, the comparison of synchronous costs represents a comparison between what each alternative of accumulation gives to the national economy with what it takes from it.

In replacing numbers by letters in our discussion we have:

$$(K_{II} - K_I) E_{II/I} > (K_{II} - K_I) \beta;$$
$$(K_{III} - K_{II}) E_{III/II} < (K_{III} - K_{II}) \beta,$$

where K_I, K_{II}, and K_{III} are investments in the three alternatives, β is the prescribed rate of growth, $E_{II/I}$ is the effectiveness of additional investment in alternative II in comparison with alternative I, and $E_{III/II}$ is the effectiveness of additional investment in alternative III in comparison with alternative II.

Since the differences included in the parentheses are positive,

$$E_{III/I} > \beta > E_{III/II} . \qquad (6.1)$$

The norm of effectiveness of the investment alternative that corresponds to the minimum of synchronous outlays of labor

$$E_{II/I} \geqslant r_K \geqslant E_{III/II} \qquad (6.2)$$

is also included among the indicators of the effectiveness of additional investment.

It is obvious that the more we examine alternatives of investment for producing the entire consumption fund, the smaller will be the difference between indicators of the effectiveness of two alternatives similar in size of investment.

Given a large number of alternatives of the volume of investment for producing the entire consumption fund, the effectiveness of additional investment of two adjacent successive outlays is practically equal.

If alternative S is optimal, then

$$E_{S/S-1} = E_{S+1/S} . \qquad (6.3)$$

Taking into consideration (6.1), (6.2), and (6.3), we conclude:

$$r_K = \beta, \qquad (6.4)$$

i.e., the norm of effectiveness of investment of the alternative of accumulation that ensures the minimum synchronous outlays on the entire prescribed consumption fund is equal to the rate of growth of production.

In this way the calculation of the time factor in outlays on individual products with the aid of the norm of effectiveness of investment is linked with the calculation of the time factor in synchronous outlays of labor on the entire consumption fund with the aid of the rate of growth of production. Thus, both r_K and β serve to minimize the value of the entire consumption fund. The norm of effectiveness of investment (r_K) serves this purpose in the problem of finding the most effective distribution of the given volume of accumulation among different purposes, and the coefficient of growth of production (β) serves the same purpose in the problem of finding the optimal volume of accumulation.

189

Equality $r_K = \beta$ characterizes the potential optimum of accumulation that ensures the maximum synchronous labor productivity with a given rate of growth of production. But this equality says nothing about the realism of the given rate of growth nor whether it is the largest of the possible rates.

The realism of the rate of growth can be checked by balance calculations. That rate of growth is realistic which can be attained with a real increase in the fund of working time of workers in material production and with a long-term growth in their labor productivity. Assuming the complete utilization of these possibilities in a sufficiently long-term plan we will obtain the maximum possible stable rate of development.

Then the equality $r_K = \beta'_{max}$ characterizes the real optimum of accumulation. Since the norm of effectiveness of investment (r_K) expresses the permissible minimum effectiveness of investment (E_{min}), the achievement of the real optimum of accumulation will be expressed by equality

$$E_{min} = \beta_{max}. \tag{6.5}$$

The meaning of this equality is simple. The left side expresses the minimum economy of labor that accumulation gives the national economy in a unit of time in its optimal use. The right side of the equality expresses what accumulation takes from the national economy under a stable maximum possible rate of growth of production. The stable maximum rate of growth of production is the criterion of the optimum on whose basis this equality is derived. This criterion had already been established in the resolutions of the 15th Party Congress. "On the question of the *rate* of development . . . we should proceed not from the maximum rate of accumulation for the *next* year or for several years, but from that relationship of elements in the national economy that would provide the most rapid rate of development over the *long run*." [9]

Thus, in analyzing the factors involved in the development of the national economy, those factors that determine the norm of effectiveness of investment have become more apparent. This norm directly depends on the national economy's volume of accumulation and on the distribution of possible investments according to their effectiveness. This is precisely the conclusion that follows from the formulation of the problem of finding the overall maximum effect of investment in a socialist economy that was presented in Chapter 4. But this answer is inadequate. The question of what determines the volume of accumulation arises.

We can answer this question only by examining the long-term problems and conditions of development of the national economy.

We saw that with optimal planning, accumulation must provide for the maximum rate of development of the national economy over the long run. This principle also controls the level of the norm of investment effectiveness. The average long-run norm of investment effectiveness is connected with the maximum possible rate of growth of labor productivity. Thus the entire system of value norms for calculating costs must, in the final analysis, be determined by the maximum rate of steady growth of labor productivity. All value norms — prices of means of production, differential rent, rent payments for the use of productive capital, and the norm of investment effectiveness — are connected with each other. Then the principle of calculating not only the national economic plan as a whole but also every part of every machine becomes what V. I. Lenin considered the most important and the major factor in the victory of the new system.

Formula (6.5) characterizes a very important relationship between the rate of growth of production and the norm of effectiveness of investment. The essence of this relationship is not in the equality of magnitudes, but in the fact that the norm of investment effectiveness not only depends on the volume of accumulation (as was demonstrated in Chapter 4) but also influences it. An optimal relation is formed between consumption and accumulation on the basis of this interrelationship. Equality $(E_{min} = \beta_{max})$ is based on the firm suppositions that technology is unchanged and that the growth of production occurs in consequence of an increase in manpower with an absence of limitations on natural resources, and that the product of the preceding year (period) enters into consumption. It is sufficient to change even one of these assumptions and formula (6.5) will change. Thus, if we reject the latter of the assumptions and accept the fact that investment in the national economy begins to yield an effect within year (periods), then formula $(E_{min} = \beta_{max})$ will be transformed into the formula [10]

$$E_{min} = \beta_{max} (\beta_{max} + 1)^t. \tag{6.6}$$

In actuality the factors determining the optimal share of accumulation in the national income are so complex and variable that they do not fit into a simple formula.

191

At the beginning of the 1960s several works appeared on the problem of the optimum in accumulation. The equality of the marginal effectiveness of capital to the growth rate received the name of the golden rule of accumulation.

A generalization of the results of a number of works was given in Koopmans' (1963) and Malinvaud's (1963) studies. [11] An interesting attempt was made here to take into account predictable technological progress. Particularly worthy of attention is the analysis of the problem without the assumption that future goods will be valued lower than present goods in terms of use value, and at the same time within the framework of an infinite time horizon.

By proceeding from a most simple model of the optimal path of development we can then shed light on complications introduced by technological progress. Let us consider two consequences of technological progress, namely, changes in the period of social production and changes in the norm of investment effectiveness. If technological progress uniformly reduces both labor in production and capital investment, then the average period of social production does not change. Under such conditions the equality $E_{min} = \beta_{max}$ obviously retains its force as the characteristic of the optimal growth path. For in this case technological progress influences the growth of production similarly to an increase in the number of workers, without changing the capital stock in production. When technological progress promotes those methods of production for which the subsequent growth of synchronous labor productivity is connected with a lengthening of the period of social production, thresholds arise on the path of lowering synchronous labor costs. Overcoming these thresholds can be a complex problem.

7. Thresholds [Porogi] on the Path of Growth of Production

We examined synchronous outlays of labor under conditions of uniform growth, when accumulation is counterposed to labor savings from capital with the same effectiveness and with the same turnover time. This does not mean that reproducible capital must be the same technologically as existing capital. New capital must be more effective than the old. This is one of the foundations for the growth of production. But the norm of investment effectiveness must not change. Such a condition for a stable growth rate directly follows from equality (6.5).

However, this equality does not take into account the

conditions of transition of the national economy to a technology that promises an increase in growth rates, but only at the price of an increase in the average production time. Moreover, these conditions are not exceptional. Without considering periods of industrialization, periods of increase in the average production time are possible in the process of subsequent development of the economy. Such periods lead to new economic heights, but only through thresholds of temporary increases in synchronous labor costs and possibly a relative decline in the profitability of new technology.

We will present simple model of these thresholds.

We will denote the labor costs of producing the annual consumption fund with old implements as C_c, and with new implements as C_H. We will denote the investment necessary for producing these products by means of old implements as K_c and by means of new implements as K_H. In this case $K_H > K_c$, and $C_H < C_c$, from which $\dfrac{K_H}{C_H} > \dfrac{K_c}{C_c}$.

Since $\dfrac{K}{C} = \bar{t}$ ($\bar{t}$ is the average production and circulation time), then $\bar{t}_H > \bar{t}_c$.

The growth rate with old production equipment equals β_c. The norm of effectiveness of investment with old technology is $r_c = \beta_c$.

Suppose that the effectiveness of investment in new technology is higher than the previous norm:

$$\frac{C_c - C_H}{K_H - K_c} > r_c. \qquad (6.7)$$

It follows that with the old growth rate (β_c) new technology ensures (after its assimilation!) lower synchronous labor costs than the old technology. Indeed, by taking into account that $r_c = \beta_c$, we can rewrite inequality (6.7) as follows:

$$C_c + K_c \beta_c > C_H + K_H \beta_c. \qquad (6.8)$$

Under such conditions the opportunity exists not only to reduce the synchronous labor costs of the same output but also to increase its growth rate. In fact, it is apparent from inequality (6.8) that we can select a new growth rate $\beta_H > \beta_c$ for which the synchronous labor costs of creating the same consumption fund will be lower for new technology than for old technology, i.e.,

$$C_c + K_c \beta_c > C_H + K_H \beta_H. \qquad (6.9)$$

193

On the way to this goal we will have to pass through a temporary increase of synchronous labor costs of producing the given consumption fund, since for a certain period of time additional outlays of labor on the production of new technology will not be compensated by labor savings from its utilization. In fact, synchronous outlays of labor on the production of the consumption fund at the beginning of the production of new technology will amount to

$$C + (K_\text{н} - K_\text{c}) \gamma + K_\text{н} \beta_\text{c}, \qquad (6.10)$$

where γ is the share of the productive capacity of renewable capital in the entire productive capacity of old capital.

Moreover, synchronous costs with old technology and the same growth of production will be equal to

$$C_\text{c} + K_\text{c} \beta_\text{c}. \qquad (6.11)$$

Since $K_H > K_c$, expression (6.10) is greater than expression (6.11).

As long as the share of new technology in the productive power of the national economy does not attain a sufficiently high level, synchronous costs per unit of the consumption fund will be higher on the average than those that would occur with old technology and the previous rate of growth of production. In this way the first threshold arises on the path from the old to the new technology, namely, the threshold of increasing synchronous outlays of labor. New technology will begin to lower synchronous costs from the year in which its share in the national economy's productive capacity attains the following magnitude[12]:

$$\alpha = \frac{K_\text{н} - K_\text{c}}{(C_\text{c} - C_\text{н}) + (K_\text{н} - K_\text{c}) \gamma} (\beta_\text{c} + \gamma). \qquad (6.12)$$

(We note that γ approximately expresses the rate of depreciation of old technology.) Then the expression

$$\frac{K_\text{н} - K_\text{c}}{(C_\text{c} - C_\text{н}) + \gamma (K_\text{н} - K_\text{c})} = T_{\text{н/c}} (6a) = \frac{1}{E_{\text{н/c}} (6a)}$$

will be the period of recoupment of additional investment in new technology in comparison with old technology, calculated without reckoning depreciation $6a$ in operating costs.

By taking this into account we can write formula (6.12) in a shorter and economically clearer form:

$$\alpha = \frac{\beta_\text{c} + \gamma}{E_{\text{н/c}} (6a)} = \frac{r_\text{c} + \gamma}{E_{\text{н/c}} (6a)} \qquad (6.13)$$

194

This means that new technology will raise synchronous labor productivity only after the year in which its share in the national economy's productive capacity attains a magnitude equal to the ratio of the sum of the norm of effectiveness of old technology and its rate of depreciation to the effectiveness of new technology, calculated without including depreciation in the production costs of output.

The growth of synchronous labor costs in the transition from the old to the new technology is accompanied by a relative reduction in the profitability of the new technology in comparison with the old. The profitability of old technology increases to a greater extent than that of new technology, and ultimately the old technology can become more profitable than the new. We will prove this.

Suppose that the new technology, before its introduction, was more profitable than the old:

$$\frac{P - C_H}{K_H} > \frac{P - C_c}{K_c}, \tag{6.14}$$

where P is the sum of prices of consumer goods before the introduction of new technology. (Since the other magnitudes in inequality (6.14) are expressed in units of labor, P also must be represented in the same units.) Since $P = C_c + K_c \beta_c$ (i.e., P is equal to the demand for consumer goods), inequality (6.14) can be written as follows:

$$\frac{C_c + K_c \beta_c - C_H}{K_H} > \beta_c. \tag{6.15}$$

Inequality (6.15) obviously corresponds to inequality (6.8).

With the rise in prices *(P)* that occurs in consequence of the growth in demand associated with the production of new, more expensive technology, the right side of inequality (6.14) increases more rapidly than the left side. Indeed, $K_c < K_H$, and the increase in the numerator increases the fraction all the more as its denominator is smaller.

As a result, inequality (6.14) can change as follows:

$$\frac{P + \Delta P - C_H}{K_H} < \frac{P + \Delta P - C_c}{K_c}, \tag{6.16}$$

i.e., the old technology will become more profitable than the new. In this way *a second threshold on the path from the old to the new technology arises, namely, the threshold of the rate of profit.* However, this threshold is not always formed, but only with a certain relation between the effectiveness and capital-output ratio

195

of new and old technology. Let us find this relation. The sum of prices of consumer goods at the beginning of the replacement of old by new technology is equal to the sum of workers' incomes. In terms of labor it is equal to (6.10):

$$C_c + (K_H - K_c)\gamma + K_H\beta_c.$$

The condition that this old technology becomes more profitable than the new at the beginning of its replacement will be expressed by the following inequality:

$$\frac{C_c + (K_H - K_c)\gamma + K_H\beta_c - C_c}{K_c} > \frac{C_c + (K_H - K_c)\gamma + K_H\beta_c - C_H}{K_H}.$$

Hence

$$\frac{K_H - K_c}{K_c} > \frac{C_c - C_H}{K_H(\beta_c + \gamma) - K_c\gamma}. \qquad (6.17)$$

The right half of this inequality represents a special index of the effectiveness of the new technology in comparison with the old. The annual economy of labor from the replacement of old by new technology is in the numerator of this index, and the national economy's additional annual costs associated with the replacement of old by new technology are in the denominator. If the ratio of additional investment in new technology to investment in old technology is larger than this index of the effectiveness of new technology, then its introduction involves a threshold of profitability. The old technology becomes more profitable than the new, in spite of the fact that in the future the new technology will become more effective (6.8) and more profitable than the old ((6.5) and (6.15)).

Let us clarify what has been said by a numerical example. Let us take the following initial data: C_c = 100, C_H = 90, K_c = 50, K_H = 100, β_c = 0.1, and γ = 0.1. Hence the coefficient of effectiveness of the new technology in comparison with the old is 0.2 per year, and without considering depreciation it is 0.3.

Sychronous labor costs with a growth rate of 0.1 will amount to 105 for old technology and to 100 for the new. In the period of transition from the old technology to the new the greatest synchronous labor costs for the same product at the previous growth rate (β_c) will amount to 115. In proportion to the growth in the share of new technology in productive capacity these outlays will decrease and will attain the previous level (105) when this share (a) increases to two-thirds.

In the period of the greatest synchronous costs (at the beginning of the production of the new technology) the old technology will become more profitable than the new:

196

$$\frac{115-100}{50} > \frac{115-90}{100}.$$

The threshold of profitability (the rate of profit) arises in this example because it contains inequality (6.17)

$$\frac{K_н - K_c}{K_c} = 1 > \frac{C_c - C_н}{K_н(\beta_c + \gamma) - K_c\gamma} = \frac{2}{3}.$$

If K_H were equal to 80 (instead of 100), then, given the other conditions of the example, the threshold of profitability would not occur, although synchronous labor costs in the transition period would be higher than with the old technology (a maximum of 111).

In analyzing the conditions of the emergence of the threshold of profitability on the path of technological progress we did not examine changes in the general rate of profit. It was sufficient to compare movements of the rates of profitability of new and old technology. But the analysis of changes in the general rate of profit in periods of technological renewal of fixed capital leads to the same conclusion, providing we accept this rate as the index of the time factor. In fact, a rise in prices caused by an increase in synchronous labor costs leads to a rise in the general rate of profit. By using this rate to compare production costs and capital investment we obtain a reduction in the relative effectiveness of new technology in periods of its assimilation. Suppose that r' is the general rate of profit. Then the costs of production with the old and the new technology, with the time factor reckoned according to this rate (r') before the introduction of new technology will be

$$C_c + K_c r' > C_н + K_н r'. \tag{6.18}$$

Since $K_H > K_c$, the increase of r' increases the right half of the inequality to a greater extent than the left half. Consequently, the growth of r' (the general rate of profit) can make the left half of inequality (6.18) become smaller than the right half.

Hence it is apparent that the rate of profit, like the norm for calculating the time factor, has an important defect. It reflects the current situation and short-run conditions, whereas the planning of investment requires reckoning with conditions relating to a sufficiently long period of time and consideration of development prospects. Accordingly, a change in the rate of profit occurring under the influence of implementation of the plan of capital investment can fundamentally change the relative evaluation of its

197

effectiveness. New technology effective *before* its realization can prove to be insufficiently effective *during* its introduction. If these changes in the rate of profit were taken into account as changes in the time factor and influenced the direction of investment, the planned economy would undergo economic fluctuations. Periods of extensive implementation of new technology would be replaced by a decline in rates of construction.

This property of the rate of profit was of particular significance in the years of socialist industrialization. If the rate of profit had been accepted then as the criterion of effectiveness of investment, it would have been necessary at the peak of construction to change its direction, curtailing certain construction projects that had been started.

The defect of the rate of profit noted here exists even now. That is why the analysis of inequalities (6.14) and (6.17) explains not only why socialist industrialization is possible only given a certain disturbance of the profitability principle, but also why in a socialist economy there is not, and must not be, either a general rate of profit or prices of production in the exact sense of the term. In order to overcome the threshold on the path of growth that is posed by the general rate of profit (see inequalities (6.14), (6.16), and (6.17)), it is necessary that temporary fluctuations in the profitability of Department II influence neither the profitability of Department I nor the relative effectiveness of long-term investments. The multiplier for calculating the time factor must reflect not so much current conditions as future ones.

The norm of investment effectiveness which is calculated by the methods of optimal planning for a sufficiently long planned period satisfies this requirement. It does not depend on those fluctuations of prices of consumer goods with which the threshold of profitability is associated.[13]

It is apparent from formula $E_{min} = \beta_{max}$ that the norm of investment effectiveness must be uniform for all branches of the national economy. Branch norms of effectiveness of capital investment have as little justification as branch prices for coal, cast iron, or other means of production. Branch differences in prices for the same commodity exclude the possibility of the correct calculation of labor costs. In the same way branch differentiation of norms of effectiveness would overstate labor costs associated with the time factor in some cases and understate them in others.

But it does not at all follow from formula $E_{min} = \beta_{max}$ that the multiplier for calculating the time factor must be identical whatever the costs. The principle of a uniform price pertains to a commodity of the same quality. Those differences that have important significance from the standpoint of the time factor are inherent in investment, namely, differences in its turnover periods and in the degree of reliability of the expected effect. It also does not follow from formula (6.5) that the norm of effectiveness of investment must remain constant. On the contrary, to the extent that the rate of growth of production will change, the multiplier for calculating the time factor must also change. In the case of investments of long duration we must take into account norms not only for the immediate future but also for the distant future.

In a planned economy the threshold of profitability can be completely removed with smaller limitations of the principle of profitability than those that have actually existed until now in the USSR. That is why we still have great possibilities for expanding the sphere of operation of this principle without fearing the appearance of thresholds caused by it on the path of growth of production.

Matters are different with the threshold of synchronous labor costs. It depends not on methods of calculating effectiveness (like the threshold of profitability), but on the conditions of the growth of production. It is best overcome as part of long-term planning as a whole. In our most simple model of the threshold of synchronous costs we proceeded from certain premises that, of course, can be different in reality. For example, we assumed that the production of consumer goods would increase at the same rate (β_c). If we assume that at the beginning of the assimilation of the new technology the rate of growth of the national economy's productive capacity drops somewhat, then the threshold of synchronous costs will become less steep but, on the other hand, more prolonged.

8. The Problem of Calculating Future Changes in the Norm of Effectiveness of Investment

The norm of effectiveness of investment will change from time to time in connection with change in the conditions determining it. It probably will change before the most durable means of labor that come into being under it wear out. In these cases the means of labor created under the previous norm of effectiveness of investment will no longer correspond to the new norm of investment effectiveness. Losses will arise in consequence of the nonconformity of certain means of labor that have not yet been worn out to the new conditions of the national economy. These

199

losses can be prevented or decreased by selecting certain investment alternatives involving short periods of wear and tear. Such alternatives may not correspond to the overall maximum effect of investment under the previous norm of effectiveness. But in return they make it possible to adapt the economy more rapidly to new conditions reflected in the new norm of investment effectiveness.

On the other hand, long-term investment alternatives must be evaluated not only from the standpoint of the existing norm of investment effectiveness, but also from the standpoint of future norms of effectiveness.

For example, if the norm of investment effectiveness is calculated for a period of five or six years it would be incorrect to construct enterprises only on this basis that have a useful life of 50 years or more.

However, it is also impossible to carry out all construction by proceeding from future norms of investment effectiveness. In making calculations according to future norms, the balance of accumulation and investment would not work out.

Consequently, tending toward future norms of effectiveness in choosing alternatives with the longest periods of obsolescence is associated with deviations in the opposite direction (from the existing norm) in choosing alternatives with short periods of obsolescence. The purpose of these deviations must be the maximum continuous growth of labor productivity.

We will demonstrate with a very simple example the losses that arise in consequence of the nonconformity of previously made long-term investments to the new conditions. Let us examine a combination of alternatives of two construction projects A and B. The indicators of these alternatives are presented in Table 34.

Table 34

Number of alternative	Investment, in millions of rubles	Production costs of annual output, in millions of rubles per year	Effectiveness of additional investment, in % of investment	Period of obsolescence of fixed capital, in years
I_A	100	115	—	20
II_A	200	105	10	20
I_B	100	117	—	5
II_B	200	105	12	20

Suppose that the existing norm of effectiveness of investment is equal to 11% per year. Suppose that within five years the norm of investment effectiveness will be reduced to 8%. The combination $I_A + II_B$ of alternatives A and B corresponds to the norm of 11% per year.

If the construction of projects A and B is carried out according to alternatives $I_A + II_B$ the replacement of this combination by another one corresponding to new conditions is possible only 15 years after establishing the new norm of effectiveness of investment, since the useful life of the fixed capital of alternative I_A is equal to 20 years. Thus, the nonconformity between project A's fixed capital and the new conditions of the national economy will last for 15 years. But if instead of combination $I_A + II_B$ another combination were accepted with the same total of investment, namely, combination $II_A + I_B$, then in five years alternative I_B could be replaced by alternative II_B.

It is true that for the five years the combination of alternatives $II_A + I_B$ would require additional production costs in comparison with combination $I_A + II_B$. These additional costs would amount to $(105 + 117) - (115 + 105) = 2$ million rubles per year. On the other hand, during the remaining 15 years the combination of alternatives $II_A + II_B$ would yield savings of production costs in comparison with combination $I_A + II_B$. These savings would amount to 10 million rubles per year $[(115 + 105) - (105 + 105)]$.

It is also necessary to take into account the fact that the combination of alternatives $II_A + II_B$ requires 100 million rubles more investment than the combination $I_A + II_B$. This sum of investment could yield savings of production costs by operating with a new norm of effectiveness (8% per year) to the extent of a million rubles per year. This means that the net savings of production costs yielded by the combination of alternatives $II_A + II_B$ in comparison with combination $I_A + II_B$ would amount to 2 million rubles per year $(10-8)$.

In this way the successive implementation of the combination of alternatives $II_A + I_B$ and the combination $II_A + II_B$ yields, over the course of 20 years, savings of production costs equal to $(2 \cdot 15) - (2.5) = 20$ million rubles in comparison with costs in the combination of alternatives $I_A + II_B$.

Hence it is apparent that in finding the long-run maximum effect of investment in the national economy the principle of uniformity of the norm of investment effectiveness is applicable only when this norm does not change in the course of the longest useful life of fixed capital. In the absence of this condition future norms of effectiveness of investment must also be taken into account together with the existing one. It is obviously impossible to accomplish this by establishing different norms of effectiveness for long-term and short-term investments. We can show this by our example. Indeed, the norms of investment effectiveness indicate that the best combination is the combination of alternatives II_A + I_B, if:

(1) additional investment in alternative II_A will be more effective than the norm of effectiveness of long-term investment;

(2) additional investment in alternative II_B will be less effective than the same norm.

As can be seen from Table 34, the effectiveness of additional investment in alternative II_A is equal to 10% per year, and that of additional investment in alternative II_B is equal to 12% per year. This means that in selecting the combination of alternatives II_A and II_B with the aid of norms of effectiveness it is necessary that the norm of effectiveness of long-term investment be less than 10% but more than 12% per year. Such a norm is obviously impossible.

True, we can escape from this difficulty by establishing such a low norm of effectiveness of short-term investment that alternative I_B proves to be more effective than alternative II_B even in the case of evaluating the effectiveness of long-term investment on the basis of a norm smaller than 10%. Thus, if we accept a norm of investment effectiveness for long-term investment of 9%, and a norm of effectiveness for short-term investment of less than 6%, the combination of alternatives II_A and I_B will be the best one. In fact, under these conditions the most effective one for project A will obviously be alternative II_A. We must apply two norms of effectiveness for project B, one for alternative I_B — we accept it as equal to 5% — and the other for alternative II_B at 9%. By subtracting the sum of production costs from the product of investment and the norm of its effectiveness, we obtain:

for alternative I_B: $\quad$ $117 + 100 \cdot 0.05 = 122$ million rubles;

for alternative II_B: $\quad$ $105 + 200 \cdot 0.09 = 123$ million rubles.

The smaller of these two sums occurs for alternative I_B. In this way it follows that with norms of effectiveness equal to 9% per year for long-term investment and to 5% per year for short-term investment our problem is solved. This solution is valid only for

202

the two projects in our example, not for the entire national economy. According to the conditions of our example, the existing norm of effectiveness of investment is equal to 11%. Consequently, if instead we establish norms (9% and 5%) for all projects, the balance of investment and accumulation will not work out. The investment requirements will be larger than accumulation.

Thus, taking future norms of investment effectiveness into account limits the role of the single present norm of investment effectiveness, because in certain cases alternatives must be selected not in conformity with, but in spite of, this norm. However, this limitation on the single norm of effectiveness must be accomplished not by replacing it by several different norms of investment effectiveness, but by introducing corrections in the balance of investment and accumulation that is compiled on the basis of the single present norm.

The procedure for introducing these corrections is as follows:

1. We construct the optimal balance of accumulation and investment according to rules presented in Chapters 4 and 5. In this way the norm of investment effectiveness will be determined. We will call it the "present" norm as opposed to the "future" one.

2. We develop the perspectives for changes in the norm of investment effectiveness. We generalize these perspectives in the future norm of effectiveness.

3. We separate two groups of alternatives from those project alternatives that did not enter into the balance of investment and accumulation.

The first group consists of alternatives with short periods of capital turnover and with greater effectiveness of investment than the present norm (in our example, alternative I_B).

The second group consists of alternatives with long periods of capital turnover and with an effectiveness of investment intermediate between the present and future norms (in our example, alternative II_A).

4. We introduce the following corrections in the balance of investment and accumulation compiled according to point 1:

(a) we replace part of the accepted alternatives with long useful lives by alternatives of the first group for the same projects (so that final output does not change); as a result, the total sum of investment in the balance will be reduced (in our example we replace alternative II_B by alternative I_B);

(b) we replace another part of the accepted alternatives (with long useful lives) by alternatives of the second group for the same projects (so that final output does not change); this replacement must increase investment in the balance (in our example we replace alternative I_A by alternative II_A).

5. The indicated corrections of the balance of investment and accumulation must satisfy the following conditions:

(a) the sum total of investment after all rearrangements of alternatives must remain at the previous level, i.e., equal to planned accumulation;

(b) losses from rearrangements during the operation of the present norm of investment effectiveness must be less than the increase in the effect of investment during the remaining life of fixed capital of alternatives of the second group.

Let us give the last condition a mathematical form.

We introduce the following notation. The effectiveness of investment in the alternative that is replaced by an alternative of the first group is r_0; the effectiveness of investment in the alternative of the second group is r_2; the "present" norm of investment effectiveness is r_H; the "future" norm of investment effectiveness is r_6; the useful life of the alternative of the first group is τ_1; the useful life of the alternative of the second group is τ_2; and the remaining period of operation of the "present" norm of investment effectiveness is t.

A rearrangement of investment from the alternative with effectiveness equal to r_0 (this alternative is replaced by the alternative of the first group with smaller investment) to the alternative of the second group will cause losses equal to $K(r_0 - r_2)$ rubles per year, where K is the sum of investment that undergoes rearrangement. During the entire useful life of the alternatives of the second group these losses will amount to

$$K\tau_2 (r_0 - r_2) \text{ rubles.} \tag{6.19}$$

This replacement of alternatives has its advantageous aspect. Alternatives of the first group will be replaced in τ_1 years by alternatives with an effectiveness equal to r_0 (i.e., by those alternatives that previously yielded their places in the balance of investment to alternatives of the first group). This new replacement will increase investment by K. The effectiveness of investment K is higher than the new ("future") norm of investment effectiveness, i.e., $r_0 > r_6$.

Consequently, the replacement of alternatives will yield an increase in the annual effect of investment K equal to $K (r_0 - r\ )$.

In the period from $(\tau_1 + 1)$ years to τ_2 years inclusively this increase in the effect of investment will amount to

$$K(\tau_2 - \tau_1)(r_0 - r_6). \tag{6.20}$$

By comparing the increase in the effect of investment (6.20) with the losses (6.19) we find the conditions under which the replacement of alternatives in the balance of investment increases the total effect of investment during time τ_2:

$$K(\tau_2 - \tau_1)(r_0 - r_6) > K\tau_2(r_0 - r_2). \tag{6.21}$$

This gives the following inequalities:

$$(\tau_2 - \tau_1)(r_0 - r_6) > \tau_2(r_0 - r_2); \tag{6.22}$$

$$(\tau_2 - \tau_1)(r_2 - r_6) > \tau_1(r_0 - r_2); \tag{6.23}$$

$$\frac{r_2 - r_6}{r_0 - r_6} > \frac{\tau_1}{\tau_2}. \tag{6.24}$$

Inequality (6.23) reproduces the procedure explained above for calculating savings and losses from the rearrangement of alternatives in our arithmetical example. Inequality (6.24) most simply expresses the conditions of effectiveness of the rearrangement of alternatives.

However, all these inequalities are not completely accurate. They are based on the assumption that a ruble of loss in the immediate future is equal to a ruble of loss in the more distant future. This is wrong. Indeed, in our example we will replace the immediate loss by a loss in the distant future of an equal amount. Then it will appear possible, without limiting consumption and without increasing costs, to increase immediate investment by the corresponding sum of rubles. During the period for which the loss was postponed this sum of investment will permit us to obtain certain savings in production costs of output, savings that would not have been obtained if the immediate loss had not been postponed to the future.

On the other hand, the increase in the effect of investment resulting from the replacement of alternatives also can be invested in production. While losses are aggravated by the lost effect from their possible investment, the growth of the effect is increased due to the possible effect from its investment in production. As a result of this refinement, inequality (6.24) will be replaced by a much more complex inequality [14]:

205

$$\frac{r_2-r_6}{r_0-r_2} > \frac{(1+r_6)^{\tau_2-\tau_1}\left\{\dfrac{r_6}{r_H}[(1+r_H)^t-1] + (1+r_H)^{t-1}(1+r_6)\left[(1+r_6)^{\tau_1-t}-1\right]\right\}}{(1+r_6)^{\tau_2-\tau_1}-1}. \quad (6.25)$$

This inequality draws the lower limit r_2 closer to r_0 to a greater extent than did inequality (6.24).

For example, if $r_0 = 0.1$ $(=r_H), r_6 = 0.05, t = \tau_1 = 10$ years, and $\tau_2 = 30$ years, it follows from inequality (6.24) that $r_2 > 0.067$, and it follows from inequality (6.25) that $r_2 > 0.078$.

Of course, we know in our project practice that in planning long-term investment we must take account of conditions not only in the immediate future but also in the more distant future. Accordingly, the effectiveness of long-term and short-term investment is determined in our project practice by proceeding from different recoupment period for investment.

In this way the variety of norms of investment effectiveness applicable in practice reflects not just the absence of obligatory norms in this matter. There is a rationale to this variety. The applicable norms of investment effectiveness in general will conform to their turnover periods. Such a principle obviously rests on the concept that along with the growth of accumulation the norm of effectiveness will be reduced, since possibilities for effective investment will be used more broadly and completely.

However, the actual differences between the normative periods of recoupment for long-term and short-term investments are apparently too great. Inequalities (6.24) and (6.25) justify comparatively modest differences between indicators of the effectiveness of long-term and short-term investments. For example, if $r_2 = 0.04, r_0 = 0.3$, and $\tau_1 / \tau_2 = 0.1$, then r_6 must be no larger than 0.01. Such a low norm of investment effectiveness is hardly possible with intensive technological progress and high rates of growth of labor productivity. Accordingly, a considerable difference between the effectiveness of long-term and short-term investments (for example, $0.04 - 0.3$) is not justified if we take account only of the quantitative aspect of the question.

9. The Law of Economy of Labor and the Time Factor

Formula $E_{min} = \beta_{max}$ reveals a very important connection between the calculation of the time factor and the law of economy of labor. It demonstrates that the calculation of the time factor is directed in the final analysis at maximizing the growth rate of labor productivity. In other words, the calculation of the time factor in economics is dictated by the law of economy of labor as the law of economic development. It would be incorrect to interpret the law of economy of labor only as the law of minimum outlays on a product. The static aspect of this law is useful in solving particular planning problems, but it is insufficient either for understanding the most important problems of economic dynamics or for long-term planning. Furthermore, the law of economy of labor can hardly be understood even as the law of minimum synchronous outlays of labor on a product for a sufficiently long period. Formula (6.5) refers to a high and stable maximum growth rate of labor productivity. This maximum obviously is an objectively existing force, breaking through a multitude of obstacles of specific historical circumstances. Its operation under the conditions of socialism is almost obvious. Under capitalist conditions its operation is hindered by the planless nature of the economy and by the huge waste of energy and resources. But the principle of maximum profit is nothing other than a particular economic aspect of the maximum growth rate. Thus even under capitalism the law of economy of labor functions as a law of dynamics and not of statics. Finally, the entire historical process of replacement of economic systems represents a series of transitions from systems with lower rates to systems with higher rates of growth of labor productivity.

Maximizing the growth rate rather than the level of labor productivity is the objective principle for calculating the time factor. It is interesting that this principle can sometimes contradict the principle of minimum synchronous labor costs. For example, providing the national economy with new technology that, with a previous maximum growth rate (β_c) lowers synchronous labor costs of creating the consumption fund, permits an increase in growth rates so that synchronous labor costs per unit of output will temporarily become higher than with the old technology. This is precisely the conclusion that can follow from the principle of the optimum expressed in formula (6.5).

Indeed, let us introduce, in the notation used earlier, sychronous outlays of labor on the creation of a consumption fund with the old technology:

$$C_c + K_c \beta_c = C_c + K_c r_c,$$

and synchronous outlays of labor on the same product with new technology as:

$$C_{\text{н}} + K_{\text{н}}\beta_{\text{н}}.$$

According to (6.4) β_H, the new growth rate, must be equal to the new norm of investment effectiveness r_H. Thus $\beta_H > \beta_c$ and this means that $r_H > r_c$.

Suppose

$$r_{\text{н}} = E_{\text{н/c}} = \frac{C_{\text{c}} - C_{\text{н}}}{K_{\text{н}} - K_{\text{c}}}.$$

This means that

$$\beta_{\text{н}} = \frac{C_{\text{c}} - C_{\text{н}}}{K_{\text{н}} - K_{\text{c}}}.$$

Then the condition that synchronous labor costs with old technology will be higher than with the new technology and the new growth rate is expressed by the inequality

$$C_{\text{c}} + K_{\text{c}}\beta_{\text{c}} > C_{\text{н}} + K_{\text{н}} \frac{C_{\text{c}} - C_{\text{н}}}{K_{\text{н}} - K_{\text{c}}}. \tag{6.26}$$

Hence

$$\beta_{\text{c}} > \frac{C_{\text{c}} - C_{\text{н}}}{K_{\text{н}} - K_{\text{c}}}.$$

Since $\beta_c = r_c$ (according to formula (6.4), $r_c > (C_c - C_H) / (K_H - K_c)$ or $r_c > r_H$, which contradicts the initial inequality $r_c < r_H$. The contradiction refutes inequality (6.26). In words, this means that the new maximum growth rate can be so much higher than the previous one (with old technology) that synchronous outlays of labor on the same output can be temporarily higher than with old technology.

This temporary threshold will be overcome by virtue of the same factor that caused it, namely, the higher growth rate, as a result of which C_H will be reduced more rapidly than C_c.

10. The Technique of Reckoning the Time Factor in Project Calculations

From what has been said it follows that calculating the time factor in a socialist economy involves the determination of the degree of correspondence of given costs and benefits to the optimum development of the national economy, i.e., to the maximum growth rate of labor productivity. This means that the norms necessary for this calculation must arise from the optimum plan of development of the socialist economy for a sufficiently long period. Formulating such a plan is the most difficult part of

208

all the work that must be fulfilled in order to calculate the time factor. The technique of this calculation in project calculations is comparatively simple. It arises from the rule of identity, namely, that we can compare only synchronous costs and results. Accordingly, all costs incurred at different times and results obtained at different times must be adjusted to a single time, either to a single period or to a single moment of time. Adjustment to a single period of time answers the question as to how much synchronous labor costs will increase for the national economy's final product in consequence of the production of the given product. The formula for this adjustment is $C_i + K_i E$, where E is the norm of investment effectiveness.[15]

Adjustment to a single moment of time answers the question concerning the amount of labor that must be expended in a given year in order to obtain as much output as can be produced during the entire time of operation of the given project. The simplest formula for this adjustment is $K_i + (C_i/E)$.

Both formulas are recommended in the *Standard Procedure* of the Academy of Sciences of the USSR, with the difference from those presented above being that instead of a single norm E for the entire national economy it is proposed to use branch norms of the effectiveness of investment.

Both formulas do not take into account either construction periods or changes in costs C_i in different years of operation. In particular, no account is taken of the possibility of cessation of operation as a result, for example, of exhaustion of natural sources of raw materials. In essence, both formulas assume an unlimited (infinite) time horizon. Accordingly, calculation according to any of these formulas leads to the same result. However, the possibilities for improving each of these formulas are different. Increments of synchronous outlays of labor on the national economy's annual output (according to formula $C_i + K_i E$) can be calculated only on the assumption that costs C_i remain constant. But formula $K_i + (C_i/E)$ can be extended to cases in which C_i and K_i change over time. Indeed, this formula contains, as a matter of fact, the sum of operating costs for an infinite number of years with consideration of the time factor. This means that costs in year t are adjusted to the outlay of labor in the first year of operation that, in being used for expanding production, would yield the same product as outlay C_i in the year t. By assuming that the effect of investment equal to C_i in the first year will be used again and again for expanding production during t years we obtain the result that in year t the product of outlays C_i in the first year will be equal to the product from outlays $C_i (1 + E)^t$ in the year t. Hence outlays C_i in the year t are equivalent (in their product) to outlays $C_i/(1 + E)^t$ in the first year.

If we add the value C_i for an unlimited number of years, with due regard for the time factor (using compound interest), we will obtain

$$\sum_{t=1}^{\infty} \frac{C_t}{(1+E)^t} = C_t \sum_{t=1}^{\infty} \frac{1}{(1+E)^t} = \frac{C_t}{E}. \qquad (6.27)$$

This formula can be written in a more general form, replacing the infinite period of operation by a limited one (T) and assuming that operating costs depend on time C_i (t). Applying the same method to the calculation of construction periods, we divide capital investment into parts according to the time at which they are expended $K_i(t)$. Then we obtain a more general formula for all synchronized costs [16]:

$$\sum_{t=1}^{T} \frac{K_i(t)}{(1+E)^t} + \sum_{t=1}^{T} \frac{C_i(t)}{(1+E)^t} = \min. \qquad (6.28)$$

Further generalization of this formula is possible by taking account of changes in the norm of effectiveness. To do so we must substitute $E(t)$ for E in formula (6.28). It is true that it is difficult to determine the values of $E(t)$. Nevertheless, in time such a refinement of plan calculations will obviously become not only possible but even necessary.

11. Final Considerations

The norm of investment effectiveness is the most controversial and the most puzzling of the plan indicators. This is natural. It is the indicator that regulates the conformity of plan and project decisions to the long-term (dynamic) optimum, and there is much that is still unclear in this optimum. Even the conditions of existence of this optimum are unclear. Difficult problems arise in connection with the infinite nature of time and the limited nature of foresight. Nevertheless, we will try, by using the considerations presented above, to provide answers to the questions posed at the beginning of this chapter.

The norm of investment effectiveness differs from differential rent in that rent is a norm for taking account only of feedback costs, whereas the norm of investment effectiveness is, in addition, a norm of outlays of surplus labor for accumulation. This is apparent from the simple formula for the optimal value of this norm, namely, $E_{min} = \beta_{max}$. The left half of this formula characterizes this norm as a norm of feedback costs, and the right half as a norm of accumulation (the rate of growth of productive capital). Consequently, the norm of investment effectiveness not only is a means of minimizing actual costs of production but, in addition, is a norm of real costs. However, the outlays of labor that are reflected in this norm differ from the costs of production of an individual product. The costs of production are causally connected with the production of a product, and therefore are composed of asynchronous elements. The norm of investment effectiveness arises on the basis of the synchronous measurement of outlays of labor on the consumed product. The comparison of investment effectiveness in each individual case with the norm of effectiveness provides an answer to a twofold question: (a) does the given investment correspond to the overall maximum effect of all investment in the national economy; and (b) does the given investment correspond to the optimal ratio of accumulation to consumption? If the effectiveness of investment in the given large-scale project surpasses its norm by far, this means that we should revise the national economy's accumulation plan for the purpose of increasing it. In this way the norm of investment effectiveness is linked with the volume of accumulation not in a one-sided way (as was assumed in Chapters 4 and 5), but by a mutual connection.

Now we can illuminate the problem of uniformity of the norm of investment effectiveness. Accumulation is always embodied in specific means of production. By introducing these means into the model of the optimal plan we necessarily obtain a multitude of different limitations on resources, to which a multitude of different multipliers (Lagrange, Kantorovich) must correspond, i.e., a multitude of different norms of effectiveness.

Which one general limitation on resources reflects the single norm of investment effectiveness? The answer is the scarcity of the surplus labor that is associated with the length of the period of production and circulation. Since this surplus labor applies to the entire national economy and is drawn from a single source of manpower, the norm of effectiveness of labor for accumulation must be uniform. Complete shiftability exists only for future, not yet trained, manpower (students). Shiftability is somewhat limited for occupations requiring long preparation, and for different kinds of highly qualified labor it is almost impossible. That is why the possibilities of adapting production time and the structure of investment to a single norm in different lines of production are not identical. That is also why the actual effectiveness of productive capital in different branches can vary in different ways from the common norm of effectiveness of investment even in the optimal plan.

But it does not at all follow that norms of effectiveness of investment must be branch norms. The norm of investment effectiveness is a plan regulator (a controlling norm) acting over a long period, which is intended to influence the most important factors in the national economy's development (the division of labor into necessary and surplus labor, the technological structure of production, and the relationship between the amount of manpower and the number of job vacancies) by directing the national economy's development so as to sustain the highest growth rates. Accordingly, deviations of the actual effectiveness of capital from the overall norm of investment effectiveness indicate the direction of solution of the most important problems of long-term planning. Orientation toward branch norms of investment will reinforce errors in the distribution of investment among branches that arose in the course of nonoptimal planning.

Notes

1. Of course, not every change in production time is accompanied by changes in labor productivity. However, in these cases there is no problem of calculating the time factor.

2. K. Marx and F. Engels, *op.cit.*, Vol. 24, p. 354.

3. Let us check this conclusion. If the expression $\sum_{i=1}^{n} c_i t_i$ is equal to productive capital, then by dividing this expression by the value of produced output in a unit of time we will obtain its average production and circulation time, weighted according to labor costs. The value of output produced in a unit of time is equal to

$$\sum_{i=1}^{n} c_i.$$

$$\frac{\sum_{i=1}^{n} t_i c_i}{\sum_{i=1}^{n} c_i} = \bar{t} \left(\frac{\text{rubles}}{\text{rubles per year}} = \text{years} \right).$$

Before us is the average production and circulation time, weighted according to labor costs.

4. See *Ekonomicheskaia effektivnost' kapital'nykh vlozhenii i novoi tekhniki.* Moscow, Sotsekgiz Publishing House, 1959, p. 16.

We remark that by giving to indicator $\sum_{i=1}^{n} t_i c_i$ the scale of ruble-years (or man-years) we must relate it not to output in a unit of time, but to one-time output. In this sense the weighted production time is usually called linked time [*sviazyvaniem*]. The term "linking"[*sviazyvanie*] is borrowed from capitalist practice (linking — the release of monetary capital). It does not altogether successfully characterize the meaning of indicator $\sum_{i=1}^{n} c_i t_i$ Nevertheless, other names for this phenomenon ("immobilization" or "idleness" of costs, etc.) are still less successful.

Since it is not one-time production but the continuing reproduction of output that is usually being planned, the time factor is most often calculated on the basis of capital investment.

5. "Surplus labor generally, as labor beyond the extent of given requirements must always exist. But under the capitalist system, as under the slave-holding one, etc., it has only an antagonistic form, and is supplemented by the complete inactivity of a certain part of society" (K. Marx and F. Engels, *op. cit.*, Vol. 25, Part II, pp. 385-386).

6. *Ibid.*, p. 386.

7. Certain bourgeois economists include "abstinence" or "waiting" in the composition of real costs of production, together with labor costs. In so doing, it is assumed that both elements of costs — workers' labor and capitalists' "waiting" — must be paid for (see, for example, A. Marshall, *Principles of Economics*, 6th Edition, 1910, p. 389). We can construct a model which demonstrates that under conditions of a capitalist economy the restriction of consumption in the process of expanding production ("waiting") falls on workers, while capitalists receive payment (growth in profit) for this "waiting." Moreover, how we can add such dissimilar elements as labor and production time remains unclear in this theory.

8. See Z. F. Chukhanov, "The Time Factor and Economic Effectiveness of Socialist Production, *Voprosy ekonomiki*, 1960, No. 9, pp. 90 *et. seq.*

9. *KPSS v resoliutsiiakh i resheniiakh s'ezdov, konferentsii i Plenumov TsK*, 7th Edition, State Political Literature Publishing House, 1954, Part II, p. 454.

10. We substantiated formula (6.6) in the doctoral dissertation *Metody soizmereniia narodnokhoziaistvennoi effectivnosti planovykh i proektnykh variantov*, Part I, Leningrad, 1940, pp. 378 *et seq.*

11. See *Study Week — The Econometric Approach to Development Planning*, October 7-13, 1963, North Holland Publishing Company, Amsterdam, 1965.

12. a is determined from the equation

$$(1 - a)C_c + a\,C_{\text{н}} + (1 - a)\,(K_{\text{н}} - K_c)\gamma + K_{\text{н}}\beta_c = C_c + K_c\beta_c,$$

which expresses the fact that synchronous outlays of labor on consumed output (in the year in which the share of new technology in production capacity is equal to a) are equal to synchronous outlays of labor with old technology. Thus, the rate of growth of the national economy's production capacity remains equal to β_c. If $a = 0$, the left half of this equality is transformed into expression (6.10).

13. This norm must be revised as the planning perspective changes.

14. We omit its derivation.

15. In this section of the chapter we use the notation that was accepted in the *Standard Procedure for Determining the Economic Effectiveness of Capital Investment and New Technology in the National Economy of the USSR* of the Academy of Sciences of the USSR.

16. The first part of formula (6.28) has already received recognition. The influence of construction periods on costs is thus taken into account. Calculating the time factor in the reckoning of operating costs (the second part of the formula) is still disputed. The opponents of such calculation obviously ignore the fact that it corresponds both to logic and to practice, where in essence this calculation in the form of formula

$$K_t + \frac{C_t}{E}$$

is already being applied.

CHAPTER 7

NORMS OF EFFECTIVENESS AND THE USEFUL LIFE OF MEANS OF LABOR

The norm of investment effectiveness must be distinguished from norms of effectiveness of productive capital. The first is linked with the use of surplus labor, whereas norms of effectiveness of capital are linked with the utilization of specific means of production. Therefore, a multitude of norms of effectiveness of productive capital are counterposed to a single norm of investment effectiveness. Means and objects of labor do not have that universal substitutability that is characteristic of potential manpower. The substitutability of means of production is limited not only by the range of means similar in purpose, but also, within the limits of this range, by differences in effectiveness. Accordingly, norms of effectiveness of means and objects of labor must differ not only according to branches or enterprises but even according to individual kinds of means of production. Furthermore, they must change for each specific means of labor, depending on its physical deterioration and obsolescence. This diversity and variability of effectiveness of means of labor can be reflected in their valuation in such a way that payments for capital are calculated in terms of the same share of this appraised sum (for example, a share equal to the norm of investment effectiveness). Such a procedure does not free us from the necessity of determining the effectiveness of specific implements of labor in the course of assessing them.

With all their variety, norms of effectiveness of reproducible means of labor (in optimal planning) are enclosed within two boundaries. The upper boundary is the norm of investment effectiveness. The lower boundary is zero. The effectiveness of capital cannot exceed the norm of investment effectiveness, since an excess in its effectiveness must be removed either by differential rent (if this excess is caused by using better natural resources) or by expanding production of the corresponding means of labor (if this excess is caused by a shortage of new, highly effective means of labor). But the effectiveness of productive capital must not be lower than zero. With a negative effectiveness the use of means of production brings only losses. In this way the useful life of means of labor is determined economically by the period during which their use yields a nonnegative effect. How do we calculate the effectiveness of available means of labor?

1. The Fundamental Difference Between Calculations of the Effectiveness of Replacing Existing Means of Labor by New Ones and Calculations of the Comparative Effectiveness of New Means of Labor

In the reproduction of existing fixed capital the following questions must be decided:

(1) In what form do we reproduce existing means of labor?

(2) How do we determine the optimal time for replacing existing means of labor by new ones?

The second of these questions presumes the previous solution of the first. In fact, the solution of the second question consists of determining the effectiveness of replacing existing means of labor by the most effective of the new means of labor. Consequently, finding the most effective alternatives of new means of labor is a necessary condition for determining the limits of utilization of existing means of labor.

Calculations necessary to solve the latter question differ in an important particular way from calculations associated with the first question. Neither the value (investment) of existing implements nor the cost of renewing them enter into the costs of utilizing these implements, whereas both investment and its depreciation completely enter into the costs of alternatives of new capital.

Indeed, in plan calculations of effectiveness we always look for the minimum costs of reproduction, not the minimum costs of production, i.e., the minimum of future costs, not the minimum sum of future and past costs.[1]

215

But future costs consist of the following:

(1) In the use of new means of labor: (*a*) costs of producing these means; (*b*) costs of their operation, including depreciation.

(2) In the use of existing means of labor, costs consist only of operating expenditures, excluding expenditures for renovation, but including those for maintenance. In this way, the initial investment and outlays on its renovation are excluded from the cost of utilization of existing means of labor.

This special feature of calculating the effectiveness of the replacement of existing means of labor by new ones is usually ignored. But it has considerable importance in determining the optimal time of replacement and in determining payments for capital. Neglect of this special feature leads to understanding the effectiveness of use of old implements, prompting their premature replacement by new ones.

2. Factors Reducing the Effectiveness of Existing Means of Labor

Means of labor can be used for an indefinitely long period providing they are appropriately maintained. This fact has been known from time immemorial. Plutarch relates that the ship on which Theseus left on the legendary voyage and safely returned was preserved by the Athenians for centuries. They removed old boards and beams as these decayed and put other strong ones in their place.

With the development of machine production the technical possibility of a long-lasting life for means of labor became a usual occurrence. A machine consists of a multitude of parts that have different periods of wear and tear. Accordingly, it is technically possible by replacing each worn-out part in time by a new one to extend indefinitely the machine's useful life.

In actuality the useful lives of machines are not long. Furthermore, they have become shorter than previously. Machines no longer outlive the periods of wear and tear of their most long-lasting parts. The limits to their lives are now posed not by technology, but by economics.

A worsening of the indicators of effectiveness of use of means of labor, such as a reduction of labor productivity, an increase in the consumption of raw materials, fuel, and electric power, an increase of outlays on maintenance, etc., are the economic consequence of wear and tear.

When this process of wearing out occurs in the absence of

216

technological progress in the designing and production of implements for the same purpose, the relative effectiveness of use of old implements for the given purpose is reduced, whereas the effectiveness of new implements remains unchanged. The limit of effectiveness of use of old implements is approached in this case only by virtue of the economic consequences of physical deterioration. If deterioration occurs while there is a growth in the effectiveness of new means of labor, the useful life of old implements is still further reduced in comparison with the economic limit of physical deterioration.

3. Fundamental Equalities Determining the Limits of Wear and Tear

How do we find the economically optimal moment for replacing old means of labor by new ones? We must calculate and compare the costs of reproducing the given output with old means of labor and with new, more effective means.

For simplicity of explanation we will assume that the old and new means of labor produce the same output and that differential rent is absent. We will first find the most effective new means of labor with respect to minimum differential costs (or, in monetary terms, with respect to minimum full production costs of output):

$$C_{\text{н}} + K_{\text{н}} r_{\text{к}} = \min,$$

where C_{H} is the production cost of output with a new, more effective means of labor, K_{H} is capital investment in new means of labor, and r_{K} is the norm of investment effectiveness.

We will denote the production costs of the same output (without outlays on renovation) when it is produced with old means of labor by e_{c}. Then the condition of effectiveness of use of old equipment will be expressed by inequality

$$e_{\text{c}} \leqslant \min \left(C_{\text{н}} + K_{\text{н}} r_{\text{к}} \right). \tag{7.1}$$

The optimal moment for replacing an old means of labor by a new one comes when this inequality is transformed into the equality [2]

$$e_c = \min \left(C_{\text{н}} + K_{\text{н}} r_{\text{к}} \right). \tag{7.2}$$

For calculating production costs with new implements we must determine the useful life of new means of labor. How do we do this?

In calculating production costs with new implements we must proceed from a useful life for these implements such that the average production costs of output over the entire life will be the lowest.

Increasing the useful life of a means of labor influences the production costs of output in two ways:

(1) it reduces depreciation per unit of output;

(2) it increases other operating costs, apart from depreciation.

Hence it is not difficult to conclude that too short and too long useful lives increase the production costs of output. Too short ones do so because higher charges for depreciation exceed savings on other outlays, and too long ones do so because higher charges for other expenses, apart from depreciation, exceed savings on depreciation.

It is clear that there exists a useful life of means of labor for which the average production costs of output over the entire life are lowest.

Different kinds of means of labor wear out in different ways. Accordingly, the growth of operating costs caused by the wearing out of means of labor is expressed by different curves. But no matter how different these curves are, a general condition exists for finding the optimal useful life of means of labor. This condition is the equality of marginal operating costs (excluding depreciation) relating to a unit of output at the end of the useful life of old means of labor to the average production costs of the same output with new implements, taken over the entire period of their life.

Let us examine the conditions for the optimal period of wear and tear, at first without considering technological change. (Later we will take into account the role of technological progress.)

4. Finding the Optimal Useful Life of
Means of Labor Without Consideration
of Technological Changes

We assume that during the period of wear and tear of a given means of labor neither the production costs of producing the given means with new implements nor the value of new implements for the same purpose changes.

We also ignore the possibility of several successive applications of means of labor. We confine ourselves thus far to cases in which the means of labor generally loses its use value after the completion of its useful life for one purpose.

Let us assume that with a certain useful life the average production costs are higher than operating costs, excluding depreciation, applicable per unit of output producible at the end of the useful life of the means of labor. Then, having lengthened the useful life, we can reduce the average production costs of output. For the lengthening of the useful life adds only expenses other than depreciation. According to our assumption these expenses are less than the average of production costs.

Lengthening the useful life of means of labor will reduce average production costs only as long as the magnitude of operating expenses other than depreciation does not attain the level of average production costs. Beyond this point each additional unit of output will require larger expenditures than those each unit cost before this increase in the useful life of means of labor. Consequently, the average production costs of a unit of output over the entire life will increase.

To sum up, the minimum average production costs can be neither higher nor lower than the maximum allowable production costs without depreciation, i.e., these quantities must be equal. This reasoning can be elaborated as follows.

We will denote outlays on means of labor by K, the quantity of output producible with the aid of these means of labor during their life by x, and the operating costs, apart from depreciation, applicable to the last unit of output by $f(x)$.

Then the entire sum of operating costs for producing x units of output during the life of a means of labor will be expressed as follows:

$$\int_0^x f(x)\, dx.$$

Hence the average production costs of output during the entire life of the means of labor will amount to

$$\overline{C} = \frac{\int_0^x f(x)\, dx}{x} + \frac{K}{x}. \tag{7.3}$$

219

Let us find the conditions for the minimum of these production costs.

Differentiating expression (1) with respect to x and setting the first derivative equal to zero, we have:

$$\frac{f(x)}{x} - \frac{\int_0^x f(x)\, dx}{x^2} - \frac{K}{x^2} = 0,$$

from which

$$f(x) = \frac{\int_0^x f(x)\, dx}{x} + \frac{K}{x}. \tag{7.4}$$

The left half of equality (7.4) represents operating expenses (apart from depreciation) occurring for the last unit of output, and the right half of the equality expresses the average enterprise cost of producing output.

5. The Rule of a Machine's Useful Life as a Multiple of the Periods of Wear and Tear of Its Parts

The conclusion presented above is based on the condition that the form of the curve of operating costs does not depend on the useful life, i.e., it does not depend on the point of this curve at which we replace the machine with a new one. In reality, the form of this curve changes depending on the point at which we interrupt the "life" of the means of labor. This relationship is explained by two factors.

(1) The nature and periodicity of maintenance depends on the desired useful life of the means of labor, namely, on whether we have in mind using the means of labor for a short period or, on the contrary, extending its use for a long time.

(2) For a given kind and periodicity of maintenance the useful life of a means of labor influences the sum of outlays not yet used for maintenance.

These factors complicate the problem of finding the optimal useful life. Instead of one curve we must deal with several curves and solve the question by means of comparing the production costs of output for different useful lives.

By means of such a comparison we find the useful life for which the average (over the entire period) production costs of output will be lowest. In doing so it would be incorrect to make calculations of future useful lives of machines on the basis of given maintenance practices without adjusting this basis. Optimal useful lives of parts of means of labor are the basis for calculating useful lives of machines. The nature and periodicity of maintenance must be calculated not only for systematically supporting complete operating serviceability of the machine but also by proceeding from the problem of attaining minimum outlays on output.

We will investigate the influence of the multiple of the useful lives of different parts on the optimal useful life of a machine. In so doing we will make the following assumptions at the start:

(a) Operating costs (per unit of output) increase in connection with wear and tear only due to an increase in maintenance, in the absence of a worsening of the quality of the means of labor and with other operating expenses remaining unchanged, apart from maintenance and depreciation.

(b) The cost of repair reproduction of parts of means of labor is equal to the cost of their reproduction in the manufacture of the means of labor.

The useful life of means of labor influences the cost of still unused outlays on maintenance. Suppose that the machine consists of parts with useful lives of 1, 2, 3, 4, and 5 years. Then at the end of the 5th year of its life the most durable group of parts will wear out. However, parts with periods of wear and tear of 2, 3, and 4 years that were replaced in the course of maintenance will not yet be completely worn out. Thus, parts with a period of wear and tear of 4 years will be only ¼ worn out, parts with a period of wear and tear of 3 years will be ⅔ worn out, and parts with a period of wear and tear of 2 years will be ½ worn out.

If we limit ourselves to a 5-year useful life of such a machine, the value of the parts that are not worn out must be added to the operating cost of preceding years. The sum of operating costs together with depreciation costs will considerably exceed their possible minimum. The complete wearing out of all parts coincides only with a useful life that is the common general multiple of the period of wear and tear of all groups of parts. Accordingly, the sum of average annual outlays on maintenance and depreciation of means of labor reaches a minimum with a useful life of the machine that is a multiple of the periods of wear and tear of all of its parts. We will call this proposition, for short, "the multiple rule."

Let us clarify what has been said by a simplified example. We will assume that outlays on repair (or replacement) of parts amount to (in rubles):

Parts with a period of wear and tear of 1 year   1
Parts with a period of wear and tear of 2 years   2
Parts with a period of wear and tear of 3 years   3
Parts with a period of wear and tear of 4 years   4
Parts with a period of wear and tear of 5 years   5

Let us assume that the machine consists of five parts (with a single part of each kind) and that its renewal cost amounts to 15 rubles (i.e., 1 + 2 + 3 + 4 + 5).

Then we can trace from Table 35 all the values of absolute and average outlays on maintenance, depreciation, and their sums.

Table 35

The Dynamics of Average Annual Outlays on Maintenance and Depreciation

Useful life, in years	Outlays on maintenance					Average annual outlays on depreciation, with limitation of the useful life to the given period	Total (groups 6 and 7), with limitation of the useful life of the given period
	Current year outlays	From the beginning of the useful life	Expenditure applicable to the given year, with prolongation of the useful life	Remainder at the end of the year of expenditures of future years	Average annual expenditures for the entire period, including expenditures of future years (groups 3 and 1)		
1	2	3	4	5	6	7	8
1	0	0	0	0	0	15.0	15.0
2	1	1	1	0	0.5	7.50	8.0
3	3	4	2	1	1.33	5.00	6.33
4	4	8	3	2	2.00	3.75	5.75
5	7	15	4	5	3.00	3.00	6.00
6	6	21	5	6	3.50	2.50	6.00
7	6	27	5	7	3.85	2.15	6.00
8	1	28	5	3	3.37	1.88	5.25
9	7	35	5	5	3.89	1.67	5.56
10	4	39	5	4	3.90	1.50	5.40
11	8	47	5	7	4.27	1,36	5.63
12	1	48	5	3	4.00	1.25	5.25
13	10	58	5	8	4.46	1.15	5.61
14	1	59	5	4	4.21	1.07	5.28
15	3	62	5	2	4.13	1.00	5.13
16	9	71	5	6	4.43	0.94	5.37
17	7	78	5	8	4,60	0.88	5.48
18	1	79	5	4	4.39	0.83	5.22
19	6	85	5	5	4.47	0.79	5.26
20	1	86	5	1	4.30	0.75	5.05
21	12	98	5	8	4.67	0.71	5.38
22	4	102	5	7	4.63	0.68	5.31

Table 35 (Continued)

Useful life, in years	Current year outlays	Outlays on maintenance			Average annual expenditures for the entire period, including expenditures of future years (groups 3 and 1)	Average annual outlays on depreciation, with limitation of the useful life to the given period	Total (groups 6 and 7), with limitation of the useful life of the given period
		From the beginning of the useful life	Expenditure applicable to the given year, with prolongation of the useful life	Remainder at the end of the year of expenditures of future years			
1	2	3	4	5	6	7	8
23	3	105	5	5	4.57	0.65	5.22
24	1	106	5	1	4.42	0.625	5.045
25	10	116	5	6	4.64	0.600	5.24
26	6	122	5	7	4.52	0.58	5.10
27	3	125	5	5	4.63	0.56	5.19
28	4	129	5	4	4.61	0.54	5.15
29	7	136	5	6	4.68	0.52	5.20
30	1	137	5	2	4.57	0.50	5.07
31	11	148	5	8	4.77	0.48	5.25
32	1	149	5	4	4.67	0.47	5.14
33	7	156	5	6	4.73	0.46	5.19
34	4	160	5	5	4.70	0.44	5.14
35	3	163	5	3	4.66	0.43	5.09
36	6	169	5	4	4.70	0.42	5.12
37	10	179	5	9	4.83	0.41	5.24
38	1	180	5	5	4.73	0.40	5.14
39	3	183	5	3	4.70	0.39	5.09
40	4	187	5	2	4.67	0.375	5.045
41	12	199	5	9	4.86	0.365	5.225
42	1	200	5	5	4.76	0.357	5.117
43	6	206	5	6	4.80	0.349	5.149
44	1	207	5	2	4.70	0.341	5.041
45	7	214	5	4	4.75	0.333	5.083
46	9	223	5	8	4.84	0.326	5.166
47	3	226	5	6	4.81	0.319	5.130
48	1	227	5	2	4.73	0.312	5.042
49	10	237	5	7	4.84	0.306	5.146
50	1	238	5	3	4.77	0.300	5.070
51	8	246	5	6	4.82	0.294	5.114
52	4	250	5	5	4.81	0.288	5.099
53	7	257	5	7	4.84	0.283	5.087
54	1	258	5	3	4.78	0.278	5.058
55	6	264	5	4	4.80	0.273	5.073
56	6	270	5	5	4.82	0.268	5.088
57	7	277	5	7	4.86	0.263	5.123
58	4	281	5	6	4.84	0.258	5.098
59	3	284	5	4	4.81	0.254	5.064
60	1	285	5	0	4.75	0.250	5.000
61	15	300	5	10	4.92	0.246	5.166
62	1	301	5	6	4.87	0.242	5.112

As Table 35 shows, attaining minimum annual outlays requires a considerably longer useful life of the machine than the period of wear and tear of the most durable parts. The optimal useful life in this example, equal to the smallest multiple of the useful life of all parts, which is 60 years $(3 \times 4 \times 5)$, is 12 times larger than the period of wear and tear of the long-lasting parts.

It is clear that the more complex the machine and the larger the number of major parts with different useful lives included in it, the larger must be the least common multiple of these terms. This means that the useful life of the machine for which outlays on maintenance of means of labor are most completely used must be all the longer. However, excessively long useful lives of machines are inadvisable because of the technical obsolescence of means of labor.

Accordingly, we can limit ourselves to periods for which surplus payments for maintenance will be sufficiently small. Such periods must be ones that are multiples of the useful lives of the most expensive parts. In our example average outlays on maintenance and depreciation have already dropped by the 20th year to 5.05 rubles, which exceeds the lowest magnitude by only 1%. The 20-year period is equal to the multiple of the useful life of four of the five parts, including the most expensive ones with useful lives of 4 or 5 years. With a 24-year period, costs decline to 5.045 rubles. This decline is connected with the fact that the given period is also a multiple of four parts, with underutilization of the fifth part only during one year. We may note that even a 15-year period (a multiple of three parts, with a slight underutilization of two parts) also ensures a comparatively small (2.6%) deviation from the minimum possible outlays. Hence it is clear that the minimum of production costs of output is attained when the useful life of a machine is equal to the lowest multiple of the useful lives of all parts or (approximately) of the most expensive of the parts.

Thus, in our example the general rate of depreciation (with consideration of maintenance costs) will amount, for a 60-year period, to 33.3%; for a 20-year period, to 33.7%; for a 24-year period, to 33.6%; and for a 15-year period, to 34.2%.

The question arises as to whether "the multiple rule" eliminates the equality of the average (over the entire period) production costs of output to the highest operating costs (excluding depreciation) at the end of the useful life.

It is apparent from Table 35 that each year's maximum outlays on maintenance amount to 5 rubles, which is equal to the lowest average production costs (with a useful life equal to the lowest multiple of the useful life of all parts). Thus, the multiple rule does not abolish the fundamental property of the optimal useful life. The optimal useful life is always determined by the time at which average production costs and operating costs (excluding depreciation) are equalized. The multiple rule makes specific only the conditions under which this equality is approached. According to the multiple rule this equality is approached with a useful life of the machine equal to the least common multiple of the periods of wear and tear of all of its parts.

6. The Optimal Useful Life and the Wear and Tear of Means of Labor as a First Approximation

From what has been said above it follows that, in the absence of technological progress, the optimal useful life is that period of service of the machine at the end of which all parts, both those originally installed and those installed during repairs, are completely worn out in the machine.

(a) With the period of wear and tear of the most long-lasting part as a multiple of the periods of wear and tear of all other parts, the optimal useful life is equal to the period of wear and tear of the most long-lasting part.

(b) In the absence of this condition the optimal useful life is equal to the least common multiple of the useful lives of all parts.

However, the optimal period does not always have such a technical meaning. It does have this meaning only under our initial assumptions, i.e., in the absence of technological progress and with the equality of repair reproduction costs of parts to the costs of reproducing them in machine-building plants. But if the cost of the repair reproduction of parts is higher than their cost in the manufacture of means of labor as a whole, the optimal useful life of the machine is less than the lowest multiple of the periods of wear and tear of all parts and can be less than the period of wear and tear of the most long-lasting parts.

We can see this by means of the following reasoning. Suppose that a means of labor consists of four groups of parts with periods of wear and tear of 1, 2, 4, and 8 years. Here the period of wear and tear of the most long-lasting part is a multiple of the useful lives of other parts.

Let us assume that the value of parts amounts to (in rubles):

Part No. 1 with a period of wear and tear of 1 year
Part No. 2 with a period of wear and tear of 2 years
Part No. 3 with a period of wear and tear of 3 years
Part No. 4 with a period of wear and tear of 4 years
The value of the means of labor   15

If the replacement of parts during repair costs as much, the curve of operating costs will be expressed by the staggered line AB in Fig. 1. In this case the optimal useful life, as is apparent from the graph, coincides with the period of wear and tear of the most long-lasting part.

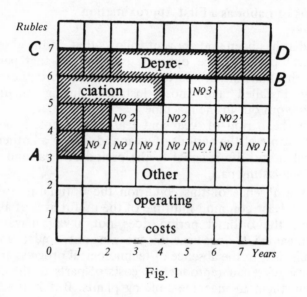

Fig. 1

But let us assume that replacing parts during repair of the machine costs three times as much as producing them in a machine-building plant in the course of manufacturing the same machine. Then the curve of operating costs will be expressed by line AB in Fig. 2. To find the optimal useful life of the machine under these conditions we must draw a straight line $C_1 D_1$ parallel to the abscissa, so that the area $AC_1 D_1$ represents 15 rubles.

226

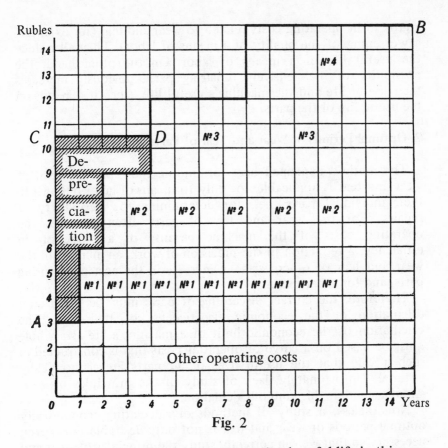

Fig. 2

As we can see from the graph, the optimal useful life in this case will be equal to 4 years, which is one-half of the period of wear and tear of the most long-lasting parts.

In this case replacing parts with useful lives of 1 and 2 years causes surplus payments smaller than savings in depreciation which result from lengthening the useful life to 4 years. But the surplus payments for replacing parts with periods of wear and tear of 4 years exceed savings in depreciation that result from increasing the useful life of the machine to 8 years. Accordingly, to attain the lowest production costs of output with the given machine we must replace it by a new one after 4 years of service, although the parts with an 8-year useful life will thus not yet be completely worn out.

Here we have examined the influence of the high costs of repairs on the optimal useful life of a means of labor. It is clear that a similar influence is exerted on this life by all other causes of

227

a growth in operating costs related to wear and tear (for example, a worsening of the quality of a means of labor). They all reduce the useful life of a means of labor. On the other hand, the possibility of inexpensively repairing parts obviously increases their useful life and the machine's useful life, since it depends on the useful life of the parts.

7. Optimal Periods of Wear and Tear of Parts and Assemblies

The method explained here for finding the economic limit of wear and tear is applicable not only to means of labor but also to their individual parts, i.e., for determining the periodicity of repairs. For the wear and tear of parts often increases the operating costs of the machine because of a reduction in efficiency, a reduction in the precision of work, an increase in the wear and tear of other parts, an increase in the cost of repairing parts, and for other reasons.

Therefore, the correct discarding of parts must be based on a calculation of the economic effectiveness of their use. The calculation of the economic limit of a machine's life as a whole must be based on a curve of operating costs that is constructed in such a way that the useful lives of all parts are economically optimal. Unfortunately, lack of study of the principles of wear and tear hinders this kind of calculation.

Nonetheless, a study of methods of calculating economically optimal periods of wear and tear is not only desirable but is even necessary so that we can correctly study the principles of wear and tear, i.e., in order to know which technical indicators of wear and tear are necessary for determining its economic limits.

8. The Optimal Useful Life of Means of Labor with Respect to Technical Obsolescence ("a Second Approximation")

The procedure explained here for determining optimal useful lives are only first approximations. They ignore such an important factor in this problem as technological progress. This means that they give us only an approximation of the optimal useful life with respect to technical obsolescence. It is precisely because we have ignored technological progress that we have been able to demonstrate that the limits of technical obsolescence are determined ultimately by economics. But the minimum production costs of an individual product cannot be considered as the

228

criterion of the greatest effectiveness of outlays. The minimum production costs of an individual product may be incompatible with minimum production costs for all of the national economy's final output. This is precisely what occurs in determining the useful life of means of labor according to the minimum average production costs of output during this period.

True, when equipment outlives the period for which average production costs of output attain a minimum, its further use will be associated with higher production costs for the given output. But in return this use will yield a postponement of renovation. Postponement of renovation will make it possible to invest the corresponding sum in new construction. The effect brought about by the use of the amortization fund for new construction may exceed the losses associated with the increase in the useful life of the existing means of labor. Therefore, the useful life of a means of labor corresponding to the minimum production costs of output can be called partial-optimal, since it corresponds to minimum outlays on a part of the national economy's output, precisely to minimum outlays on output producible with the aid of the given implement.

If we take account only of technical obsolescence, the optimal useful life of means of labor must be, as a rule, greater than the partial-optimal period. In fact, as long as the operation of old means of labor requires surplus payments smaller than the savings in production costs that result during the same time period from investment equal to the additional outlays on the renewal of these means of labor, the use of old implements requiring surplus payments for the given output will yield savings in the total sum of outlays on reproduction.

This means that the economic limit of technical obsolescence approaches when surplus payments on the output of given means of labor are equalized with the normative effect of investment equal to cost of reproduction of these means of labor, i.e., when equality $e_H - c_H = K_H r_H$ is realized, where e_H is the expected production costs of output without outlays on renovation with new means of labor beyond the limit of their partial-optimal useful life. This equality is obviously equivalent to equality (7.2), formulated for the case when technological progress is absent.

The optimal useful life with respect to technical obsolescence can be calculated according to the following formula:

$$f(x + x_1) = f(x) + Kr_K, \qquad (7.5)$$

where K is costs of reproduction of the given means of labor (equal to outlays on its production); x is the amount of output producible with the aid of this means of labor during its partial-optimal useful life; $x + x_1$ is the amount of output producible with the aid of the same means of labor during its optimal useful life with respect to technical obsolescence; $f(x)$ is operating costs, apart from depreciation, related to a unit of output at the end of the partial-optimal useful life of the given means of labor; and $f(x + x_1)$ are those expenditures at the end of the optimal useful life with respect to technical obsolescence of that means of labor.

By substituting expressions $f(x)$ and $f(x + x_1)$ in the equation (7.5) we obtain one equation with two unknowns. But we can determine x either graphically or analytically.

Finding x by one or the other method, we then find x_1 for the equation (7.5).

Having determined $(x + x_1)$, we find the time during which this amount of output can be produced, i.e., the optimal useful life with respect to technical obsolescence.

9. Analysis of the Conditions Determining the Economic Limits of the Service of Means of Labor

Formula (7.2) is the most general expression of the economic limits of the service of means of labor:

$$e_c = \min{(C_H + K_H r_K)}.$$

We can see from this formula that the economic limit of the service of means of labor depends on the following factors:

(1) factors influencing e_c, i.e., operating costs of old means of labor;

(2) factors influencing C_H and K_H, i.e., indicators of the effectiveness of work with the aid of new means of labor;

(3) factors influencing the norm of investment effectiveness r_K.

Technical obsolescence is the fundamental factor of the first kind. It increases e_c, which raises the effectiveness of replacing old means of labor by new ones.

Factors of the second kind are mainly technical innovations and discoveries of new natural resources. They decrease costs of production or raise the effectiveness of those implements of labor on which C_H and K_H depend in formula (7.2), which increases the

230

effectiveness of replacing old means of labor by new ones.

Finally, as is apparent from formula (7.2), the optimal useful life of means of labor depends on the norm of investment effectiveness. The higher the norm, the longer the life.

The norm of investment effectiveness in turn directly depends on:

(a) the volume of possible investment with high (average and low) effectiveness (i.e., the distribution of investment alternatives according to their effectiveness);

(b) the national economy's volume of accumulation;

(c) the planned rate of growth of final output.

Other things being equal, the larger the values of quantities designated in a and b, the higher is the norm of investment effectiveness, and the larger the value of the quantity designated in b, the lower this norm must be.

In turn, these conditions are associated with a number of other conditions, namely, the rate of growth of population, technological change, and the volume of accumulation in preceding years. Of these conditions, it is especially important to examine the influence of technological progress in determining the economic limit of the service of old means of labor.

Technological progress expands the range of highly effective investments. This means that, other things being equal, technological progress raises the norm of investment effectiveness. But a rise in the norm of investment effectiveness in turn extends the economic limit of the service of old means of labor. The higher this norm is, the higher is the allowable limit of operating costs in the course of wear and tear, i.e., the higher e_c can be in formula (7.2). Consequently, general technological progress lengthens the useful life of means of labor by raising r_K.

In this way technological progress exerts a twofold and, moreover, a directly contradictory influence on the limit of use of existing means of labor. Inventions lower this limit in the lines of production affected by them, but they raise it in all remaining lines of production. Hence we can conclude that general technological progress probably exerts a much smaller influence on the average useful life of means of labor than is usually thought on the basis of data for individual branches.

As we see, the principles of calculating the economic limits of use of means of labor are identical both in the case of technical obsolescence and in the case of technological progress in the sphere of their production. This is understandable. In both cases a relative reduction occurs in the effectiveness of production with the aid of old implements of labor in comparison with the effectiveness of production with the aid of new implements. In both cases the limit of the service life of old implements approaches when this relative reduction goes beyond a certain boundary. The difference consists only in the fact that in the case of physical deterioration a reduction occurs in the effectiveness of production with old implements while there is a constant effectiveness of production with new implements, whereas in the case of technological progress in the production of implements a change in the relative effectiveness occurs by means of raising the effectiveness of production with new implements while there is a constant effectiveness of production with old implements.

It would be an error to think that the reduction in the useful life of old implements caused by technological progress is associated with some kind of losses for the national economy. If this reduction is correctly calculated according to formula (7.2), on the basis of given e_c, C, and K and a correct norm of investment effectiveness, it yields savings in costs of reproduction, not losses. Calculation according to formula (7.2) is precisely intended to find the alternative ensuring the minimum of all outlays in the national economy; and, if according to this calculation it appears that replacing equipment that is still not technically worn out by new equipment is the more effective alternative, the further use of this equipment will cause losses. Replacing the equipment will ensure the minimum of future outlays in the national economy to the extent that these outlays depend on a choice between old and new equipment.

10. The Optimal Useful Life of Means of Labor, with Consideration of Technological Progress ("a Third Approximation")

How do we find the useful life of means of labor that is optimal in all respects? Formula (7.2) determines the retirement time of means of labor, not their useful lives. It permits us to establish whether this time has arrived, but says nothing about when this time will arrive. However, formula (7.2) is the basis for deriving formulas for optimal useful lives of means of labor. For this purpose the following data are necessary:

(1) a curve of the relationship of operating costs of old means of labor (excluding depreciation) to the useful life $f(t)$ (this curve expresses the economic consequences of technical obsolescence);

232

(2) curve of the reduction of production costs of a given output with new implements under the influence of technological progress $\varphi(t)$;

(3) a curve of the change in capital investment in new equipment $g(t)$.

Then the initial formula for the optimal limit of service (with consideration of technical obsolescence and technological progress) can be written as:

$$f(t) = \varphi(t) + r_{\kappa}g(t). \qquad (7.6)$$

Of course, it is difficult to foresee future technological progress, even with respect to qualitative changes. It is still more difficult to take account of its influence on outlays, production costs, and capital investment. Therefore, useful lives, optimal in the true sense, can be calculated with consideration of technological progress in the given line of production only within a certain range of probability.

Let us investigate the conditions under which the optimal useful life of an implement becomes shorter than the optimal period of technical obsolescence.

These conditions can be understood on the basis of formula (7.6).

Indeed, suppose that a means of labor has been used for a period during which x_2 units of output have been produced with it. It has not yet reached a useful life that is optimal with respect to technical obsolescence. This situation can be expressed as:

$$f(x_2) < f(x + x_1) + K_{\text{н}}r_{\kappa}. \qquad (7.7)$$

Yet it would already be effective to replace the given means of labor by a new, better implement. In accordance with formula (7.6) we will express this situation thus:

$$f(x_2) = C_{\text{н}} + K_{\text{н}}r_{\kappa}. \qquad (7.8)$$

It follows from (7.7) and (7.8) that

$$f(x + x_1) + Kr_{\kappa} > C_{\text{н}} + K_{\text{н}}r_{\kappa}. \qquad (7.9)$$

Inequality (7.9) signifies that an old implement must be reproduced in a new form, not in its previous one. By comparing (7.7), (7.8), and (7.9) we conclude that technological progress reduces the useful life of old means of labor when they become

233

obsolete for reproduction and it becomes more effective to reproduce a means of labor of a new type instead.

Since technological progress proceeds at rapid rates, means of labor usually become obsolete for reproduction long before the completion of the optimal useful life with respect to technical obsolescence. But means of labor that are obsolete for reproduction usually remain in operation for a more or less extended period. For only in exceptional cases can obsolescence for utilization appear simultaneously with the emergence of obsolescence for reproduction. Obsolescence for reproduction is characterized by an inequality different from that of obsolescence for utilization:

obsolescence for reproduction

$$C_c + K_c r_\text{K} > C_\text{H} + K_\text{H} r_\text{K},$$

obsolescence for utilization

$$e_c > C_\text{H} + K_\text{H} r_\text{K}.$$

But, at any moment of time during the optimal useful life with respect to technical obsolescence,

$$e_c < C_c + K_c r_\text{K}.$$

Consequently, the simultaneous approach of obsolescence for reproduction and for utilization is possible only in the case of a sharp reduction in the costs of producing output with new implements from the level $C_\text{H} + K_\text{H} r_\text{K} = C_c + K_c r_\text{K}$ (the absence of obsolescence for reproducing old implements) to that of $C'_\text{H} + K'_\text{H} r_\text{K} = e_c$. This means that the costs of production of output with new implements must be immediately reduced to a sum not less than $C_\text{H} + K_\text{H} r - e_c$.

But this is not all. If a similar reduction occurs in many branches it is impossible to replace all obsolete equipment by new equipment immediately. This impossibility is reflected in a growth of the norm of investment effectiveness from r_K to r'_K such that inequality $e_c > C'_\text{H} + K'_\text{H} r_\text{K}$ changes its sign, i.e., $e_c < C'_\text{H} + K'_\text{H} r'_\text{K}$.

If the norm of investment effectiveness is not raised in accordance with the growth in the effectiveness of investment and the production program for new technology, the value calculations will lose their reliability. They will show effectiveness of replacing all of the old equipment by new equipment $(e_c > C'_H + K'_H r_K)$, but the given directive will be capable of fulfillment not in all cases, but only in certain ones. In this process it will remain unclear in which cases such replacement should be carried out. An understated norm of investment effectiveness hinders the calculation of effectiveness in the same way as understated norms of material outlays (for example, an understated norm for consumption of fuel). The possibility of following the directives of the calculation is lost.

As a rule, the optimal life is less than the optimal useful life with respect to technical obsolescence. In the case of intensive, general, technological progress the norm of investment effectiveness (r_K) may increase, which will increase both the optimal useful life and the optimal life with respect to technical obsolescence. In this process, the simultaneous growth of the optimal useful life of a means of labor and of its obsolescence is possible. This will occur when an increase in the norm of investment effectiveness will increase the optimal useful life with respect to technical obsolescence by more than the increase in the optimal useful life with respect to normal obsolescence.

Inequality (7.9) shows how incorrect it is to judge the degree of obsolescence of implements only according to the higher production costs of output with a given implement in comparison with the production costs of the same output with a new implement. In fact, it is apparent from this inequality that technological progress can reduce production costs with new implements to any extent in comparison with production costs with old implements without reducing the useful life of old implements provided that this progress requires a growth in capital per unit of annual output for which the effectiveness of reproducing capital in the new form will be lower than the norm of investment effectiveness.

This means that not every kind of technological progress that raises the productive power of labor in a given line of production justifies a reduction in the useful lives of existing means of labor compared to optimal ones with respect to technical obsolescence. A reduction of the useful life (and obsolescence) is caused only by that kind of technological progress that raises the effectiveness of investment in the given technology above the norm of effectiveness.

However, let us recall how technological progress influences the norm of investment effectiveness. Other things being equal, increasing the possiblility of investment with an effectiveness higher than the norm raises this norm. This means that technological progress in the sphere of the given capital reduces its useful life because the rates of technological development in the given sphere are higher, on the average, than for the national economy. Hence, with a given volume of accumulation a uniform rise in the effectiveness of investment in new technology in all branches may not be reflected in the useful lives. A reduction in C_H may be compensated by a growth in r_K.

But if a general rise in the effectiveness of new technology is accompanied by growth in the national economy's volume of accumulation, the norm of investment effectiveness may not rise. Then a general reduction in the useful lives of the means of labor will occur.

11. Measuring the Degree of Wear and Tear of Means of Labor

How do we determine the extent of wear and tear of a means of labor? This depends on the kind of wear and tear being discussed — technical (physical) wear and tear, obsolescence, or general wear and tear. All three kinds of wear and tear are measured according to the same principle, namely, on the basis of a reduction in the economic effectiveness of a means of labor in comparison with the most effective of the new means of labor.

General wear and tear can be defined as the difference between the initial value of a means of labor and its value at a given moment of time, calculated as the sum of all that economy of labor that the means of labor can yield until the time it is replaced:

$$U_0(t_1) = \frac{K_c - K_0(t_1)}{K_c}, \qquad (7.10)$$

$$K_0(t_1) = \sum_{t=t_1}^{t_m} \frac{C_H(t) + r_K K_H(t) - e_c(t)}{(1+r)^{t-t_1}} \quad (t = t_1, \ldots, t_m), \qquad (7.11)$$

where
$U_0(t_1)$ is the indicator of general wear and tear in year t_1;
K_c is the initial value of the old means of labor;
$K_0(t_1)$ is its general value in year t_1;
$e_c(t)$ is the operating cost (without depreciation) of output in year t;
$C_H(t)$ is the production cost of the same output in producing it

236

with a new means of labor in year t;

$K_H(t)$ is capital investment in a new means of labor in the year t;

t_m is the year of replacement of old by new equipment, when $e_c(t) = C_H(t) + r_H K_H(t)$.

Thus, $K_0(t_1)$ will express the sum of savings in reproduction costs that can be obtained with the aid of the given means of labor during the entire subsequent time of use, i.e., during the entire time while $e_c(t) \leqslant C_H(t) + r_H K_H(t)$. When this inequality is transformed into an equality, the old means of labor is replaced by a new one. The savings obtained at different times are added, with due consideration for the time factor.

Technical wear and tear is determined according to the formula

$$U_m(t_1) = \frac{K_c - K_m(t_1)}{K_c}, \tag{7.12}$$

$K_m(t_1)$ is calculated here on the assumption that the means of labor has not yet become obsolete, i.e., according to the formula

$$K_m(t_1) = \sum_{t=t_1}^{t_m} \frac{C_c + rK_c - e_c(t)}{(1+r)^{t-t_1}} \quad (t = t_1, \ldots, t_m), \tag{7.13}$$

where $K_m(t_1)$ is the value of the means of labor in year t_1 on the assumption of the absence of obsolescence in the past and in the future;

C_c is the initial production cost of output with the old means of labor;

$e_c(t)$ is the operating cost (excluding depreciation) with an old means of labor in year (t).

In this formula $e_c(t)$ changes over time, while C_c and K_c remain constant.

Obsolescence is measured by the difference between general wear and tear and technical wear and tear:

$$U_\mu(t_1) = U_0(t_1) - U_m(t_1) = \frac{K_m(t_1) - K_0(t_1)}{K_c}. \tag{7.14}$$

A.S. Konson recommends a different economic measure of physical wear and tear:[3]

$$a_\Phi = \frac{R}{K_1},$$

where a_Φ is the economic measure of a machine's physical wear and tear (in fractions of the cost of reproducing it);

237

R is the estimated cost of repair necessary for renewing all worn-out assemblies;

K_1 is the cost of the complete reproduction of this machine at the moment when it is determined to be physically worn out, with consideration of its depreciation associated with the appearance of new, more advanced designs with better operating properties.

This formula is appealing in its simplicity. Nevertheless, it is incorrect. Its denominator (K_1) reflects obsolescence not only of the first but also of the second kind. Thus K_1 does not at all express the cost of reproduction, but rather the price that a machine of the old design would have if it were a new one. Such a basis for calculating physical wear and tear does not correspond to the meaning of the indicator. As a rule this indicator will exaggerate the extent of physical wear and tear by the total obsolescence of the second kind. For example, suppose that repair requires replacing half of the parts and is so well organized that its cost is equal to one-half of the cost of reproduction of the machine. By virtue of the appearance of machines with better designs the price of a new machine of the old type can be equal to only one-half of its cost of reproduction. Naturally, the machine must not be reproduced. However, it does not follow from this that the degree of its physical wear and tear is equal to 1, as suggested by A. S. Konson. With more accurate calculation of the denominator of the same formula we obtain the result that the machine's physical wear and tear is equal to only 0.5.

Konson proposes measuring obsolescence by the reduction in the cost of the machine as a result of technological progress in accordance with the formula [4]

$$a_M = \frac{K_0 - K_1}{K_0},$$

where a_M is the indicator of obsolescence, K_0 is the initial cost of the machine, and K_1 is the cost of completely reproducing it with consideration of obsolescence of the first and second kinds.

The correctness of this formula depends on how K_1 is determined. In Konson's opinion the present value of the new model of an old machine $(K_{c\,1})$ will amount to

$$K_{c1} = K_{H1} \left(\frac{q_c}{q_H}\right)^\alpha \left(\frac{C_H}{C_c}\right)^\beta,$$

where q_C and q_H are the annual productivity of an old and a new machine, respectively, and C_c and C_H are the operating costs per unit of output of an old and a new machine, respectively.

Indicators of the extent of a and β can be found on the basis of studying the data for similar machines. The author does not substantiate this formula.

Calculations of the indicators of general wear and tear, physical (technological) wear and tear, and obsolescence are not an end in themselves. They must result from calculations of the effectiveness of use of machines and serve to determine the limits and remaining useful lives. Formulas (7.10) through (7.14) are a "by-product" of calculations of the optimal use of means of labor. The formulas proposed by Konson are not connected with these calculations and require independent and, moreover, quite complex calculations (for determining indicators of the extent of a and β). Therefore, they can hardly be of practical significance. In particular, the indicator of physical wear and tear (a_Φ) for the most part will only lead to error.

12. Determining Optimal Useful Lives in Cases of Utilization of Worn Out Means of Labor for Other Purposes ("a Fourth Approximation")

The rules and formulas presented above for determining periods of wear and tear do not take into account the possibility of using a worn-out implement for another purpose. They assume that upon completion of its useful life a means of labor is unsuitable for anything else. In reality, means of labor worn-out for one purpose can be effectively used for other purposes. The possibility of a different use must be taken into account in determining useful lives for given purposes.

This possibility can be taken into account in the formula for the economic limits of wear and tear in the form of the residual value of a worn-out means of labor. We will denote this residual value by $K_{c\,\dot{o}}$. Then formula (7.2) must be changed in the following way:

$$e_c + r_{\text{к}} K_{co} = \min^{\cdot}(C_{\text{н}} + r_{\text{к}} K_{\text{н}}). \qquad (7.15)$$

It is apparent from formula (7.15) that the higher the residual value of old capital, the closer is the economic limit of its service for a given purpose. This is understandable. If the residual value of an old means of labor is high and the effect from its use for a given purpose is small, then it is better to use a still valuable implement for anoth;r purpose, for which it will be used more effectively.

How do we determine the residual value? If the matter concerns the use of a worn-out machine as scrap for an open-hearth furnace, this question does not present special difficulties. True, the problem of evaluating scrap (as part of the problem of evaluating waste products) is still controversial. Nevertheless, there is no doubt that the price of a ton of scrap must be many times smaller than the cost of a ton of a new machine. Accordingly, product $(r_K \cdot K_{co})$ in formula (7.15) will be close to zero, so that even relatively large errors in evaluating K_{co} will have practically no significance in determining the useful life of machines.

But if an old machine can be used for another purpose and also as a machine, the question of determining its residual value assumes considerable significance. Moreover, we have no generally accepted principles for this evaluation.

At first glance the residual value of a means of labor can be determined as the still undepreciated part of its initial (or renewal) cost. But in order to find this part we must already know the useful life of the machine for all of its successive purposes. Thus a vicious circle is formed. To determine the useful life of a means of labor we must know the residual value, and to determine the residual value we must know the useful life.

Formula (7.11) for determing K_{co} breaks this circle. Accordingly, this formula can be substituted for formula (7.15). It is apparent from formula (7.11) that we can solve our problem without any evaluation of a partially worn out means of labor. This does not signify that we set the value of the means of labor as equal to zero. This signifies only that we replace this evaluation by other magnitudes that perform, in our problem, the same function performed by the evaluation of fixed capital.

Indeed, what is the function performed in our problem by evaluating replaceable means of labor? According to (7.11) the evaluation must reflect the entire future effect that a means of labor can yield in its most effective use, with due consideration for the time factor. But if this is the case, then we can solve the problem by means of direct calculation of its effect for other purposes.

Let us demonstrate how this can be done.

When we determine whether an implement for producing product A has reached its economic limit of wear and tear, we compare the following alternatives:

I. Given the condition that the implement cannot be used in another line of production:

Alternative 1: producing product A with the aid of the old implement.

Alternative 2: producing the same amount of product A with the aid of the new implement.

II. Given the possibility of using the old implement for producing product B:

Alternative 1: producing product A with the aid of the old implement.

Alternative 2^I: producing the same amount of product A with the aid of the new implement plus producing product B with the aid of the old implement (which can be used in the given period for producing product A).

It is obvious that alternatives 1 and 2^I do not yield identical output. Alternative 1 yields output A and alternative 2^I yields output $A + B$.

In such a form the effectiveness of these two alternatives is incommensurable, for they yield different output. Moreover, the fundamental condition for comparing the national economic effectiveness of project alternatives is the identity of their national economic effect.

But alternatives 1 and 2^I can be adjusted to an identical output. For this purpose it is necessary to foresee by which method and with what outlays we can produce product B if alternative 1 is realized. By joining to alternative 1 the supplementing alternative of production of product B (in the amount in which it is obtained according to alternative 2^I), we adjust alternative 1 to the same output that alternative 2^I yields. Then adjusted alternative 1 (we will denote it by 1^1) and alternative 2^I will be commensurable with respect to the effectiveness of outlays. Given the identity of the national economic effect of compared alternatives, their relation to the national economic effectivenesses is inversely proportional to the relation of outlays required by these alternatives.[5]

Table 36

Number of the alternative	Output	Annual costs of Output	Investment
1^I	Production of product A with the aid of an old implement	e_a (without renovation	0
	Production of product B with the aid of new implements*	C_b (production costs)	K_b
2^I	Production of product A with the aid of a new implement	C_a	K_a
	Production of product B with the aid of an old implement (previously used for producing product A)	e_b (without renovation)	0

*We recall that C_b and C_a are average production costs for optimal useful lives of the corresponding means of labor.

241

We see from Table 36 that each of these alternatives yields identical output $A + B$. Owing to the identity of the effect we can compare the effectiveness of investment in the new implement for producing A (alternative 2^1) and the utilization of the old implement for the same purpose (alternative 1^1). For this purpose we use formula (7.2), assuming that:

$$e_c = e_a + C_b + r_\kappa K_b,$$
$$C_{\scriptscriptstyle H} = C_a + e_b,$$
$$K_{\scriptscriptstyle H} = K_a.$$

Then the limiting condition for the service of the old implement in the first of the two purposes will be expressed as:

$$e_c + C_b + r_\kappa K_b = e_b + C_a + r_\kappa K_a. \qquad (7.16)$$

When the left half of this equality becomes larger than the right half it is more effective to shift the old implement used for producing A to producing B, and to install a new means of labor for producing A instead of using the old one.

As we see, there is no estimate of old fixed capital in formula (7.16). The task of determining the limits of service of means of labor for one purpose can be solved without evaluating the means of labor that are transferred to another purpose. The advantage of this method is that it requires only such data as can be objectively determined. Only outlays figure in formula (7.16). Instead of an evaluation of old means of labor we additionally took into account, on the one hand, the output that they can yield in another use (output B), and expenditures for their operation in this use; and, on the other hand, we took account of investment in producing the same output (B) and its production costs in producing it without the use of old means of labor.

On the basis of the formula for the limit of service of the implement in the first of the two uses, we can derive the formula for the optimal useful life in this use. For this purpose we must express e_a as a function of the magnitude of output A produced during the preceding period of service, i.e., $e_a = f_a(x_a)$.

However, initial operating costs in the second use (e_b) also depend on the useful life of implements in the first use. The more an implement is worn out in the first use, the higher, as a rule, are the initial operating costs of this implement in the second use:

$$e_b = f_b(x_a).$$

Then the initial formula (7.16) for the optimal useful life will assume the following form:

$$f_a(x_a) + C_b + K_b r = f_b(x_a) + C_a + K_a r_\kappa. \qquad (7.17)$$

The amount of output B produced during the period of service of the same implement in the second use will correspondingly be determined from the formula

$$f_b(x_b) = C_b + r_k K_b, \qquad (7.18)$$

where $f_b(x_b)$ denotes annual operating costs (without depreciation) depending on the useful life, and x_b is the sought-for amount of output B.

We can find the total useful life of the implement in both uses by determining the calendar time in which $(x_a + x_b)$ can be produced.

13. Under What Conditions Can Obsolescence Cause Harm?

We have shown that from the standpoint of society obsolescence does not cause losses, but is the condition for reducing outlays on reproduction. We determined optimal useful lives by seeking to find minimum outlays. However, some economists assume that the loss in value of old means of labor caused by the growth of labor productivity represents a loss requiring compensation.

This viewpoint is readily explicable with reference to capitalism. For the capitalist, the loss of part of the value of his equipment, buildings, and installations is in fact a loss. It is a loss of part of his capital. The antagonistic nature of the capitalist economy is manifested in these losses of private wealth occurring in consequence of an increase in the national wealth. However, obsolescence under capitalism is also associated with national economic losses. Capitalists whose interests are threatened by technological progress strive to delay the implementation of inventions that are dangerous for them. This restraining of new technology also causes national economic losses.

Thus, under capitalism technological progress and the obsolescence caused by it are actually linked with both particular and national economic losses. But how can correctly calculated obsolescence cause any losses in a socialist economy? Academician S. G. Strumilin assumes that a reduction in the value of means of labor requires compensation.[6] Unfortunately, Strumilin has not offered convincing proof of his thesis. Therefore, this thesis has not been accepted by Soviet economists. Nonetheless, there is a certain amount of truth in it.

The question of whether obsolescence causes losses is resolved

243

in different ways depending on what is used as the base for comparison in calculating losses. If optimal useful lives of old means are determined after their obsolescence is discovered, the recognition and calculation of obsolescence are not only not a loss but also a means of attaining the greatest savings. Continuing the use of obsolete means of labor would be a loss. Exaggeration of their depreciation could also cause losses if it led to rejecting their use when this was still effective.

But obsolescence does involve a loss if the possibility is not grasped of anticipating and reducing it by choosing means with shorter useful lives or those less subject to obsolescence, achieving in this way still greater labor economies.

Suppose that the production of output is possible with two types of machines, A and B. Machine A is longer-lasting and is more subject to the effect of obsolescence. If we consider only physical wear and tear, machine B is less economical; but, on the other hand, it is less subject to obsolescence.

Given identical investment, these machines have the following indicators (see Table 37).

Table 37

Type of Machine	Average production costs of output, in rubles per unit for useful lives	
	Optimal with respect to technical wear and tear	Optimal*
A	10	15
B	12	13

*With respect to technical wear and tear, and obsolescence.

If we do not foresee technological progress and obsolescence, we must prefer machine A. But if we foresee obsolescence, then B will be the optimal type of machine. In comparison with this possibility, the choice of machine A — as a result of obsolescence — will cause, over a certain period, losses of 15 − 13 = 2 rubles per unit of output.

14. The Varying Influence of Technological Progress on Optimal Useful Lives of Machines and Their Parts

Technological progress influences the useful lives of parts and of machines in different ways. These varying influences are explained by the varying tendencies of technological progress in regard to the useful lives of parts and machines. Rapid wear and tear of

244

parts not only increases outlays on repair and idle periods associated with it, but also reduces the reliability of machines and instruments. With the development of complete mechanization and automation of production, the economic significance of reliability of parts increases by many times, approximately as much as the value of the complex of technologically related machines.

That is why technological development is directed toward increasing the durability and wear-resistance of parts, above all, of the least long-lasting of these.[7] This tendency is also strengthened by the advisability of drawing closer together periods of technical wear and tear of different kinds of parts and of lengthening periods between repairs.

On the other hand, technological progress is directed toward reducing the useful lives of machines. The shorter the useful life of a machine, the less is its obsolescence.

These opposing tendencies have a common basis. Both arise from the principle of the lowest costs per unit of machine output. If we try, giving rein to our imagination, to think of a conceivable final point of development of these two tendencies, then at this point the useful lives of all parts will be equalized with each other and with the useful life of the machines as a whole. Of course, such a situation is impossible. The conditions of wear and tear of individual parts are so different that the influence of these differences can hardly be compensated by the more precise adaptation of the properties of materials to the functions of parts manufactured from them. A roundabout route to the same goal has been found in practice, namely, the modernization and replacement of relatively less long-lasting parts and assemblies by new ones with different designs that better correspond to the changing requirements of technology. With modernization an old machine ends its existence before its longest-lasting parts wear out. It is replaced by a new one manufactured through use of its long-lasting parts. In this way modernization can draw together the useful life of a machine as an aggregate of specific parts and the useful lives of less long-lasting parts and assemblies.

15. Problems of the Practical Applications of Methods and Procedures Recommended by Us for Selecting Material

We have presented only the basic rules for determining the optimal useful lives of means of labor in a socialist economy. The application of these rules remains difficult. The regularities of

245

technical wear and tear have been little studied. The economic consequences of technical wear and tear have been still less studied. But this is not all. The study of the economic consequences of technical wear and tear is hindered by the fact that plant bookkeeping is not arranged for this purpose.

The study of the methods of determining useful lives illuminates the goal toward which we must strive. It shows which materials must be produced, in which direction to conduct the study of the wear and tear of means of labor, and what should be the objectives of methods of determining useful lives.

We have become convinced that the curves of the relationship of operating costs to the period of service of a means of labor and to the amount of "work" performed by it are the most important data for calculating optimal useful lives. Such curves are necessary for all means of labor, both old and new. True, a curve of these costs with old implements is not necessary for determining the limits of use of old means of labor. In this case a similar curve for new means of labor is necessary. Without this curve it is not possible to determine correctly the production costs with new implements, which is necessary for determining the limits of use of old implements.

The dependence of operating costs on technical wear and tear can be determined only on the basis of a great deal of empirical material. The production costs of output producible by means of the fixed capital studied and indicators of its physical wear and tear must be the initial data.

The calculations must be worked out so that influences of all factors other than technical wear and tear are eliminated. This is not an easy task. Therefore, we must seek its solution by various methods:

(1) by studying indicators of the effectiveness of "work" of the same fixed capital for different segments of time of its service;

(2) by studying indicators of the effectiveness of "work" of fixed capital of the same form but of varying ages;

(3) by technical analysis of the operating conditions of machines during their useful lives and through construction on this basis of a typical curve of changes in costs during these lives;

(4) by experimental study of technical wear and tear and the determination of its economic consequences.

The economic consequences of physical wear and tear must be studied to begin with, if only for the most important forms of means of labor.

The empirical study of obsolescence is a most difficult problem. Its difficulty involves the fact that we must determine the future

246

dynamics of economic indicators without knowing those economic means with the aid of which it will be realized (because if such means were already known they would be realized as new means of labor). It is not possible to replace curves of future changes of indicators of effectiveness of machines for one or another purpose by data on the average growth of labor productivity in the country. The rates of technological progress in different lines of production differ greatly from each other. Therefore, the use of an average magnitude of growth of labor productivity for the entire country will, for example, sharply exaggerate the future obsolescence of new textile machinery and understate this obsolescence for internal combustion engines, electronic devices and equipment, etc. Furthermore, the study of the principles of obsolescence of machines for a specific purpose must be based upon the investigation of progressive tendencies in changes in individual technological-economic indicators. For example, for conveyors it is necessary to study changes in the average lifting capacity, the consumption of fuel, the weight of the machine per unit of power, etc. Only such detailed study of the principles of technological development can yield sufficiently reliable data for calculating the curve of future changes of economic indicators, namely, value of machines and the production costs of machine output.

16. Obsolescence, Price Formation, and Payments for Capital

Investigation of the economic limits of service of means of labor sheds light on certain controversial questions of calculating costs and of price formation.

The equality of prices to marginal costs is often questioned on the grounds that it is equivalent to orienting production toward obsolete technology. The equality of prices to marginal costs of production with old implements would signify orientation toward old technology only if marginal costs with old implements were not determined by minimum costs with new implements. But with optimal planning, as we saw, the upper limit of reproduction costs with old implements is determined by the lowest reproduction costs with the most effective of the new implements. This equality is possible only because reproduction costs with old implements have a different composition from costs with new implements, namely, $e_{\bar{c}}$ and not $C_H + K_H r_K$.

Thus, determining prices by marginal costs according to formula (7.2) signifies orientation toward the newest technology (the right half of the formula) and toward *the most effective use of old means of labor.*

The differences noted in the composition of reproduction costs with old and new implements were not taken into account in the practice of calculation and price formation. Calculating the service limits of implements of labor and obsolescence was thereby hindered.

Formula (7.1) provides the key to the determination of payments for capital. In fact, the effect (future economies of labor) of the use of an old means of labor in period t according to this formula will amount to

$$r_f(t) = \min\,(C_{\text{H}} + K_{\text{H}} r_{\text{K}})\,(t) - e_{\text{c}}(t), \qquad (7.19)$$

where $r_f(t)$ is the effect of the use of an old means of labor in period t. If $e_{\text{c}}(t)$ is determined according to socially necessary norms, payments for the use of the corresponding means of labor must be equal to $r_f(t)$. In particular, for new means whose sum $(C_{\text{H}} + K_{\text{H}} r_{\text{K}})$ is a minimum, payments for capital according to formula (7.19) will amount to $K_{\text{H}} r_{\text{K}}$ plus outlays on renovation. Including this payment in full production costs of output would equalize costs for new and old enterprises. With normal operation, full production costs of output for all enterprises would be equal to $C_{\text{H}} + K_{\text{H}} r_{\text{K}}$. Thus not only would the time factor (within r_{K}) be taken into account but all enterprises would be placed in equal conditions of application of labor. In this way, with the correct calculation of physical wear and tear and obsolescence of fixed capital, production costs of the same articles produced with different implements would tend toward a common level, one that was characteristic of normal work. Deviations from this level would characterize the quality of each enterprise's work.

Of course, the formula presented here for payments for capital is extremely simplified. It provides only the basic idea for determining these payments. The formula for evaluating means of labor with consideration of technical wear and tear and obsolescence (7.11) is based on the same idea. Accordingly, payments for capital could also be determined as a share of the assessment of means of labor, if they were calculated according to formula (7.11). Calculating payments for capital according to formula (7.19) would be an important verification of the norm of investment effectiveness (r_{K}). Thus, if with a given value of this norm a large part of the available means of labor were unprofitable, this would signify that the norm of investment effectiveness was understated.

Notes

1. For this see pp. 144-145.

2. A. S. Konson, in his work *Ekonomika remonta mashin* (Moscow, Machinery State Publishing House, 1960, p. 120), proposes a different formula for determining the degree of economy of repair (and thereby the degree of economy of use of old equipment):

$$R < K_1$$

where R is the cost of a major overhaul of the machine, and K_1 is its complete reproduction cost (in prices of the same year).

Nevertheless, this formula is correct only under very inflexible assumptions:

(a) a machine's wear and tear influences only the cost of a major overhaul, but not other operating costs and not the quality of output;

(b) technological progress does not occur in the given branch (in consequence of which the most effective new machine will be a machine of the same type as the old one);

(c) reproduction of the machines completely satisfies requirements for them (demand for them).

Formula (7.1) requires neither the first nor the second of these assumptions. The third assumption remains. It signifies that the law of value is used not only according to its content but also according to its form (i.e., the correspondence of supply to demand is observed). Without this condition, value indicators are insufficient for determining the effectiveness of these or other outlays.

3. *Ibid.*, p. 11.

4. *Ibid.*, pp. 25-27.

5. For the rule of identity, see Chapter 3.

6. See S. G. Strumilin, "The Time Factor in Planning Capital Investment," *Izvestiia Akademii Nauk SSSR, Otdelenie ekonomiki i prava,* 1946, No. 3.

7. For this see A. S. Konson, *op. cit.,* Chapter IV, especially pp. 68 *et seq.*

CHAPTER 8

THE PROBLEM OF MEASURING RESULTS OF LABOR IN A SOCIALIST ECONOMY

In the measurement of the effectiveness of labor, two problems arise:

(a) measuring the effectiveness of labor in the production of specific products, and

(b) measuring the effectiveness of certain outlays of labor (by collectives and by individual workers).

We must solve problems in practice.

Measuring the effectiveness of the production of output is necessary above all for the distribution of labor among different uses.

Finding the minimum of outlays on a given final output is an important but insufficient condition for constructing an optimal plan for the national economy. It is also necessary that the volume and composition of the final output correspond to the national economy's requirements. As was demonstrated above, to construct a production plan we must compare ("mutually weigh") the "useful effects" of different objects of consumption and compare them with outlays of labor.

Measuring the effectiveness of specific expenditures of living labor is necessary for organizing production and distribution according to labor. The correct management of production in the enterprise, the shop, and at the working place cannot be ensured only by knowledge of what expenditures each product costs society. We must also know what the expenditures of living labor in each of the national economy's links give to society. In fact, how could enterprises, shops, and workers conduct the struggle for raising labor productivity if they did not know the results of their

250

own labor? If indicators of the results of living labor are incorrectly formed (for example, if they are raised when they should be lowered), then the struggle to raise them will lead to lowering labor productivity.

The correct measurement of the results of living labor is of enormous significance. Of all social systems, only socialism is characterized by distribution according to labor, and only under socialism does the principle of the worker's individual material interest in the results of his labor take on full force. But the measurement of what each producer gives to society is the necessary condition for the operation of this principle. The more accurately the results of living labor are determined, the more completely the law of distribution according to labor can act and the closer the connection between individual and social interests can be. The accuracy of distribution according to labor is, in turn, the most important condition for the continuous growth of labor productivity and of well-being.

But this is not all. The accuracy of measurement of the results of living labor is also of enormous significance for the planned direction of the national economy as a whole. On it depends the effectiveness of economic calculation. If indicators of the results of labor (at enterprises, shops, and by individual workers) incorrectly reflect what labor gives to society, economic calculation will inevitably hinder the operation of the law of development according to plan. It will encourage less productive expenditures and counteract the fulfillment of more productive assignments established by the plan.

We repeat: there are two problems in measuring the effectiveness of labor. The first one, measuring the effectiveness of social labor in the production of specific products, is the fundamental one. The solution of the second problem is connected with the solution of the first one.

1. The Problem of the Comparison

Heterogeneous use values are incommensurable, but in practice they are nevertheless compared. What are called indicators of the physical volume of output, of commodity circulation, of national income, and the like are calculated as masses of use values. The results of enterprises' work are measured in money. In practice costs are compared with results in order to determine the profitability of production.

251

What is the economic meaning of comparing heterogeneous use values? How do we best carry out such a comparison?

It is obvious that we cannot solve this problem directly. But, given the impossibility of direct measurement, indirect measurement is sometimes possible, i.e., measurement of a quantity that is associated with all incommensurable quantities (such as the measurement of temperature according to changes in the volume of mercury).

Precisely such a possibility exists in the sphere of comparing use values. All production is associated with one general quantity — expenditure of labor. This connection creates the possibility of indirectly comparing different use values.

Assuming either outlays per unit of each product or outlays on the entire producible mass of use values to be constant, we relate change in outlays only to changes in use values, to changes in their amount (if outlays per unit of each product are constant), or to changes in the relative value of the "weights" of different use values (if outlays on total final output are constant).

Comparing the total amount of outlays by proceeding from the assumption of the invariability of outlays per unit of each product lies at the basis of constructing indices of the physical volume of output, commodity circulation, national income, etc. Comparing outlays on each product — given the condition of invariability in total outlays on all output — lies at the basis of the comparison of costs and results with respect to their conformity to requirements.

The essence of this latter comparison lies in the fact that outlays appear in a double role: (1) as the sum of outlays on consumer goods, and (2) as the sum of consumers' incomes. If goods are sold at prices corresponding to the balance of supply and demand, the relationship of prices to outlays on different goods will show the extent to which the production of each commodity corresponds to needs. In fact, prices that equilibrate the supply and demand for consumer goods reflect equally effective "weighing of useful effects" of different products by the mass of consumers. Accordingly, the results of production calculated according to these prices can be used to compare costs and results, taking into account the conformity of production to needs. Thus, if prices that equilibrate supply and demand for each product are equal to differential costs, this means that production corresponds to needs.

However, demand reflects needs that have already been influenced by the distribution of incomes. The more unequal is the distribution of income, the less does demand reflect the population's needs, and the more does it reflect the distribution of income.

The enormous inequality in the distribution of incomes under capitalism is associated with similar inequality in the relative importance of different classes of consumers in demand. Therefore, it appears that outlays on producing luxury items are socially necessary, while outlays on producing objects of primary necessity for raising consumption by the majority of the population to the level of a subsistence minimum are socially unnecessary.

Distribution according to labor under socialism links each person's demand with his individual participation in the production process. For different individuals the monetary unit represents an unequal although not very different part of individual income. Accordingly, the population's demand under the conditions of socialism is incomparably more closely linked with needs than under capitalism. But since earnings conform to the quantity and quality of labor, the needs of different groups of the population still constitute unequal shares of the population's total demand.

Hence it follows that the most exact reflection of needs in demand is conceivable only given a distribution of monetary incomes according to needs. Thus demand will accurately reflect needs only under communism, i.e., when it would seem that demand will have ceased to exist. This unexpected conclusion compels us to ask whether it is correct that estimation of needs by means of demand will disappear under communism. Doesn't demand represent an imperfect form of the system of estimating that can best of all be realized only under communism?

In order to uncover "hints of the higher" in the law of equating supply and demand, let us try to present the principles of the most effective distribution according to needs at the stage of complete communism, i.e., a distribution such that the utilization of the consumption fund will yield the highest degree of general satisfaction of needs.

Distribution according to needs presumes a sufficiently high level of labor productivity, so that labor becomes the first vital requirement (by virtue of changes in the nature of physical labor, improvement in its conditions, shortening of the working day, etc.).

But distribution according to needs should not be understood as the absence of any limitations on consumption. An abundance of products does not mean that they become free goods. Under all conditions products will remain the result of labor; and, although the results of labor can be very great, they cannot be unlimited.

Of course, certain needs are limited by their very nature (for example, the consumption of food). With an abundance of products such needs can be satisfied without limitations, and the volume of production of goods necessary for this can be calculated according to scientifically valid norms. However, even in this case products with special taste properties and special usefulness may remain scarce by virtue of the limited natural conditions of their production.

With a growth in well-being there is an increase in the relative importance of needs that do not have definite limits. To make the transition to communism dependent on the possibility of unlimited satisfaction of these needs means to postpone it for an indefinite period. Moreover, the transformation of labor into the primary vital requirement is the necessary and obligatory condition for the transition to communism. Precisely this transformation will allow us to pass from distribution according to labor to distribution according to needs. As experience shows, such a transformation is possible in individual cases even with a comparatively low level of satisfaction of needs. In this respect the major factor is the nature of labor, the dependence of its result on the worker's creative efforts. Labor that in its content is absorbing for the worker is creative labor, which inevitably becomes a vital requirement and moves into the background requests based on vanity. In addition, such labor is more productive than labor associated with external compulsion, even an economic one, i.e., than labor prompted by material interest in the results of labor. This property of labor performed in accordance with an internal incentive was long ago observed in the proverb "Where there is a will, there is a way." Although a certain level of satisfaction of needs is necessary for "willing" labor to prevail, on the other hand, "willing" labor, forming an important part of the content of vital interests, limits the development of certain needs. Therefore, the transformation of labor into a vital requirement obviously does not require the complete and absolute satisfaction of all individual needs, but only a sufficiently high level of satisfaction.

By proceeding from this hypothesis we will present the measurement of the results of production under conditions of distribution of scarce goods according to needs.

The distribution of material wealth according to needs can be implemented not only in kind but also in the form of shares of participation in the consumption fund. Both forms have been tested in practice, to one extent or another. Distribution in kind is applicable both in the absence of any limitations on individual consumption (for example, in supplying water or gas) and in a situation in which such limitations are necessary (for example, in the distribution of products through rationing, and of apartments according to orders, and so on). Distribution of shares of participation in the consumption fund presumes the limited nature of this fund in comparison with social needs. Above all, the distribution of incomes in monetary form is applicable here. A share of the consumption fund equal to I/CF, where I is the recipient's monetary income and CF is the consumption fund expressed in the same monetary unit, is granted to each recipient of income. Distribution of goods according to labor certificates is also applicable here. The share of participation in the consumption fund is expressed in work-hours or in work-days. Historical experience has rather completely disclosed the properties of each of the forms of distribution of consumer goods.

Distribution in kind is natural either with the possibility of complete satisfaction of the consumer's needs or in those cases in which the consumer himself cannot correctly determine what he needs. An example is the need for a sanatorium or for drugs for medical treatment. But for many goods the composition of needs (with due consideration of their comparative value and of outlays for satisfying them) can be established best of all by the consumers themselves. For this purpose each consumer must have his share of participation in the consumption fund, established according to the general extent of his needs, with due consideration of age, family situation, and other objective bases for calculating needs.[1] The unit in which costs are measured must be the unit for measuring these shares. If this was not the case, results and costs would be incommensurable, and consequently it would be impossible to determine needs. In determining the needs both of society as a whole and of each of its members, the costs associated with satisfying these needs must be taken into account.

Distribution of shares of participation in the consumption fund is necessarily linked with the establishment of consumption valuations expressing the amount of labor that society considers it necessary to expend on the given product according to the conditions of consumption. Without such valuations it is not possible to create "a connection between the amount of social working time that can be expended on producing a specific object and the magnitude of social needs subject to satisfaction by means of this object."[2]

255

The necessity of consumption valuations is clearly revealed in the mathematical formulation of the problem of optimal planning, if by this means we seek the production program that corresponds to social needs.

In the preceding chapters we assumed the production program for the national economy's final output to be given, and we solved the problem for a general minimum of labor costs. If, in proceeding from this problem, we formulate a double problem, one for a maximum of national income, this maximum will be attained only when the differential costs for each product equal its consumption valuation.[3] The conformity of the amount of working time expended on each final product to the social need for it, i.e., to the amount of labor that society considers it necessary to expend on it, will also be expressed in this equality.

Consumption valuations are necessary not only for determining the production program for consumer goods but also for planning the production of means of production. Without them it is not possible to determine which means of production must be produced and in what amounts. Furthermore, we have already introduced such valuations into our model of the plan, minimizing labor costs for prescribed output. Norms of effectiveness of all available means of production (r_h) are valuations of their use value in industrial consumption. Thus, by ignoring at the start of the investigation the complex and controversial problem of valuations of consumer goods, and by limiting our problem to questions of producing the prescribed output, we nevertheless were unable to do without consumption valuations of means of production. The reason is that in the production of means of production it is also necessary to determine to what extent their "useful effects" (use value) justify outlays on their production. "The increase of labor that is caused by the production of the means of labor themselves — machines, coal, etc. — must be less than the labor that is saved by the use of the machines."[4]

Norms of effectiveness of means of production (or what amounts to the same things, norms of feedback costs) express the minimum economy of labor that these means must yield in the optimal plan. A comparison of these norms with costs of reproduction yields an answer to the question of whether the production of these or other means of production is effective.

For an *object of labor*, r_h expresses the consumption valuations for the full utilization of a unit of the hth means of production. If this valuation (r_h) is less than the differential costs of producing

256

the given object, it will not be reproduced. (Remaining reserves can be used.)

For a *means of labor,* r_h expresses the consumption valuation for the partial utilization (during a unit of time) of this means, i.e., it expresses rent. This rent must cover outlays on its renovation plus the normative effect of investment in this means of labor. If rent (the norm of effectiveness) for the means of labor does not meet this sum of outlays, such means of labor will not be reproduced, but could be used up to a certain limit of wear and tear (for this, see Chapter 7).

In this way consumption valuations of means of production help us to find the plan for producing prescribed final output that can be implemented with lowest outlays of labor. Consumption valuations of consumer goods are necessary for the purpose of finding the program for producing such goods that yields the maximum satisfaction of needs.

The optimal production program for means of production is attained when differential costs are equated to the marginal effectiveness of utilization of these means of production. The optimal production program for consumer goods is determined by a similar condition, namely, by the equality of differential costs to the minimum consumption valuation of the product (i.e., by the marginal effectiveness of its utilization). If consumption valuations of the increment in production are larger or smaller than outlays of labor on this increment, it means that the production of this product exceeds requirements or does not meet them. Equality of the marginal consumption valuation to differential costs signifies that all possibilities of satisfying requirements are exhausted and that the proportionality of production to requirements is ensured.

However, this brief formula for the optimum is incomplete and therefore inaccurate.

In the first place, we must introduce precision into the consumption valuations. Both the individual and the social consumption valuations have a specific meaning only as extreme quantities no higher than a certain sum for a given mode and volume of consumption.

The social consumption valuation is the maximum price at which the entire given amount of the product in a specific interval of time can be realized. In addition, this price coincides with the minimum valuation for the least effective method of consumption of this product in the optimal plan. In this way consumption estimates are "maximins," and in this respect they are also similar to norms of effectiveness of means of production, for example, to the norm of effectiveness of capital investment.

257

In the second place, differential costs are "minimaxes." These are the minimum costs at which the entire given amount of the product can be produced, and they are the maximum costs with the least effective method of production, but they are still necessary for meeting requirements in the optimal plan.

However, despite this formal similarity between consumption valuations of consumer goods and consumption valuations of means of production there is a great difference between these kinds of valuations. The effect of the utilization of means of production is objective and measurable. The effect of the consumption of consumer goods is subjective and immeasurable. This does not mean that it does not have an objective aspect. If use values did not have the objective capability of satisfying needs, they would not, as a rule, have subjective utility. But the useful properties of consumer goods enter into economic calculations only through the valuations of individual or social consumers. If we assume that a higher consumption effect corresponds to a larger valuation, the overall maximum effect from the consumption of a given amount will be of the product attained under conditions similar to the attainment of the overall maximum effect from capital investment, namely, under conditions of equality of the marginal effectiveness of consumption of the product for all modes of consumption (i.e., by all consumers). However, this assumption is too rigorous. It means that the distribution of incomes according to needs is already being realized and that it is being done in the form of issuing labor certificates or even money. At the present time such a distribution would have a negative influence on production, and consequently on the level of consumption. The problem of maximizing benefits cannot be solved apart from the problem of minimizing costs. They are linked by the dependence of both on the distribution of incomes. On the one hand, the distribution of incomes must stimulate cost savings and the growth of production, and on the other hand it must be directed at maximizing the general level of satisfaction of needs that is possible with a given level of production.

Thus, maximizing the population's well-being cannot be reduced to an extremal problem for a minimum of costs and a maximum of benefits. It is not possible to determine the maximum of well-being without optimizing the distribution of incomes, i.e., estimating its influence both on the standard of living (the level of satisfaction of needs) and on the level of production. If we assume that the system of distribution of incomes is sufficiently favorable both for production and for

258

consumption, the problem of maximizing benefits has a simple solution. The maximum consumption effect is yielded by the composition of production that:

(a) requires the lowest costs among all allowable methods of producing the same consumed output;

(b) corresponds to requirements in the sense that the differential costs of each product are equal to its differential social valuation.

The scale of consumption valuations is established by the average payment for one hour of labor. Consumption valuations can also be expressed in units of average working time. Their function is more graphically represented in such an expression. They show the amount of labor that society considers it necessary to expend on producing each product. Hence it follows that the sum total of labor consumption valuations of the entire fund of consumer goods cannot exceed the outlays of labor. The equality of the sum of prices to the sum of values in this way standardizes the general level of consumption valuations.

Social consumption valuations are subdivided into two forms according to their method of formation:

(1) valuations expressing the sum of personal (individual) needs of a society;

(2) valuations expressing collective needs.

Valuations of the first kind are necessary in solving the problem of "granting to each member of society material and cultural goods according to his growing needs, and according to individual requirements and tastes . . . ."[5]

Valuations of the second kind are necessary in problems of long-term planning of the national economy and in the solution of those questions that determine the long-term structure, rates, and direction of development of the economy. These problems are so complex and important both in the scales of means required and in their influence on the fate of the country that their solution is conceivable only on the basis of centralization of power and resources. For example, the population's demand does not at all solve the problems of accumulation and the rates of expansion of production. It is not possible to make the question of accumulation depend on the volume of workers' individual savings (with respect to accumulation, the population's demand is expressed in its savings). This would mean limiting the share of accumulation in the national income within much narrower limits than under capitalism. In the solution of this problem by a socialist state the share of accumulation in the national income and its growth rates surpass the corresponding indicators of capitalist countries.

But the optimal planning of accumulation presupposes its social consumption valuation. This valuation is the norm of investment effectiveness. The optimum in accumulation is attained when its volume is such that this consumption valuation of accumulation is equated with the individual expenditure of surplus labor on the further expansion of production at the same rate. Precisely in this lies the meaning of equality[6]

$$r_K = \beta \text{ max.}$$

Having established the fundamental relationships in the national economy and their dynamics, the long-term plan in addition develops those controlling norms that must compel (by economic methods) all executors of the plan—both local planning and project organizations and enterprises — to direct their activity in conformity with the prospects marked out for the development of the national economy. Not only the norm of investment effectiveness but also the norm of payments for capital, rent payments, and the entire system of price must serve this purpose. In particular, price policy is an extremely effective means of liquidating every kind of disproportion between branches. The establishment of a higher plan price for scarce goods not only provides the information that the consumption valuation of the commodity exceeds its differential costs but, in addition, is an economic order to expand the production of this commodity.

2. Minimizing the Cost of the Social Product and Maximizing Welfare

Production is not an end in itself. It is a means of satisfying needs. Accordingly, it is natural to accept as the initial task of optimal planning the maximization of the welfare function (or the function of the standard of living, the social utility function, the preference function, or the consumption function — all these are different names for the objective function of the results of the public economy). Then the dual problem will consist of finding norms of effectiveness of resources (of manpower and means of production) that minimize the sum of costs of producing maximum welfare. These norms are found by solving the direct problem. In so doing the law of economy of labor can be expressed by including free time in the welfare function as a special good. The model is thus directed toward seeking the optimal length of the working day. The welfare function, according to certain investigators, can compare not only different goods at the same moment of time but also identical goods at different moments of time, i.e., it can take account of the time factor in economics.[7]

The properties of the task of maximizing welfare that is taken as the initial task in optimal planning are, of course, extremely attractive, but they are illusory. It is not possible to realize them by virtue of the incommensurability both of use values and of their subjective utility. True, individual and social preferences for some goods instead of others and for some consumption structures instead of others are facts, observable everywhere and every day. However, order of preferences can be expressed only in relationships of "larger" or "smaller," not by way of commensuration. In other words, we can assign a larger number to the preferred good and a smaller number to the rejected good, but it is not possible to assign to these numbers all the properties inherent in numbers. It is not possible to add these numbers or to subtract one from another. They denote only the order of preferences.

Moreover, it is not possible to identify the order of preferences with the order of utility or with the level of welfare. ". . . It is easy to jump to the assumption that one pattern is preferred to another because it has a large concealed index of 'satisfaction' or 'utility.' This is a fruitless assumption. More than that it is a trap we must carefully avoid. Such a concept was formerly the object of intense disputes in economic literature, but it has been completely discredited. One of the reasons for this is the obvious nonhomogeneity of the index."[8] ". . . One alternative has greater utility than another because it is preferable, but the reverse is not true."[9] This means that the investigation of preferences does not yield material for determining the utility or welfare function. But this is not all. It is very difficult to determine experimentally an individual utility function, even under ideal conditions. "If it is so difficult to determine the utility function even under the most favorable conditions, there is, of course, no hope that it can be found under real conditions for situations of practical interest."[10]

The mass demand and structure of consumption of the population is a different matter. In observing it, individual and random factors will be mutually offset and the regularities detected can be used for predicting demand. Functions of the dependence of demand on the average income of consumers, on prices of a given commodity and other commodities, and on other factors serve this purpose.

V.A. Volkonskii proposes that we determine, instead of demand functions, the objective consumption function, which would permit us to compare the preferability of different consumption structures. This function is not clearly defined. "In fact, if $u(x)$ is the objective consumption function and $g(u)$ is any monotonically increasing function, then function $u(x) = g[u(x)]$ will also be the objective consumption function. This means that the value of the objective consumption function itself does not reflect any real quantitative regularity."[11] Hence it follows that the level of the objective consumption function becomes determinate and assumes economic meaning via the given prices. The welfare function (in any of its alternatives, in particular as the preference function of the mass of consumers) does not have its own unit of measurement. The scale for consumption valuations must be given from without.

But this is still not the main difficulty in determining the preference function. Let us assume that it can be overcome by establishing a common scale for all consumption valuations. The major difficulty consists in the fact that as long as labor costs are unknown, at least within any limits of possible values, and as long as producers' incomes are unknown, neither consumption valuations nor preference functions can be determined. It is not possible to foresee all possible values of the preference function for all possible values of the amounts of goods and incomes.

The preference function can be determined only given comparatively narrow limits of changes in prices and incomes, which in turn are determined by the conditions of production and distribution. Precisely here we can see the profound meaning of the primacy of production as a principle of Marxist economic science, and the idea of the determination of value by labor costs. It only seems that we can proceed from maximizing the welfare function and then calculate, by solving the dual problem, prices of resources. In reality, we can only proceed from experimental data and by using plan calculations for costs of production and for the distribution of incomes.

On this basis the need for different products with certain possible values of costs can be calculated. By proceeding from the most probable alternative of costs and the needs corresponding to it, the problem is raised of the minimum labor costs required to meet these needs. Data on labor costs obtained in solving this problem will permit us to correct the calculation of needs and again to solve the problem for a general minimum of labor costs with consideration of the corrected composition of needs. In this way the level of welfare can be maximized by means of repeated minimization of the cost of the national economy's final output with repeated recalculations of the need for different goods on the basis of data on the labor costs of these goods obtained at the preceding stage of the calculations.

In this case, maximizing the national income is the dual problem. It permits us to find those prices of final output for which the greatest profitability is attained when the composition of production corresponds to needs. This conformity also signifies the achievement of the maximum satisfaction of needs possible with the given outlays of labor and with the given distribution of incomes. As we will see below, the function of the conformity of production to needs attains in this process a maximum – zero. With nonconformity of output to needs, part of the outlays do not create value, and consequently the sum total of prices proves to be less than the sum of values, and the function of the conformity of production to needs assumes a negative value.[12]

3. Measurement of the Results
and Effectiveness of Living Labor

The measurement of the results of living labor is based, on the one hand, on the measurement of output and, on the other hand, on the measurement of material outlays. Living labor not only yields but also absorbs output (means of production). Consequently, the product of living labor can be represented as the difference between what labor yields and what it absorbs from the national economy, i.e., as the increment in the mass of use values produced by living labor. It is not possible to measure this difference in kind owing to the heterogeneity of the use values of output and of the means of production expended on it. But it can be measured indirectly in units of value or in units of labor costs. In measuring the productivity of labor it is necessary that this indirect measurement reflect the "physical volume" of the produced increment of use values. If we measure the result of living labor with due consideration of its conformity to needs (i.e., in current prices), the relationship of the result of labor costs will express its effectiveness.

263

As we know, the result of living labor is best measured by net output, i.e., by the difference between the value of produced output and the value of means of production expended on it. The relationship of net output to actual labor costs shows the fulfillment by living labor of norms of expenditure of living and embodied labor. This essence of the measurement of the productivity of living labor can be most easily clarified if we ignore the monetary measurement of outlays. Then the relationship of net output (expressed in normative working time) to actual working time will be the general indicator of the fulfillment of all norms, both norms of output and norms of expenditures of past labor. For example, if this relationship is equal to two, this means that the given labor's contribution to the national income was double the planned norms or, in other words, that the given worker expended on the creation of output one-half the living and past labor required according to norms of output and norms of material expenditures.

In the value measurement of net output the productivity of living labor is expressed not by a dimensionless but by a dimensional relative quantity, for example, in rubles per man-hour. In its meaning this is similar to the index of norm fulfillment expressed in man-hours. Indeed, if three rubles of net output are yielded, on the average, by one man-hour of labor, and in the given case six rubles are yielded, this means that the worker expended, in general, on the creation of output one-half of the living and past labor required according to norms of output and material expenditures.[13]

However, net output is calculated by the Central Statistical Administration of the USSR only for determining the national income. It is not calculated at enterprises. An obvious inconsistency results, namely, the most important national economic index appears to be unacceptable for individual parts and links of the national economy.

What are the factors that obstruct the measurement of the results of labor at individual enterprises by net output?

It is customary to think that net output is not calculated at enterprises because the wholesale prices of industry and the procurement prices for means of production are not proportional to the corresponding values. However, the problem of measuring the results of living labor at enterprises is not resolved by the coincidence of prices with values. Net output depends on the conditions of application of labor, namely, the nature of its technical equipment, the quality of usable resources, locations,

264

and other conditions. The conditions of application of labor in producing the same output are usually different. Differences in these conditions cause two substantial defects of net output. The first one is the incompatibility of particular maxima of net output of enterprises, branches, and regions, in a word, of individual parts of the national economy. The second one is that net output cannot serve as the basis for distribution according to labor.

Let us examine each of these defects.

The limited nature of better conditions of application of labor in comparison with the need for them gives rise not only to a feedback between outlays on different products but also to a feedback between the results of the labor of different links in production. Consequently, if all of the links in the national economy strive to achieve a maximum of their net output, these strivings will prove incompatible with each other, for they could be realized only by allotting to all enterprises the best conditions of application of labor, both natural and technological ones, which is impossible.

Thus, the feedback between costs signifies not only the incompatibility of particular minima of costs of production but also the incompatibility of particular maxima of the results of living labor.

Because of the incompatibility of particular maxima of net output, its dynamics do not reflect the dynamics of national income for any part of the national economy. An increase in an enterprise's net output by one million rubles does not mean that the national income increases by the same sum as a result. If an enterprise increases its net output by using scarce raw materials that were previously consumed by other enterprises, the national income may drop as a result. This will occur when the net output of other enterprises is reduced by more than one million rubles owing to a transition to poorer raw materials.

The divergence between the dynamics of an enterprise's net output and the dynamics of the national income is explained by the fact that one enterprise's net output may grow as a result of a reduction in other enterprises' net output. In this way the striving of individual enterprises toward a maximum of net output may be incompatible not only with similar strivings of other enterprises but also with the maximum growth of the national income.

Another defect of net output is its unsuitability for distribution according to labor. Payment for labor on the basis of net output would violate the principle of distribution according to the quantity and quality of labor. Workers of better equipped enterprises, those using better natural resources, etc., would obtain higher pay for the same labor than workers of enterprises located in less favorable conditions.

When the defects of the index of net output are associated with inequality in the conditions of application of labor, in order to remove these defects we must adjust net output to equal conditions of application of labor so that:

(1) for each increase in adjusted net output there would be a corresponding increase in national income;

(2) labor identical in quality and quantity would yield identical adjusted output under any conditions necessary for society.

How to accomplish these requirements is the major and most difficult problem in measuring the effectiveness of living labor. The paramount importance of this problem was perceived in practice long ago, and attempts were made to solve it.[14]

In practice we have tried to isolate profitability from the influence both of changes and of differences in the conditions of application of labor. Thus, changes caused by factors that do not depend on the production activity of the enterprises were taken into account in determining the amount of above-plan profits or of economies from reducing production costs. Included here are changes in prices of raw materials, semifinished products, fuel, and other materials, changes in railroad and other rates, replacement in a planned way of basic kinds of raw materials and fuel, changes in wage rates and supplements, in depreciation rates, in selling prices, and so forth.

Matters are more complex with respect to the removal of the influence of differences in the conditions of application of labor on the results of labor at enterprises. For this purpose we use the turnover tax, intrabranch accounting prices, the regulation of prices for interchangeable means of production in conformity with their degree of economy, and different forms of extraction of differential rent.

The turnover tax was mainly used for smoothing out the differences in the profitability of production of different goods that were caused by price policy.

Accounting prices within a branch with a uniform wholesale price smooth out the influence of different natural sources of raw materials on the calculated profitability of their production. Thus the uniform wholesale price is formed on the basis of average branch production costs of output. This system prevails in the extractive industry of the USSR.

The conformity of wholesale prices of means of production to

266

their degree of economy is attained by establishing higher prices for the more economical, and lower prices for the less economical, output serving a given purpose. Differences in prices thus compensated to some degree for differences in the degree of economy of the applied means of production. For example, we would include here the higher prices for scarce kinds of material and fuel (nonferrous metals, fuel oil).

Payments similar to differential rent can eliminate the influence of differences in natural resources and transport conditions on the production costs of output. Such a system has been applied in the timber industry since 1949, when stumpage fees for lumber were introduced.

As we see, in actual practice we have available several means of isolating profitability from external influences. The use of all of these means of adjusting profitability to equal conditions was inadequate before the 1965 economic reform. Therefore, in planning it was necessary for each enterprise to take account of those differences in the conditions of application of labor that remained unequalized. Nevertheless, in this process subjective factors exerted a strong influence on the extent to which actual production possibilities of enterprises were considered. The greatest rewards were sometimes received not by those enterprises that achieved the greatest increase growth in results, but by those that obtained the smallest assignments.

When the planning of assignments proceeded from the level attained by the enterprise, other negative consequences arose. Only those results attained by the enterprise collective that were realized during the planned year were taken into account in above-plan profits. But technological progress and progress in the organization of production usually do not yield a rapid effect. A long time is often necessary for its realization. That is why the planning of assignments according to the level attained hindered the development of technology and the organization of production.

The problem of adjusting the net output of enterprises and their associations to equal conditions of application of labor is most accurately resolved under optimal planning. Payments for capital investment (for credit) and for the use of productive capital and natural resources place all executors of the plan under equal conditions of application only if these payments are calculated according to the principles of optimal planning. The best conditions are thereby created for complete economic calculation. Net output is adjusted to equal conditions of application of labor

267

by deducting from it the normative effect of the use of capital and natural resources. The difference obtained can be compared both with labor costs and with payments for this labor. The relationship of adjusted net output to outlays of living labor may be called the adjusted productivity of labor. This index will reflect the fulfillment of norms of output, of the quality of output, of material outlays, of the effectiveness of use of fixed and working capital, and of the use of natural resources, all adjusted to equal conditions. The comparison of adjusted net output to wages is possible in the form of the difference between adjusted net output and wages, in the form of the ratio of these quantities and, finally, in the form of the ratio of their difference to wages. These three forms of comparison will yield indicators of adjusted net income, adjusted gross earning capacity and, finally, profitability. The latter is the most synthetic of these.

But this profitability has a meaning quite different from that of the relationship of profits to productive capital. The relationship of adjusted profits (from which rent and payments for productive capital are excluded) to wages may be called the profitability of labor. This is the index of conformity of payments for labor to its results; the rate of profit is the index of conformity of the distribution of surplus value to invested capital. It is obvious that the index of the profitability of labor corresponds more to socialist economics than the rate of profit. Accordingly, we can foresee that in the future, calculation of profitability on the basis of productive capital will give way in the practice of socialist countries to calculating the profitability of labor.

Conditions have not yet been created for measuring labor productivity on the basis of adjusted net output. Furthermore, in the future it will not be necessary to calculate this index at each working place. The accuracy of all measurements (both in technology and in economics) must be economically valid. It must be sufficient, but not excessive. Excessive accuracy is unprofitable. Calculating the results of labor by the adjusted net output is economically valid only where many elements of material outlays depend on the workers and where the costs of calculating net output will not exceed savings derived from the completeness of this calculation. Therefore, the results of labor of small collectives (sections and brigades) and of individual workers must encompass only those elements of net output that depend on the workers. There are more of these elements in the results of joint labor than in the results of individual labor. Consequently, a more complete accounting of the elements of net output is necessary in the measurement of the results of joint labor than in the measurement of the results of individual labor. But a correct understanding of the results of labor as adjusted net output gives us the key to the "weighing" and the measurement of each of the particular indicators of the results of living labor.

Notes

1. At the present time such a task is almost an impracticable one. This is natural, since until the present there has been neither any practical experience in completing it nor any scientific development of this problem. But it can hardly be doubted that with the further development of physiology, psychology, sociology, and statistics it will be possible to investigate the dependence of certain objective attributes of welfare (for example, the state of health, of longevity, indicators of mental statistics) on the level and composition of consumption, and also to study the dependence of needs on sex, age, profession, and climatic conditions. Such investigations will not only enable us to place the problem of optimizing consumption on an objective basis, but will also sketch out the means of its solution.

2. K. Marx and F. Engels, *op. cit.*, Vol. 25, Part I, p. 205.

3. See Chapter 9 on this.

4. K. Marx and F. Engels, *op.cit.*, Vol. 23, p. 453.

5. *Programma Kommunisticheskoi partii Sovetskogo Soiuza*, State Political Literature Publishing House, 1961, p. 64.

6. See page 190.

7. See V. F. Pugachov, "Criteria of Optimality of the Economy," in *Ekonomiko-matematicheskie metody. Narodnokhoziaistvennye modeli. Teoreticheskie voprosy potrebleniia*, Moscow, Academy of Sciences of the USSR Publishing House, 1963, pp. 64 *et seq.*

8. R.D. Luce and H. Raiffa, *Igry i resheniia* (translated from the English), Moscow, Foreign Literature Publishing House, 1961, p. 38.

9. *Ibid.*, p. 66.

10. *Ibid.*, p. 63.

11. V. A. Volknoskii, "On the Objective Mathematical Characterization of Consumption," in *Ekonomiko- mathematicheskie metody . Narodnokhoziaistvennye modeli. Teoreticheskie voprosy potrebleniia*, Moscow, Academy of Sciences of the USSR Publishing House, 1963, p. 204.

12. More detail is given on this in Chapter 9.

13. The meaning of the measurement of productivity of living labor as an index of norm fulfillment will become even clearer if we express labor costs in the same units as those in which net output is measured. Of course, it would be incorrect to replace labor costs by wages actually paid. Wages depend not only on the quality and quantity of labor expended but also on other factors (on the branch, region, results of labor, etc.). Here the relationship of actual wages to the results of labor is especially important. By virtue of this dependence outlays on wages become to a certain degree an index of results rather than of costs. In the measurement of labor productivity the monetary expression of its costs must depend only on the quantity and quality (skill) of labor. For this purpose a uniform system of fixed time rates is necessary, similar to the system of constant (comparable) prices, but much more simple (such a system of rates would be useful not only for measuring labor productivity but also for analyzing wages).

Such an index of labor productivity would be a dimensionless quantity expressing the general level of fulfillment by workers of all norms of expenditures of living and past labor.

14. The necessity of adjusting net output to equal conditions of application of labor is a particular case of the general principle of the equal difficulty (homogeneity) of all norms in a socialist economy. This principle is the basis of distribution according to labor. The standardization of labor costs is based on it. The measurement of the results of living labor must be based on it. If this were not the case, payment according to results would frequently violate the law of distribution according to labor. As we demonstrated above, the relationship of net output to labor costs is nothing other than an index of the fulfillment by living labor of all norms of outlays of both living and past labor.

CHAPTER 9

THE LAW OF VALUE AND
PLANNED PRICE FORMATION

The role of the law of value in a socialist economy is still underestimated. It is true that at present Soviet economists (with certain exceptions) recognize the operation of the law of value in a socialist economy. But how this law operates remains an unclear and controversial question. It is assumed that the law of value is limited by the plan in some respects.

At first glance this agrees with the facts. In the first place, planned prices may deviate from prices that correspond to the law of value. They may be both considerably higher and lower than production costs. They may not correspond to conditions of supply and demand. In the second place, planned proportions between branches may differ substantially from those dictated by the law of value. Bodies performing the planned management of the national economy may establish production assignments without considering their profitability, since the obligatory nature of these assignments ensures their fulfillment and even overfulfillment.

There is no doubt concerning these facts. But is it correct to interpret them as signifying a restriction of the law of value? There are two possibilities. If the law of value operates in a socialist economy, it cannot be restricted. If it does not operate, it is not necessary to restrict it. The very idea that an objective law can be restricted in its operation by subjective factors is inherently contradictory. Therefore, the plan cannot restrict the law of value, any more than it can restrict the law of gravity or equality of the square of the hypotenuse to the sum of squares of the sides. If planned prices do not correspond to the law of value, this does not mean that the plan can restrict the operation of the law of value. The nonconformity of planned prices to the law of value causes negative economic consequences. This thought was clearly expressed by A. G. Kulikov at the scientific conference on the law of value conducted in 1957 by the Institute of Economics of the Academy of Sciences of the USSR. "Ignoring the law of value and nonobservance of its requirements in the practice of managing the economy does not mean that the law of value ceases to function. Such an assertion would be equivalent to the denial of the law of value. If the law of value is not used according to plan in managing the economy, its operation in this case emerges in a spontaneous form and leads to negative consequences in the development of the economy." [1]

The lag in agriculture, the irrational use of means of production, errors in the location of production, the weakening of economic calculation in industry, and the construction of unprofitable enterprises were noted among these negative consequences.

Nevertheless, the idea of the restriction of the law of value by the plan is still the prevailing opinion of Soviet economists. K. V. Ostrovitianov considers that "the restriction of the operation of the law of value is the condition for its greatest possible use." [2] Many other Soviet economists think likewise. [3] But the essence of the law of value is the connection between the labor equivalence of exchange and the proportionality of commodity production. This connection is an objective one, independent of human will. It can be manifested in a spontaneous form, but it can also be planned.

The idea that the plan limits the operation of the law of value has its origin in the identification of an objective law with the spontaneous form of its manifestation. S. G. Strumilin long ago warned against this error. Thus, in 1930 he indicated that the plan must oppose not the law of value, but spontaneity. [4]

The identification of the law of value with the spontaneous form of its manifestation unavoidably leads to the conclusion that the law of value and the law of development according to plan are incompatible with each other. A logical dead end is reached. It appears that incompatible, mutually exclusive laws act jointly in the real world. [5]

But in reality the law of value and the law of development according to plan not only do not exclude each other but only jointly can be most completely realized. This means that only with the realization according to plan of the law of value can its action be freed from the influence of chance, and that only with the

271

complete conformity of planned prices to the law of value can the greatest development according to plan and proportionality in development of the national economy be achieved.

Let us begin with general considerations. We know that with its uncontrolled, spontaneous realization the law of value functions only in an average sense, i.e., through deviations of prices from socially necessary costs. Under these conditions the law of value influences production according to the following rule: first cut it and then try it on. The rationality of costs is verified only after they have been incurred. Hence, "The proportionality of individual branches of production will be reproduced from disproportionality as a constant process . . . ."[6]

The constant proportionality of branches, and, consequently, the constant conformity of prices to socially necessary labor costs are conceivable only in a planned economy. "A constant, consciously sustained proportionality would in fact signify development according to plan, but not that proportionality which is established only as an average quantity from a number of constant fluctuations."[7]

On the other hand, with scientifically valid planning, economic laws form the content of plans. In particular, the better the law of value is taken into account in the plan, the smaller is the role of this law as a negative regulator of production. Consequently, the most complete realization of the law of development according to plan is attainable when the law of value is used most precisely in managing a socialist economy; and, vice versa, the "restriction" of the law of value by the plan is transformed in the final analysis into the "restriction" by the plan . . . of the law of development according to plan. This conclusion needs further explanation and substantiation.

1. The Law of Value and the Problem of Optimal Organization of Management of a Socialist Economy

The law of development according to plan of the national economy is an objective one, and consequently it cannot be restricted any more than the law of value. When we speak about its "restriction," we use this term in the same provisional sense in which we speak of the "restriction" of the law of value, i.e., in the sense of "violation of its requirements." With regard to the law of value, this violation consists of the nonconformity of planned prices to this law. With regard to the law of development according to plan, this violation consists of the nonconformity of the methods and organization of management of the national economy to its laws of organization. These laws have not yet been adequately studied. But the fundamental tendency in the organization of economic management is already sufficiently clear, namely, the development of democratic centralism.

We have seen that the most complete combination of democratization of management of the economy with centralization is achieved only when local indicators of costs and benefits are completely coordinated with national economic indicators, when the minima of cost accounting expenditures indicate conformity of local decisions to the overall minimum of outlays, and when the maximum of local benefits signifies conformity of local decisions to the overall maximum of benefits.

Accordingly, the degree of conformity of local indicators to overall indicators can serve as the criterion of optimality for the organization of economic management. The complete coordination of local indicators with overall ones opens the greatest opportunities for developing the creative activity of the workers in an optimal direction for all society, i.e., with observance of optimal proportions given the maximum growth of labor productivity and with the best use of the workers' material and moral interest in the results of their labor. We will demonstrate below that such a system of prices and economic calculation is an expression of the law of value in its most precise planned use.

However, the maintenance of conformity of planned prices to the law of value is a very difficult task. It is complex because socially necessary expenditures of labor assume both proportionality in the structure of production (conformity between the production of each product and the need for it) and the achievement of levels of costs that are normal for the given social conditions. This means that the conformity of planned prices to the law of value is attainable when the principle of proportionality of production and the law of economy of labor are realized not only in the plan but also in managing the national economy. This follows from the fact that the exchange of labor equivalents and the proportionality of prices to socially necessary expenditures of labor are the attributes of proportionality of production.

This means that the complete realization of the law of value as an objective necessity, without deviations caused by random factors, assumes the optimal organization of a socialist economy, ensuring not only the formulation but also the fulfillment of optimal plans. The theory of duality of linear programming corresponds to this statement. This theory demonstrates that optimal prices are another aspect of the optimal plan. Only optimal plan prices possess the remarkable properties noted. They coordinate local indicators with overall indicators and local with state advantage.

But it is not possible to formulate a plan under the conditions of democratic centralism without having prices. At first glance this appears to be a vicious circle. Optimal prices arise from the optimal plan, and an optimal plan must be compiled on the basis of optimal prices. [8] In actuality we are confronted with a relationship characteristic of economics, in which optimal values of interconnected magnitudes are determined jointly by successive approximations.

Mathematics has elaborated several algorithms for the simultaneous solution of the direct and dual task of linear programming. Although much remains to be done in order to adapt such methods to planning the national economy, nonetheless the possibility of the joint determination of the optimal plan and optimal prices has been mathematically proved and confirmed by experience in solving a number of tasks. The problem here is not the "vicious circle" mentioned above (there is an exit from this circle), but the colossal scale of the task. It is not possible to compile so detailed a national economic plan that the prices of all goods could be determined in connection with this plan. Furthermore, even if it were technically possible, it would hardly be advisable. Detailing the optimal plan for the national economy can be accomplished best of all by detailing (disaggregating) optimal prices established in the course of compiling the national economic plan for the most important products and resources. In this way the interrelationship of the plan and prices not only does not form a vicious circle but, on the contrary, it puts into the hands of the planning apparatus an effective instrument for optimizing the economic structure, namely, approximately optimal prices. Such prices, formed on the basis of prices of the most important products and on the basis of norms of effectiveness of the most important resources (capital investment, natural resources), would be the organizing principle in detailing the plans of branches, regions, and enterprises. We can assert this because the organizing role of prices has been demonstrated by experience. If the law of value ensures a certain proportionality of production even under conditions of anarchy in production, then it can be so much more effective for automating the course of a planned economy.

The fundamental properties and formulas of optimal prices are already well known (we will examine them below). By proceeding from these and being guided by prices and norms of effectiveness of the national economic plan we can calculate approximately optimal prices. At first they will not be perfect. But each step in approximating them to the optimal level will be at the same time a step toward optimizing the management of a socialist economy.

2. The Law of Value as the Regulator of Production

The question of the planned restriction of the action of the law of value is connected with the problem of the regulator of production proportions. The operation of the law of value under socialism was denied by many Soviet economists precisely because it seemed that the recognition of this operation also signified its recognition as the regulator of the socialist economy — of its rates, proportions, and so forth. At the present time certain economists identify the recognition of the operation of the law of value with the recognition of this law as the regulator of socialist production proportions.

However, this view is based on neglecting the difference between the planned and unplanned operation of an economic law. It is the relationship between spontaneity and the plan in the formation of socialist production proportions that is the subject of study and dispute in the question of the regulator of social production. The recognition of the operation of the law of value by itself does not solve this question. It is further necessary to determine how the law of value operates. Does it operate in conformity with the plan or in spite it?

The planned use of the law of value can subordinate all economic decisions to the plan, if planned prices and the system of economic calculation are formed in conformity with the law of value. Such a use of the law of value imparts an enormous breadth of action to the plan. The national economy's plan must not, and cannot, determine all details of economic activity. It cannot determine what every enterprise must make every day of its operation and from what parts each machine and each of its parts must be made, etc. But each of these decisions must be linked with the national economic plan not only qualitatively but also quantitatively.

For example, in choosing a material for a part of a machine it is not sufficient to know that nonferrous metals must be economized. We must also have data for calculating the extent of

275

this saving. If this were not the case, either excessive savings of metal would be possible, causing great losses, or excessive expenditures of it connected with losses at other enterprises.

If prices of metal are established at a level such that the demand for it in all effective uses [9] is in balance with its production, this metal will be usable only in those cases in which its entire output will be most effectively utilized. This does not mean that such planning of prices restricts the operation of the law of value. It means that the plan creates those conditions under which economic laws are directed toward the realization of tasks formulated in the plan. By knowing the quantitative relationships of prices to those conditions that are accessible to the influence of planning management, we can so change these conditions and establish such planned prices that the law of value will assist rather than counteract the realization of planned proportions. In this case proportions dictated by the law of value will coincide with the planned ones, but it would be incorrect to consider that production is regulated by the law of value.

Production proportions under socialism are determined by many conditions and factors, among which planning management is a more powerful factor the better it takes account of economic laws. Thus, the question of the regulator of socialist reproduction is in principle resolved simply. The plan as a form of realization of economic laws must be the regulator. But the accomplishment of this principle depends on the scientific level of planning work and, in particular, on the accuracy of quantitative economic analysis.

3. Foundations for Developing a Mathematical Model of Price Formation

Marx first demonstrated that systematic deviations of prices from values not only do not contradict the labor theory of value but can even be explained only on the basis of this theory. Marx was not able to complete his main work, *Das Kapital*. Nonetheless, this work contains the foundations necessary for constructing a mathematical model of price formation.

Without presenting an exposition of Marx's theory of value as a whole, we will turn our attention only to those propositions that are necessary for constructing a mathematical model of price formation in optimal planning. The objective function and limitations are the most important elements of the model of optimal planning of a socialist economy. The law of economy of labor is expressed most clearly in a mathematical model if the

276

overall labor costs of the national economy's necessary final output are the minimized objective function of the model and if national income expressed in socially necessary labor is the minimized objective function in the dual problem. Such a solution of the question of the model's objective function requires additional explanation. But the greatest differences of opinion arise not on the grounds of refinement of the objective function, but on the grounds of the limitation of the model. The presence of limitations on resources causes the emergence of modifications (of transformed forms) of value in a socialist economy.

Which limitations on resources must be reflected in the model of the optimal plan?

The necessity of a certain limitation of social production time is the most complex and controversial matter in this question. (By social production time we mean the entire period between expenditures of social labor made for producing the given product and the receipt of the given product for consumption.) Limitation of the social production time emerges as a limit on accumulation. The optimal relationship between consumption and accumulation is a most complex problem. Here we will deal with it only from the standpoint of the necessity of considering the limited nature of accumulation in the course of calculating costs and benefits, and this means also in the process of price formation.

There are no doubts concerning the necessity of considering limitations on natural resources. In a socialist economy not only the better national resources but also relatively poorer ones are used.

In the same way all productive capital must be taken into account in compiling the plan. Some of the implements of labor have become obsolete for reproduction but can still be effectively used. Consequently, the quantity of these implements cannot be immediately decreased, and their valuation does not reach their costs of production.

In optimal planning models, the value accounting of limitations is essentially done according to the prinicple of prices of the law of value that prices of nonreproducible resources tend toward levels at which the demand for them is covered by supply.

According to Marx's teaching, the equilibrium of supply and demand is a necessary condition for realizing the law of value. It can be said that in his theory of value the price of equilibrium of supply and demand is a form of manifestation of the law of value. "Even an ordinary economist . . . must agree that no matter what

277

the market value is, supply and demand must be equalized in order for it to be realized." [10]

Some of our economists believe that this norm is not obligatory for a socialist economy. This is correct in the sense that planned prices can deviate from prices of equilibrium of supply and demand. Nevertheless, as we will see later, experience demonstrates and mathematics proves that the rejection of this form directs the operation of the law of value against the law of economy of labor. In the mathematical model of the law of value the price of equilibrium of supply and demand is the necessary means for taking account of limitations of resources and requirements.

Mathematics demonstrates that prices of equilibrium of supply and demand help us to find the minimum or maximum attainable with certain limitations. By using this method in models of the operation of the law of economy of labor we become convinced that the extremal role of the form of manifestation of the law of value is connected with the general law of economy of labor, not with a special economic law of any system. Under communism the overall minimum of labor costs can be determined only with the aid of those norms of effectiveness of use of natual resources and investment that balance the demand for these resources with their planned availability. [11] Accordingly, those who believe that the form of manifestation of the law of value is not obligatory for a socialist economy are wrong. The balance of supply and demand is even more important for a socialist than for a capitalist economy. On the other hand, only planning can ensure a stable balance of supply and demand. Not only the theory of optimal planning but also the development of our practice leads to this conclusion. In practice we take increasingly better account of the state of supply and demand. Although it was previously felt that in our situation demand must outstrip supply (this was seen as one of the advantages of a socialist over a capitalist economy), in recent years general opinion on this question has changed. The program of the CPSU poses the task of the complete satisfaction of the growing demand for consumer goods.

In addition, important changes in the system of satisfying requirements for means of production have been projected in our practice. The 23rd Congress of the CPSU decreed: " . . . To prepare the gradual transition to planned distribution of equipment, materials, and semi finished products by means of wholesale trade . . . . " [12]

As a rule the consumer knows his needs better than do the

278

supply organizations. It is only necessary that he should not be interested in presenting exaggerated claims. Such an interest is unavoidable if demand is larger than supply. Experience also demonstrates that if the demand for a commodity is not covered by its supply, it is difficult to ensure the distribution of the commodity in conformity with actual need. This is obvious in regard to consumer goods. Queues, speculation, and other negative phenomena appear in the distribution of goods.

Less evident but still more urgent is the need for equality of supply and demand of means of production. With effective economic calculation the demand for means of production can better express actual requirements than the demand for consumer goods. Consumer demand would correctly reflect needs only if the distribution of monetary incomes is according to needs rather than according to labor. But if demand originates from enterprises guided by the principle of "the maximum of results and the minimum of costs," then prices of equality of supply and demand ensure a distribution of means of production among enterprises such that these means are most effectively used and an overall minimum of costs of producing the national economy's final output is attained.

The concept of necessary working time as the quantitative limit of "those parts of social working time that can be appropriately expended on various particular spheres of production"[13] is of great importance in Marx's teaching concerning socially necessary labor. This concept reflects the aspect of the law of value that involves taking account of the limitation of needs and realizing that to do so it is necessary to know not only the amount of labor expended on producing a product but also the amount of labor that society considers it advisable to expend on this product. The necessary working time in this sense of the concept is clearly revealed in the mathematical modeling of the law of value. A special auxiliary (or resolving) Lagrange-Kantorovich multiplier must correspond to each limitation in the model.

True, certain economists object to the use of these multipliers in planning prices on the ground that these multipliers have a marginal (limiting) character; and, as we know, Marxism cannot be combined with marginalism. However, this objection is based on a dogmatic simplification of Marx's economic teaching. Marginal magnitudes play a substantial role in it. It is sufficient to recall the role of the least productive expenditure of labor and capital in Marx's theory of ground rent, and also the defense of this concept by Lenin in his dispute with Bulgakov. Bulgakov objected to the concept of the last, least productive expenditure of labor and capital, which concept plays a large role in Ricardo's and Marx's theories of ground rent. Bulgakov asserted that the price of grain is determined by the average productivity of capital. Lenin called Bulgakov's reasoning on this "average productivity" an empty arithmetical exercise. He wrote: "Bulgakov . . . overlooked a *trifle,* the limited nature of land. This limited nature — completely independently of any *ownership* of land — creates a certain kind of monopoly, namely, since the land is entirely occupied by farmers, and since demand is presented for all grain produced on all land, including the very poorest plots and the ones most distant from the market, it is clear that the price of grain is determined by the cost of production on the poorest land (or the cost of production associated with the last, least productive expenditure of capital)." [14]

Lenin linked the role of the least productive expenditure of capital with the limited nature of land. But not only natural resources are limited. The volume of accumulation is also limited. It is smaller than the number of possibilities for effective investment. Accordingly, it is not by chance that we find in Marx an indication of the limiting nature of the general rate of profit. "Special rates of profit in different spheres of production are themselves more or less indeterminate; but to the extent that they appear, it is not their uniformity but their differences that emerge. The general rate of profit itself emerges only as a minimum limit of profit, not as an empirical, directly perceptible form of the actual rate of profit." [15]

Here Marx links the limiting nature of the general rate of profit with differences in particular rates of profit in different spheres of production. This idea is also present in Marx's observation that "differential rent . . . is nothing other than additional profit existing in any sphere of industrial production for any capital functioning in better than average conditions. Only in agriculture is it consolidated, since it rests on such a solid and (relatively) stable basis as different degrees of natural fertility of different categories of land." [16]

Accumulation in a socialist economy is also limited, although differently than in the case of land. Accordingly, we must also apply to capital investment Lenin's comments on the decisive role of its least productive expenditures in price formation.

Under the conditions of socialism, marginal quantities (Lagrange multipliers) have incomparably greater importance than under capitalism. In a socialist economy these quantities are a necessary instrument of optimal planning, whereas under capitalism "marginal measurement" is accomplished spontaneously, only as a tendency that is constantly disrupted and that cannot lead to an optimum.

It is not Lagrange multipliers that are incompatible with Marxism, but rather the economic content of those bourgeois theories that make extensive use of these multipliers. The same mathematical methods can be applied in theories constructed on diametrically opposed premises.

In reflecting the form of operation of the law of value, the methods of the Lagrange-Kantorovich multipliers can be filled with any content. Bourgeois economists use them in models in which they seek a maximum of subjective utility. Then the multipliers take on the content of marginal utility. If a minimum of labor costs for all of the national economy's output is sought in optimal planning, the multipliers reflect labor costs in this scheme. Multipliers always reflect the content of the objective function of the model.

The use of marginal magnitudes in planning is linked not with a subjective theory of value, but with search for the maximum benefits or the minimum costs of organizing the economy on the principles of democratic centralism. Accordingly, the indicated quantities can be excluded from the sphere of calculating costs and determining prices only by rejecting the use of those mathematical methods that are necessary for achieving the greatest economy of labor and the best results.

We see that all the premises necessary for the model of planned price formation, namely, for determing objective functions of the model, constraints, and prices that take account of these constraints in value form, are contained in Marx's theory of value.

The category of the transformed form of value is the most complex part of the Marxian theory of value. Marx investigated it only with reference to capitalist conditions. As we know, Marx and Engels believed that under socialism the law of value would lose its force, and naturally the question of the forms of operation of the law of value could not rise in socialist economy.

Marx associated modifications of value with the formation of the general rate of profit in a capitalist economy. But, in addition, Marx took the position that the price of production has a material basis. [17] Hence it follows that the price of production (or the modification of value similar to it) must occur not only in a capitalist economy but also in a socialist one, since the material basis of the price of production is retained in it and the law of value operates.

But then the question arises, Which labor costs of the product does its price of production express?

The answer to this question should be sought in Marx's observation that the price of production "is determined not only by the value of the given commodity but also by the aggregate value of all commodities."[18] From this we can draw the conclusion that the price of production is a partial derivative of the aggregate value of all commodities with respect to the quantity of the given product. If this is so, then the price of production proves to be the same reflection of expenditures of social labor on the given product as the price which is proportional to the value of this product. Both are partial derivatives of the value of the aggregate product with respect to the quantity of the given product, but are formed under different conditions (limitations). The price that is proportional to the value of the product is a partial derivative, formed under conditions of limitations only of needs. The price of production is a partial derivative, formed under conditions of limitations not only of needs but also of certain resources (of accumulation, of natural resources). The mathematical model of the law of value confirms that this is precisely how the matter stands.

4. Socially Necessary Working Time

The concept of socially necessary working time is the basis of Marx's theory of value. The influence of the law of value of production is based on the comparison of individual costs with socially necessary costs. Socially necessary costs are the criterion that permits us to distinguish in each individual line of production between necessary and unnecessary costs.

This criterion reflects not only costs but also their social effect, not only the conditions of production but also the conditions of distribution and consumption. The qualitative[19] and quantitative[20] conformity of the results of labor to social need (in its specific expression for a given society) are taken into account in socially necessary labor.

Furthermore, socially necessary working time is a social norm of costs stimulating cost economies. "The determination of value by socially necessary working time manifests itself by cheapening commodities and compelling the production of goods under identically favorable conditions."[21]

This function of the law of value assumes especially great

282

significance under socialist conditions. The approximation of prices to socially necessary labor costs is the basis of solving the most important practical tasks of a socialist economy, namely, improving economic calculation, measuring the effectiveness of project alternatives, regulating distribution according to labor, and democratizing economic management. The main practical difficulties in these questions stem from the fact that in determining the effectiveness of expenditures it is necessary to deal with several indicators for which rules of weighing comparison have not been established. [22] Thus, if some indicators of the effectiveness of any alternative are "better" and others are "worse" than in the compared case, it is difficult to draw a general conclusion concerning the effectiveness of the given alternative. Strictly speaking, a multiplicity of indicators of effectiveness excludes the possibility of a generalized calculation of this effectiveness. On these grounds some economists have become convinced that a single indicator of effectiveness is generally impossible.

But if prices corresponded to socially necessary labor costs, the effectiveness of project alternatives and the degree of success of work by an individual sector of the national economy would be measured by the relationship of socially necessary costs of output to individual costs.

So refined and logically clear a formula for the effectiveness of expenditures is not yet applicable in practice. Planned prices are not yet adjusted to proper conformity to socially necessary costs. The reason for this is not only the complexity of the problem but also a lack of attention to it. The generally accepted definition of socially necessary expenditures of labor rests on only part of Marx's theory. Only the range of ideas included in Volume I of *Das Kapital* is usually used in the treatment of this problem, and the development of the category of socially necessary expenditures under the conditions of formation of the price of production and of other modifications of value is not taken into account. Moreover, in Volume III of *Das Kapital,* Marx laid the foundations for the general theory of socially necessary labor, encompassing not only those economic conditions in which prices tend toward values but also those conditions in which prices are proportional to modified value.

In Volume I of *Das Kapital* Marx gave the following definition of socially necessary labor, forming the substance of value: "Socially necessary working time is that working time which is required for producing any use value under the existing socially normal conditions of production, and with a level of skill and labor intensity which is average for the given society."[23]

The concept of socially necessary labor is not completely covered by this definition. Indeed, if we assume that socially necessary labor is expressed only in average costs, we must conclude that any modifications of value are not proportional to socially necessary costs. But this would mean that modification of value contradicts the law of economy of labor, disrupts the conformity of production to needs, and requires that goods be produced not under socially necessary conditions, but under different ones.

Marx thought otherwise. Thus in Chapter 37 of Volume III of *Das Kapital* we read: "If this division [of labor within the entire society – V. N.] is proportional, products of different groups are sold at their values (with subsequent development according to their prices of production) or at prices that are essentially modifications of these values in accordance with prices of production, and are determined by general laws. In reality, the law of value appears not in relation to individual goods or objects, but rather always in relation to the entire totality of products of individual social spheres of production, which appears as distinct owing to the division of labor, so that not only is it true that only necessary working time is expended on each individual commodity but that of the total social working time only the necessary proportial quantity is expended on different groups." [24]

The meaning of this statement is completely clear. The equality of market prices of modifications of value is just as much a sign of conformity of prices to socially necessary labor costs as the equality of prices to values.

5. A Series of Socially Necessary Costs and Its Most Important Characteristics, Given the Scarcity of Only One Kind of Resource

How is it possible that both value and its modifications reflect socially necessary labor costs?

This is conceivable under conditions in which socially necessary costs represent not a single quantity but a series of quantities. Then one characteristic of this series (the average) can determine value and another one can do so for its modification. Such a solution of the question is prompted by logic and is confirmed by further study of the question.

In Volume III of *Das Kapital* we find an extensive investigation of the formation of a series of costs that differ greatly but that are necessary for meeting requirements, and the determination of prices by two characteristics of this series, namely, its average and marginal (largest) values.

If a commodity is produced everywhere under identical technical and natural conditions, then differences in the labor costs of producing it depend wholly on only the particular features of the workers.

In Marx's view, "in every branch of industry the individual worker, Peter or Paul, varies more or less from the average worker. Such individual variations, called 'errors' in the language of mathematics, mutually offset and cancel each other when we select a considerable number of workers."[25]

Under such conditions the normal, necessary level of costs is expressed by their average magnitude. It is sufficient to know average costs in order to determine to what extent the individual costs of producing a commodity correspond to socially necessary ones.

This is precisely the case that Marx investigated in Volume I of *Das Kapital.* In his definition of socially necessary costs he assumed the existence of socially normal conditions — the normal character of material factors of labor and the existence of socially prevailing means of labor, abstracting in this case from differences in the utilized natural resources. [26]

Such conditions obviously existed during the entire period of simple commodity production. [27] Such a situation assumes both a low level of development of productive forces and an extremely slow rate of their growth. The low level of labor productivity is associated with uniformity of utilized natural conditions (by virtue of the labor intensity of use of poor resources), and the extremely slow rate of development of technology ensures the existence of "socially prevailing means of labor."

But with the growth in the level and, especially, in the rate of development of productive forces, substantial differences in the conditions of application of labor arise. This is obvious with reference to natural resources. Technological progress draws into use, together with better natural resources, poorer ones that it was previously inadvisable to use. But similar differences in the effectiveness of utilized means are created by modern technological progress in the means of labor. New, more effective means of labor now appear in many branches within such small intervals of time that it is economically impossible to reduce the useful lives of previously produced means of labor to these intervals. Accordingly, implements with varying effectiveness function simultaneously. These differences are smoothed out by the depreciation of obsolete means of labor (obsolescence). However, the dimensions of the obsolescence of machines indicate the great range of differences in the effectiveness of simultaneously utilized technology.

With the emergence of substantial differences in the effectiveness of utilized means, the conditions of formation of socially necessary costs changed. A series of the distribution of these costs appeared. If, in producing a commodity, for one or another reason it is socially necessary to use means of production differing in effectiveness, costs incurred under both average and better conditions of production, as well as under poorer ones, are socially necessary. This is so because differences in costs arising from differences in the effectiveness of conditions of application of labor do not have an accidental character, but a regular one. Accidental deviations from the average are distributed according to the law of normal distribution, and they more completely offset one another close to the same average as the number of observations is larger. But the distribution of deviations from the average that are linked with the necessity of using different conditions of application of labor is of a different character. Given an increase of this kind in the number of observations, deviations are not mutually offset close to the former average, but rather change the average level itself.

Suppose, for example, that a commodity is produced on units of land with varying fertility — better, average, and poor. With an increase in the number of plots that can be cultivated, average costs change. The reason for this is the scarcity of the relatively better plots of land. Therefore, in taking additional plots into cultivation, the relationship between the plots of varying quality changes. We will illustrate this with an example.

Let us assume that the production of wheat is possible on four different categories of land. Costs and the possible volume of production on the different kinds of land are shown in Table 38. [28]

Table 38

Category of land	Price of production of a quarter, in shillings	Amount of production, in quarters per year
A	60	1
B	30	2
C	20	3
D	15	4

The average price of production of wheat under these conditions depends on the total volume of its production and the quality of land utilized. For example, four quarters per year can be produced on land D, also on land B, and C, and, finally, on land A, B, and C. That composition of utilized land for which the average price of production will be least corresponds to the law of economy of labor. Let us show the dependence of the minimum average price of production on the amount of production of wheat (Table 39).

Table 39

Utilized units of land	Amount of production of wheat, in quarters per year	Minumum average price of production, in shillings per quarter	Difference between highest and average prices of production, in shillings per quarter
D	4	15.0	0
D, C	7	17.1	2.9
D, C, B	9	22.5	7.5
D, C, B, A	10	24.0	36.0

As we see, increasing the number of plots that can be cultivated leads to changing the minimum average quantity and to growth in deviations of the largest socially necessary expenditures from the average ones.

If wheat requirements amount to 10 quarters per year, in order to satisfy this it will be necessary to produce wheat on all plots of land considered in Table 38. Then Table 39 will show a series of the distribution of socially necessary costs of producing wheat. This means that in order to satisfy requirements, not only costs of 15 and 20 shillings per quarter (which are lower than the average of 24 shillings) but also costs considerably surpassing the average must be incurred, namely, 30 and 60 shillings per quarter. In a capitalist economy the commodity price in such cases will be equal to the highest socially necessary price of production, and the entire excess of the commodity price over average costs will form a "false social value," the realization of which yields rent to the landowners. In a socialist economy, differential rent as landowners' income disappears, but the equality of prices to the highest socially necessary costs retains significance. Only with this equality can prices be used to distinguish between necessary costs (corresponding to the law of economy of labor) and unnecessary ones in each individual case.

Average socially necessary costs cannot fulfill this function. Let us observe Tables 38 and 39. If the price of wheat were equal to average costs (24 shillings), the production of wheat on land A

287

and B would be unprofitable, whereas the indicated average would presuppose the use of these units of land.

The equality of prices to marginal costs is necessary not only when differences in costs arise in consequence of the involvement in operation of less and less effective means of labor but also in changing to more effective means of labor. True, the idea of price determination by marginal costs was originally associated with the proposition that production required the use of less and less effective means of labor. This proposition lay at the basis of West's, Malthus', and Ricardo's theory of rent.[29]

However, Marx demonstrated that differential rent can occur in the change to increasingly better land. This idea was expressed by Marx as early as 1851. Thus, in a letter to Engels of January 7, 1851, he wrote: "The law of rent, in the form of the simple thesis put forward by Ricardo, if we leave aside subsequent conclusions drawn from it, does not at all assume decreasing fertility of land, but only the circumstance that, *in spite of the universal growth of fertility of land with which the development of society is accompanied,* the fertility of different plots of land is still *different* or that, with the systematic application of capital to the same plot of land, a different result is obtained." [30]

This statement is now more relevant than when Marx lived. Rates of technological progress are now much higher than a hundred years ago. This statement is important not just in explaining prices of agricultural products: it is of fundamental importance in explaining the law of value as a whole. It substantiates the necessity of the equality of prices to marginal costs, with a continuous reduction in their level, so long as differences in the effectiveness of utilized implements continue to exist, for whatever reasons. Such a situation usually occurs in agriculture and in industry owing to differences not only in nonreproducible means of labor but also in reproducible ones. Consequently, Marx's scheme, which explains price formation in agriculture under conditions of increasing fertility of the soil, can be used to explain the role of marginal costs under conditions of technological progress in the sphere of reproducible implements.

In particular, this scheme refutes the idea that the equality of prices to marginal costs is equivalent to orienting production toward obsolete technology. [31] Marginal costs depend on the amount of production of the commodity under the better conditions of application of labor, namely, on the better pieces of land and on the better machinery. "If production on land B, C, and D exceeded requirements [see Table 39 -- V. N.], land A would cease to play a regulating role." [32]

In a similar way, the use of obsolete machines ceases as better ones are reproduced and marginal costs of production drop. Consequently, in the change to better conditions of application of labor (to better units of land and to better machines), marginal costs themselves are determined by the progress of production under better conditions.

As we already noted, the role of marginal costs in price formation does not depend on the reasons for the emergence of differences in conditions of application of labor. It is sufficient that these differences exist. However, the causes of the formation of these differences are important for their stability, their tendencies of development, and the limits of their fluctuations. In this regard, nonreproducible means of labor differ from reproducible ones. Hence there are certain peculiarities of differential rent in comparison with profits. Among these special features an important one is the circumstance that differential rent begins at zero, whereas profits presuppose a certain minimum rate. Nonetheless, differential ground rent can be viewed as a particular case of supplementary profits from the use of better (more effective) means of production.

This concept of differential rent allows us to generalize the scheme of price formation under conditions of change to better means of labor, i.e., to construct on this basis a general scheme of price formation under conditions of change to better means of labor, both to nonreproducible and to reproducible ones.

Let us present a quantitative model of price formation under conditions of change to better means of labor. These means can be both better units of land and better machines, appearing as a result of technological progress. Then the old, less effective machines will be similar to relatively poorer plots of land, the reduction in profits from these machines will be analogous to the reduction in rent from plots of land previously taken into cultivation, the obsolescence of obsolete machines can be compared to the reduction in the price of plots of land in consequence of taking into cultivation better plots of land, and the removal from operation of worn-out equipment will be analogous to the cessation of production of goods on land whose differential rent has become a negative quantity.

Let us examine three successive periods in the production of a certain product. We will assume that the dependence of the demand for the product on its price is expressed by the following series (Table 40).

289

Table 40

Price, in rubles per unit*	Demand, in units per time period
10	4
9	5
8	6
7	7

* Here each unit can express millions or even billions or ordinary units.

In the first (initial) period four means of labor differing in quality are used with the indicators presented in Table 41.

Table 41

Number of means of labor	Amount of production, in units per period	Costs of producing the commodity, in rubles per unit	Price of the commodity, in rubles per unit	Profit, in rubles per unit of output	Price of the means of labor, in rubles
1	1	10		0	0
2	1	9	10	1	10
3	1	8		2	20
4	1	7		3	30
Total	4				

At the beginning of the second period, means of labor No. 5 is introduced with a production capacity equal to 2 units per period, and with costs of production of 6 rubles per unit of the product. Then the indicators for production of the second period will change as follows (Table 42).

Table 42

Number of means of labor	Amount of production, in units per period	Costs of producing the commodity, in rubles per unit	Price of the commodity, in rubles per unit	Profit, in rubles per unit of output	Price of the means of labor, in rubles
2	1	9		0	0
3	1	8	9	1	10
4	1	7		2	20
5	2	6		3	30
Total	5				

290

At the beginning of the third period means of labor No. 6 is introduced with a capacity of 2 units per period with costs of production of 5 rubles per unit of the commodity. Production attains 6 units per period, and the price is reduced to 8 rubles per unit of the commodity (Table 43).

Table 43

Number of means of labor	Amount of production, in units per period	Costs of producing the commodity, in rubles per unit	Price of the commodity, in rubles per unit	Profit, in rubles per unit of the commodity	Price of the means of labor, in rubles
3	1	8	⎫	0	0
4	1	7	⎬ 8	1	10
5	2	6	⎪	2	20
6	2	5	⎭	3	30
Total	6				

If by means of labor in this scheme we have in mind nonreproducible natural resources, then under the heading of "profit" we include differential rent, and the "price of the means of labor" will express capitalized rent.

If by means of labor we want to signify reproducible resources (for example, machines), we must introduce additional assumptions:

(1) the costs of production of the means of labor do not exceed its price in the period in which this means is introduced into operation;

(2) the term of technical obsolescence of each means of labor is not less than four periods;

(3) during each period only the newest technology will be produced, and it will be placed in operation in the following period.

Then the costs of production of the newest technology that has been placed in operation in the given period set a limit to the costs of production with old implements and also lower the profits and valuation of old means of labor. These relationships can be traced from Table 44.

Table 44

Number of means of labor	First period			Second period			Third period		
	Costs of production, in rubles per unit of output	Profit, in rubles per unit of output	Price of the means of labor, in rubles	Costs of production, in rubles per unit of output	Profit, in rubles per unit of output	Price of the means of labor, in rubles	Costs of production, in rubles per unit of output	Profit, in rubles per unit of output	Price of the means of labor, in rubles
1	☐10	0	0	10	−1	0	10	−2	0
2	9	1	10	☐9	0	0	9	−1	0
3	8	2	20	8	1	10	☐8	0	0
4	7	3	30	7	2	20	7	1	10
5				6	3	30	6	2	20
6							5	3	30

Prices equal to the marginal costs of each period are placed in boxes. To the extent that they are reduced, profits from the use of old means of labor fall below the general rate of profit. Accordingly, the reproduction of obsolete means of labor ceases. But means of labor that are obsolete for reproduction can be used as long as this does not become unprofitable. Naturally their valuation must be reduced in conformity to the reduction in their effectiveness (profitability).

Thus, obsolescence equates the rate of profit from the use of old implements to the general rate of profit (in the optimal plan — with the norm of effectiveness of capital investment).

In the given model the range of distribution (the difference between the largest and smallest quantities) of socially necessary costs of producing the commodity remains constant (three units of labor per unit of output). In actuality it is variable. It is linked with norm of effectiveness of capital investment. The lower this norm is, the shorter (with other conditions remaining equal) the useful lives of old means of labor can be,[33] and the smaller is the difference between the largest and smallest quantities of the series of socially necessary costs. If the norm of effectiveness of investment is equal to 0.15 in our model, then with a product price in the first period equal to 10 rubles per unit it would not be possible to produce means of labor No. 5. The expected profit from its use would be lower than should follow from a norm of 0.15 (10 − 6 < 30 · 0.15). Means of labor No. 5 could be used only

292

with a product price of 10.5 rubles. But with such a price it would be advantageous to use means of labor No. 1.

The norm of investment effectiveness is linked, in turn, with the rate of growth of production in the national economy as a whole.[34]

Consequently, the range of distribution of socially necessary costs per unit of the product with reproducible means of labor and the useful lives of these means are larger as the national economy's growth rate is higher.

6. Socially Necessary Labor Costs Under Conditions of Scarcity of Several Kinds of Resources

In examining the process of formation of a series of socially necessary costs, we assumed that differences in costs of production were caused by the scarcity of only one kind of resources — land of relatively good quality. For this reason the price of the product in the schemes presented is proportional to the labor costs of producing it on land that does not yield rent. In reality, differences in the costs of producing the same product are caused by the scarcity of many kinds of resources, with many products being directly or indirectly produced (i.e., through the means of production used) with two or more scarce resources. In consequence of this, prices become nonproportional to labor costs in lines of production using only inferior resources of a given type that do not yield rent. In this case marginal costs include rent from one (or more) kinds of resources. Marx examined this case in Chapter 44 of Volume III of *Das Kapital.* He demonstrated that "by means of differential rent of type II, relatively better land that already yields rent can become the regulating price and, because of this, *all* land, including that which has not yielded rent up to this time, can be transformed into land that yields rent."[35] Although in this case the proportionality of prices to marginal labor costs remains the law of price formation, nevertheless the concept of marginal costs acquires here a different, more complex content. These are not the marginal (highest) costs of the series of socially necessary costs of the given product, but rather the marginal increments of socially necessary labor expended on the national economy's entire final output, increments that are caused by the production of the given commodity with given resources. (The formula for socially necessary labor and its substantiation will be given below.)

7. The Equality of Prices to Marginal Socially Necessary Costs, and False Social Value

The equality of prices to marginal socially necessary costs under capitalism is connected with the realization of false social value. The average price of production according to Table 39 is 24 shillings per quarter, and the marginal one is 60 shillings. The excess of the marginal price of production over the average one forms the false social value. The question may be raised as to whether the determination of prices by marginal costs leads to the emergence of false value under socialist conditions.

Marx assumed that with the "replacement of capitalist production by association" value of agricultural products would drop because of the disappearance of false social value. Under the conditions of Table 38 the value of a quarter's worth of wheat decreased by 2.5 times. Marx linked this conclusion with the cessation of the action of the law of value under socialism and, in particular, with the disappearance of the uniformity of the market price of goods of the same kind and quality. [36]

However, the conclusion concerning the disappearance of false social value in a socialist economy remains valid also given the operation of the law of value. False social value is based not on the law of value as such but also on private ownership of land and the appropriation of differential rent by landowners. With the transfer of this rent to society, part of the payment for labor that previously entered into capitalist costs of agricultural production can be compensated for out of differential rent. The production costs of agricultural output will correspondingly decrease so that the new marginal production costs (or even the price of production) may become equal to the previous average price of production. [37] To explain this we will rework Table 38 into a single-product model for a capitalist economy (Table 45), proceeding from the following assumptions:

(1) the entire social product consists of wheat;

(2) the product of the preceding year enters into consumption; necessary means of production are reproduced at the same time;

(3) the rate of growth of production is equal to 0.1 per year (in conformity to the annual rate of profit, equal to 0.1);

(4) the relations between costs on different units of land are the same as in Table 38;

(5) all rent is distributed according to labor;

(6) the overall monetary payment for labor, including payment for it from rent, remains unchanged.

Table 45

A Single-Product Model for a Capitalist Economy

(in shillings)

Category of land	Product		Advanced variable capital	Profit (including rent)	Rent	Individual price of production	
	Quarters	Price of production for all output (including rent)				All output	One quarter
A	1	60	50	10	–	60	60
B	2	120	50	70	60	60	30
C	3	180	50	130	120	60	20
D	4	240	50	190	180	60	15
	10	600	200	400	360	240	24

Table 46

A Single-Product Model for a Socialist Economy

(in shillings)

Category of land	Product		Payment for labor		Value of the surplus product		Individual value		Individual price of production		Rent
	Quarters	Price of production of all output (including rent)	Wages	From rent	From rent	Profit	Total product	One quarter	Total product	One quarter	
1	2	3	4	5	6	7	8=4+5 +6+7	9=8:2	10=4 +7	11=10 :2	12=3 −10
A	1	24	20	30	6	4	60	60	24	24	–
B	2	48	20	30	6	4	60	30	24	12	24
C	3	72	20	30	6	4	60	20	24	8	48
D	4	96	20	30	6	4	60	15	24	6	72
	10	240	80	120	24	16	240	24	96	9,6	144
			200		40						

Let us turn our attention to the fact that the marginal price of production of a unit of the product in this model is equal to the average value, i.e., to 60 shillings per quarter. With the replacement of capitalist relations by socialist ones, and with the previous natural indicators of production, we obtain a single-product model for a socialist economy which is presented in Table 46. By comparing model 2 with model 1 we see that:

1. The price of a unit of the product was reduced by 2.5 times, i.e., from 60 to 24 shillings per quarter with unchanged expenditures of social labor per unit of output, and with unchanged payments for labor.

2. This reduction in the price was caused exclusively by the disappearance of false social value, which in model 1 was 1.8 times larger than the advanced capital.

3. Differential rent remained in model 2, and the relationships among rent from units of land of different categories remained unchanged, as well as the relationship of the sum total of rent to the wage fund (144/80 = 360/200 = 1.8). The relationship of rent to the sum total of workers' incomes decreased by 2.5 times (144/200 : 360/200 = 1/2.5).

4. The sum of product prices relative to wages remained unchanged (240/80 = 600/200 = 3), but it decreased in relation to the sum total of workers' incomes by 2.5 times (240/200 : 600/200 = 1/2.5).

5. Equality of the marginal price of production to the average value of a unit of output was retained in model 2. Consequently, both models show how the determination of relative prices by marginal costs is combined with the determination of their level by average costs. Marginal costs are calculated in a category of costs different from average ones. Average costs are related to value and marginal costs, to its transformed form − in the given model, to the price of production.

In model 2 the disappearance of false social value was represented in the form of a reduction in the product price by 2.5 times, retaining the previous fund of workers' monetary incomes. But an essentially similar result is possible with the retention of the previous product price and an increase in workers' incomes by the payment for labor from differential rent. The difference will be only in the scale of prices.

8. Modification of Value

The equality of prices to marginal socially necessary costs is not a special case but the general law of price formation. It also encompasses price formation according to the formula for value, namely, in the absence of substantial differences in the conditions of application of labor, average socially necessary costs coincide with marginal costs. However, with different conditions of

296

application of labor, price formation according to marginal socially necessary costs is necessarily connected with the modification of value, i.e., with the formation of a system of prices in which relative prices of commodities are proportional to marginal socially necessary costs, and the general price level relative to labor costs is determined by average socially necessary costs. The necessity for such a transformation of value is based on the fact that the realization of final output cannot yield more than the sum of its values.

But how is it possible that the sum of such prices, which express marginal costs, should be equal to the sum of values expressing average costs? In other words, how is it possible that the sum of prices calculated according to the formula for "actual costs of production plus the means of their minimization" should be equal to the sum of actual costs of production?

This is possible if marginal costs are expressed in a scale of prices different from average costs (for example, if marginal costs are expressed in terms of production costs and average costs are expressed in terms of value). Marginal production costs can be equal to the value of the same product.

Let us assume that society produces only one product — grain. It is produced on two plots with differing labor productivity. Indicators of output and costs are presented in Table 47. Output and costs are expressed in kind, and other indicators are in monetary units.

Expenditures of labor are here expressed in production costs in a scale different from value (see columns 6 and 1).

Table 47

Plots	Output	Expenditures of labor	Wages	Labor for society	Individual value of output	Value of a unit of output	Production costs of a unit of output	Social value of output	Net income
	1	2	3	4	5=3+4	6=5:1	7=3:1	8	9=8−3
1	100	100	75	25	100	1	0.75	150	75
2	100	200	150	50	200	2	1.5	150	—
Total	200	300	225	75	300	1.5		300	75

It follows from Table 47 that the average value of a unit of the product is equal to 1.5 monetary units (300:200). Multiplying this

297

by the amount of output (column 1), we obtain the social value of each plot's output (column 8).

The marginal production cost of a unit of output is apparent from column 7. The demand for the product is composed of the totals of columns 3 and 4, and is equal to 300 monetary units (225 + 75). It is equal to supply if price = value = 1.5 monetary units per unit of the product.

Thus, the price of equality of supply and demand in our example is equal both to the marginal production cost and to the average value. At the same time, it is also equal to full production costs with consideration of differential rent. For both plots it is also equal to 1.5 monetary units per unit of product.

Let us make our example more complex. Let us assume that many products are produced, and that each of them is produced under different conditions of application of labor. Then if the sum total of all feedback costs (all rent and profits) is equal to the value of the surplus product, the sum of prices of all consumed products will be equal both to the sum of their values and to the sum of their marginal production costs, and finally, to the sum of full production costs.

Thus prices can be determined simultaneously as average and as marginal socially necessary costs. Marginal production costs indicate the limit of allowable outlays on each individual product. At the same time, with prices equal to these production costs, there are no enterprises that are planned to operate at a loss, and the sum of prices can be equal to the sum of values. If marginal measurement is applied to value, the sum of prices in this case cannot be realized, since it will exceed the sum of values. In our example the sum of values is equal to demand (300). If the volume of supply is equal to the sum of marginal values ($200 \cdot 2 = 400$), it will exceed demand by 100 monetary units.

We will demonstrate with a similar numerical example the possibility of the equality of the marginal price of production to the average value. Let us assume that only one product is being produced on two plots of land. But, in contrast to the preceding example, production requires capital investment. In this case profit and rent will be consumed unproductively. Indicators of output and expenditures are given in Table 48. Indicators of output and labor costs are expressed in kind, and other indicators, in a monetary unit.

Table 48

Plots	Output	Capital investment	Labor costs	Wages	Surplus value	Individual value	Social value		Distribution of surplus value			Rate of profit
							Of a unit of output	Of all output	Total	Including		
										Ground rent	Profit	
1	100	150	100	75	58	133	2	200	125	100	25	16.7
2	100	300	200	150	117	267	2	200	50	–	50	16.7
Total	200	450	300	225	175	400	2	400	175	100	75	16.7

It is apparent from the table that the average value of a unit of the product is equal to the marginal price of production and to the price of equilibrium of supply and demand, i.e., to two monetary units per unit of the product.

The transformation of value is linked with its redistribution. Marx demonstrated the relationship between these processes under capitalism. Under the conditions of socialism the transformation of value also presupposes its redistribution. But the social and economic content of this process are different from those under capitalism. The equality of prices to marginal costs under capitalism is necessarily linked with the appropriation by the owners of better resources of the total effect of production with costs lower than marginal costs. Accordingly, the value of the surplus product here cannot be less than the overall economy of labor from the use of relatively better resources.

In a socialist economy the surplus product is not linked by a similar relationship to the effect of better resources. The need for surplus labor for expanding production and for other purposes is determined by considerations entirely different from the overall effect of relatively better means of production. This effect depends on the deviations of marginal socially necessary costs from average costs. With a large range of distribution of socially necessary costs it can exceed the optimal size of the surplus product. Such a situation is more probable the higher the technological level and the more intensive its development. Accordingly, equating the surplus product to the overall effect of better resources can prove to be incompatible with the optimal amounts of the surplus product. In the practice of socialist construction a system of distribution of the national income has been worked out that allows any relationships between the overall effect of better resources and the surplus product. The incomes of workers in socialist countries do not consist only of wages. Social consumption funds, distributed among workers free of charge, are also included. Therefore, the overall effect of better resources can exceed the surplus product by virtue of that part of the necessary product that is distributed through social consumption funds.

9. The Fundamental Equality Determining Socially Necessary Working Time

The concept of socially necessary labor reflects not only the conditions of production but also the conditions of consumption of a commodity. Only that labor is necessary for society whose product qualitatively and quantitatively corresponds to social needs.

This limitation can be exactly fulfilled only by means of special consumption valuations expressed in the labor that society can spend on each product. The existence of such labor valuations is logically necessary in order to separate socially necessary costs from the series of the distribution of costs that are possible according to the conditions of production. Let us look at Tables 39 and 40 (pp. 287, 290). These show only the costs that are possible according to the conditions of production. But as long as the extent of needs for a commodity is unknown, socially necessary costs are also unknown. As a rule, costs per unit of output depend on the amount of production. In some cases they will increase, and in others they will decline with the growth of production. But in both cases socially necessary costs become definite only when the social need for the given commodity has been determined. This need can be set in a twofold manner: (1) according to the amount of the commodity; (2) according to its price. Table 39 becomes a series of the distribution of socially necessary costs under one of the following assumptions: (1) the need for wheat equals 10 quarters per year; (2) the price of wheat equals 60 shillings per quarter.

Each of these definitions of the necessary volume of production is connected with the other. The need for any output is not fixed. "The quantitative definiteness of this need is extraordinarily elastic and variable." [38] It depends on the price of the given commodity, on the prices of other commodities (especially substitutes), and on the level and distribution of the population's

300

income.

The law of value determines the necessary amount of commodities through the price of equality of supply and demand. The labor that, according to the conditions of consumption, society considers it necessary to spend on a given supply of the commodity is also reflected in this price. If this price coincides with the marginal costs of production for the same amount of production, this means that the necessary working time is expended on the commodity.

The measurement of output according to prices that balance needs and production corresponds to the law of economy of labor. If the price of equilibrium of needs and production is lower than expenditures on producing the commodity, the loss will show how much unnecessary labor is expended on producing the given commodity. If the commodity is produced in an insufficient quantity in comparison with needs, then the excess profit shows the economy of labor that society can receive from expanding the production of this commodity.

However, demand usually gives only a distorted expression of social needs. The reflection of needs in demand is affected by the distribution of incomes. The more unequal the distribution, the less accurately does demand reflect the population's needs and the more accurately does it reflect the distribution of incomes.

Only with the distribution of monetary incomes according to needs is the equality of outlays on a product to the equilibrium of supply and demand an accurate indicator of the conformity of production to the law of economy of labor.

A socialist economy cannot be guided only by the population's demand in deciding on the production of final output. This is not just because incomes are distributed according to labor rather than according to needs. We have already seen that the population's demand does not completely solve the problems of accumulation and the expansion of production. By its very nature this problem requires a centralized solution. But it is also not possible to consider the population's demand as the final arbiter in the determination of the composition of production of consumer goods. The transition to communism presupposes the development of needs and their rationalization. It is wrong to assume that each consumer knows best of all what he needs. Even highly cultured people are often mistaken in determining what kind of nutrition is most beneficial for them and what clothing is most suitable for them. These and many other questions concerning consumption can be correctly solved only on the basis of special study.

Moreover, it is not possible for each person to be a specialist in all those spheres of knowledge that in one way or another are linked with questions of rationalizing consumption.

One of the chief means of rationalizing consumption – providing education to develop new needs and to struggle against needs rooted in remnants of the past – is the regulation of prices. This is no accident. It is characteristic of education concerning the development of new needs among the population. Distribution according to labor in connection with the rationalization of consumption makes it possible for a socialist society to use the consumption fund much more effectively than was possible for a capitalist economy. In other words, with a given production of consumer goods per capita of the population a socialist economy attains a much higher level of welfare, i.e., a higher general level of satisfaction of needs, than does a capitalist economy.

Hence it follows that, although prices of consumer goods under socialism take account of demand, production is determined not just by demand. It is not the equality of demand prices to the costs possible according to the conditions of production, but the equality of demand prices to the costs necessary from a social standpoint, that is the condition for proportionality of socialist production. Only this equality determines socially necessary costs. We will illustrate this with an example. Suppose that the dependence of demand and full production costs on the amount of production of a product is expressed by the series presented in Table 49.

Table 49

Amount of production, in thousands of units per year	Marginal costs of production of a unit of output, in rubles	Demand, in thousands of units per year
5	30	10
10	20	25
25	15	40
60	12	60
100	10	80
120	9	100

As the table shows, the production of a commodity and the demand for it are balanced with an output of 60,000 units and a price of 12 rubles per unit. But this does not mean that production must be equal to 60,000 units. If the given product is one whose useful effect is underestimated by demand, the amount of production must be more than 60,000 units, for example, 100,000 units. Then the price must be equal to 9 rubles per unit, which is lower than the costs associated with this volume of production, i.e., 10 rubles.[39] If the given product is one for which the consumption must be limited to 10,000 units per year, the demand price will be higher than costs (30 rubles versus 20 rubles per unit).

Thus, in a socialist economy necessary costs represent not a simple summary of the population's individual "orders" expressed in demand, but an organized collective order, the result of a scientific "mutual weighing" of the useful effects of the given product in comparison with other products and with costs. Since this order depends on the amount of costs, it must be expressed in the form of a series of quantities, i.e., in the form of a conditional order similar to Table 49. Each line of such a table would represent a conditional supply of the following form: if costs are such-and-such, then scientifically valid needs (not demand) for a given product would be such-and-such. Only on the basis of a comparison of this series of costs, possible according to the conditions of production, can we calculate beforehand the amount of production corresponding to needs and, in addition, calculate socially necessary costs. The study of the dependence of demand prices on the extent of supply is a necessary but not sufficient condition for determining a series of socially necessary costs. A scientific investigation of the objective useful effects of different products and of the regularities of development of needs during the transition to communism is also necessary.

Thus, the prices of consumer goods must correspond to demand, but production must not always be oriented to prices. It must always be oriented to socially necessary costs, which may not coincide with equilibrium of supply and demand. Hence it follows that the measurement of results by the sales prices of consumer goods (reflecting demand) cannot serve as the basis for a comparison of costs and results. For this purpose socially necessary costs are necessary. Since the results are realized at demand prices, the determination of results according to socially necessary norms can be done only by introducing corrections into the actually realized results. The economic function of the turnover tax consists precisely of this.

The turnover tax compensates for the deviations of demand prices from socially necessary costs. Results measured without the turnover tax must reflect socially necessary costs. Consequently, socially necessary time is determined by the following equality: labor, necessary according to the conditions of production, is equal to labor, necessary according to the conditions of consumption. This equality was formulated by Marx in Volume III of *Das Kapital.* In Chapter 37 of this volume we read: "Suppose, for example, that a disproportionally large amount of cotton fabrics is produced, although in this entire product and in these fabrics there is only the working time necessary for this purpose under the given conditions. But in general too much social labor is expended on this particular branch, i.e., part of the product is useless. Accordingly, the entire product can only be sold under the same conditions that would prevail if it were produced in the necessary proportions. This quantitative limit of those parts of social working time that could be appropriately spent on different particular spheres of production is only a more developed expression of the law of value in general, although *the necessary working time here acquires a different meaning. A certain amount of working time is necessary for satisfying social needs. The limiting factor is manifested here by means of use value* [my emphasis — V.N.]. Under the given conditions of production, society can expend only so much of its aggregate working time for such-and-such a product of a specific kind."[40]

These statements by Marx substantially develop and complete that concept of socially necessary labor that he presented in Volume I of *Das Kapital.* Marx distinguishes between working time necessary according to the conditions of production and working time necessary according to the conditions of consumption. Socially necessary time is determined only on the basis of both conditions. Proportionality in the distribution of labor among different kinds of manufacturing means that the working time, necessary according to the conditions of production, that is expended on the production of each commodity (both on the total amount of it and on each unit of it) is equal to the working time necessary according to the conditions of consumption. This equality also determines socially necessary time.

10. Tendencies in the Development of Socially Necessary Labor Costs and the General Law of Price Formation

The calculation of costs is a social process. Accounting and computation are only its concluding stage. Initial data for

304

computation — prices and other value norms — form the most important elements of economic relationships. Accordingly, the calculation of costs and the formation of their socially necessary levels has a history and is subordinated both to general and to specific economic laws. Not just methods, but even laws of calculating costs do not remain unchanged. They change together with economic development. The general direction of development of the measurement of costs is linked, for example, with the law of the obligatory conformity of production relations to productive forces and with the law of economy of labor. By virtue of the law of economy of labor the fact that actual costs of production consist only of labor is the general law for calculating costs at all stages of economic development.

The law of economy of labor not only determines the content of actual costs of production but also subordinates the calculation of labor costs to extremal problems, i.e., to problems of maximizing the growth rate of labor productivity. For a known degree of economic development the subordination of the calculation of labor costs to extremal principles is linked with the necessity of considering such auxiliary quantities as social norms of the effectiveness of utilization of means of production. The norms serve as means of minimizing the sum total of expenditures of labor in the national economy (statics) and as means of maximizing the growth rate of labor productivity (dynamics). These auxiliary items of expenditures arise on the grounds of differentiation of conditions of application of labor. Differentiation of conditions of application of labor is the reverse side of the development of productive forces.

With technological progress and a growth in the effectiveness of labor, the use of relatively poor natural resources is extended, and more effective means of labor are applied together with less effective ones. In this way the differentiation of the conditions of application of labor is the result of the growth in the productive power of labor with a certain scarcity of the better natural resources and of surplus labor associated with the length of production time. The law of economy of labor can be realized in the presence of inequality in the conditions of application of labor only by including auxiliary quantities in the calculation of costs (beyond actual costs of production). These quantities permit us to find that overall minimum of actual costs that is allowable with the scarcity of certain resources. Under capitalist conditions these auxiliary quantities arise spontaneously and are linked with obtaining surplus value. Under socialism they become means of

305

managing the economy on the principles of democratic centralism.

Just as differences in the conditions of application of labor increase with the growth of productive forces, so does the role of the means of minimization in the composition of costs grow in calculating socially necessary costs. This general tendency first clearly appeared under capitalism. The price of production emerged. With the formation of the price of production the content of socially necessary working time changed. Whereas in the age of exchange according to value the equality of equilibrium prices of supply and demand to values was the sign of proportionality in production, with the appearance of prices of production the equality of equilibrium prices of supply and demand to prices of production became the sign of proportionality in production.

Let us recall that Marx considered as the sign of proportionality in the division of labor the sale of goods not only at their values but also (with subsequent development) at prices of production, or "at prices that are essentially modifications of these values and correspond to prices of production, and are determined by general laws."[41]

But the price of production is the value expression of differential labor costs. Consequently, even under capitalism socially necessary labor costs began to be determined not by average costs of producing the product (by value), but by those differential costs incurred by the national economy for the given product such that the amount of its production coincides with needs. Of course, in a planless economy this equality characterizes only a constantly disrupted tendency.

And what about under socialism? History does not repeat itself. With the socialist transformation of the economy, that uniformity of conditions of application of labor which was characteristic of the precapitalist economy does not return. That is why it is not possible to fit socialist price formation into the formula for socially necessary labor that is inherent in simple commodity production.

Thereby we are confronted with the hypothesis of the necessity of calculating costs according to formulas for transformed values. Experience in socialist construction confirms this hypothesis. The norm of effectiveness of capital investment has long been used — since the end of the 1920s — by many planners in calculating the effectiveness of project alternatives.

The *Standard Procedure for Determining the Effectiveness of Capital Investment* of the Academy of Sciences of the USSR

(1960) in essence only adjusted, legalized, and expanded previously formed project practice. Unfortunately, norms of effectiveness of productive capital and natural resources were introduced into economic calculation only in connection with the 1965 economic reform. Before this the correctness of the hypothesis concerning the necessity of calculating costs according to formulas for transformed value was mainly confirmed through the negative consequences of calculating costs according to formulas from the long past age of simple commodity production. An insufficient yield of productive capital and natural resources was obviously linked with the fact that they were free of charge.

Nevertheless, the price of production formula is not suitable for a socialist economy. From the very laws of such an economy there emerges its own formula for socially necessary labor costs, differing from the price of production formula.

In a planned economy, with optimal organization the national economy's minimum differential costs for a given product are the socially necessary labor costs of each product, given the condition that production is equal to requirements. With such differential costs, not only the overall minimum of outlays on all of the national economy's final output but also the overall maximum of satisfaction of needs is attained.

The overall minimum of outlays is attained because differential costs express the increment in actual costs of producing the entire final product that is caused by producing the given product. It is not difficult to conclude that the overall minimum of actual costs of production is attained when the production of each product causes the minimum increment in these costs. The overall maximum of satisfaction of needs is attained because the composition of production corresponds to needs, and the greater this conformity — other things being equal — the higher the level of satisfaction of needs.

This formula for socially necessary costs presupposes the optimal organization of a planned economy, which not only has not yet been attained but in general is attainable only gradually and with a certain degree of approximation. Consideration of this law of price formation is absolutely necessary under the conditions of socialism. The program of the CPSU says that "prices must to an increasing degree reflect socially necessary expenditures of labor and ensure compensation for costs of production and distribution and a certain profit to each normally operating enterprise."[42] This requirement signifies not only an approximation of prices to differential costs but also the gradual

307

optimization of planning and management of the Soviet economy. How do we find planned socially necessary differential costs?

For this purpose we must know two distribution series, namely, the distribution of different possibilities (methods) of producing the given product with respect to the magnitude of costs and the distribution of different possibilities (methods) of consumption with respect to the amount of the consumption valuation.

Formation of the equality of costs necessary according to the conditions of production to costs necessary according to the conditions of consumption can be represented by the simplified numerical model presented below.

Table 50

Expenditures of average manpower, in man-hours per unit of product A	Possible volume of production for these expenditures, in units of product A	The consumption valuation of a unit of product A, in man-hours	Possible volume of consumption with a given valuation, in units of product A
1	10	5	10
2	20	4	20
3	30	3	30
4	40	2	40
5	50	1	50

Let Table 50 express both distributions mentioned above for product A, in which each line refers to a single method of production and a single method of consumption, the number of methods of production being equal to the number of methods of consumption. In Table 50 the methods of production are placed in increasing order of expenditures per unit of the product, and methods of consumption are placed in decreasing order of the consumption valuation for a unit of the product. It is immediately apparent that the maximum possible satisfaction of needs with minimum costs will be attained with the utilization of the first three methods of production and the first three methods of consumption (beginning from the top). The volume of production is then equated with consumption on the basis of marginal costs equal to three man-hours per unit. With the further expansion of production for each unit of the product, more labor will be expended than corresponds to the labor consumption valuation, which contradicts the law of economy of labor.

Having established rent payments for better resources for the first two methods of producing product A, we equate: (1) the entire sum of incomes to the sum of consumption valuations, and (2) differential costs per unit of output for all utilized means of production. At the same time these differential costs (equal to three man-hours per unit of product A) will be the smallest of all that are possible with the given methods of production when production is equal to the greatest satisfaction of needs.

Of course, our numerical model is simplified in the extreme. However, in its main features it agrees with more complex models, namely, for different conditions of application of labor planned prices must be proportional to differential costs rather than to average socially necessary costs. Still, average socially necessary costs continue to control prices. This is the case because differential socially necessary costs serve to minimize the sum total of labor costs of the society's necessary final product, which is equivalent to minimizing the average value of a unit of real national income, i.e., of the aggregate final product of the necessary composition. Thus, the reduction of the general level of average labor costs is the goal served by price formation according to marginal costs.

As we see, in combining theoretical analysis of the law of value with historical analysis, tendencies not only in the development of socially necessary labor costs but also in the general law of price formation clearly emerge.

If we recall that with the equality of the conditions of application of labor marginal and average socially necessary costs are equal, we will immediately find the general law of price formation. This law says that prices always tend toward differential (marginal) socially necessary labor costs. In other words, in contrast to value, the price reflects socially necessary expenditures for the growth of production of a given commodity, not the average costs of producing its entire volume. In commodity production, in solving the question of the production of each individual commodity, not the total production of the commodity is examined but only its comparatively small increase. To determine the economic advantage of a growth in the production of any commodity we must know not the average value of outlays on a unit of the commodity, but outlays per unit of growth in production. These outlays may be greater than average but, as a rule, they are smaller than average by virtue of technological progress. Therefore, price formation according to average socially necessary costs usually orients production toward new technology to a lesser degree than price formation according to differential socially necessary costs. It is necessary to remember only that differential socially necessary costs are not actual costs but planned costs in the optimal plan, and that they are formed at advanced enterprises equipped with the newest technology, not at obsolete ones, whose degree of economy of use is determined by costs at new, advanced enterprises.[43]

11. A Model of Differential Socially Necessary Labor Costs in Optimal Planning

Socially necessary labor costs contain two kinds of information. On the one hand, they express labor costs necessary according to the conditions of production; and, on the other hand, they express costs allowable according to the conditions of consumption. The coincidence of both these costs signifies that the production of the commodity corresponds to the need for it and is being conducted sufficiently economically. With optimal planning, socially necessary costs express the minimum necessary labor costs according to the conditions of production, and the maximum allowable ones according to the conditions of consumption. As we will see later, this characterization is incomplete. More exactly, the properties of socially necessary labor costs are revealed only with the aid of a mathematical model of the optimal plan. We will begin with a linear model. The two problems of linear programming — the direct and the dual — can represent both aspects of the formation of socially necessary labor costs, namely, costs allowable according to the conditions of consumption. The direct problem demonstrates how labor costs for the national economy's final output are minimized with a given need for this output. The dual problem demonstrates how national income is maximized as a result of adjusting the composition of final output in conformity to needs.

As we know, the maximum of the general objective function is equal to the minimum of the other objective function. With reference to our double problem this signifies that total working time is distributed among lines of production so that: (a) the production of each final product corresponds to the need for it, and (b) the minimum working time is expended on the entire program of the final product.

Let us examine what the formula for socially necessary labor costs will be in the static model (i.e., the formula encompassing one period of time).

Suppose that:

c_i^l are full labor costs in the planned period for producing a unit of the national economy's ith final output according to the lth technological process. This means that all labor costs for the means of production used are part of c_i^l

$$(i = 1, 2, ..., n),$$
$$(l = 1, 2, ..., s);$$

a_{ij}^l is the full expenditure (for objects of labor) or the complete time of utilization (for means of labor) of resource j per unit of the ith final product according to the lth technological process (with consideration of all preceding stages of production) $(i = 1, 2, ..., n)$, $(j = 1, 2, ..., m)$, $(l = 1, 2, ..., s)$;

q_i^l is the amount of ith final product produced according to the lth process during the planned period;

Q_j is the amount of resource of type j available at the beginning of the planned period;

q_i is the demand for final product i during the planned period;

r_j is the norm of effectiveness of utilization of the jth resource;

P_i is the consumption valuation of the ith final product, expressed in labor.

The optimal plan is formed by solving the following problem of linear programming:

Find the production plan, i.e., those nonnegative q_i^l ($i = 1, 2, ..., n$; $l = 1, 2, ..., s$), which minimize $\sum_{i,l} c_i^l q_i^l$ (overall expenditures on the necessary final output) $\quad\quad$ (9.1)

with constraints $\sum_{i,l} a_{ij}^l q_i^l \leqslant Q_j$ (the demand for resource j must not exceed its availability)

$$(j = 1, 2, ..., m); \quad\quad (9.2)$$

$\sum_l q_i^l \geqslant q_i$ (the production of each product must not be less than the demand for it)

$$(i = 1, 2, ..., n). \quad\quad (9.3)$$

Norms of effectiveness of use of resources and consumption valuations in the optimal plan are determined by solving the dual of the preceding problem.

In order to facilitate drawing up the dual problem we will rewrite constraints (9.2) in the following form:

$$\sum_{i,l} \left(-a_{ij}^l\right) q_i^l \geqslant -Q_j \quad\quad (j = 1, 2, ..., m).$$

Then we will find the nonnegative p_i and r_j which maximize

$$\sum_j r_j (-Q_j) + \sum_i p_i q_i \quad \text{(national income)} \quad\quad (9.4)$$

with constraints: $\quad\quad p_i \leqslant c_i^l + \sum_j a_{ij}^l r_j$

311

(the consumption labor valuation of each product must not be higher than the national economy's differential labor costs for this product)

$$(i = 1, 2, ..., n; l = 1, 2, ..., s).$$ (9.5)

Let the optimal plan of the dual problem $\{\hat{r}_j; \hat{p}_i\}$ correspond to the optimal plan of the direct problem $\{\hat{q}_i^l\}$. In this case $\hat{r}_j$ are norms of effectiveness of resources, and $\hat{p}_i$ are consumption valuations of the products in plan $\{\hat{q}_i^l\}$. Then

$$\hat{r}_j = 0, \text{ when } \sum a_{ij}^l \cdot \hat{q}_i^l < Q_j,$$ (9.6)

$$\hat{q}_i^l = 0, \text{ when } \hat{p}_i < c_i^l + \sum_j a_{ij} \cdot \hat{r}_j.$$ (9.7)

Thus, for all production processes included in the optimal plan, inequalities (9.5) are transformed into equality

$$c_i^l + \sum_j a_{ij}^l \cdot \hat{r}_j = \hat{p}_i.$$ (9.8)

We will explain the basic elements of this model.

The model represents the national economy as a single whole, in which intermediate products of the planned period are treated as unfinished production. In accordance with this, labor costs c_i^l and expenditure coefficients a_{ij}^l represent full costs in the planned period, i.e., with consideration of expenditures on all intermediate products necessary for producing a unit of the ith final product.

Q_j ($j = 1, ..., m$) denotes the amount of resources available at the beginning of the planned period. Here both reproducible and nonreproducible means of production, and both means of labor and objects of labor are included. In this process, with respect to the means of labor, Q_j expresses the effective fund of time of utilization in the planned period of the amount of means of labor that is available at the beginning of the period, and with respect to the objects of labor, Q_j expresses the amount of these available at the beginning of the period.

One of the Q_j denotes the planned limit of capital investment. The limitation on capital investment has a substantially different nature from the limitation on the remaining material resources. This is a limitation on consumption in the planned period. It must be one of the sought-for quantities (unknowns) in the problem of optimal planning of the national economy. Taking its magnitude as given, we considerably simplify the task. Nevertheless, this simplification does not introduce substantial changes in the formula for socially necessary labor.

Condition (9.3), which fixes the extent of requirements for each final product, is an even greater simplification. In actuality, the requirements for each product depend not only on its price but also on the prices of many other products, and above all of interchangeable products. Prices are determined by socially necessary labor costs. Thus, fixing planned requirements can only be done conditionally, based on expected (but not yet calculated) expenditures of socially necessary labor. Consequently, a single solution of the problem does not yield an optimal plan, since the prices P_i found may not coincide with those assumptions on whose basis the required quantities q_i were calculated. Then we must again calculate q_i in accordance with the p_i ascertained and once more solve the problem. In this way, solution of the problem stated yields only a conditionally optimal plan, based on the assumption that the required amounts q_i of final products are determined correctly. Since the required amounts q_i depend on prices p_i, prices depend on costs (9.8), and costs per unit of output depend on the amount of production, the determination of requirements and the compilation of the optimal plan are possible only by means of iteration.

Expression $\sum_i p_i q_i - \sum_j r_j \cdot Q_j = $ max is the objective function of the dual problem.

This requires explanation. Since $\sum_i p_i q_i$ represents the sum of prices of final output, it may seem that this sum also expresses the labor value of the national income. However, it is apparent from equality (9.8) that besides complete labor costs c_i^l, a normative effect (economy of labor) from the use of material resources, i.e., $\sum_j a_{ij}^l r_j$ also enters into prices $\hat{p}_i$. For all final products together this sum will amount to $\sum_{i j, l} a_{ij}^l \cdot q_i^l \cdot \hat{r}_j = \sum_j \hat{r}_j Q_j$. This means that the sum of labor prices of final output exceeds its labor value by $\sum_j \hat{r}_j Q_j$. Consequently, in determining the labor value of the national income it is necessary to deduct $\sum_j \hat{r}_j Q_j$ (material costs) from the sum of prices of final output, as is apparent from formula (9.4).

Condition (9.5) means that in the optimal plan prices can be lower but not higher than differential costs. As we will see later, the sum $c_i^l + \sum_j a_{ij}^l \cdot r_j$ expresses differential socially necessary costs.

This means that condition (9.5) indicates that prices in the optimal plan cannot be higher than socially necessary costs. This is an almost obvious property of optimal prices. Less obvious is why prices of certain goods can be lower than their costs of reproduction. The explanation is apparent from (9.7). If differential costs of some process of producing a given commodity exceed the price of that commodity, this process is not used.

313

When a similar situation occurs for all processes of producing a given commodity, it will not be reproduced, although it can be used if its price is set below the costs of production. An example is the case in which the production of a better machine reduces the valuation of an old machine used for the same purpose below the costs of reproducing it. Such an old machine will not be reproduced although it can continue to be used for a long time, as long as its use does not prove to be on the edge of unprofitability.

Condition (9.5) can be explained differently. Not only the costs that are now reflected in production costs of output but also planned profit and differential rent calculated according to optimal plan norms $(\hat{r}_j)$ enter into the sum $c_i^l + \sum a_{ij}^l \cdot \hat{r}_l$. Consequently, condition (9.5) means that prices must yield profit and rent no higher than the norms of the optimal plan. This is natural. If some technological progress for producing the ith product yields higher profit and rent than follows according to the norms, this is a sign that the optimal plan is not yet complete. It is necessary to expand the application of this process, limiting certain other processes. Norms of effectiveness of resources also change in conformity to this. Accordingly, in the optimal plan socially necessary costs are identical for all processes of producing the given commodity. See equality (9.8) in reference to this. This does not mean that the labor costs of reproducing a given commodity are equal in all processes. It means that each process of producing the given commodity accepted in the optimal plan causes an equal increment in the labor involved in reproducing all of the national economy's final output.

Since our model of the optimal plan reflects the law of economy of labor, the content of costs and results in this model reflects the law of labor value. We must only remember that working time serves as the unit of measurement in the model (we do not deal with the question of reducing complex labor to simple labor, since one or another solution of this question will not change the conclusions).

Let us begin with the fundamental relation between social costs and results. According to the duality theorem,

$$\min \sum_{i,l} c_i^l q_i^l = \max \left(\sum_i p_i q_i - \sum_j r_j Q_j \right). \qquad (9.9)$$

This means that the national income in its labor expression cannot exceed the labor costs of producing it. The maximum of the national income is equal to the minimum labor costs of

314

producing it. But the national income can have a smaller labor value than the labor costs of producing it in the case of nonconformity of production to needs. If more labor is expended on some products than society can expend according to the conditions of consumption (i.e., more than $\hat{p}_i$), it will be necessary for society to expend less labor on other products than would be necessary to satisfy needs.

Disproportions between production and consumption mean that a certain part of the aggregate labor was expended uselessly. In this case the national income expressed in labor will be less than the expenditures of labor on it. In our simplified model if

$$\sum_i \hat{q}_i^l > q_i, \text{ then } p_i = 0. \tag{9.10}$$

Thus, in our model, maximizing the value of social results (of the national income) involves only the establishment of the greatest possible conformity of production to needs. This is precisely why the overall results may be lower but no higher than the sum of expenditures. This corresponds to the statement that "the magnitude of value of a given use value is determined only by the amount of labor or by the amount of working time socially necessary for producing it."[44]

In turn, (9.10) harmonizes with Marx's idea that, with unnecessary expenditure of labor on any branch of production, part of the produced product is useless.[45] Since our model encompasses only one planned period, (9.10) expresses the loss in value of excess products in extreme form, because it does not take account of the possibility of using them beyond the limits of the given period.

Equality (9.9) determines socially necessary labor for society as a whole. In the optimal plan, socially necessary labor costs are minimum overall (total) expenditures of labor on output that most corresponds to needs.

Equality (9.8) is the criterion of conformity of one or another alternative (process) of producing the ith product to the optimal plan. This means that equality (9.8) determines differential socially necessary labor costs for each individual product. The left half of this equality expresses the increment in minimum expenditures of labor on all of the national economy's final output that is caused by producing a unit of the ith product with the lth technological process. The right half of equality (9.8) represents the increment in maximum national income that is caused by obtaining a unit of the ith product. Let us explain this in more detail.

315

It is apparent from equality (9.9) that in the optimal plan the sum of differential costs for all final products is equal to the sum of prices of these products.

$$\sum_i \hat{p}_i q_i = \sum_{i,l} c_i^l \hat{q}_i^l + \sum_j \hat{r}_j Q_j. \tag{9.11}$$

Since

$$\sum_j \hat{r}_j Q_j = \sum_{i,j,l} a_{ij}^l \hat{q}_i^l \hat{r}_j, \tag{9.12}$$

then (9.11) can be rewritten as:

$$\sum_i \hat{p}_i q_i = \sum_{i,l} c_i^l \hat{q}_i^l + \sum_{i,j,l} a_i^l \hat{q}_i^l \hat{r}_j. \tag{9.13}$$

Since with small variations in resources $\Delta Q_j \hat{r}_j$ does not change (by virtue of the linearity of the problem), equality (9.8) can be written in the form

$$\frac{\Delta \left[\sum_{i,l} c_i^l \hat{q}_i^l + \sum_{i,j,l} a_{ij}^l \hat{q}_i^l \hat{r}_j \right]}{\Delta \hat{q}_i^l} = \hat{p}_i = \frac{\partial \sum_i \hat{p}_i q_i}{\partial q_i}. \tag{9.14}$$

We note that the minimum of the overall sum of differential costs $\left[\sum_{il} c_i^l q_i^l + \sum_{ijl} a_i^l \cdot q_i^l \cdot r_j \right]$ is determined by the conditional minimum of labor costs $\sum_{il} c_i^l q_i^l$. With fixed $\hat{r}_j$ and $\hat{q}_i^l$, sum $\sum_{ijl} a_{ij}^l \cdot \hat{q}_i^l \cdot \hat{r}_j$ is also fixed. Consequently, differential socially necessary labor costs of each individual product are expressed by the equality of two partial derivatives, namely, by $\hat{q}_i^l$ from the conditional minimum of labor costs of the required final output, and by q_i from the conditional maximum of the consumption labor valuation of the same final output.

Let us turn to a more general model of socially necessary labor, encompassing a linear model as a particular case. This change permits us to use the Kuhn-Tucker theorem of the saddle point of the Lagrangian function. It has been proved for linear and concave programming. Production with increasing effectiveness of successive expenditures remains beyond its limits when marginal costs are lower than average costs. For simplicity of explanation we will again confine ourselves to the linear case.

On the basis of the Kuhn-Tucker theorem of the saddle point of the Lagrangian function[46] we can write that the overall minimum

316

of labor costs (9.1) and the overall maximum of results (9.4) are realized with such $\hat{q}_i^l$, $\hat{p}_i$, and $\hat{r}_j$, for which the Lagrangian function

$$L\left(q_i^l,\ p_i,\ r_j\right) = \sum_{i,l} c_i^l q_i^l + \sum_j r_j \left(\sum_{i,l} a_{ij}^l q_i^l - Q_j\right)$$
$$- \sum_i p_i \left(\sum_l q_i^l - q_i\right) \tag{9.15}$$

attains a saddle point, i.e., of the minimum as a function of q_i^l with fixed $\hat{p}_i$ and $\hat{r}_j$, and of the maximum as a function of p_i and r_j with fixed $\hat{q}_i^l$.

Then equality (9.9) will be expressed in the form of the equality of the minimum value $L_1 = L(q_i^l\hat{p}_i, \hat{r}_j)$ to the maximum value $L_2 = L(\hat{q}_i, \hat{p}_i, r_j)$. L_1 corresponds to the direct problem of linear programming and L_2 to the dual one.

$$\min L_1 = \min \left\{\left[\sum_{il} c_i^l q_i^l\right.\right.$$
$$+ \left| \sum_j \hat{r}_j \left(\sum_{i,l} a_{ij}^l q_i^l - Q_j\right) - \sum_i \hat{p}_i \left(\sum_l q_i^l - q_i\right)\right| \right\}$$
$$= \max L_2 = \max \left\{\sum_i p_i q_i - \sum_j r_j Q_j\right.$$
$$+ \left| \sum_{i,l} \hat{q}_i^l \left(c_i^l + \sum_j a_{ij}^l r_j - p_i\right)\right| \right\}, \tag{9.16}$$

where r_j and p_i in function L are Lagrange multipliers that take into account constraints on resources (9.2) and needs (9.3).

After the solution of the problem the values of quantities included in the rectangles become equal to zero. Indeed, if $\sum_{il} a_{ij}^l q_i^l < Q_j$ (the need for a resource is less than its availability), then $r_j = 0$. If $\sum_l q_i^l > q_i$ (production of the ith product exceeds the need for it), then $\hat{p}_i = 0$. If conditions (9.2) and (9.3) represent equalities, then differences $\sum_{il} a_{ij}^l q_i^l - Q_j$ and $\sum_l q_i^l - q_i$, and the products of these differences and $\hat{r}_j$ and $\hat{p}_i$, are equal to zero. Consequently, the minimum of function L_1 is equal to the conditional minimum of labor costs $\sum_{i,l} c_i^l q_i^l$ and norms of effectiveness of resources ($\hat{r}_j$) play an auxiliary role. If $L_1 = \min$, they are either multiplied by zero or themselves become equal to zero.

317

This means that the use of scarce resources does not create value. Norms of their effectiveness $(\hat{r}_j)$ cause only transformation of value, i.e., the formation of stable but mutually offsetting deviations of prices from values.

The maximum of function L_2 is equal to the maximum value of national income $\sum_i p_i q_i - \sum_j r_j Q_j$, because in this case the quantity included in the second rectangle becomes zero. This is apparent from (9.8).

Consequently, equality (9.16) determines the socially necessary costs of all of society's final output. Partial derivatives for q_i^l from min L_1 determine socially necessary costs per unit of each individual product.

With condition $\hat{q}_{ii}^l > 0$ these derivatives become zero at point $q_i^l = \hat{q}_i^l$:

Hence
$$\frac{\partial L_1}{\partial q_i^l} = c_i^l + \sum_j a_{ij}^l \hat{r}_j - \hat{p}_i = 0. \tag{9.17}$$

$$c_i^l + \sum_j a_{ij}^l \cdot \hat{r}_j = \hat{p}_i. \tag{9.18}$$

We again obtain equality (9.8), which determines socially necessary labor costs in optimal planning.

The left half of this equality expresses differential costs of the ith product, i.e., that increment in the conditional minimum of expenditures of labor on society's final output that is associated with the production of the ith product with technological method l.

Indeed, the left half of equality (9.18) is a partial derivative of the minimum of that part of the Lagrangian function that is included within square brackets, considering this part with reference to each variable q_i^l separately from the fixed optimal values of the remaining $\hat{q}_i^l$

$$\frac{\partial \left[\sum_{i,l} c_i^l q_i^l \quad \sum_j r_j \left(\sum_{i,l} a_{ij}^l q_i^l - Q_j \right) \right]}{\partial q_i^l} = c_i^l + \sum_j a_{ij}^l r_j. \tag{9.19}$$

The right half of equality (9.18) expresses that increment in the conditional maximum of the national income that is caused by the appearance of a unit of the ith product.

$$\frac{\partial \left[\sum_i \hat{p}_i q_i - \sum_j \hat{r}_j Q_j + \sum_{i,l} q_i^l \left(c_i^l + \sum_j a_{ij}^l \hat{r}_j - \hat{p}_i \right) \right]}{\partial q_i^l} = \hat{p}_i. \tag{9.20}$$

Consequently, socially necessary labor for an individual product will be determined by the following equality. The increment in the conditional minimum of expenditures on society's final output, caused by the production of a unit of the ith product with technological method 1, is equal to the increment in the conditional maximum of the national income caused by the appearance of a unit of the ith product, or, more briefly: differential costs of the ith product with production method 1 are equal to society's differential income for the same product.

We have already called the reader's attention to the fact that multipliers $\hat{r}_j$ are not included in real costs. Consequently, the sum of labor prices must be equal to the sum of labor costs for the same output:

$$\sum_i \hat{p}_i q_i = \sum_{i, l} c_i^l \hat{q}_i^l. \tag{9.21}$$

But it is apparent from (9.11) and (9.13) that the sum of prices must also be equal to the sum of differential costs.

Equality (9.21) is incompatible with (9.13). The left halves of these equalities are identical, whereas the right half of equality (9.13) is larger than the right half of equality (9.21) by a sum that is not a source of value but serves as a means of minimizing it, i.e., by $\sum_{i,j,l} a_{ij}^l \hat{q}_i^l \hat{r}_j$. However, since in economic calculations the means

equated to zero (it is not paid out of costs).

By decreasing the sum of labor costs by a certain proportion, we will obtain the sum of paid labor. We must also decrease multipliers p_i and r_j in the same proportion (in order to preserve the relationship between the quantities in function L).

Dividing differential costs by $(K + 1)$, where K is the norm of labor for society, i.e.,

$$K = \frac{\sum\limits_{i,j,l} a_{ij}^l \hat{q}_i^l \hat{r}_j}{\sum\limits_{i,l} c_i^l \hat{q}_i^l},$$

we have

$$\sum_{i,l} c_i^l \hat{q}_i^l = \frac{1}{K + 1} \left(\sum_{i,l} c_i^l \hat{q}_i^l + \sum_{i,j,l} a_{ij}^l \hat{q}_i^l \hat{r}_j \right). \tag{9.22}$$

We correspondingly change formula (9.8):

$$\frac{1}{K + 1} \left(c_i^l + \sum_j a_{ij}^l \hat{r}_j \right) = \frac{1}{K + 1} \hat{p}_i. \tag{9.23}$$

319

In a capitalist economy the entire sum of feedback costs is realized by the owners of means of production in the form of surplus value. In a socialist economy the sum of feedback costs is realized in the form of labor for society, the amount of which can only accidentally coincide with the required amount of surplus labor. If the required volume of surplus labor is less than the entire sum of feedback costs $\sum_{i,j,l} a_{ij}^l \hat{q}_i^l \hat{r}_j$, the remainder may be distributed among workers in material production in proportion to their labor (for example, in the form of bonuses from profits and rent), or according to needs.

12. The General Formula for Price Formation

Marx presented two formulas for price formation. One was for simple commodity production (value) and the other was for capitalism (the price of production). He showed that the two formulas were connected, but he did not derive from them a general formula for price formation expressing the law of value as such for any commodity economy.

The absence of a general formula for price formation has served until the present time as the main target for bourgeois critics of Marx's theory of value. The existence of two formulas for expressing the operation of a single law is considered by them as an inherent contradiction in a scientific system.

Furthermore, conditions have matured in the socialist economy that are favorable for generalizing the laws of price formation. Rich experience in planning prices has been accumulated, and the beginning of the mathematical theory of optimal planning has been created. On the basis of this theory we can derive a formula for the optimal planned price – a price that corresponds to the best utilization of the law of value. By comparing it with formulas for the price of production and value we can find those features of price formation that are common to all three formulas.

The model of socially necessary labor in the optimal plan leads us to this goal. Let us turn, in this model, from labor costs and labor prices to value and monetary prices. Let w be the coefficient of proportionality of values to labor costs, and let π_i be the optimal price, expressed in a monetary unit. By considering (9.23) we have a formula for the monetary price in optimal planning:

$$\hat{\pi}_i = \hat{p}_i \frac{w}{K+1} = \frac{w}{K+1}\left(c_i^l + \sum_j a_{ij}^l \hat{r}_j\right), \qquad (9.24)$$

320

from which it is clear that the optimal price is proportional to the partial derivative of the conditional minimum of the value of the total final output with respect to the amount of the given product.

Formula (9.24) recalls the price of production. This similarity is not accidental. Even under capitalism the law of economy of labor operates under conditions of scarcity of the better material resources. The competition among capitalists that is the basis for the formation of a general rate of profit is also subject to this law to a certain extent.

However, the price of production differs from the optimal plan price.

In the first place, the price of production is formed on the basis of a partial derivative of the actual, not the minimum, value of society's final product (under capitalism this minimum is not realized).

In the second place, individual prices of production with feasible technological processes are, on the average, equal only to the market price while, according to formula (9.24), outlays on each process of producing the commodity included in the optimal plan are equal to the price.

In the third place, the elements of the price of production are formed under conditions of private ownership of the means of production. Accordingly, the sum total of surplus labor cannot be less than the general normative effect of material resources, less than the sum total of feedback costs. Denoting the norm of surplus labor by K_n, we write the formula for the price of production ($\hat{\pi}_i$):

$$\bar{\pi}_i = \bar{p}_i \frac{w}{K_n + 1} = \frac{w}{K_n + 1}\left(\bar{c}_i^l + \sum_j a_{ij}^l r_j\right). \qquad (9.25)^{47}$$

Under the conditions of simple commodity production, when the value of implements of labor is insignificant and relatively better natural resources are incompletely used (i.e., $r_j = 0$), formula (9.25) is transformed into the equality of average prices to values:

$$\bar{\pi}_i = \bar{p}_i w = \bar{c}_i^l w. \qquad (9.26)$$

This reasoning leads to the general formula for the law of value:

$$\bar{\pi}_i = \frac{w}{K + 1}\left(\overline{c_i^l + \sum_j a_{ij}^l r_j}\right), \qquad (9.27)$$

where K is either the norm of labor for society (in a socialist economy) or the norm of surplus labor (in a capitalist economy).

321

The economic meaning of formula (9.27) is that the law of economy of labor under the conditions of commodity production is realized through the proportionality of average prices to average partial derivatives of the value of society's final product with respect to the quantity of each given product.

The general formula for the law of value is of wide-ranging significance:

1. It follows from this formula that the formation of the transformed form of value is not at all a distortion of this law. The transformation of value is an expression of the law of value under conditions of a sufficiently high level of development of productive forces, when not only the better material resources but also less effective ones are used. Under the conditions of commodity production the scarcity of better resources can be taken into account in economic calculations only by means of Lagrange multipliers. This law also applies under socialism. If these multipliers are not used in price formation, they are applied in project calculations in the form of unofficial norms of the recoupment period on capital investment, coefficients of scarcity, and similar procedures.

The tendency for the transformation of value in socialist countries is caused not only by the limited nature of accumulation in comparison with the possibility for effective investment but also by the scarcity of better natural resources. (This is clear from formula (9.27): r_j for natural resources is differential rent.)

Hence it is apparent how invalid is the objection against Marx's theory of value that it does not correspond to the facts, since prices are proportional to values only under certain conditions. Marx's theory of value does not state that prices are proportional to labor values, but that prices are derived from value. Mathematics aids us in explaining precisely which derivatives from value are prices.

2. It follows from formulas for socially necessary labor (9.9) and (9.16) that the limited nature of material resources does not create value. The mathematical formula for the law of value yields a clear delimitation of the actual costs of production from the means of minimizing them.

Hence it is obvious how wrong are those bourgeois critics of Soviet economic science who assume that in the mathematical scheme of the optimal plan each primary factor is an independent source of the creation of value and that the relative scarcity of each manifests itself as a measure of value. Mathematics by itself cannot demonstrate of what actual costs of production consist. The qualitative premises of the scheme are given by economic

322

science. If the law of economy of labor enters into the premises of the scheme for price formation, then it is not possible to derive from this law price theory different from the theory of labor value and a theory of profit and rent different from the theory of surplus value.

3. Mathematical models of the law of value illuminate the difference between price and value, generalize the concept of price, and demonstrate its existence in the economy with a labor unit of costs and benefits. The following properties of price clearly emerge in these models:

(a) Price differs from value not only quantitatively but also qualitatively. In a certain sense price is related to value as a means is to an end.

In the optimal plan the law of value minimizes the overall value of society's final output and maximizes the national income, with the aid of prices derived from the overall minimum of labor costs and the maximum of national income.

Hence a formal difference emerges between value and price. The value of society's final output is the model's objective function, and prices are Lagrange multipliers r_i and p_i, which take into account limitations on resources and needs.

(b) The price is the means of minimizing expenditures of labor on all of society's final output. Accordingly, the price of an individual commodity can deviate by any amount from its value, up to the point that objects can have a price that do not have value (for example, r_j for usable natural resources is, as a rule, larger than zero).

(c) Prices and norms of effectiveness of all material goods are derived from the value of society's final output. We have already demonstrated this for p_i. We will remark that all r_j (norms of effectiveness and prices of resources) are partial derivatives of the conditional minimum of expenditures of labor on the final product with respect to the amount of the given resource:

$$\hat{r}_j = \frac{\partial \min L_1}{\partial Q_j} \; ;$$

(d) The price as a consumption valuation of the product, different from labor costs, is necessary not only in the case of monetary measurement of costs and benefits but also in the case of labor measurement of this kind.

(e) All prices, both monetary and labor, of final output and resources equalize demand and availability. This is the essential attribute of commodity production.

13. Socially Necessary Labor and Prices in Models of the Development of a Socialist Economy

The optimal plan for one period of time can be constructed only as part of a long-term plan. Only by considering long-term development can we establish certain constraints on the plan for one period, namely, the limit of capital investment and the program for producing final output with respect to those means of production that are intended for the subsequent growth of production. But if we assume that these constraints are set by the optimal long-term plan, the formulas for socially necessary labor and price formation that are derived from an analysis of the static model will be suitable for calculating prices that are also optimal from the standpoint of long-term development. Consideration of long-term development takes away nothing from formulas for price formation that are derived from an analysis of the static model; rather, it adds something.

In the first place, in the long-term plan the volume of accumulation is not given, but is sought. Accordingly, in the dynamic model of the optimal price the norm of effectiveness of investment should be replaced by an expression of its dependence on factors determining it.

In the second place, in the dynamic model socially necessary labor costs depend on time. In time both average and differential socially necessary labor costs change.

In the third place, under the conditions of continuous technological progress and the development of needs, optimal prices must assist these processes in the best possible way. The equality of differential costs to consumption valuations can hardly satisfy this requirement. Furthermore, with continuous changes in the conditions of production and consumption this is hardly practicable. It is natural to assume that some sort of (changing) optimum exists for the gap between the consumption valuation and differential costs. If this is correct, the fundamental equality that determines socially necessary costs changes. Profit — positive in some lines of production and negative in others — is added to differential costs.

In the fourth place, in models of economic development the problem of optimizing the movement of prices, i.e., the relationships between prices in different periods of time, must be solved. In dynamic models of optimal planning the equality of consumption valuations to differential costs must occur not only within the limits of the given period but also between periods. Let us assume that the production time for a commodity is equal to one period. Then the commodity produced in period t must have in the $(t + 1)$ period a consumption valuation equal to its differential costs in period t. Problems of monetary circulation and financing are thereby introduced into the model. Financing the growth of production and the payment of surplus labor connected with it can be implemented both by deductions from wages (loans, direct taxes) and out of profits (including the turnover tax in it). In both cases the equality of differential costs of period t to the price of the $(t + 1)$ period necessary in the optimal plan is possible. But the composition of full production costs in the first case will be different from that in the second. With the payment of surplus labor out of deductions from wages, the sum total of profits of all enterprises is equal to zero. Under such conditions credit financing is possible only if credit is free.

In the second case, i.e., with the financing of the growth of production out of accumulated profit, the money necessary for its realization enters into circulation through the payment of the surplus labor that produces this profit. The emission of money can occur in this case through credit arrangements. Payments for credit will then enter into the composition of full production costs.

The first scheme of the dynamics of prices is similar to the action of the objectively conditioned valuations in the dynamic model of the optimal plan proposed by L.V. Kantorovich. In this model, objectively conditioned valuations of products decline, on the average, in proportion to the growth of production. Accordingly, the economic growth rate in this model represents a quantity inverse to the index of change in objectively conditioned valuations, weighted by current amounts of products.[48]

The second scheme of the dynamics of prices is similar to price formation in J. von Neumann's model of an expanding economy.[49] In this model the production of all goods increases at the same rate, prices do not depend on time, and the increase in production is financed through the investment of profit.

The reduction of prices in conformity to the growth of production would be possible only if the total fund of money wages remained unchanged over time, both with a growth in labor productivity and in the number of workers. This is an unrealistic supposition (at least under the conditions of distribution according to labor). With a growth in production we must pay either additional workers (if growth occurs by virtue of an increase in the number of workers) or the inventors, efficiency experts, and scientific workers whose activity caused the growth of labor productivity. Technological progress is absent in Neumann's model. Accordingly, the condition of equilibrium in this model is expressed in an identical rate of development of all branches, with a constant level of real wages. In that case, prices naturally remain constant.

Under conditions of continuous technological progress a gradual reduction in the price level is more probable, but at a slower rate than the growth in production. Such a concept of the dynamics of prices is based on the hypothesis that the greatest growth in production due to progress in technology and organization is attainable by making payments to inventors, organizers, and efficiency experts that are dependent on the effectiveness of achievements; but, in addition, these payments must constitute only a certain portion of the effect. Then the total fund of money wages can grow at a slower rate than the consumption fund, and the general level of prices will decrease. Such dynamics of the price level are more advisable than the action of objectively conditioned valuations or the stability of the price level.

However, the conditions of development of production may be extremely varied. Accordingly, we must be careful in defining this movement of the price level as an optimal one. In the long-term plan the dynamics of prices depend not only on the norms of payment for the creative achievements of workers in production, but also on changes in the relationships between accumulation and consumption, on the nature of technological progress (in particular, on change in the full capital intensity of final output), on changes in the relationship between working time and free time, and on changes in the size of the unproductive sphere. All these relationships have their own optimal values. That is why the best dynamics of prices can be found only in connection with the solution of a whole series of problems that have not yet been adequately worked out.

Notes

1. *Zakon stoimosti i ego ispol'zovanie v narodnom khoziaistve SSSR,* State Political Literature Publishing House, 1959, p. 65 (cited henceforth as *Zakon stoimosti*).

2. *Ibid.,* p. 25.

3. *Ibid.,* p. 39.

4. See *Planovoe khoziaistvo,* 1930, No. 4, pp. 155-157.

5. "The law of proportional development according to plan and the law of value are laws that, by their nature, are mutually exclusive," *Zakon stoimosti,* p. 227.

6. K. Marx and F. Engels, *op.cit.,* Vol. 25, Part I, p. 282.

7. V. I. Lenin, *op.cit.,* Vol. 3, p. 620.

8. A. Ia. Boiarskii presents such an objection to the theory of optimal planning. See his *Matematiko-ekonomicheskie ocherki,* Moscow, State Statistical Publishing House, 1962, p. 369.

9. That is, those applications in which the use of the given metal ensures the least expenditures on output.

10. K. Marx and F. Engels, *op.cit.,* Vol. 25, Part I, p. 210.

11. For more detail on this see *Primenenie matematiki v ekonomicheskikh issledovaniiakh i planirovanii,* Collection, Moscow, Socialist Economics Publishing House, 1959, pp. 160 *et seq.* (cited henceforth as *Primenenie matematiki).*

12. *Direktivy XXIII s'ezda KPSS po piatiletnemu planu razvitiia narodnogo khoziaistva SSSR na 1966-1970 gody,* Political Literature Publishing House, 1966, p. 14.

13. K. Marx and F. Engels, *op.cit.,* Vol. 25, Part II, p. 186; see also Vol. 26, Part I, pp. 220-221.

14. V.I. Lenin, *op cit.,* Vol. 5, p. 118.

15. K. Marx and F. Engels, *op.cit.,* Vol. 25, Part I, p. 403. For the significance of this statement in Marx's theory, see the collection *Primenenie matematiki,* p. 182.

16. K. Marx and F. Engels, *op.cit.,* Vol. 30, p. 220.

17. See Chapter 1.

18. K. Marx and F. Engels, *op.cit.,* Vol. 25, Part I, p. 225.

19. *Ibid.,* Vol. 23, p. 49.

20. *Ibid.,* Vol. 25, Part II, p. 186.

21. *Ibid.,* p. 195.

22. The existence of a norm for weighting the different indicators of effectiveness is equivalent to combining them into one index.

23. K. Marx and F. Engels, *op.cit.,* Vol. 23, p. 47.

24. *Ibid.,* Vol. 25, Part II, p. 185.

25. *Ibid.,* Vol. 23, p. 334.

26. *Ibid.,* pp. 47, 207.

27. *Ibid.,* Vol. 25, Part II, p. 474.

28. Compiled according to Table 1, Chapter 39, Volume III of Marx's *Das Kapital.* The units of measurement may be in millions. (See K. Marx and F. Engels, *op.cit.,* Vol. 25, Part II, pp. 204 and 212.)

29. See D. Ricardo, *Nachala politicheskoi ekonomii i podatnogo oblozheniia,* Moscow, Socialist Economics Publishing House, 1935, p. 35.

30. K. Marx and F. Engels, *op.cit.,* Vol. 27, p. 151.

31. See K. Ostrovitianov, "The Building of Communism and Commodity Production," *Voprosy ekonomiki,* 1961, No. 10.

32. K. Marx and F. Engels, *op.cit.,* Vol. 25, Part II, p. 210.

33. See Chapter 7.

34. See Chapter 6.

35. K. Marx and F. Engels, *op.cit.,* Vol. 25, Part II, p. 297 (note by F. Engels).

36. *Ibid.,* p. 213. See also Vol. 27, p. 151: "The entire gist of the question of rent consists in the fact that rent emerges through the equalization of prices of commodities produced at different costs of production, but this law of market price is nothing but a law of bourgeois competition."

37. Marx calculated false social value by proceeding from the price of production. We also retain this expression of costs in the model of a socialist economy only for comparability with Marx's calculations, and do not consider as yet the question of the existence of the law of the price of production in a socialist economy.

38. K. Marx and F. Engels, *op.cit.,* Vol. 25, Part I, p. 206.

39. This does not mean that production of the given commodity will necessarily *be* unprofitable, i.e., will not yield a net income. Labor for society is included in costs.

40. K. Marx and F. Engels, *op.cit.*, Vol. 25, Part II, p. 186. See also Vol. 26, Part I, p. 221.

41. *Ibid.*, Vol. 25, Part II, p. 185.

42. *Programma Kommunisticheskoi partii Sovetskogo Soiuza*, State Political Literature Publishing House, 1961, p. 90.

43. See Chapter 7.

44. K. Marx and F. Engels, *op.cit.*, Vol. 23, p. 48.

45. *Ibid.*, Vol. 25, Part II, p. 186.

46. See G. Kuhn and A. Tucker, editors, *Lineinye neravenstva i smezhnye voprosy*, Moscow, Foreign Literature Publishing House, 1959, pp. 192-194.

47. The lines over the symbols are signs of average quantities.

48. See L.V. Kantorovich and V.L. Makarov, "Optimal Models of Long-Term Planning," in *Premenenie matematiki v ekonomicheskikh issledovaniiakh*, Moscow, Mysl Publishing House, 1965, Vol. 3, p. 40.

49. On von Neumann's model see V.V. Novozhilov, "Mathematical Models of the Economy in Bourgeois Political Economy and Their Criticism," in *Trudy nauchnogo soveshchaniia o primenenii matematicheskikh metodov v ekonomicheskikh issledovaniiakh i planirovanii*, Moscow, USSR Academy of Sciences Publishing House, 1962.

CHAPTER 10

AN ANSWER TO CRITICISM

We have already noted that the ideas and methods of optimal planning that arose in the USSR were rejected for a long time by the majority of Soviet economists and theoreticians, and consequently were hardly used in practice. For some time the ideas of optimal planning underwent criticism from bourgeois economists. Especially sharp disputes flared up concerning the question of the application of the method of multipliers (controlling norms) in measuring costs and benefits and in price formation. Some Soviet economists, while accepting the application of this method to tasks of local planning, have denied the validity of its use in planning the national economy.[1] In our opinion this would mean that it would be permissible to use the method of multipliers where it could be replaced by other methods of optimal planning, but that it could not be used where it was indispensable.

1. The Version of the Absence of Multipliers in Tasks of National Economic Planning

A number of fundamental objections have been advanced against the use of the method of multipliers in national economic planning. The most categorical of these is the assertion that there is no place for multipliers in tasks of national economic planning.

A. Ia. Boiarskii begins his criticism of L. V. Kantorovich's concept with this "theorem of nonexistence." "The transition

329

from brigades or enterprises of a branch to the totality of branches means a transition of a qualitative nature, a transition to tasks of quite a different kind. The attempt to reduce them to the same intraplant task leads to a situation in which the entire table is so filled with 'forbidden squares' that nothing remains for the application of the method." [2]

As proof, Boiarskii presents the example of a distribution of a production program among plants in which each plant can produce only one product by a single method. Having presented this example in a table designed for the task of selecting the optimal alternative, he filled many boxes with zeros and infinity signs. These zeros and infinity signs expressed the fact that there were no other alternatives of utilization of each plant. [3] Where there is no opportunity for choice there is also no task for an optimum.

Having demonstrated in this way that the method of multipliers cannot solve a problem that does not exist, Boiarskii repeats the same proof, completing the criticism of the norm of effectiveness of investment that I defended. He so changes the conditions of the example taken from our article that only one alternative of investment remains for each product of the program. Then the critic states triumphantly, "In this case the possibility of establishing a limiting norm of effectiveness vanishes, and thereby his [V. V. Novozhilov's — Ed.] entire concept collapses. So much the worse for it."[4]

Is this really so? Boiarskii's entire proof is based on the assumption that in tasks of national economic planning, in contrast to tasks of plant planning, there are no alternatives, that there is no problem of selecting an optimal alternative. There is not only no semblance of truth in this assumption, but it is even contrary to the truth. The transition from the plans of brigades, enterprises, etc., to the national economy's plan is associated with an enormous growth in the number of alternatives. All these brigades, enterprises, etc., are part of the national economy; they are its sectors. Accordingly, plan alternatives of individual enterprises must be chosen from the standpoint of the national economy, i.e., they must be directed toward the realization of a *national economic* optimum. This means that each enterprise must use limited resources (natural resources, capital investment, productive capital) with consideration of other possibilities for their use in the national economy.

The theorem of nonexistence of multipliers in tasks of the national economic plan is, as a matter of fact, proof of the existence of these multipliers. It is a reverse proof. Indeed, if the norm of effectiveness of investment, for example, disappears only if we make a completely unrealistic assumption (the absence of alternatives of technology!), this means that in real conditions it must exist.

M. V. Kolganov proves the nonexistence of multipliers in national economic tasks differently. In the task of minimizing the overall sum of labor costs, differential costs are essentially increments in this sum caused by the production of a unit of the given product. But "with a growth in labor productivity labor expenditures on each kind of output may remain unchanged while output in kind may grow."[5] Since an increment in expenditures does not actually occur, we cannot determine differential costs.

This criticism is based on an incorrect interpretation of differential costs as increments in actual costs over time in comparison with their previous level. Differential costs express increments in minimum possible costs, and such increments always exist. Minimum possible outlays on the given amount of products serve as the basis for computing these increments. If additional production of a commodity does not cause an increment in costs, this means either that the plan is not an optimal one and its costs are not the minimum costs or that the additional production of the commodity does not require expenditures of labor.

2. Other Misunderstandings Based on the Incorrect Interpretation of Differential Costs

Critics of calculation of differential costs as an instrument of optimal planning often neglect their characteristic property — that of expressing the overall minimum of expenditures of labor. Boiarskii's objection is based on this omission when he says that my "structure is turned toward the past" and "the norm of effectiveness is determined according to the effectiveness of the last ruble in the sense of savings in costs in comparison with the past." But only plan alternatives are compared in finding minimum planned costs. The norm of effectiveness is the minimum effectiveness of alternatives of investment accepted in the optimal plan. The plan pertains to the future, not to the past. How could Boiarskii think that the effect of investments in our schemes is determined "by savings in costs in comparison with the past?" This can only be explained by the fact that he identified the investment necessary for fulfilling the program with productive capital, and the production program with the previous period's output. However, productive capital (the result of investment in previous years) plays no part in those examples of mine that Boiarskii used for criticism.[6]

Boiarskii's assertion that investment for increasing the production of output is not considered in our scheme is obviously based on the same identification of existing capital and investment. In our example, presented by Boiarskii (see above), the minimum sum of investment (not of existing capital!) necessary for fulfilling the program amounts to 250 million rubles. This sum also ensures the growth of output over the level previously attained. In this example there is no indication of how much the production program exceeds the previously attained level. This is unimportant. The conclusion that there is an absence of investment for increasing production is valid only under one of the following two conditions: either by assuming that the major part of investment (250 million out ot 340 million rubles) yields no effect, neither a growth in production nor a reduction in production costs, or by identifying the 250 million rubles of investment with productive capital.

One of the prevalent objections against the use of the method of multipliers in calculating costs is that it is not possible to add actual expenditures of labor to possible, but neglected, savings. Double accounting of certain costs results.

When it is a matter of the method, its effectiveness is the major consideration. The effectiveness of the method of multipliers has been accurately demonstrated. Auxiliary multipliers in all tasks have the same property that seems inadmissible to critics, namely, that either costs are added to their sacrificed savings, or that the effect is added to its sacrificed increment. Moreover, none of the critics has decided to deny the effectiveness of this method in particular planning problems. It has been repeatedly demonstrated not only theoretically but also in practice. We do not see the grounds on which the same property of multipliers should hinder their application in tasks of national economic planning.

However, we cannot confine ourselves to stating this obvious inconsistency of the criticism. Let us try to uncover the reasons for it. It seems to us that the critics are most confused by the use of multipliers in taking account of actual costs. In fact, at first glance it may appear strange that sacrificed savings are included in actual costs. This confusion vanishes as soon as we recognize the necessity of using multipliers in planning. The necessity of using multipliers in the calculation of actual (ex post) costs arises from the use of these multipliers in compiling the optimal plan. Ex post indicators must be calculated by the same methods that are used to calculate plan indicators. This is a general rule of socialist statistics. In the sphere of calculating costs the method of multipliers has as its basis the primacy of costs of reproduction over costs of production in calculating value and determining prices. The primacy of costs of reproduction has not only a quantitative aspect but also a qualitative one. Planned costs determine prices not only quantitatively but, first of all, qualitatively. They determine the composition of those costs that must be considered in the price. This aspect of the matter is usually forgotten. Hence there arises the difficulty of understanding why it is necessary to consider sacrificed savings in actual costs and thereby to accept the double accounting of certain costs.

3. Does the Use of the Method of Multipliers in Price Formation Contradict Marxism?

It would seem that proof of the nonexistence of multipliers completes the criticism. Why should there be other objections to them if they do not exist? Boiarskii obviously does not believe in the persuasiveness of his own example with the forbidden boxes and presents a further series of arguments. First is the one that multipliers are limiting ("marginal") quantities and that Marxism and marginalism are incompatible.

Other critics of the method of auxiliary multipliers have presented this argument, in connection with which schemes for its application in planning the national economy are described as schemes of the marginal utility school.[7] Defenders of these schemes are included in the ranks of revisionists who are reviving the ideas of bourgeois apologists.[8]

The method of multipliers is mathematics. Mathematical means are formal, i.e., they are devoid of content. That is why the same mathematical means can be used in different economic theories — both in valid and invalid ones. The idea that the use of marginal multipliers contradicts Marxism is based on a dogmatic simplification of Marx's theory. Marginal magnitudes play an important role in this theory.[9]

It is not multipliers that are incompatible with Marxism, but rather the economic content of those bourgeois theories that make extensive use of multipliers. Thus, J. B. Clark's theory of marginal productivity is incompatible with Marxism. According to this theory each class receives what it produces. Workers receive the product of labor, capitalists receive the product of capital, and landowners receive the product of land.

But this saving conclusion arises neither from the definition of marginal productivity nor from the proposition that each worker can receive no more than the marginal (least productive) worker receives. The reverse follows from these statements, namely, that workers are exploited.

Indeed, if the productivity of labor of different workers is different, and if according to the laws of competition each of them can receive no more than the marginal worker receives, this means that all workers receive less than they produce.

Clark himself understands this well. He writes, "The theory representing society as honest and the theory representing it as a system of organized robbery of labor are distinguished by two dissimilar definitions of the term 'marginal productivity.' "[10]

In Clark's opinion each worker's product is equal to the product of the marginal worker. This means that the products of all workers except the marginal worker are simultaneously both larger than and equal to the marginal worker's product. By definition they are larger than the marginal worker's product. That is why something remains for the share of capital. But at the same time they are equal to the marginal worker's product, as a result of which each worker, in receiving only the marginal worker's product, nonetheless has all that he has produced. Clark takes credit not for discovering the role of marginal magnitudes in economics, but for discovering that each worker's product is equal to the marginal worker's product.[11] "When the term marginal productivity is defined differently, it leads to the theory of exploitation of labor. If labor units located at early stages of a series produce more wealth than they obtain, then labor is cheated."[12] Of course, Clark's "marginalism" is incompatible with Marxism. But nothing and no one prompts Soviet economists to repeat Clark's error and to consider the unequal as equal. Accordingly, they can use marginal magnitudes (multipliers) without fear of becoming unintentional defenders of capitalist procedures.

Analysis of Clark's theories demonstrates how unfounded is the idea that it is marginal magnitudes that impart an apologetic character to it.

Yet how do we combine Marxism and marginalism (without quotation marks) if, according to Marx, value is determined by average expenditures of labor and, according to marginalism, prices are determined by the highest costs of production? It would seem that one excludes the other. Prices cannot be simultaneously determined both by average and by marginal costs. It would seem that with prices equal to marginal costs the sum of prices will always be larger than the sum of values.

This is correct if the average and marginal costs pertain to the same expression of costs, for example to value. But it is incorrect if the marginal measurement is applied to another expression of costs. We have already demonstrated that marginal production costs can be equal to the average value of the same product, and the marginal price of production can be equal to the average value.[13]

4. The Fundamental Objection to the Use of the Method of Multipliers in Planned Price Formation

What has been said about marginalism brings us to an answer to the main argument presented against the method of multipliers. This argument involves the following reasoning. The method of multipliers reflects only the law of dependence of prices on supply and demand. Prices must be planned in conformity to the law of value. Consequently, the method of multipliers is unsuitable for planned price formation.

The first two statements are correct, but the conclusion is wrong. The conclusion would be correct if the law of supply and demand were not related to the law of value. In fact, the price of equilibrium of supply and demand is a form of manifestation of the law of value. The critics neglect this proposition.[14]

Having put this statement between the first and second ones, we conclude that the method of multipliers is a form of utilization of the law of value in optimal planning. Accordingly, by using multipliers in models of the optimal plan we can prove mathematically that the price of equilibrium of supply and demand is a necessary form of manifestation not only of the law of value but also of the law of economy of labor.

Of course, in the planned use of the law of value we must not confine ourselves to its form of manifestation. In the optimal plan all prices not only equalize supply and demand but also are proportional to expenditures of labor and have a value content. The requirement that prices have a value content is of profound practical significance. It means that prices must assist the attainment of a stable optimum for the national economy. Calculations and decisions are based on prices (especially on prices of means of production). The consequences of these calculations and decisions often extend beyond the periods of long-term plans. Static optima of the economy are often incompatible with the dynamic optimum, with the optimal direction of development. That is why prices of the current optimal plan may lead to decisions that do not correspond to the long-term plan.

But this is not all. The requirement of a value basis for prices is also necessary from the standpoint of calculation. To calculate the prices of all commodities as prices of equilibrium of supply and demand is impossible. It is impossible not only because the demand functions are unknown (let us assume that they are known!), but also because it would be necessary to repeat such a calculation with each change in the relationship between supply and demand not only for a given commodity but for all commodities having a similar purpose. The demand for each commodity depends not only on its price but also on the prices of other commodities. Therefore, the calculation of plan prices on the basis of equilibrium of supply and demand is appropriate only with reference to those conditions of application of labor in which either value is not involved (natural resources) or in which part of it has been lost and it is not being reproduced (in consequence of obsolescence). The norms of their effectiveness do not have their own value basis, but reflect savings in the value of products. For all products demand is equalized to supply through the regulation of production. This makes it possible, through a calculation of costs, to find prices for a stable balance of supply and demand.

True, prices of obsolete means of production, and in part of new technology, must be set with consideration of the effectiveness of their application. Accordingly, prices can be conceived of as feedback costs. However, the natural way of finding these multipliers is to calculate the value of production of means of production and of new technology with subsequent consideration of differences in the effectiveness of their application.

The value calculation of nonreproducible limitations of production is expressed in the calculation of costs according to the following formula: actual costs of production plus the means of minimizing them.

Such a scheme of price formation reflects both the content and the form of manifestation of the law of value. In this process the means of minimization do not enter into value. They only cause stable deviations of prices from values and the formation of a transformed form of value.

5. Objections to the Use of Multipliers
   in Long-Term Planning

Can the method of multipliers be applied in dynamic models (of long-term planning)? Critics of this method apparently assume that it can be applied only in static planning tasks, in tasks of current but not of long-term planning.

However, these multipliers are applied in problems of both linear and nonlinear programming, in static and dynamic problems. In particular, the norm of effectiveness of investment is necessary first of all in long-term planning for determining the optimal amount of accumulation. The static model of the optimal balance of capital investment still has theoretical and practical significance. True, it starts from the prescribed investment limit, but if we assume that planned accumulation to some degree approximates the optimum, then finding the plan that ensures the most effective use of this accumulation solves the problem of a dynamic optimum to the same degree. Therefore, the criticism of the methods I proposed for finding the overall maximum effect of investment should have demonstrated at least one of the following propositions:

(1) the proposed methods do not yield a solution of the problem (i.e., they contain errors);

(2) our plans of accumulation are far from the optimum, in consequence of which static models of distribution of capital investment are not of practical significance at the present time.

In criticizing the static model of an optimal plan that I proposed, A. Kats asserts both of these propositions.[15]

(1) Kats sees the fundamental defect of this model in the fact that it is based on the production program and the investment limit prescribed by the plan. As a result of this, in order to adhere to the limit of capital investment and the fulfillment of the general production program for individual kinds of output, the technological alternatives chosen are not the best ones. It appears that backward technology is embedded in the plans themselves — in the relationship between the production program and the investment limit.

(2) On the other hand, Kats disputes the principle of an overall minimum of labor costs. He believes that better technology is ensured by choosing alternatives according to particular minima of labor costs for each kind of output. For this purpose he recommends "alternately ensuring minimum labor costs for individual kinds of output," which "at first changes but little the

initial unfavorable relationship in the balance of means of production and social needs, reflecting the shortage of material resources. But the greater the interval between the current period and the initial one, the more favorable is the change in the balance of means of production and social needs under the influence of alternately ensuring minimum labor costs for individual kinds or parts of output." [16]

Kats presents three arguments in support of this thesis.

(1) The most advanced technology conceals within itself the best possibilities for increasing the yield of fixed productive capital by means of insignificant additional investments.

(2) The most advanced technology is the basis for subsequently creating the most advanced technical means.

(3) The full capacity of new kinds of equipment is disclosed only in the process of their productive utilization. [17]

Each of these statements is plausible. But they pertain not to the technology that ensures the minimum production costs of output, but to the most effective technology. Nowhere in the world is the effectiveness of technology determined in practice according to the minimum production costs of output, without taking account of capital investment in technical means. Thus the quotations from the American journal with which Kats supports the statements mentioned pertain not to that technology he considers the most modern (according to the criterion of minimum production costs), but to another kind, selected according to the criterion of profit or the minimum individual price of production.

Kats neglects the fact that labor-saving investment is also possible without changes in the level of technology. Such investment is usually directed to reducing various kinds of losses. For example, increasing the cross section of electrical conductors reduces power losses, thickening the walls of buildings reduces thermal losses, decreasing the controlling gradient of a railroad track reduces the cost of transportation (by increasing the weight of the train), and increasing the diameter of a pipeline reduces the costs of transporting gas or oil. The number of such examples could be indefinitely increased. Investment that does not involve a rise in the technological level differs from investment in new technology by the fact that its effectiveness falls as investment rises. Thus, the realization of Kats' proposal would lead to the full utilization of the possibilities of low-effectiveness investment involving no change in the technological level, at the expense of a reduction in highly effective investment in new technology. This

338

would greatly slow down the growth in the technological level of the economy.

To support his thesis Kats presents a table that shows how the production costs of output change in the optimal balance of investment and in the balance in which alternatives with the lowest production costs are accepted for three lines of production and alternatives with the highest production costs of output are accepted for two lines of production. In so doing he assumes that in the optimal balance the production costs of output will decline annually by 1% in all lines of production. In the same balance that he constructed, the rates of decline in production costs will be 2% per year in three lines of production and 0.5% per year in two lines of production.[18] The relative share of the last two enterprises in the overall production costs of all five lines of production is less than a third. This means that Kats, in proving that his method of constructing the investment balance is better than the optimal one, puts into the numerical models of the compared balances a condition under which the average rate of reduction in the production costs of the balance proposed by him will be one and a half times larger than in the optimal method. The difference in the rates of reduction in the production costs of the two balances was necessary for Kats because without this the optimal investment balance would yield the most inexpensive output not only in the first years but also in the subsequent period of operation. Since he did not present any data to support this difference, there is no subject for scientific dispute.

It is hardly worth considering another numerical model of Kats' that shows that the greater the renewal of previously produced means of labor, the more rapidly social labor productivity grows.[19] It is constructed on just as arbitrary assumptions as the investment balance.

But this is not all. The author's assertion that with a growth in the renewal of means of labor the growth rates of social output increase "and at an increasing rate" (!) is absurd. It means that with an unlimited decrease in the useful lives of means of labor, output will grow to a still greater extent. The author does not notice that an excessively rapid replacement of equipment transforms the national economy into production for the sake of production.

Kats' fundamental error consists of ignoring the time factor. He prefers high rates of growth of the economy in the more distant future as a result of low rates in the next few years. Thus he does not even mention the necessity of any limits on recoupment periods of investment. He thereby essentially replaces considerations of gaining time by a proposal involving a loss of time in the competition between the two systems. After all, in capitalist practice the time factor is always considered in economic calculations.

6. M. V. Kolganov's Objections

M. V. Kolganov presents several objections to the concept of differential socially necessary costs. We have already answered one of them. Three still remain:

1. The application of Lagrange multipliers in models of minimization of labor costs is invalid, since the derivatives of a linear function cannot be set equal to zero. They are equal to a coefficient with an unknown, i.e., to a constant number. [20]

2. The equality of minimum labor costs of final output to maximum national income, which corresponds to the duality theorem of linear programming, is an identity signifying that national income is equal to national income. One can derive neither the volume of products nor prices from this identity. [21]

3. Price formation according to marginal costs increases the general level of prices, but it does not free the poorer enterprises from unprofitability. In this process the costs of poorer enterprises rise. [22]

All three of these arguments are unfounded.

1. Partial derivatives (5.2) of the Lagrangian function also become equal to zero in the solution of the task involving cases of a linear relationship. In models of price formation these derivatives represent sums of a negative increment (i.e., savings) of labor costs caused by expenditure of a unit of the given resource on the prescribed product $\delta c_i / \delta q_h$ with a constant positive quantity — multiplier λ_h. The economic meaning of the equality to zero of this partial derivative consists of the fact that the marginal economy of labor from the use of the given resource is equal to the norm of effectiveness of this resource in the optimal plan.

2. The equality, obtained according to the duality theorem, of minimum labor costs of the final product to the national income is not an identity. It is obtained not with any level of costs, but only with minimum costs, and not with any composition of final output, but only if there is complete conformity of its composition to needs.

3. Kolganov's objections to price formation according to marginal costs would be valid if prices were constructed according

340

to marginal values. But, as we demonstrated above, the value level of prices is compatible with price formation according to marginal transformed value.[23]

7. Self-Refutation by Critics

Criticism has its own laws. If they are violated, then the criticism can become additional proof of the correctness of the disputed statement. We noted above that some of A. Ia. Boiarskii's objections turn out to be proof (from the contrary standpoint) of the need for multipliers in planning. But this is not all. Boiarskii completed his article with a complete refutation of the fundamental thesis of his criticism. He gave a characterization of the tasks of linear programming from which it clearly follows that national economic planning is the first task of linear programming. Let us present this characterization.

"If the given problem of linear programming is not a trivial one, then its solution means that in specific cases – in individual enterprises, regions, brigades, lines of production, etc. – the method of operation that is most profitable from their standpoint must be replaced by a different, somewhat less profitable one. The loss from the latter, however, is exceeded by the gain from the use of corresponding resources in another place or for another purpose."[24]

In other words, the problems of linear programming are not trivial when a feedback effect exists among the costs or among the results of different economic units. This means that the choice of the most profitable alternative for one sector of the national economy raises costs or reduces results in other sectors. This is obviously the same feedback effect between costs of different sectors of the national economy that none of the critics of the method of multipliers disputes, and that was to be taken into account by means of multipliers according to proposals made long ago. It is also obvious that the overall maximum of results and the overall minimum of costs for the national economy as a whole must be the main criterion. Boiarskii agrees with this. This is apparent from the fact that he refers negatively to capitalist practice, which does not solve problems of use of scarce resources "from the standpoint of minimum overall costs for all enterprises." Boiarskii's fundamental thesis that problems of national economic planning do not pertain to the class of problems to which the method of multipliers is applicable is thereby completely refuted.

P. S. Mstislavskii has presented the idea of a replacement of the method of the multipliers that in its impracticability proves, on the contrary, the necessity of using this method in calculating costs. He proposes determining the effectiveness of one or another alternative of the plan "according to the sum total of labor costs for all products."[25] This means that in choosing a plan alternative, for example, in choosing material for a part, we must calculate outlays on all of the national economy's products for different alternatives of material for the given part. Such a possibility is conceivable, but not feasible. Furthermore, it is not worth accomplishing even if it were possible. "The result would be the same as in the calculation . . . of indirect cost by L. V. Kantorovich's method," but determining the total outlays on all products would require tremendous, excessive calculations.

8. Substance as Form and Form as Substance
(Concerning the Foreign Treatment of the Method of Multipliers in the Economy of the USSR)

In refuting the view of the incompatibility of Marxism and marginalism we have thereby responded to certain remarks of Western economists on the subject of our work. However, since bourgeois economists criticize this work from fundamental positions different from those of Soviet economists, their arguments require special analysis.

In an article devoted to Soviet discussion of the principles of determining the effectiveness of capital investment, G. Grossman[26] notes that the method we have proposed for finding the overall minimum of costs[27] is closely analogous to the system of general equilibrium of Walras and other Western economists. Grossman is surprised that the author could continue in this case to adhere to the labor theory of value and undertake the improbable task of synthesizing Marx's theory with Walras' theory. Nonetheless, he recognizes that the concept of feedback costs fulfills, to a certain extent, the task of reducing all costs to labor as the unit of measurement (*numéraire*). Grossman explains this result by the fact that we proceeded from premises different from those on which systems of general equilibrium are constructed. Choosing working time as the quantity to be minimized determined the unit of measurement of the model and permitted us to express the value of means of production in labor (the task of deriving prices of means of production from the value of utility of final output was thereby eliminated). Grossman

342

emphasizes that this would be impossible if we had set as our goal the minimizing of different costs than labor or the maximizing of a different final output than leisure time (time free from work).

Grossman is undoubtedly correct in regard to the fact that it is not possible to combine Marx's theory with Walras' theory. But he is mistaken in assuming that we posed and fulfilled this task to any extent. He himself notes that our scheme originates from premises different from a system of economic development ["equilibrium" rather than "development" was probably intended — Trans.]. The premises involved are the major factor in every theoretical model. A model in which the law of the economy of labor is embedded differs from models of economic equilibrium in a most important aspect, namely, in determining the content of the objective function to be minimized, i.e., in determining costs. (In the economic model costs are expressed not with respect to limitations but with respect to the objective function to be minimized.) Therefore, Grossman is wrong in believing that in our model costs are reduced to labor only formally, as in an accounting unit. On the contrary, costs are expressed in this model in a labor unit precisely because they consist of labor.

It is easy to see this if we replace the labor unit in our model by a unit of any commodity. For this purpose it is necessary only to divide all quantities expressed in labor units by the labor value of a unit of the chosen commodity. Relative prices do not change as a result of this; and minimum costs expressed in units of the given commodity will, as before, minimize the labor involved in reproducing the social product. This means that in our model costs are not only formally expressed in labor but they actually consist of labor. This is precisely why all prices in this model are derived from the labor value of the entire social product.

Hence it is clear how wrong Grossman is in assuming that the choice of the objective function of an economic model solves only the formal question of the accounting unit (numéraire). The choice of the objective function to be minimized determines the content of costs, the content of value, and the law of price formation. A unit of any commodity (for example, gold) can become, in this case, the accounting unit (numéraire).

The choice of the objective function of a model is a fundamental question. If the quantity that is reduced to a minimum in reality is not minimized in the model, the model will distort essential features of reality.

The choice of the objective function of an economic model is a question concerning the most important economic law, a question

343

of the content of costs, of the elements of the economy that people strive to reduce to a minimum, in contrast to those elements and conditions that they strive to utilize to the maximum. Divergences between Marxist-Leninist political economy and bourgeois economic science are concentrated precisely on these questions.

Systems of general equilibrium (Walras and others) do not reflect the law of economy of labor, and consequently they also do not reflect the labor theory of value. Thus the model reflecting these laws differs from models of general equilibrium not formally, but in the most essential premises, even if identical mathematical means (marginal magnitudes) are used.

Marx's theory cannot be synthesized with Walras' theory, not because marginalism is supposedly incompatible with Marxism, but because we cannot simultaneously assert that costs consist only of labor and not only of labor.

The use of marginal magnitudes in Marxist economic models necessarily arises from the law of economy of labor and from the limited nature of certain resources. As we know, Marx repeatedly noted both this limited nature and the necessity for considering it from an economic standpoint. In our schemes this limited nature is taken into account. The means for doing so (multipliers) pertains to mathematics, not to economics.

Grossman mistakenly took the mathematical form of our model for its economic content and mistakenly took its economic content (costs consist only of labor!) for the accounting unit (numéraire).

Campbell's[28] article consists of the "expanded reproduction" of a similar error together with other errors. It begins with a brief account of the different destinies of the development of Western economic theory and Marxism. According to the author, in the last half-century Western science achieved not only the reduction of different theories of value to the common denominator of utility but also combined this theory with the question of what determines the relative output of different products — the problem of the distribution of scarce resources among different purposes. Marxists have not noticed this achievement. The limited nature of the Marxist legacy in economic theory consists, in Campbell's opinion, not so much in the incorrectness of the idea that value is created only by labor as in a failure to understand the fundamental problem of economic science — the distribution of resources among different purposes. In supposedly not finding in Marx an answer to the question of the interrelationship of the

344

problem of distribution of resources and the problem of value, Soviet planners are tirelessly trying to solve the problem themselves. In many cases they have found correct answers to particular questions of the effective distribution of resources. However, the combination of these answers into a general theory has been slowed, says Campbell, since it would unavoidably contradict certain propositions of Marxism. The application of mathematics in Soviet economic science has aggravated this contradiction and requires that Soviet economists be freed from the limitations of Marxist theory, which supposedly has already almost occurred in the works of L. V. Kantorovich and V. V. Novozhilov. But these authors, in Campbell's opinion, have not carried matters to a conclusion. In their schemes the structure of the final product is taken as given, whereas in actuality it is a very important element in the economic system. Nevertheless, the theory of consumption is already being worked out in the USSR. When someone combines it with the works of Kantorovich and Novozhilov, then a second discovery of the Western theory of value will have occurred.

Such is the essence of Campbell's article.

Theories are verified by their conformity to facts and by their application in practice. In this respect we must first of all introduce an important correction into Campbell's account of the destinies of economic science in the last half-century. There is a gap in this account. It is not mentioned that at the beginning of this period the most important verification in the history of economic theories occurred. Socialism arose. Marxist theory predicted this fact and explained it as a regular stage of development. Western theory not only did not predict it but even now cannot satisfactorily explain how this could occur and how a planned economy is possible.

The problem of the effective distribution of labor (and consequently of other resources) among different purposes, which according to Cambell was worked out by Western science, is one of the central ideas of Marxist economic theory. More than a hundred years ago Marx wrote: "The saving of time, as well as the planned distribution of working time among different branches of production, remains the first economic law at the basis of collective production."[29]

Marx repeated this statement many times in different formulations. Questions of the effectiveness of capital investment and similar questions are being developed on this basis in Soviet practice and in Soviet economic science. How can one speak of a

345

lack of understanding by Marxists of the problem of distribution of resources among different purposes?

The characterization of our viewpoint also does not correspond to the facts. If we are to believe Campbell, then Kantorovich and Novozhilov have attained some success thanks to the fact that they have almost freed themselves from the labor theory of value and have constructed schemes of distribution of resources on the basis of utility. In reality, subjective utility is not considered at all in these schemes. This means that prices in these schemes are derived not from utility but from something else. From what else, precisely?

Campbell acknowledges that in our concept all elements of value are expressed in labor units and that labor as the unit of measurement (*numéraire*) of value is scrupulously retained. But he considers this conformity to the labor theory of value as completely illusory. He understands that this conformity is based on minimizing expenditures of labor in the model. Therefore, he concentrates the main fire of his criticism on refuting this premise. In his opinion minimizing expenditures of labor for a given set of products is an absurd goal (especially in the Soviet Union). Novozhilov's assertion that minimizing expenditures of labor is equivalent to maximizing output, since economized manpower can be used for increasing output, does not save matters.[30] "In Novozhilov's method labor is minimized under conditions of utilization of all remaining outlays with which it cannot be combined."

Campbell neglects two features of our scheme:

(1) only those means of production are completely utilized in our scheme whose norms of effectiveness are higher than zero; [31]

(2) it embodies a multitude of alternatives of production of a unit of each product, alternatives that differ in amount of capital investment.

Accordingly, if it is advisable to increase the production plan, this is possible both by using the resources that it would not be necessary to exploit with a smaller program and by choosing less capital-intensive investment alternatives (if it is not advisable to increase the investment limit).

It seems to us that minimizing the expenditures of labor on the production of the prescribed set of products is the only real method of constructing an optimal balance of production and needs. Needs are determined by proceeding from expected expenditures (per unit of each product) and from labor resources. The minimum expenditures necessary for the satisfaction of needs are then found. Corrections in needs and in the production program are introduced in conformity to the minimum expenditures obtained for each product. A similar process is continued until the volume of production for each product coincides with social needs, given full employment of the able-bodied population and an optimal length of the working day.

To prove the absurdity of minimizing any one kind of cost, Campbell presents a situation in which planners working in the area of railroad transport set the goal of minimizing the cost of fuel, leaving all other costs unchanged. Under these conditions, says Campbell, Novozhilov's national economic production costs would be expressed in fuel (as the *numéraire*). Here Campbell repeats Grossman's errors, carrying them to an extreme and thus facilitating their disclosure.

In the first place, in minimizing the total consumption of fuel the national economic production cost will have a fuel content, even if it is expressed in rubles or even in man-hours. In this case the minima of outlays will minimize the total consumption of fuel. The choice of the quantity to be minimized is determined not by the *numéraire* but by costs in the model.

In the second place (and this is the main point), this choice cannot be arbitrary for the national economy as a whole. Costs in the social economy actually consist only of labor. This does not mean that only labor is scarce. Certain conditions of its application are also scarce. But the scarcity of labor is different from the scarcity of the conditions of its application. People strive to minimize expenditures of labor and to make maximum effective use of the conditions of its application. Therefore, in the model of the social economy expenditures of labor enter into the objective function to be minimized, and the conditions of its application are included in the constraints. But the objective function to be minimized expresses costs. This means that minimizing labor signifies nothing other than the fact that costs consist only of labor.

In answering critics from the camp of bourgeois economists we consider it not superfluous to repeat several important points that were already made in Chapter 5.

The fundamental defect of theories of general economic equilibrium (Walras and others) consists of ignoring differences between the scarcity of labor and the scarcity of means of labor. In essence these theories do not consider differences between the subjects and the objects of the social economy.

The social economy's scarce means (natural resources, capital investment) are not special types of costs but are those conditions of the application of labor whose limited nature imparts a conditional character to the problem of a minimum of labor costs. In the mathematical model of the social economy the difference between outlays and the conditions of their application is expressed in the difference between the objective function to be minimized and those constraints (equations or inequalities) that must be observed in finding the indicated minimum.

Mathematics thus makes it possible to formulate accurately the difference between the limited nature of labor and the limited nature of the conditions of its application.

Even a static model in which labor costs are minimized is formed in a direction diametrically opposed to the construction of systems of general equilibrium, i.e., not from prices (or utility) of consumer goods to prices of factors of production, but from labor costs to prices of consumer goods. The cognitive force of the models that reflect the law of economy of labor and the law of value is fully revealed only in investigating the development of the economy. Then it is clearly observed that people strive to decrease expenditures of labor and to make maximum use of the conditions of its application, i.e., to shorten the working day and to expand capital investment and the development of natural resources.

But this is not all. The law of economy of labor explains not only quantitative relationships within the limits of a particular society but also qualitative changes in the social structure.[32] The transition to socialism of countries with a relatively low level of development of capitalism is explained by the historic necessity for these countries to accelerate rates of growth of labor productivity by changing to a higher mode of production.

Theories of general economic equilibrium that do not reflect the law of economy of labor ignore the main factor of the economy both in its static and, especially, in its dynamic aspects. That is why the defenders of the theory of economic equilibrium could not predict and explain the main feature of recent economic history — the appearance of socialism.

If the law of economy of labor has such great significance in Marxist economic theory, then obviously there can be no talk about a decline of the labor theory of value nor about a "second discovery" by Marxists of the Western theory of value.

The process that appears to Campbell as the decline of the labor theory of value is a development and, accordingly, a strengthening of this theory.

In fact, the concept of differential costs and full production costs represents a generalized expression of the law of labor value. According to this concept, prices that balance the need for, and the production of, each product are always derived from the value of the final social product. The law of minimization of labor costs for the required output can be realized only if prices are proportional to differential costs per unit of product, i.e., partial derivatives of the conditional minimum of the value of the social product with respect to the production of the given commodity. Under certain conditions these derivatives are equal to labor values, whereas under others they are equal to prices of production, and under still others are equal to full production costs.

Thus, prices that are proportional to values, as well as prices that are proportional to prices of production, are explained on the basis of the same law and according to the same principle.

True, we have not yet carried the generalization of Marx's theory of value to its conclusion. We must introduce a demand function into our model. Noting this, Campbell predicts that when this occurs the breakdown of the labor theory of value will be complete and there will be a "second discovery" of the Western theory of value (the theory of marginal utility) by Marxists.

This is an illusion. We foresee a completely different perspective, namely, a second discovery by Western economists of the law of economy of labor. The study of demand does not contradict Marx's theory of value. On the contrary, the concept of socially necessary labor presumes the conformity of the production of the product of this labor to social wants. Thus, the study of wants does not lead in any way to a decline of the labor theory of value in the USSR and to its replacement by the theory of marginal utility.

The difference between these theories consists not of the fact that one of them does not consider wants and the other does so, but rather that one of them reflects the law of economy of labor and the other does not.[33] Therefore, for a second discovery by Marxists of the Western theory of value it is not sufficient to add to the concept of differential costs the theory of consumption. It is also necessary to "subtract" from this concept the law of economy of labor, i.e., the determination of costs by labor. Such a prospect is obviously unreal. The law of economy of labor is confirmed by the entire course of history.

On the other hand, another prospect is extremely probable — the recognition of the law of economy of labor by Western economists. The increasing difficulty of defending a theory that puts labor and the conditions of its application on the same level is leading to this. The reality of this prospect is unintentionally confirmed by none other than Campbell himself. In rejecting the problem of minimizing labor costs he contrasts to it — as an authentic problem — the maximization of free time and the production of output.

However, the problem of a maximum of the consumption function that includes free time among the objectives demanded differs only formally from the problem of a minimum of expenditures of labor on the necessary output. In both problems labor enters directly or indirectly (i.e., through free time) into the objective function, and the conditions of its application are included in the constraints.

We think that the minimization of labor costs on the required output is a more suitable form of expressing the law of economy of labor than the maximization of output and free time. Labor costs can be calculated, whereas it is very difficult to measure subjective utility even under the most ideal conditions. Such is the result of the prolonged and hot disputes on the measurability of utility, a result attested to by mathematicians free from what Campbell calls "the limitations of Marxist theory."

We saw that in analyzing our concept Campbell ascribes a formal significance (*numéraire*) to the most important premise of our model (the determination of costs in terms of labor and the task of minimizing labor that arises from it), and consequently he easily transfers a similar premise into his formulation of the problem. The same tendency to "stylization" of the concept of differential costs under the theory of general equilibrium is manifested in his detailed presentation of the concept of differential costs.

Thus, according to Campbell, in Novozhilov's work value is viewed only as the reflection of production limitations, i.e., national economic production costs are identical with feedback costs. This is a very inaccurate presentation. Feedback costs constitute only part of the national economic (full) production costs. Expenditures of labor on the production of the given commodity constitute another part, and moreover the fundamental part. Prices would be the reflection of production constraints only in a model in which all resources in production, including labor, were included in the constraints. In the model in which labor is included in the objective function, costs and prices are constructed according to the following formula: expenditures of labor plus feedback costs.

350

To sum up, we are justified in saying that Campbell's article is extremely biased. By virtue of his obvious antipathy toward Marxism, substance appears to him as form, form as substance, the real as illusory, and illusion as reality. This loss of the measure of things and people was reflected in the very title of his article, "Marx, Kantorovich, and Novozhilov: Stoimost' versus Reality."

However, sooner or later truth wins out. It is already clearing a way for itself. Not all Western economists see in Kantorovich's and Novozhilov's works a retreat from Marxism. Thus, M. Dobb (Cambridge University) examines our scheme of costs as a special type of price of production. The price of production constitutes an important element of Marx's theory of value. In other words, it is not a matter of a retreat from Marxism, but of the application of the price of production category to the conditions of a socialist economy. [34] It seems to us that the national economic (full) production costs differ so significantly from prices of production that it is hardly advisable to call them a special form of prices of production. However, this question is already beyond the scope of the subject matter of this chapter. M. Dobb disputes neither the use of the method of multipliers in planning the national economy nor the conformity of this practice to Marx's theory of value.

* * *

In defending the use of the method of multipliers in national economic planning we do not, by any means, suggest that the schemes we have proposed for its use do not have any defects. On the contrary, they are still far from perfect. They require criticism. Are the initial data of the model correctly chosen? Do they reflect the essential features of reality? Is the method of finding the optimum sufficiently effective? Is it possible to apply simpler or more effective procedures for solving the same problem? All these questions require scientific discussion.

But if the initial data of the model take account of the essential features of reality and the method of finding the optimum is effective, then we cannot consider as incorrect those concepts (marginal magnitudes) that are necessary for solving the problem.

In objecting to the defects in models of the use of the method of multipliers, critics forget that all conditions of application of the multipliers remain in full force, namely, the scarcity of the best conditions of application of labor and democratic centralism in managing the economy. Critics forget that the scarcity of the best conditions of application of labor is important not only for individual parts of the national economy but also for the whole, and must be considered not just in current but in long-term planning. Accordingly, defects in particular models of optimal planning must be removed by proposing more perfect schemes, not by criticizing the method that is necessary not only for the optimal planning of the national economy but also for developing economic calculation, for perfecting distribution according to labor, and for the further democratization of management of the economy by strengthening the planning principle.

Notes

1. See A. Boiarskii, "On the Question of Applying Mathematics to Economics," *Voprosy ekonomiki,* 1961, No. 2; L. Gatovskii and M. Sakov, "On the Basic Foundation of Economic Studies," *Kommunist,* 1960, No. 15; A. Kats, "An Incorrect Concept of Economic Calculation," *Voprosy ekonomiki,* 1960, No. 5; A. Kats, "Economic Theory and the Application of Mathematics to Economics," *Voprosy ekonomiki,* 1960, No. 11; A. Kats, "On So-Called National Production Costs," *Voprosy ekonomiki,* 1965, No. 2; M. Kolganov, "Political Economy and Mathematics, *Voprosy ekonomiki,* 1964, No. 12; M. Kolganov, "Value and Planned Price," *Voprosy ekonomiki,* 1966, No. 5; P. Mstislavskii ,"On the Quantitative Expression of Economic Relationships and Processes," *Voprosy ekonomiki,* 1961, No. 2.

2. *Voprosy ekonomiki,* 1961, No. 2, p. 65.

3. A zero in the box for output means that an automobile plant, for example, cannot produce textiles.

4. *Voprosy ekonomiki,* 1961, No. 2, p. 70.

5. *Voprosy ekonomiki,* No. 5, pp. 71-72.

6. In the general scheme for the optimal plan, productive capital is taken into account in its material form — as specific means of production available at the beginning of the planned period (see the collection *Primenenie matematiki v ékonomicheskikh issledovaniiakh,* Mosgow, Sotsekgiz Publishing House, 1959, pp. 164-165).

7. See *Voprosy ekonomiki,* 1961, No. 2, p. 69.

8. *Ibid.,* p. 101

9. For this, see pp. 279 *et seq.*

10. J. B. Clark, *Raspredelenie bogatstva,* Moscow and Leningrad, OGIZ Publishing House, 1934, p. 67.

11. *Ibid.,* p. 229.

12. *Ibid.,* p. 67.

13. For this, see pp. 296 *et seq.*

14. For this, see pp. 277 *et seq.*

15. *Voprosy ekonomiki,* 1960, No. 11.

16. *Ibid.*

17. *Voprosy ekonomiki,* 1966, No. 2, pp. 115-117.

18. *Voprosy ekonomiki,* 1964, No. 2, p. 119.

19. *Voprosy ekonomiki,* 1965, No. 2, pp. 122-123.

20. *Voprosy ekonomiki,* 1964, No. 12, p. 113.

21. *Voprosy ekonomiki,* 1966, No. 5, pp. 68-69.

22. *Ibid.,* p. 67.

23. See pp. 296 *et seq.*

24. *Voprosy ekonomiki,* 1961, No. 2, p. 70.

25. *Ibid.,* p. 102.

26. See his article "Scarce Capital and Soviet Doctrine," *Quarterly Journal of Economics,* 1953, Vol. LXVII, No. 3.

27. See V. V. Novozhilov, "Methods of Finding Minimum Costs in a Socialist Economy," *Trudy Leningradskogo politekhnicheskogo instituta,* 1946, No. 1.

28. See *Slavic Review,* October 1961.

29. *Arkhiv Marksa i Engel'sa,* Vol. IV, Partizdat Publishing House, 1935, p. 119.

30. Campbell obviously has in mind the following observation of ours: "If these expenditures [minimum ones — V.N.] are so small that it would be advisable to increase the production program, it can be reexamined (*Primenenie matematiki v ekonomicheskikh issledovaniiakh,* Moscow, Sotsekgiz Publishing House, 1959, p. 167).

31. "All those natural resources and previously produced means of labor that, even with a zero norm of effectiveness, do not enter into a single one of the alternatives with lowest differential costs must remain beyond the limits of the balances." *Ibid.,* p. 167).

32. See p. 347.

33. Thus, the newest treatment of the Walras-Cassel equations includes labor together with other factors of production in the constraints, not in the objective function (see *Lineinye neravenstva i smezhnye voprosy,* edited by Kuhn and Tucker, Moscow, Foreign Literature Publishing House, 1959, p. 364).

34. M. Dobb, "Notes on Recent Economic Discussion," *Soviet Studies,* 1961, Vol. XII, No. 4 (April).

353

CHAPTER 11

CONCLUSION

Planning the national economy cannot, and must not (even if it could), embrace all economic decisions. The national economic plan is compiled according to highly consolidated (aggregated) indicators encompassing large groups of phenomena. Accordingly, prices calculated in compiling the optimal plan for the development of the national economy should pertain only to the most important groups of commodities. The same must also be said about norms of effectiveness of material resources (capital investment, productive capital, natural resources).

In breaking down (detailing) the national economic plan by regions, branches, and enterprises we must ensure conformity of all local plans and decisions to the national economic optimum. This means that further work on the plan for the development of the national economy involves the division of the huge extremal task into parts and finding a general optimum by solving a multitude of particular extremal tasks. Here the use of the law of value is necessary.

1. The Main Practical Conclusion

The planned management of a socialist economy can be optimized only through *combining optimization of national economic plans with optimization of price formation.* Under optimal planning prices and economic accountability, constructed with due consideration of the law of value, coordinate the profitability of a multitude of particular decisions with the national economic plan. (The uncoordinated remainder of the decisions can be adjusted by means of subsidies, the turnover tax, and similar means.) On the other hand, if prices and economic accountability do not consider the law of value and, so to speak, contradict it, then discord between the plan-directive and economic accountability is inevitable, and the planning apparatus is burdened with the impracticable task of centrally solving a multitude of local planning problems and of providing purely administrative methods for fulfilling them.

Thus, detailing the national economic plan is possible only on the basis of optimizing disaggregated prices and norms of effectiveness. The role of the law of value in this matter consists not only in the fact that value categories become the controlling norms of the planning apparatus (the centralized management of the economy) but also of the fact that the "principle of value," i.e., the equality of optimal prices to differential labor costs, is the basis for calculating most of these norms. Hence the possibility arises of approximating optimal prices by calculating them not as a whole, like consumption valuations, but in parts, like differential labor costs. The range of the search for optimal values of the norms is thereby limited within comparatively narrow bounds, which are determined by the conditions of production. A different route for determining prices, by proceeding from consumption valuations, is complicated by the fact that the range of change in these valuations, depending on the amount of products, is much broader than the range of change in costs.

Knowing the formulas for differential costs, we can substitute in them approximate values for prices of means of production and for norms of effectiveness, and then we can verify to what extent the results obtained conform to other prices. If, for example, a price obtained in this way diverges considerably from the price of another commodity similar in purpose, or from a price of the same commodity calculated for a different region, it is necessary to correct the prices so that an equal price corresponds to an equal consumption valuation. Thus, by correcting price calculations step by step (best of all, in the course of planning these prices, not at the stage of realization) we will coordinate them with each other and with the material balances.

The process of optimizing both prices and the planning calculations based on them, which make specific the national economic plan, is included in this process of coordination of prices. Prices coordinated in this way can already be approved as selling prices. True, these will only be approximately optimal prices. Nevertheless, they will aid not only the fulfillment of the optimal plan for the national economy on the principles of economic calculation but also the introduction from below of proposals for compiling the new plan that will be closer to a new optimal plan than proposals based on nonoptimal prices.

2. The Main Theoretical Conclusion

Optimal plan prices are the most accurate expression of the law of value. The law of value is realized in these prices with the smallest random deviations. Such a situation is possible only in a socialist economy. Under capitalism the conformity of prices to expenditures of labor is realized "through nonrealization," i.e., only on the average, with constant deviations and disturbances. Only in a planned economy can we attain a stable proportionality in the development of the economy and a stable conformity of prices to expenditures of socially necessary labor. But it is not easy to accomplish this possibility. To the extent that prices incorrectly reflect expenditures of socially necessary labor, to that extent the law of value can give rise to disproportions, the prevention of which requires excessive centralization of management of the economy. It seems to us that the main consequence of nonconformity of planned prices to socially necessary expenditures of labor is not disproportions in production (as a rule they are prevented by planning management), but those discrepancies between local and overall benefits that greatly complicate the tasks of planning management, disturb normal economic calculation, hinder distribution according to labor, and restrain the democratization of economic management and the creative activity of working people in production.

As we know, we took little account in the past of the law of value in the process of price formation. Accordingly, it was necessary to struggle against the negative consequences of its violation. On these grounds the false conviction developed and became strengthened that the plan and the law of value are incompatible with each other, and that the operation of the law of value under socialism can, and must, be limited by the plan. In reality, the law of value (like any other law) cannot be limited. We can, and must, limit only the negative consequences of deviations of planned prices from socially necessary expenditures. But the approximation of prices to socially necessary expenditures of labor is the most effective means for this.

However, in spite of prevailing opinion, Marx's teaching concerning socially necessary working time is not completely stated by the assertion that this time is expressed in average expenditures of labor under average (socially normal) conditions. This assertion fully applies only to those economic conditions in which prices are attracted toward values. We must not forget that in analyzing the process of formation of prices of production Marx established that the sale of commodities at prices corresponding to modifications of value is just as much a sign of the conformity of prices to socially necessary expenditures of labor as is sale of commodities at value.

This development of the labor theory of value has not yet attracted proper attention. Moreover, the prerequisite for price formation in proportion to values — uniformity of conditions of application of labor — occurs neither in capitalist nor in socialist countries. Naturally, in mathematical schemes of optimal planning also, prices are not proportional to values. In the light of the traditional concept of socially necessary costs (as average costs under socially normal conditions), prices of the optimal plan appear to be severed from socially necessary costs. Moreover, optimal plan schemes of price formation are ranked by certain economists with subjective theories of value — in the spirit of marginal utility.

Such an attitude toward optimal plan prices greatly hindered not only the improvement of planning but also the organization of economic management on the principles of democratic centralism. In reality, *optimal plan prices are the most complete and the most ideal expression of socially necessary expenditures of labor.* It is only necessary that this plan reflect the law of economy of labor.

By finding the formula for socially necessary labor in optimal planning we will obtain an expression of the law of value, so to speak, in pure form, i.e., as a necessity not covered by chance occurrences. In joining to this formula an expression for the action of random factors we will obtain a general formula for price formation.

In different periods the law of value operates under different conditions, namely, with varying differentiation of the conditions of application of labor and with different conditions of exploitation of the direct producer. Therefore, prices in various periods are in a very different relationship to the values of commodities, and they stimulate the economy of labor in a nonuniform way. But in all stages of development of commodity production the general law of price formation — that average

357

prices tend toward average partial derivatives of the value of the social final product with respect to the amount of the given commodity – remains valid.

3. On the Discussion of Problems of Price Formation

Marx's theory of value reflects the laws of price formation in their relationship to other economic laws, above all to the law of economy of labor. Marx did not develop all parts of this theory to the same extent. Certain elements of the theory of value were only outlined by him.[1] In particular, he did not sufficiently work out the concept of socially necessary time in a different sense, in the sense of time necessary according to the conditions of *consumption,* in contrast to working time necessary according to the conditions of production. Marx devoted a few lines directly to this concept.[2] But it is logically included in that statement of his theory of value that asserts that the qualitative and quantitative conformity of a commodity to the need for it is a necessary condition for the labor expended on it to create value. The degree of conformity of a commodity to the need for it can be determined only with the aid of consumption valuations that indicate that "a certain amount of working time is necessary for satisfying social needs." [3]

Without such valuations the fundamental equality determining socially necessary expenditures is not realizable. This equality says:

Labor necessary according to the conditions of production } is equal to { labor necessary according to conditions of consumption. *

Without the right half of this equality, the left half becomes indeterminate. This is obvious if costs per unit of output depend on the amount of production. But in the case in which costs per unit do not change with changes in the volume of production, it is not possible to determine without a consumption valuation whether it is necessary in general to produce the given commodity and what its general level of costs should be. This pertains not only to consumer goods but also to means of production. We have seen that in the task of minimizing expenditures of labor on the prescribed output consumption valuations necessarily arise for means of production. These valuations are norms of effectiveness of these means (in other words, they are norms of feedback costs). Putting the norm of effectiveness of a reproducible means of production in the right half of the equality makes it possible to determine the left half.

But this is not all. This equality can also be extended to the determination of socially necessary surplus labor for accumulation. In that case, differential (marginal) expenditures of surplus labor for the expansion of production will be in the left half, and the differential effectiveness of capital investment will be in the right half. In particular, the equality (*) is the logical basis for the equality of the maximum possible growth rate to the norm of investment effectiveness in the optimal plan of development.[4]

We will not examine the opportunity of extending equality (*) to the determination of socially necessary expenditures of surplus labor on nonproductive activity. (We think that valuable results can be obtained in this direction.) We will confine ourselves to the significance of equality (*) in Marx's theory of value. This equality is the foundation stone of the theory of value. It demonstrates that the conformity of production to needs (the proportionality of production) is realized under conditions of equality of consumption labor — valuations to expenditures of labor. It encompasses both sides of price formation — production and needs — and it links the law of value with the law of economy of labor, with the determination of costs by labor. The basis for measuring costs and benefits is thereby determined. All consumption valuations of both means of production and of objects of consumption are expressed in the same unit in which expenditures of social labor are measured.

The primacy of production in equality (*) is manifested by the fact that the realization of the equality *begins with the left half,* i.e., with a survey of production possibilities and of expenditures necessary for this purpose. The range of change in consumption valuations of each commodity (especially of necessities) depending on supply is very broad and can hardly be determined so long as the possible amounts of and outlays on the production of commodity are unknown. Accordingly, the maximum growth in the population's welfare is naturally to be sought by finding the minimum outlays of labor on the necessary output, with subsequent recalculations (iterations) in conformity with the revealed necessity (as a result of solving the problem) of correcting the production program and the length of the working day. Minimizing the production costs of final output and maximizing — with given wage rates — the national income are natural goals of current planning. In addition, long-term planning optimizes the relationship between accumulation and consumption, and between working time and free time.

Unfortunately, equality (*) has not yet attracted the proper attention of Soviet economists and mathematical economists. Thus, the development of problems of price formation is proceeding in two directions at the present time. Some investigators confine themselves to developing the left half of equality (*), overlooking the right half, and others seek laws of optimal price formation in models that maximize the right half of the equality, considering it in isolation from the left one as a welfare function (or a social utility function). Confining analysis of the law of value to the left half of equality (*) is characteristic of many Soviet economists. It is explained by the fact that in Marx's works the concept of the social consumption valuation is insufficiently developed.

Given the proportionality of production and the conformity of prices to socially necessary expenditures of labor, consumption valuations are equated to costs necessary according to the conditions of production. Accordingly, in order to explain the law of price formation in an unplanned economy, it was sufficient for Marx to establish equality (*). But in a planned economy this is insufficient. In order to use the law of value in planning we must know the laws of formation not only of costs of production but also of consumption valuations. That is why it is inadmissible to consider those statements of the theory of value that Marx insufficiently developed as unimportant ones. Such a simplification of the theory takes cruel revenge. Either contradictions between practice and theory arise (if defects of the simplified theory are corrected in practice), or there is a collision between practice and economic laws (if practice is guided by the simplified theory).

The first of these was observed in measuring costs, namely, the contradiction between practice and the simplified theory of value (see Chapter 1, Section 1).

The second consequence of ignoring certain important elements and relationships inherent in the law of value occurred in measuring benefits. In particular, the measurement of benefits long suffered from confusing benefits with costs. There emerged a neglect of the role of consumption valuations in the formation of socially necessary costs (see Chapter 1, Section 3).

Thus, the refusal to develop the right half of the equality determining socially necessary labor costs so impoverishes the theory of value that it partially ceases to "function," i.e., to explain facts, and it becomes transformed into a dogma that we must believe in spite of its contradicting the facts. The 1965 economic reform still further sharpened the discrepancies between the impoverished theory of value and practice. Thus, payments for capital funds do not fit within the limits of this impoverished theory of value.

One one-sided element in the theory of value led to another. Some Soviet economists and mathematicians, ardent defenders of the models and methods of optimal planning, rejected the left half of equality (*) and proposed constructing prices by proceeding from the maximization of the welfare function (or the social utility function, the consumption function, etc).

Prices in this model are obtained as partial derivatives (increments) of the maximum of the welfare function with respect to the amount of the given resource or product (manpower, means of production, means of consumption). In so doing, labor also receives a valuation. The costs of production of the product, expressed in these prices, represent those negative increments of the maximum of the welfare function that are caused by the application of resources used for producing the given product (rather than others). In other words, costs in this model express not labor but a sacrificed increase in welfare.

This model cannot be rejected on strictly logical grounds. Furthermore, we can incorporate the law of economy of labor into it by including in the welfare function time free from work as a special good. Nonetheless, this model is also incapable of being applied.

The welfare function expresses only the *order* of social preferences of one or another consumption structure. Neither zero nor the unit is determined for it. Therefore, we cannot determine its partial derivatives with respect to the amount of resources and products, i.e., we cannot determine prices that, according to this concept, are partial derivatives of the welfare function (see Chapter 8, Section 2).

Thus, ignoring either half of equality (*) leads to no good. In the most concise form this equality correctly reflects both aspects of the process of price formation, namely, expenditures of labor and the social valuation of their results.

Notes

1. According to Engels, for Volume III of *Das Kapital* "there was only one initial draft, which, moreover, was full of gaps." As a result of illness Marx could not finish the part of *Das Kapital* that is devoted to the transformation of value into the price of production. See K. Marx and F. Engels, *op.cit.*, Vol. 25, Part I, p. 4.
2. See K. Marx and F. Engels, *op.cit.*, Vol. 25, Part II, p. 186; Vol. 26, Part I, p. 221.
3. K. Marx and F. Engels, *op.cit.*, Vol. 25, Part II, p. 186.
4. See pp. 189-190.